LOVE BECOMES A FUNERAL PYRE

Also by Mick Wall:

Lou Reed: The Life

Black Sabbath: Symptom of the Universe

AC/DC: Hell Ain't a Bad Place to Be

Enter Night: Metallica – The Biography

Appetite for Destruction

When Giants Walked the Earth:
A Biography of Led Zeppelin

W.A.R.: The Unauthorised Biography of W.Axl Rose

Bono: In The Name of Love

John Peel: A Tribute to the Much-Loved DJ
and Broadcaster

XS All Areas: The Autobiography of Status Quo

Mr Big: Ozzy, Sharon and My Life as the
Godfather of Rock, by Don Arden

Paranoid: Black Days with Sabbath & Other Horror Stories

Run to the Hills: The Authorised Biography of Iron Maiden

Pearl Jam

Guns N' Roses: The Most Dangerous Band in the World

Diary of a Madman:
The Official Biography of Ozzy Osbourne

LOVE BECOMES A FUNERAL PYRE

MICK WALL

This edition first published in Great Britain in 2014
by Orion
an imprint of the Orion Publishing Group Ltd
Orion House, 5 Upper St Martin's Lane,
London WC2H 9EA
An Hachette UK Company

1 3 5 7 9 10 8 6 4 2

A CIP catalogue record for this book is
available from the British Library.

ISBN (hardback): 978 1 4091 5122 7
ISBN (trade paperback): 978 1 4091 5123 4

Typeset by Input Data Services Ltd, Bridgwater, Somerset

Printed and bound by CPI Group (UK) Ltd, Croydon, CR0 4YY

The Orion Publishing Group's policy is to use papers that
are natural, renewable and recyclable and made from wood
grown in sustainable forests. The logging and manufacturing
processes are expected to conform to the environmental
regulations of the country of origin.

Every effort has been made to fulfil requirements with regard
to reproducing copyright material. The author and publisher
will be glad to rectify any omissions at the earliest opportunity.

www.orionbooks.co.uk

For Peter N. Lewis, the only real shaman I ever knew.

Contents

Acknowledgements

I would like to extend my utmost thanks to the following people, absolutely without whom. Robert Kirby, Malcolm Edwards, Jane Sturrock, Linda Wall, Vanessa Lampert, Joe Daly, Neil Cross, Holly Thompson, Anna Valentine, Emma Smith, Mark Handsley, Susan Howe, Kate Wright-Morris, Jessica Purdue, Dave Everley, Rebecca Gray, Gail Paten, Richard King, Mick Houghton, Craig Fraser, Lynnette Lawrence, Dee Hembury-Eaton, Krystyna Kujawinska, Isadora Attab, Marianne Ihlen, Anna Hayward, Jac Holzman, Bruce Botnick, Bill Siddons, Danny Fields, Dennis Jakob, R. Merlin, Patricia Kennealy-Morrison, Pamela Des Barres, Eve Babitz, Judy Huddleston, Vincent Treanor III, Jerry Hopkins, Sam Bernett, Patrick Chauvel, Evert Wilbrink, John Haeny, Jerry Scheff, Jess Roden, Howard Werth, Jeff Kitts, Richie Unterberger, Ian Clark, Steve Morant and the all the boys of the SNC, and last, but hardly least, Ray Manzarek, Robby Krieger, and John Densmore, who always deserved better, and Jim Morrison, who always gave his best.

PART ONE
LOCKED

'Self-interest exists, attachment based on personal gain exists, complacency exists. But not love. Love has to be reinvented . . .'

ARTHUR RIMBAUD, *A Season in Hell*

ONE

Paris, 1971

This is the end . . .

Jim, alone, not in a bathtub, but on the toilet, head down; trousers round his knees, found just like his hero, Elvis, would be six years later, arms dangling lifelessly by his sides, brains fried. Gone before they'd even broken down the door to get him. Overdosed on heroin. China White. The kind Paris was awash with that summer. Jim, alone, as always, surrounded by people.

He'd been predicting his own death for months, of course. Janis had gone the previous October, Jimi just two weeks before that. 'You're drinking with the next one,' Jim would only half jokingly tell friends. Except that Jim didn't really have any friends. Certainly not Pamela, with her hell-red hair and her smack and her new boyfriend, the Count . . . Or Ray, with his touch-the-brave-sunlight trip to the public and his needy please-Jim-just-for-me shit to your face . . . Or John, that asshole, always with the long hard looks and the judgemental eyes . . . Even far-out Robby, his mind blown by the acid and the permanent midnight, all mumbled passive-aggressive bullshit. Robby the secret businessman . . .

Where were they now, hey? Now that Jim didn't need them any more? Or said he didn't, anyway. Standing up suddenly on the dance floor at the Rock and Roll Circus, loudly declaiming his crappy, drunken poetry while all around – the models and gangsters, the dealers and pop stars, the street trash blown in by the Paris summer wind – sat writhing in the shadows, laughing behind their hands, waiting for fat old Jim Morrison to shut the fuck up and sit back down again. Or fall over. Again. Whichever.

Poor old Jim, alone in Paris, surrounded by all the people he thought he'd left behind in sun-shitty L.A. Same eager faces happy to hang out, listen to his bullshit then see him home safely when he was too shitfaced to do it himself. Crazy, fat man Jim, best friend to all the waiters at Café de Flore hovering over him like flies, as he guzzled his brandy, his whisky, his beer and his endless wine. Big bearded Jim, out of breath climbing the steps to the Sacré-Coeur, out of luck lounging in his borrowed apartment waiting for fucked-up Pam to come home from the Count's, then sick of waiting, grabbing a taxi to Rue de Seine, staggering towards the red neon sign of the Rock and Roll Circus, waving hi to the blonde cloakroom girl, who always gave him the same smile even as her eyes swooped past him towards whatever was coming next down the street behind him. Tiptoeing down the narrow steps into the darkened basement of the club, the DJ in the glassed-off booth always – always, man! – playing the Stones, ever since the night Keith walked in with his knife and his entourage, gave him the gypsy eye and let him know it was all cool, baby.

Worse thing about the Circus, man, having to walk past

the Count's private room on your way down into the club . . .
The one with the floor cushions and incense and pot smoke
and the same old hippy in robes, strumming the sitar . . . the
chicks all droopy-eyed and creamed on smack and Tuinals
and cheap fizz. Jim couldn't make that scene, man. The only
time he went in there was with Pam or to score for Pam. Jim
preferred to grab a table, or stretch out on one of the couches
in one of the vaulted corners of the club, looking for his new
friend Sky Eyes, half Apache Indian, half US Army deserter.
Sky Eyes had been out there, man, Vietnam, man. Killed a
cop as a kid and was given the choice: jail for ever or five years
in Nam. Sky chose the army and he did good, man. Part of
the elite force. Killing gooks for fun. Then with less than two
years to go – the old switcheroo! He'd skied it to Amsterdam.
But why, man? 'It wasn't my war, man' was all Sky Eyes said.

The first time Jim saw Sky Eyes he was dancing barefoot
at the Circus, his shirt off, some chick's red lipstick daubed
across his face like warpaint, long dirty hair hanging down to
his waist. Man, what a beautiful sight! 'Hey, man!' Jim told
him. 'I'm going to write a song about you!' Jim with his bags
of notebooks and pens, his postcards and newspapers and his
pockets full of francs, not here for the sights or the poetry
or any of that horseshit. Here like all the other American
draft-dodgers and dropouts because there was no extradition
treaty between France and the USA, so if the shit went down
in Miami he wouldn't have to go home to jail if he didn't want
to, and Jim really, really didn't want to, man. Fuck that shit.
Jim had watched that day at the bail house in Miami as one
black after another got sent down for shit that made what Jim
did look like kindergarten stuff. Jim knew he was doomed,

man. But that didn't mean he was gonna kneel and pray for it in some roach-infested shit-box in Miami, man.

By then the Circus was like Jim's second home. 'He came in all the time,' remembers Patrick Chauvel, then a 21-year-old war photographer working part-time at the Circus as a barman. 'I'd got back from Vietnam a few weeks before and I was saving up money to get back out there. Or maybe to Northern Ireland, where everyone said the next war was going to be.' The first time Jim showed up, it was a big deal. But that had been weeks before and now he was 'just another regular, really. A nice guy to speak to when sober, a monster when drunk.' And Jim was always drunk.

It must have been two in the morning when one of his staff went to complain to Sam Bernett, the manager, about a stall in the ladies' toilets being locked. People were banging on the door and shouting for whoever was in there to hurry up, but it had been nearly an hour and nothing. Sam should do something!

Wearily Sam made his way up the steps to the toilets. It was not the first time someone had locked themselves in, but usually it was in the men's. He knocked, he banged, he shouted. Suddenly he feared the worst. Drugs – cocaine, heroin – were part of the lingua franca at an all-night dive like the Circus. It was the same for the trannies, homos and whores at the Alcazar next door. These places were tolerated without police interference. As long as nobody died in them.

Sam called for two of his men to break down the door. That's when they found him. Jim, alone, zeroed out on the john, big belly hanging out, foaming at the mouth, face blood-spotted and grey, head down.

'Merde!'

Sam spun on his heel and ordered his staff to clear the toilets out, make sure the clientele were informed they were closed for the rest of the night. Panic took over as Sam tried to find a doctor – someone discreet – who could come and give an opinion. But it didn't look good. 'That guy is dead,' said someone who said he was a doctor; another regular patron of the club. 'He's not dead, he's just fucked up,' said one of the two men that had broken down the door. Sam decided to call the cops. 'No police,' they told him. 'Not here. It will mean the end for the club.'

Then what? 'We take him home . . .'

Sam watched as Patrick helped the two men lift the body out of the toilet, wrap a blanket around it as best they could and try and drag it up the steps, towards the back of the cloakroom, where a staff-only door led to the back passageway of the Alcazar, next door. 'But the body was so big, so heavy,' says Patrick. The guys carrying the body kept falling over and dropping it. Like a scene from Laurel and Hardy if it hadn't been so macabre. 'C'était horrible!' shudders Patrick.

The important thing was to avoid a *scandale*. After Patrick helped half drag, half carry the body out through the connecting corridor from the Circus to the Alcazar, and onto the street, there was already a car waiting at the kerb, a big Mercedes. 'Yes, it was a strange thing to find oneself doing,' says Chauvel now, nervously, from his Paris home, 'But I'd just come back from Vietnam and I'd seen a lot of weird things. I helped put the body in the back of the Mercedes then went back inside the Circus. They wanted everything to look as normal as possible.'

Once the silent heavy body had been shoved awkwardly across the back seat, the two men got into the front of the car and drove off through the hot Parisian night, gliding towards Le Marais, the picturesque Jewish *quartier* where Jim and Pam had stayed these past few months. 17 Rue Beautreillis, third-floor apartment. This time of night it only took 15 minutes. But then there was the added hell of trying to get the body up the several flights of stairs. And what would have to happen next when they got it there.

Back inside the club the regulars at the bar talked about it, despite Sam telling them to keep their mouths shut. There were lots of patrons like Sam and Patrick and Dominique and Sky Eyes, who had grown used to seeing Morrison at the Circus in the small hours, and knew he would score drugs sometimes, usually for Pam, he said, though lately who knew? It didn't take much for young guys like Patrick and his American pal, Cameron Watson, who was DJing later that night at La Bulle, to come up with their own theories. 'I heard that the guy he was used to getting drugs from had changed, been arrested or something,' says Chauvel. 'So Morrison got involved with a new guy that night and the heroin wasn't the same at all. It was a lot more pure and Jim didn't know. And he overdosed.' When, later that same night, Watson muted a record he was playing to announce out of the blue, 'Jim Morrison died this morning,' nobody at La Bulle knew what to make of it. They merely shrugged and carried on dancing.

Back at the Beautreillis apartment, Pam, so far gone on her own pure-as-the-driven-snow Chine Blanche she could barely stay awake, didn't know what to do, to say, as the two heavy-set guys unloaded Jim through the door and dropped the body thumping onto the floor. She'd been through this trip before, of course, or versions of it, Jim passing out all fucked up on some poor bastard's floor, but this was different. Even Pam, in her heavy-lidded, barely there state, could dig that. Still, how bad could it be? Jim would sleep it off, as usual, and then what? She was more worried about who these fucking guys were. What did they want? Money? Her smack? Was this a fucking rip-off, man? Inside, she began to panic. Tried giving them orders but when they looked at her and she caught their faces – dark, heavy, neutral – she backed off and went into her little-girl-lost act instead. It had always worked before, it would now . . . right?

'What's wrong with him?' she slurred, trying to sound cool.

They ignored her. Spoke among themselves, heavy, meaty French accents. Then one of them went into the bathroom and began running the tub.

'What are you doing?' she said, almost laughing, like this is a big put-on, right? 'What's *going on*?'

They ignored her, began undressing the body, roughly, boots first, laying them by the door, as if he'd just stepped out of them. Then the jeans and the off-colour T-shirt, one of them, the more nervous of the two, noticing the surprisingly grey hairs on Jim's chest and pubes.

As they ran the hot water Pam finally came alive. She screamed, flew into the bathroom after them. Jumped in and lay on top of the body as the bath began to fill, screaming his name over and over. 'Jim! Jim! Jim!' Pulling at his hair and his eyes, trying to somehow get through, so they could both wake from whatever this dream did mean.

The men looked on with distaste then pulled her struggling from the bath. The water was too hot now anyway. Then they began telling her what she must do, over and over until the junkie whore seemed to get it straight in her head.

TWO

Ray of Light

Ray Manzarek was the first member of The Doors to become fully awake. To see what was going on, what might some-day be. Ray, who really knew the name of the game; who made Jim a star, and kept him there, floating in the night sky, for evermore. Ray who was the ringmaster; the whip hand; the real seer and sage of The Doors. Ray who would never be able to let go, not even as the audience began throwing chairs at the stage, as Jim hurled his mike like a spear through the hearts of the crowd, as Robby rolled his transcendentally meditated eyes and John threw down his sticks and vowed he would 'never play with that asshole again'. For Ray, who would rewrite the story again and again after Jim's death, it became not the end of a shattered career but the beginning of a new religion.

Ray, who made the whole thing up, man. Kept the train on the tracks. Kept playing through it all, hunched over his keyboards like a mad professor crooning over his microscope. Ray, who cared so much there wasn't enough room for anyone else to care at all.

When I last spoke with Ray, just a few months before he died, towards the end of the conversation he said, 'I wouldn't be surprised if I got a postcard or a phone call tomorrow from Jim, saying, "Hey, man, I'm back!"'

I had been prepared to put up with his Doors hagiography until then. It was a trip hearing Ray Manzarek of The Doors talk about 'the sacrament' of LSD. The 'hot nights on Sunset where anything seemed possible suddenly'. But when he gave me the Jim-might-not-be-dead schtick I was surprised, then disappointed, then faintly disgusted. He was insulting my intelligence. He thought I was there just to write another meaningless chapter in the bible of The Doors, the one that ends with Jim dying of a heart attack in a bathtub while his loving girlfriend sleeps peacefully in the next room. Then I realised: no, he wasn't putting me on. Ray was simply doing his job, the same one he'd been doing faithfully for over 40 years. Feeding the fire that kept him and the remaining members of The Doors and their dependants warm these many winters, keeping the myth alive for each successive generation of teenage existentialists so that they might keep buying into the whole dark fairy tale: that Ray had been the old wise man, the witness – relating this fable for so long he had actually come to believe and embrace it himself. In fact, this was always the way Ray had told himself the story, from the moment he first set eyes on his old college buddy Jim, moving through the sea mist towards him on Venice Beach that hot stoned afternoon in the nothing-doing summer of 1965, so acid-scorched and beach-combed skinny he barely recognised him as the same pudgy weirdo he'd been on head-drooping, mumbling, smoke-this terms with at UCLA.

'Jim was supposed to go to the naval academy, and didn't do that,' Ray explained earnestly when I spoke to him for a piece in *Classic Rock* magazine in 2012. 'Well, if he wasn't going to do that at least he could go and study something that would prepare him for the diplomatic field. Jim was going to be groomed, as his father saw it, as an ambassador. Perhaps an ambassador to the court of St James would have been the ideal position for Jim Morrison to occupy, according to his father. Jim Morrison instead goes to the film school at UCLA and becomes an artist. That's what I did too. I was supposed to be an attorney: Counsellor Manzarek. Instead I went to the UCLA film school . . . very serendipitous.'

So in an alternative universe, I asked, there's Mr Manzarek the attorney-at-law and there's Mr Morrison the foreign ambassador?

'Yeah, and our paths could have still crossed, you know? Being proper gentlemen, we could have gotten together at some point.'

Yeah, maybe. And then again . . .

Raymond Daniel Manzarek Junior was born on the Southside of Chicago, on 12 February 1939. Ray, for whom everything had retrospective meaning, would explain that he was an Aquarius born into the Age of Aquarius: an idealist born into an age that defined itself as a utopian age of forward-thinking nonconformity and freedom. 'Very serendipitous.' His also liked to point out that his moon sign was in Sagittarius, as was Jim's rising sign. And that he was born in the Year of the Rabbit, the lucky sign in the Chinese zodiac. Mostly, what Ray liked to tell you about himself was that he was a smart, educated, music-playing, art-loving humanitarian who believed in the good of man, and none more so than in himself. As Ray would make clear in his beautifully written autobiography, *Light My Fire*, self-doubt did not rank highly in Ray's long list of personal attributes.

As Ray tells it, his father, Ray Manczarek Senior, came from hard-working Polish immigrants – Ray Junior would later drop the 'c' from the family name. A tool- and die-maker at the local plant, Dad was a good union man who raised Ray and two younger brothers, Richard and Jim, to be upright American citizens. School was the Everett Public Elementary School; school lunches were cooked and eaten at home. They were the kind of family that sat together around the table every night for dinner. That discussed things. Hopes and dreams and how to make them a reality, the way the two previous generations of Manczareks had strived to do. It was a typically upwardly mobile, mid-Fifties American childhood with trips to the beaches of Lake Michigan, school visits to museums like the Natural History and Science and Industry; nature walks, picnicking, football at Soldier Field . . .

Ray's mother, Helen, was the musical one of the family. She had a wonderful singing voice, would treat the whole house to it every day. Helen would be the one who really encouraged her eldest son to learn to play, when she persuaded Ray Senior to buy a carved-wood upright piano. Ray Junior was seven and greatly put out when his father took him for his first piano lesson: it was a Saturday morning, a time when normally he would have been at Saturday morning pictures, catching up on the latest adventures of Flash Gordon. Instead he would now spend those precious hours in a dusty old room with an ancient European tutor, learning Beethoven and Bach.

As little Raymond got better at the piano his tutor insisted on regular daily practice: half an hour each day straight after school, practising scales and technique to the nearby sound of his classmates playing in the street. Then another half-hour after dinner, as his mother and father listened. Almost in spite of himself, he began to progress rapidly. By the time he was ten he was good enough for lessons with Bruno Michelotti, a dance band leader. It was Michelotti who introduced young Ray to musical theory; how to read a lead sheet and play simple left-hand accompaniments to melodies. It was also through Michelotti that Ray learned to play Harlem stride piano, ragtime stuff, boogie-woogie, mixing it up, trying to emulate boogie masters like Pine Top Smith, Meade Lux Lewis, Ray at the German upright piano at home, working his left-hand technique until even his parents begged him to stop. He was 12 when he mastered the left-hand boogie-woogie rhythm, the skill that would become his calling card in The Doors, where he applied the technique to the Fender Rhodes keyboard bass. The boy was tall and gangly, awkward on his feet, yet he possessed genuine rhythm. He really did

The only other things that really got his attention as a teenager were the high school softball team and because he was tall – six foot at 14 – the basketball team as well. But he stopped growing after that so the basketball fizzled out. The softball came to a more dramatic end after he overheard something astonishing blasting from the portable radio one of the cooler kids that didn't do sports had brought with him one day. Mom and Dad had always kept blues records in the house, but it wasn't until now that Ray discovered 'the far right-hand side of the dial' on the radio, where could be heard the authentic Chicago sound of John Lee Hooker, Muddy Waters, Jimmy Reed, BB King, and then later Chuck Berry, Little Richard . . .

Ray never played sports again, transitioning overnight to being one of the cool kids in their blue jeans and leather jackets who liked to smoke and dig the crazy sounds on the radio. He was 15, now attending St Rita's, a private Catholic High School, all boys – which Ray would recall in his autobiography, *Light My Fire*, as 'very depressing' – being taught by Dominican priests in their brown monks' robes.

Then came Elvis! The first time Ray saw Elvis on TV, doing 'Blue Suede Shoes' he had just turned 17, and as he later wrote, 'My eyeballs fell out of my head! Wow!' This was something else.

By now Ray had a more refined spine piano, where the white keys were black and the black keys white, a genteel cousin to the harpsichord which he nevertheless beat hell out of playing Elvis-style rock'n'roll when he should have been playing Bach. There was no turning back now. After St Rita's he went to DePaul University, one of the better Chicago-area colleges, and mixed. He was an Economics Major in the College of Commerce but all he did was chase chicks, look at art and play the piano. He was 19 when he saw Muddy Waters bring his mojo to Chicago, with, on piano, the great Otis Spann, who now became Ray's biggest inspiration. There were Otis and Johnnie Johnson, Chuck Berry's keys-man, they were the cats that showed the way for Ray. The ones that taught him to allow the singer and guitarist the space to do their things, 'comping' behind them. Until it was his turn, when, as he wrote, 'I am the lord and master. I control the destiny of the song. All must obey me . . .'

It was also now that Ray the would-be cultural attaché first came into existence. Not yet 21, but already a man of the world in his own eyes, he began to devour every art form that lent itself to his voracious gaze. Getting in on a two-buck student ticket, every Wednesday he would go to see the Chicago Symphony Orchestra play at the same Auditorium Theater where years later he would perform with The Doors. At first it was just the roaring spectacle he dug, but then he began to put it all together with everything else he was digging. How Debussy's *La Mer* would find a resonant echo in the genius-jazz of Bill Evans, another great keyboardist whose shrine Ray now worshipped at. Classical, rock, blues, jazz, it was all one to him, he now saw; all different facets of the same glorious panoply of sight and sound, of new sensation.

Then there was film, painting, theatre, literature . . . all one, Ray decided, with music, at least when it was done to its utmost, when it pushed the limits in new and challenging directions. When a touring Picasso exhibition came to Chicago he went to that. When the phrase 'world cinema' was first coined, Ray got into that too, his head nodding approvingly at showings of Truffaut, Bergman, Camus . . . *400 Blows*, *The Seventh Seal*, *Black Orpheus* . . . yeah, big daddy, what else can you show me? He didn't get it all – Michelangelo Antonioni's *L'Avventura* would remain stubbornly outside his reach. Alienation, he decided, was not his trip. Instead Ray looked to a future of inclusion and power to the people. He would see *Citizen Kane* so many times he lost count, each time taking different meanings from it. Flipping his lid over

James Dean and Marlon Brando. Those days, man, they were such special times.

There was nothing Ray didn't like seeing or doing back then. He would go from one extreme – digging *West Side Story* with the sexy Chita Rivera and the panoramic music of Leonard Bernstein – to the other – immersing himself in the great Aaron Copland: not the early *Billy the Kid* shtick, but the later 12-tone masterworks like *Piano Fantasy*. He became besotted with the plays of Tennessee Williams. When he later discovered that Jim, that other gothic Southern gentleman gone to seed, also loved Tennessee Williams, he saw it as one more sign that they were fated to meet, to work together, to shape destiny. In his book Ray claims that Jim always secretly fancied himself as a bit of a Chance Wayne, the gigolo-drifter star of *Sweet Bird of Youth*. Certainly that's one of the ways Ray always liked to think of him, especially after his death, when Jim became anything Ray, his biggest fan, said he was.

His parents saw their son's artistic leanings as a sign of intelligence, and hoped he would put that big brain of his towards becoming something serious, like an attorney. Instead he went to UCLA to study film. Oh well, shrugged Ray Senior, at least he'll get a college degree from one of the country's well-known universities. He could always get down to some serious work after that.

When Ray joined the Department of Cinematography at UCLA, it sounded grand enough to keep his ambitious parents happy. They were so excited at the prospect of their son having a career in the movie business they would soon follow him down to Los Angeles, buying a house on Manhattan Beach. But that wasn't what was on Ray Junior's mind at all.

As he told me, 'UCLA in the early Sixties was *not* the place to go for anyone thinking of a *straight* career.' Ray spoke a lot in italics – he was always so certain of what he was saying, or at least wished to give the appearance of being so. 'UCLA was really where my life and so many others began. I met my wife there, I smoked weed, took my first acid there, got in my first band . . .'

The really big event that going to UCLA triggered in Ray's life, though, wasn't to do with film or music or any other form of art. It was where he met his future wife, Dorothy Fujikawa. A beautiful, Japanese-American girl who enjoyed the same cultural pursuits as Ray but who displayed a much calmer, both-feet-on-the-ground approach to life, Dorothy was studying medicine. The same age as Ray, Dorothy had a much older head on her shoulders. She could stay up all night rapping with Ray about the finer points of Kurosawa's *Rashomon* and still make a 9 a.m. class on cardiovascular disease. She was also Ray's first big love affair. There had been a high school sweetheart he'd dated but who never let him get past second base. Then there was a beatnik chick he had started fucking on the first date. But when he went to California she went to Europe.

Now there was Dorothy. The two became inseparable and would remain that way for the rest of Ray's life. Dorothy was more than just a scintillating lover and friend. She became his muse. The one he would always try to impress, to make happy, to gain the ultimate approval from. He developed the habit of always telling anyone he hadn't already told how Dorothy's IQ – 147 – was even higher than Ray's – 135. And he dug it that Dorothy came with a certain otherness. She was

American but also more than that. They shared the same sensibility. So while Ray would not have dreamed of following his beatnik girlfriend to Europe, he vaunted San Francisco, that most European of American cities, over Los Angeles. By comparison to Frisco, he said, L.A. was 'a cowboy town'. Hippies and bohemians thrived in SF. Only the freaks survived in L.A.

When he made his first end-of-year student film, *Evergreen*, a short, black-and-white attempt at European art-house cinema – cool jazz soundtrack, off-camera dialogue laid over a collage of images – Dorothy was the co-star, along with another UCLA buddy, Henry Chrismonde, aka Hank Olguin. Hank would later have a walk-on part in the early story of The Doors.

The plot, such as it was, revolves around a young sax player and his beautiful, doomed-to-failure relationship with a jazz-loving Japanese-American girl. The movie shows the couple making love and just being together, chatting the way young lovers do about the things they like and the things they don't like. All very cool and collected, like the soporific jazz score that accompanies the disjointed dialogue. But then the girl starts talking about marriage and the young musician checks out.

The movie ends with him walking away quietly one morning, not even leaving a note, unlike in real life, where the real musician – Ray – did marry the girl. But that was Ray, or certainly how he saw himself, and maybe it was true. The musician who could be relied on, that did not walk away. Ray was such a dreamer and yet so solid, it's like watching his dream then waiting for it to come true. The good bits anyway.

Viewing the scenes on the beach in *Evergreen* now, more than 50 years later, one becomes poignantly aware of the sound of the waves crashing against the near shore that punctuates the cool jazz soundtrack, and begins to ponder how much that rasping, ghostly sound would recur throughout the story of Ray Manzarek and The Doors. From drawing up plans for The Doors on Venice Beach with Jim and the rest of the guys, to the backdrop of the crashing waves, like the sound of youthful promise. To how the last great song they would be remembered for, 'Riders on the Storm', would also be ushered in by the crashing waves of a thunder storm, only this time the mood they would summon would be elegiac, doomed. Like the word 'finis' flickering in fragile white script at the end of one of Ray's beloved French underground movies.

When Ray's second student movie, *Induction*, made it into the Royce Hall screenings, UCLA's prestigious end of year best-of screenings, he got up and made a speech, which the entire faculty applauded. But he was already seeking applause in other places too. Ray and Dorothy shared a place near the veterans' hospital complex, on Wilshire and San Vicente, halfway between Venice Beach and UCLA. Lots of young would-be musicians lived out in Venice and Santa Monica then, the rent was cheap and the living relatively easy. Lots of UCLA students now lived there too. Some, like Ray, who wanted to do both: study film and play in some hot young beat outfit.

Ray was aided in this ambition by the arrival of the rest of his family down in California in 1965, when his younger brothers, Rich and Jim, beat him to the punch by forming their own ad-hoc surfer band they named Rick & The Ravens. Like Jan and Dean but after several 'lids' of grass, Rick & The Ravens, featuring Rich on guitar, Jim on harmonica, a couple of high school buddies on drums and bass, and Ray – in his new onstage guise as 'Screaming' Ray Daniels – on vocals, were just one of a generation of likeminded surf outfits that littered the West Coast scene in the early 1960s. And just like The Jaguars, The Duals and so many others that came and went in a haze of pot smoke and surf spray, they were not destined for success. Nevertheless, with similar-thinking acts like The Marketts, who had a million-seller in 1963 with the gimmicky 'Out Of Limits' – repurposed from the name of the popular TV show of the time, *The Outer Limits* – showing there were bucks in them schmucks, Rick & The Ravens managed to score a modest deal for three singles with a local label, Aura, a subsidiary of the better-known West Coast jazz label World Pacific.

As well as releasing singles such as 'Henrietta', which Ray also incorporated into *Evergreen*, nothing happened outside of landing the band a regular gig at a less than salubrious dive called the Turkey Joint West in Santa Monica. What's interesting is how easily Ray took to the role of frontman. Eschewing the opportunity to play the keyboards, his real calling card, he elected to take off his glasses and strum a guitar while standing at the mike and belting out such hastily written crowd-pleasers as 'Just for You' (*'Baby, just for you!'*) and, their big finale each night and the closest they ever came to a hit when it got played once or twice on local radio, 'Big Bucket T', halfway between a hot-rod song and a surf anthem, with Ray affecting a voice somewhere between the Louisianan bayou and a taco stand in West Hollywood.

'We didn't know what we were doing,' said Ray, years later, still living it down. 'We were just having fun.' But clearly he did know what he was doing and while he was certainly having fun he was always looking to take the band to the next level, with his impresario role in the Ravens continuing right through their gradual, if unforeseen, transformation into The Doors.

Being in the Ravens had another knock-on effect. It was where Ray got to meet Dick Bock, the head of World Pacific. Dick viewed Rick & The Ravens for what they were: the kind of disposable shtick you threw at the wall and waited to see if some of it stuck. If it did, yoo-hoo, you would stuff the 100-dollar bills into big fat rolls and use them to buy your wife something nice. If it didn't, who cared? They were only kids out for a lark. One day they would grow up and get proper jobs. It was Dick, though, that handed Ray a double LP of the Maharishi giving lectures, which led to Ray going to his first TM classes, being held by Jerry Jarvis, the director of Transcendental Meditation West. Which is where he was first introduced to a young guy named John Densmore and his pal, Robby Krieger. Nice cats, both of whom had also played in various groups. Hmm . . .

And, of course, UCLA was the venue as well where Ray would meet the other great love of his life, Jim Morrison: Jimmy, to his friends, an overweight, quietly spoken but intense student it took a while for Ray to get to know. No sparks flew at that first meeting, or for a long time afterwards. Jim was just another one of those rich kids who'd ended up going to school in California mainly as an escape from the plans his father, a Commander in the United States Navy, had made for him.

'We didn't really get the story at first,' Ray would tell me, 'but little by little it emerged that Jim was supposed to have gone to the US Naval Academy at Annapolis, as his father had, then he was to enter the diplomatic service.' He chuckled. 'Well, that was *never* gonna happen. No more than I was going to do what my father wanted me to. Very few people at UCLA were there because their parents *wanted* them to be. I don't think Jim had been doing anything his parents wanted him to for a *long* time before he got there. In fact, he told people his parents were *dead*. A lot of people believed that for a long time, because it seemed so plausible and he said it with such conviction. But maybe by then Jim's parents really were dead. At least to him.'

THREE

Souls of the Ghosts

Jim was simply one of those guys that would never grow up. You met them on the up and you passed them again going down. They would either get left behind, or simply refuse to go any further, determined to stay forever young, whatever it took. Even if it killed them. Or until something bad happened. Something they couldn't laugh off.

It's a theme common to rock stars that make it young and never get over it, even after the circus has long since left town. But it was Jim Morrison who created that tragi-comic template, who embedded it in our minds. The idiot-savant orphan who falls to Earth bringing first heaven then hell to all they meet and touch and whose fates they alter, for better and worse.

His father was Rear Admiral George Stephen Morrison, known as Steve; his mother, Clara Clarke Morrison. Steve was born the son of a railway worker in Rome, in a remote part of western Georgia, in 1919. The upright son of old-fashioned Southern Presbyterians, who didn't drink and had a history of distinguished military service, Steve had been raised in Leesburg, Florida, a former settlement with Scottish roots then best known for its watermelon production. A short, earnest-minded young man, Steve had his life pretty well mapped out for him, following in the family tradition in his late teens when he enrolled as a cadet in the US Naval Academy in Annapolis, Maryland.

Posted to Hawaii, Steve met Jim's mother, Clara Clarke, at a US naval-base dance, in 1941, just weeks before the attack on Pearl Harbor that triggered America's involvement in the war. Clara was a blonde bundle of fun with the prettiest face Steve had ever seen. Her father was a Wisconsin lawyer and political activist who made his reputation defending local unions against maverick bosses. This made him both a hero to the working people of Wisconsin and a figure of loathing to the business community. When he ran for office on the socialist ticket some years later, he failed to get elected but remained a powerful voice of dissent for the downtrodden for the rest of his career.

With America now officially fighting the Japanese in the South Pacific, and Steve about to complete his flight training, he and Clara hurriedly married in April 1942. They set up home in Pensacola, a seaport connecting the Florida Panhandle to the Gulf of Mexico, where Steve would be active on the USS *Pruitt*, an old World War One destroyer converted into a World War Two minelayer. It was the first of many moves the family would be obliged to make as Steve's naval career gathered momentum in the years to come. By the time the couple's first-born son, James Douglas Morrison – always just Jimmy to his family – was born on 8 December 1943, they had moved again, this time to Melbourne, Florida, one of the largest cities in the county. With Steve now away flying a Hellcat, one of a fleet of elite fighter planes eventually responsible for destroying more than 5,000 enemy aircraft in the Pacific Theater – more than any other Allied aircraft – Clara and baby Jimmy moved again, this time to stay with Steve's parents, Paul and Caroline, who ran a laundry in Clearwater, east of the Gulf of Mexico. And there they stayed for the next three years, the longest period the Morrisons would ever live in one place while Jimmy was growing up.

The post-war years were no less active. Now a lieutenant, by 1947 Steve had transferred to Los Alamos, where he worked on the earliest nuclear-weapons systems. It was now, in yet another naval housing facility near Albuquerque, New Mexico, that Jimmy's little sister, Anne, was born. It was while Anne was still a baby that one of the enduring strands of the Jim Morrison mythology is said to have begun. One that nobody has ever been able to convincingly substantiate, despite the pleasingly enigmatic sheen it confers on Morrison's memory. The story of the morning, as related by Jim on tape, nearly 25 years later, he came across the 'Indians scattered on dawn's highway', as he poetically put it. Suspiciously poetic, one is tempted to add.

According to legend, early one morning in 1948 the Morrison family, along with both Jimmy's grandparents, were driving along the two-lane desert highway that connects Albuquerque to Santa Fe, when they came upon the aftermath of a head-on collision between a car and a truck carrying Pueblo and Hopi Indians. Pulling over, Steve and Paul got out of the car and went over to survey the ghastly scene. Crumpled, bloodied bodies lay strewn across the road, some dead, others seriously injured. Some were screaming out and crying for help. Jimmy, who had been dozing in the back of the car, now came fully awake and tried to clamber out of the car for a better look but was held back by his mother and grandmother. With no mobile phones in those days, the best Steve and Paul decided they could do for these poor people was to get back in the car and drive as fast as it would carry them to the next gas station, where they could use the phone to call for the emergency services. Which is what they did, an increasingly distraught Jimmy glued to the rear window as they drove away.

Overcome with excitement and fear, Jimmy pestered his folks with questions, observations, suggestions and more questions. The boy would not shut up, becoming more and more hysterical until finally, in an effort to calm him down, Steve looked over his shoulder at his son in the back seat and told him with a firm expression: 'Jimmy, it didn't really happen. It was a bad dream.'

A bad dream Jim would claim altered the course of his whole life, when, in 1970, he recalled in an interview, later used on the posthumously released Doors album, *An American Prayer*, how there had been 'Indians scattered all over the highway bleeding to death'. It was, he said, the first time he had ever 'tasted fear'. He went on to claim that he now believed that the souls of the dead Indians had somehow found their way into his soul. 'And are still there.'

It's a wonderfully cinematic story, of course, and one that fits beautifully in the telling and endless retelling of the Fable of Jim Morrison. But is it actually true? And, if so, how come Jim never told it before 1970, at a time when his habit of putting people on with crazy stories – everyone, even himself – was so well established that his closest friends no longer knew whether to believe him or not when he came out with these things? Until he died and Ray took the job over to such spectacular effect, no one built up the myth of Morrison more than Jim himself. He was an incorrigible liar who rejoiced in sending people crazy with his lurid fictions. As Robby Krieger later told me, in his understated way: 'Jim had his own way of remembering things. I'm sure *he* believed what he was saying.' Like when he would tell you with a straight face how both his parents were dead and that he had no other family. 'A leap of faith if there ever was one' is how John Densmore describes the souls-of-the-ghosts story in his autobiography, *Riders on the Storm*. And John was close enough to Jim during his crazy story-telling years to smell the bullshit better than anyone. In the end, it hardly mattered whether the story was true or not. Jim Morrison was inhabited by the souls of dead Indians? *Far out, man! I knew it!*

Less convenient to the myth but more true to reality was the fact that Jim grew up a nervous child, who would wet the bed. Something his mother found intolerable and would re-peatedly punish him for, forcing him to sleep in the wet sheets. He began to lie about it or try to hide the sheets, sleeping on his bedroom floor rather than tell his mother and face further humiliation. Whether this was down to recurring nightmares of dead Indians or the constant moving home and changing of schools and the fact his father was away so much – when Dad wasn't refusing to speak about his work at Los Alamos, he was away fighting the Korean war – cannot be said absolutely for certain. But when he later talked about the 'first time I tasted fear', it is hard to escape the notion that the adult, mother-fixated Jim was really talking about 'dawn's highway' or any other deliberately misremembered street of dreams. And that he was actually relating back to those dreadful years when he was ridden with guilt and shame because of a mother who was disgusted with him and a largely absentee father who was the embodiment of everything his son was not: strong, manly, indomitable.

Years later, he would tell his lawyer, Max Fink, that he had been molested as a boy by an unnamed male figure in his family. Max, who had worked with Jim and The Doors throughout their turbulent career, was sceptical. But Jim had cried as he told the story and Max could not be sure. Was this true too or just another of Jim's endless once-upon-a-times? Certainly there is no evidence, not even after all this time, that this story is true. But then, if Jim believed it, who knows? Perhaps he was speaking again in metaphor, in drug code, in crazy booze talk, in his increasingly rampant self-pity? What can be agreed is, he *felt* abused. If not sexually then in ways modern child psychologists would no doubt confirm. But then that was Jim, from boy to man, always just a little bit different from the rest, always the one with the special excuses. Always with the lovelorn eyes.

When Steve returned home from the Korean War in 1953, he did so as a war hero, awarded the Bronze Star for 'heroic achievement' in a combat zone. Meanwhile, with the family living in Washington, DC, before yet another move, this time to Claremont, California, to Steve's alarm his ten-year-old son was growing into a chubby bookworm who loved reading and drawing, always won at Monopoly, loved art and music

– he took piano lessons for a while – and had been recently diagnosed as asthmatic. Good at sports – he was reputedly the best kickballer in school and would later excel at swimming – he showed little or no interest in other sports, choosing instead to hide himself away in the dark fug of the local movie house, where he preferred the films of Marlene Dietrich over the shoot 'em ups other boys delighted in. Unattached to any particular football or baseball team, due partly to the family's constant moving, partly because he instinctively disliked the idea of team games, fixating instead on the anti-authority figures of the day like Marlon Brando, James Dean and Elvis Presley, Jim was one of those rivers-run-deep boys who could be wincingly shy one moment, snarky and superior the next.

His brother, Andrew, born in 1949, was closer to their sister, Annie, than big bro Jimmy. But then no one ever quite seemed to get close enough to Jimmy. The same year he was appointed president of the student council, he was kicked out of Cub Scouts after he blatantly flaunted the rules and consistently mocked the den mother. It didn't matter. In 1955 the Morrison family was back in Albuquerque, where their eldest son, on the brink of his teenage years, gave up piano arbitrarily and became an outdoorsman, spending more time wandering the desert perimeter, obsessing over lizards and snakes, than he did at home, flopped in a chair, sullenly engrossed in books and drawing. It didn't last. Years later, when he would take acid and read hidden meanings into his hallucinations, the lizards and snakes returned to commune with him again, and he would write about himself as 'the lizard king'. When his father, now Commander Morrison, was assigned to the aircraft carrier USS *Midway*, the family moved to the pleasantly dull San Franciscan suburb of Alameda, and Jim was back to skulking in his room and putting the other kids at school on their guard. By the time the 14-year-old Jimmy was enrolled into George Washington High, yet another new school, this time in Alexandria, Virginia, in 1958, classmates found him to be 'quiet', 'shy', 'weird' and, on occasion, 'angry'. Already writing poetry, though he spent most of his time reading it, becoming obsessed with music, though far too impatient to have kept up his piano studies, he was the pudgy kid with the sweet face and few friends who always kept his distance from the crowd while at the same time almost daring them to join him.

In a 1991 article in local paper, the *Alexandria Gazette*, the writer Sandy Barnes spoke to a number of Jimmy's classmates at GWH, to build an enthralling portrait of the artist as a young god. One of the kids Jimmy did hang out with was Jerry Ainsfield, who recalled 'A handsome guy, but quiet and on the shy side [who] liked to write poetry and he was a talented artist.' According to Stan Durkee, whose family would drive Jim to school each morning, 'Intellectually, Jim was head and shoulders above all the rest of us. He read every book you could imagine.' Stan and Jimmy would get the bus to nearby Washington, to search the town's bookstores for Beat Generation writers like Kerouac and Ginsberg. He recalls studying Joyce's *Ulysses* during English lessons, where 'Even the teacher was learning from Morrison's interpretation of the work.' He added: 'We all were.'

Durkee's abiding impression, he said, was of a 'detached, creative' teenager who 'few, if any, people in our class were really close to'. He said he included Jimmy's family in that equation too, claiming, 'He went for weeks without seeing his parents.' These were not things he talked about much in school, preferring enigmatic silence to chitchat. But his frustration, his isolation, would sometimes come out anyway. Like the time 'Jim got really angry and exploded', after one of the teachers dared to question his judgement. 'In a sense,' Durkee concluded, 'Morrison was rebelling against the smugness and mindlessness of the late Fifties. Jim took everything to the max.'

Not everyone remembered Jimmy quite so fondly, though. Another classmate, Dick Sparks, described him as the leader of a 'tight little intellectual group who followed him like puppies [and] made fun of other people'. Patricia Madison recalls the future agent provocateur deliberately bringing a rotting fish onto a bus one broiling summer's day just to piss the other passengers off. 'Morrison would do things we didn't dare do,' she told Barnes. Like pissing in his locker one time rather than walk the short distance to the toilets. This may, in fact, be one of the first recorded incidents of drunken bad behaviour from Morrison. He 'liked drinking bourbon', Madison said.

But though another old school buddy, Tommy Edwards, recalls seeing Jimmy 'walking down a street in Warwick Village barefoot with a guitar around his neck', not one of his classmates says they would have guessed he might end up with a musical career. That accolade, they figured, would be taken by another of Jimmy's classmates, Ellen Cohen, who sang in the school choir and a decade later became famous as Mama Cass, singer of The Mamas & The Papas, who would beat

The Doors to chart success by two years, when they broke through in 1965 with 'California Dreamin''.

But these were surface scratches, compared to the combustible teenager that was now growing into the sort of insolent young maverick neither his father nor, most especially, his mother was prepared to tolerate. The long passive silences developed into openly rebellious scowls. Jimmy learned how to antagonise and hurt his mother, who bore the brunt of his bad behaviour because his father was away so often at sea, and who grew to resent both men for it. Jim's brother, Andrew, later told the writer Jerry Hopkins how much his mother, Clara, dominated the family home, coming down hard on Steve for never being there when she needed him and going out of her way to humiliate and shame her eldest son into submission. When that didn't appear to work, she would simply leave him to his own devices, eventually talking Steve into sending the boy back to his grandparents in Clearwater to live, where he couldn't do any more harm to the family reputation. Already exhausted by his flagrant disregard for the good manners expected of a senior naval officer's son on those public occasions where the family was obliged to turn out for their father, the final straw came when Jim deliberately failed to show up for his high school graduation day.

Until then his father had held out a somewhat distant hope that Jim would come good in the end. To encourage the big turnaround, he once took him 'for a little boat ride' on his huge aircraft carrier. Telling the story years later to another credulous college buddy, Dennis Jakob, Jim told how they had 'gone for a little spin' and done some 'target practise', using the same riot guns as the marines under his father's command did to blast the hell out of dummy enemy figures in the sea. Little Jimmy had been placed on an empty provisions box by his dad and given a gun and told to have a go. 'So I fired away,' Jakob recalls in his evocative 2011 memoir, *Summer With Morrison*. 'I felt this raw sensation of power. Raw, masculine power.' Dennis listened, wide-eyed with awe. Jim said he had understood it was his father's way of giving him a glimpse of the good life he expected him to have, following in the old man's footsteps. But how it had produced a very different effect in his son, one that would turn him into a would-be poet, not a soldier.

Again, it sounds almost too good to be true. Would a serious military career officer like Steve Morrison actually give his untrained young son a gun and invite him to shoot at will? What can be verified is that his father, increasingly worn down by his wife's complaints and by his own lack of connection with his teenage son, took the decision in the summer of 1961, six months short of Jim's 18th birthday, to send him packing to Clearwater, where he enrolled at St Petersburg Junior College.

He was at SPJ for the full 1961–62 academic year, getting Bs and Cs in English, Maths and Biology. Then he transferred to Florida State University, where he completed the 1962–63 academic year and the fall trimester of 1963, achieving As in Collective Behaviour and Essentials of Acting and a B in Philosophy of Protest. By all accounts, Jimmy was a good student. But he liked to drink and this caused him problems, as it would throughout his life. In September 1963, he was arrested and charged with petty larceny, disturbing the peace, resisting arrest and public drunkenness at a football game in Tallahassee, Florida. His crime: to get wasted on beer and loudly poke fun at the football players. It was a rainy day and, leaving the ground, he and his friends were 'sword fighting' with their umbrellas when Jim spotted a helmet through the open window of a police car. Grabbing it and putting it on his head, he was immediately arrested and taken to the local police station, where the first of many mugshots he would endure throughout his life were taken of him. In them the short-haired boy appears to be smirking. The charges were later dropped after his grandparents promised to discipline the boy themselves but they never did, dismissing his antics as merely the hijinks of a high-spirited boy letting off steam.

Another time, at a house party on Clearwater beach he'd been taken to by a friend, Jim 'provoked reaction' when he stood on the couch and pissed on the floor. It was always bad when he got drunk, something he liked to do more and more. Another friend from those days, Phil Anderson, recalled him, drunk on Chianti, at a racetrack in nearby Sebring, rolling around in the dirt in a white fake-fur coat he'd found somewhere, like a polar bear covered in dirt, and tried to launch himself onto the track. Friends grabbed his ankles. 'He'd get a real pleasure out of shocking people.'

What finally cooled him out, if just for a little while, was meeting the girl who became his first real love, Mary Frances Werbelow, a 17-year-old Clearwater High junior-year grad who would dominate his life for the next three years. As Jimmy's second cousin, Gail Swift, later put it, 'I think they answered a lonely call inside each other.'

It was the summer of 1962 and Mary was sunbathing on the beach beneath Pier 60, with a friend, when both girls spotted the 18-year-old Jimmy strolling across the hot sands towards them, him and another pal, joking and flirting, shyly at first and then with more confidence. Mary was slender, almost boyish, dark auburn hair in the early-Sixties Jackie Kennedy style, very pretty. And more than a match for Jim. When he challenged her to a game of matchsticks, and lost, his forfeit was to become her 'slave for a day'. Mary took the offer seriously enough to command him to get his hair cut – that very moment. Which, bizarrely, he did, even putting up with her ordering the barber to cut it 'Shorter! Shorter!' until he was left with his head shaved into a 'buzz-cut'. Next, Mary's 'slave' was told to wash her little black Plymouth car, which she'd nicknamed 'The Bomb!' Job done, Mary's slave was then told to chauffeur her to St Petersburg, in the now sparkling black Bomb, and treat her to the pictures, where they were showing *West Side Story*.

With her orthodox Catholic schoolgirl upbringing and straight-edge friends – Mary had never drunk anything stronger than cola, and was still a virgin and proud of it – it was hard for outsiders to understand what she saw in the freaky new kid in town. But, like Jim, Mary had never felt like she properly fitted in anywhere, and related strongly with Jimmy's more obvious outsider status. Never mind the clothes he wore or the way he mumbled his words, he could challenge you to pick any book at random from the piles that covered every surface and spare space in his bedroom, read the opening lines and he'd know the book, give you the author's name, even recite the next few lines. 'He was a genius,' Mary said, years later, in a rare interview. 'He was incredible.'*

Together, they enjoyed that rare thing only couples that have a real connection are capable of: silence in each other's company. 'We connected on a level where speaking was almost unnecessary. We'd look at each other and know what we were thinking.'* They would sit and read together, or in separate rooms, they would hang out together every day practically, either at Mary's parents' place on Nursery Road or at Jim's grandparents' house. 'I hated to let him go at night. I couldn't shut the door.' The only thing they didn't do together was have sex. 'It was not happening. And it didn't for a long time,' said Mary. 'I'm surprised he held out that long.'*

Jim had begun his lifelong habit of carrying a notebook around with him. According to a Florida State contemporary, Bryan Gates, 'There was no one who wasn't under observation.' Jim's 'only purpose in life was observation'. Even when they were driving somewhere, Jim would make Mary keep his notebook open in her lap, urging her, 'Write this!' Or when he got too intense, pull the car over, grab the book, and scribble down his thoughts as fast as he could manage. Then, without looking at them, hand the notebook back to Mary and drive off again.

Jim rarely drank in front of Mary, either, 'out of respect for me', she insisted. And the stupid pranks were kept to a minimum, or saved for when she wasn't around. 'We were in love, and he didn't want to do things that I didn't like.'* Instead, he was always supportive, telling friends she was a

---

* Copyright © *St. Petersburg Times*, 2005.

great artist, who could draw even better than he did. When, in 1963, not long after Mary's 18th birthday, she had entered a beauty contest to become Miss Clearwater, a horribly bored and out-of-place Jim stayed awake long enough to see her come second.

When Jim eventually transferred to Florida State, in Talla-hassee, each weekend he would hitchhike back the 230 miles to Clearwater. He would also phone her every other day, in-structing her to stand waiting at a designated phone box, so that she could speak freely away from her parents. Mary's dad, who had begun to take against Jim, had been appalled when Mary suggested she might see Jim in Tallahassee. The couple would swap letters almost daily, too. Not that that pre-vented Mary from expressing her anger at Jim whenever she felt he had let her down. One weekend, after he'd hitched all the way back to see her, Mary ordered him out of the car at a busy intersection, and then drove off, leaving him standing there. When she finally came back she found him slumped, sobbing inconsolably, at the roadside. She stopped the car and told him to get in. He did what he was told and got in.

FOUR

Hands upon the Wheel

Drummers and singers: it's a long and rarely pretty story. They both long to be the centre of attention, yet their ways of achieving it are dependent on entirely different factors. Singers don't need a complicated kit to set up and be clashingly loud in order to hone their craft or simply have fun. Drummers do. Singing can be done anywhere anytime, loud or quiet, with people or without. Drumming can't. Drummers need others around them, an ensemble, to truly make their art come to life, to fulfil their utmost potential.

Singers get all the glory. By and large, drummers get none. Singers stand at the front. Drummers sit at the back. Singers have big mouths and plenty to say. Drummers have the loudest, most insistent voices. Eventually the two clash. Then things get nasty. It can be a fight to the death. A drummer's magic is all in his hands and feet. It's all expressed through the thunder of his heart, the syncopation of his own blood. A singer – especially one like Jim – finds his wonder in his own mind, there's the voice, the breathing, but that is merely the rug beneath his winged feet. A singer like Jim Morrison is all about the intangible, the thing that passes for consciousness, both shared and otherwise. He doesn't care for timing or even rhythm, not when the ideas are flowing. In short, the singer is every drummer's nightmare; the one loose spoke on the wheel that can never be fixed.

This can be a good thing when the drummer is Charlie Watts and he is able to punch Mick Jagger in the jaw for daring to call him 'my drummer', as happened one overeager night in the early Eighties. It took Mick down a peg and actually made life just that little bit more liveable for the other members of the band and its entourage. Or it can be bad, when it's John Densmore and all you want to do is go out there and show how good you and your band are, but Jim Morrison merely wants to bring down civilisation as we know it and start a bloody revolution. He says.

'Jim knew I disapproved of his self-destruction, that's for sure,' John told me in 2012, during an interview for *Classic Rock* magaizne. 'More than anyone else in the band, I was rather tortured by his self-destruction [but] that was the card I was dealt.' You could hear his voice tense as he said it. Not wanting to besmirch the legend all these years later, there being no real victory in beating the already beaten, he was still aggrieved and frustrated all these years and lifetimes later.

Born on 1 December 1944, a fiery Sagittarius, like Jim, John Densmore was never going to be close to someone like Jim Morrison. An earthy character rooted in the touchable, doable, achievable; a team player in the very best sense of the word, John was the kind of straight-edge guy who expected back whatever he gave you, who simply couldn't get his head around anyone who didn't believe in that fair exchange. The very opposite of how Jim Morrison saw himself, in fact: Jim the big fire-starter who had so much energy to burn he could never direct it, never control it, just letting the flames lick at and consume whatever they came into contact with, as if Jim were helpless to stop them.

John didn't dig that shit. It wasn't who he was or who he ever wanted to be. John wasn't about being an outsider. As the first snare drummer in his high school marching band, he recalled in his memoir 'the feeling of power one got when playing with 40 other musicians'. He was the train driver. All aboard! John wanted to belong, and Jim Morrison had never belonged anywhere. Not for long.

John's roots ran deep. As he discusses in his splendid 1990 memoir, *Riders On The Storm*, one of his earliest memories was attending mass every Sunday with his mother, Margaret, older sister, Ann, and younger brother, Jim, at St Timothy's Catholic Church, in West L.A. His father, Ray, did not go with them, as he was not a Catholic. Nor had any intention of becoming so.

Margaret Mary Walsh was a native Californian with a strict Catholic upbringing. She was 16 and working at the local library when the 12-year-old Ray Blaisdale Densmore and his family moved in next door. Ray was a gutsy kid. There was little time for school, Ray being forced out to work to help keep the family fed. The kind of tough, Depression-era upbringing that would crush a lesser person was taken in his stride by Ray, before he went back to school in his twenties, enrolling at USC to study for a degree in architecture. He also did work on the side as an actor with the Santa Monica Players. Margaret also made money as 'a commercial artist'.

They had been dating for years before Ray finally proposed. She agreed on condition the kids be brought up as Catholics.

It was against this sturdy background that John grew up. The middle child, he wasn't pushed in any one direction or allowed to drift too much. Enamoured of his parents' Glenn Miller records, when he expressed interest in learning the piano at eight, they rented him an old upright to take lessons on. John loved it but his parents didn't hothouse him on it the way Ray Manzarek's parents did. John mainly just played when he felt like it. His biggest piano thrill, he recalls in his book, was learning a short piece then playing it, 'especially for an audience'.

A pupil at Daniel Webster Junior High School in West L.A., when offered the chance to join the school band he had one eye on the clarinet, which had keys like a piano but looked cooler and was easier to carry around. The family dentist put the block on that though, insisting it would ruin his wonky teeth, for which he had already had a brace fitted. When the school suggested he might like to try drums instead, the inde-fatigable young boy was delighted. His parents less so, as they flinched at the noise it would make. They gave in though after seeing how serious he was, taking lessons after school on a well-worn wood and rubber practice drum pad. It wasn't long before he was dragging them to Mr Muir's Drum Shop, where John persuaded them to purchase his first shiny new kit.

One thing led to another. He was 13 when he became the timpanist in the school orchestra. After that came the school marching band, swiftly moving from bass drum, to cymbal player, to his dream gig: first snare drummer. Required as he was, however, to wear a uniform while playing, complete with plumed hat and gloves, this was *not* a cool gig. Coming lower even on the school pecking order than the tennis players, who were generally considered to be 'faggots' – and John was an active tennis player – this made him an outcast overnight; a virtual untouchable to the girls and easy meat for any passing jocks who fancied picking on him. A stigma it would take a long time to shake off.

Partial salvation appeared when he was invited to join a local youth outfit named Terry & The Twilighters, playing Top 40 hits of the day. They were all Catholic, like John, but they didn't go to Catholic school and so were cooler. There were other benefits that obtaining such a plum gig bestowed upon him. Firstly, he got to play regular gigs on the Catholic school circuit. Secondly, in an effort to help him fit in, his parents allowed him to join an ordinary 'public' state school, University High School. He would still need to attend regular catechism classes every Saturday morning, but that was a small price to pay for this newfound freedom.

Best of all, though, it was through playing drums in the Twilighters that John met his first girlfriend, Heidi. Only snag: Heidi was a virgin from a staunch Catholic school run by nuns, so she and John never got beyond 'heavy petting'. More troublesome was the fact that Heidi had been dating Terry, the singer and titular leader of the group. Suddenly rehearsals became awkward. So awkward, in fact, both Terry and John stopped going. Cue: the end of the group. John continued to play as 'a casual', a drummer-for-hire at various one-off gigs playing weddings, bar mitzvahs, birthday parties . . . good drummers were hard to find and John was becoming a very good drummer indeed. He wasn't paid well or at all sometimes, but he got to play in front of teenage girls in tight tops and short skirts and that in itself was reward enough. For now.

When John graduated he did so with average grades. Major university fodder he was not. So in the autumn of 1963 he enrolled in Santa Monica City College. It was not a happy time. He could never find a subject that fully captured his interest and he switched majors several times, without ever settling on anything outside music that he felt good at, that he felt he might actually have something interesting to say about. His only notable success came when – ensconced once again as first snare drummer in the SMCC marching band – he was part of the team that won the 1964 All-California Junior College Marching Band Competition. Their prize: to perform before 90,000 spectators at the L.A. Coliseum for the American football Pro Bowl final.

John recalls in his memoir how the summer of 1964 also saw the opening of a new type of music club along the Strip, all-ages bars where alcohol was not served but young local groups were booked to play sets of original material, without the pressing need to perform Top 40 covers in order to sell beer. Nineteen-year-old John and his best bud, Grant, would be out most nights checking out the scene at hip new joints like The Trip, Brave New World and Bedo Ledo's. Needing a car to get there, John took a part-time job in a Chinese laundry, folding the clothes, eventually saving up enough to buy a rundown 1957 Ford convertible painted silver. Wow, man!

John and Grant grew their hair long, and were hip to the more musically far-out new acts like Love, who John was utterly bamboozled by then hopelessly obsessed with. Rightly seeing Love as one of the few bands of the new L.A. rock'n'roll scene that could satisfy both his jazz leanings and still get him onto the rock stage, wearing the crazy clothes and fighting off the crazy chicks. Despite his hair and his increasingly radical musical tastes, John knew he wasn't even on the same planet as the guys in Love. Led by the boundlessly charismatic Arthur Lee, in his purple granny glasses, deep-fringe jackets, giant flared jeans and psychedelic shirts, Love were interracial, trippy, ultrafashionable . . . John found it hard to believe that they actually walked around like that on the street. But they did.

His real musical passion though lay beyond the head-rattling strains of the rock'n'roll garage bands that mainly comprised the new Strip scene, and towards the heavy-duty jazz scene then percolating just a few blocks away on Central Avenue. 'I was a jazz buff,' he would tell me in 2012. Describing himself as 'a snob about rock. I mean, I knew about Elvis and Little Richard, loved it. But then The Beatles came along and, it was like, oh, this is cool. And so I came from a sort of improvisational, experimental background, so I loved exploring the edge and kind of different [styles of music].' Love had fitted right into that new musical paradigm. But only because they were so clearly set apart from it. Where John and Grant really got their kicks was at jazz joints like the Renaissance Club, where Lenny Bruce had performed; the Manne Hole, owned by the great jazz drummer Shelly Manne; Melody Lane on Adams Boulevard; the Lighthouse; the Bit; and the Parisian Room. The kind of 'late-nite' places very few white boys would dare to go to.

A quarter of a century later, writing in the *L.A. Times*,

John recalled the 'sacred gin joints' he and Grant would start to frequent as 'intimidatingly cool', adding, 'Just the food for a hungry teenager.' It was at Shelly's Manne Hole that he saw John Coltrane's exquisite drummer Elvin Jones for the first time; the man who would become 'my muse' in The Doors, as he imitated the 'dialogue' Jones would create with Trane in epic Doors numbers like 'When the Music's Over', those echo-chamber moments where the rest of the band would fade, leaving Jim to attempt lift-off with one of his improvisatory poem-songs. Before that it had been Joe Morello, the white drummer in the Dave Brubeck Quartet, that had swallowed his attention. Now came the whole gang.

'The "press roll" in the Doors' "Wild Child" is from sitting right next to Art Blakey at the Manne Hole,' he revealed. 'The groove on "The End" is influenced by seeing Chico Hamilton down at Howard Rumsey's Lighthouse at the Sunday afternoon jazz sessions. The freeform drumming behind Jim's poetry is watching Elvin and Coltrane battle it out in "Chasin' the Trane".'

With Grant now modelling his electric-keyboard style on Trane's pianist, the great McCoy Tyner, the same guy Ray Manzarek was also then becoming obsessed with, John and he would jam together, dreaming they were sparring with Trane. They even started asking to 'sit in' with players they came across in the bars and clubs, getting by on smiles and nods. On the rare occasions they actually elicited spoken approval John would be on cloud nine for days afterwards. But you needed to be 21 to legally play in most of these places so they drove all the way down to Tijuana and scored some fake IDs off a Mexican street hustler. John used his new fake ID to obtain a regular gig at the Orbit, a smoky Santa Monica bar.

The only thing missing from the 19-year-old John's life was the ability to get laid. No matter how much he and Grant cruised around town in the old silver Ford they could not pick up chicks. They quickly divined that this also had something to do with the kind of music they had blasting out of the car. The Beatles may have had five chart-topping albums in America that year, but the Coltrane quartet also had five albums out in the same period, none of which even touched the US Top 40, yet all of which, especially *Live at Birdland* and *Crescent*, showcased the sax player's classic Jones, Tyner and double-bassist Jimmy Garrison line-up at the very height of their hard-bop, modal, avant-garde powers.

But the little girls simply refused to understand and so the boys decided their next-best strategy was to get a pad of their own and start throwing some parties. Once again using their fake IDs, they talked their way into renting a small abode in Topanga Canyon. John's parents agreed to kick in half the $70 a month rent on condition he continued his college studies, at which point he transferred to San Fernando Valley State College, in nearby Northridge. What they simply hadn't known was that, in the autumn of 1964, Topanga Canyon was Hippy Central.

John had not even smoked grass or taken uppers or any of the other usual first steps before he dived right in and took his first acid trip. One of the black cats he had sat in with more than once turned him on to the idea. A wheelchair-bound sax master named Bud who used LSD to give him back his legs and send him anywhere he wanted to go. Inspired, John invited Bud back to the Topanga house to talk him and Grant through the rudiments. Bud brought the acid in powder form, warned the boys to take only half a dose first time around in case things got too 'heavy', then split with his friend Ed, a huge black guy who carried Bud out in his arms.

Impatient, John and Grant simply shovelled the bitter-tasting powder onto their tongues and waited for lift-off. They did not have to wait long. Considering his complete lack of experience in this area, it's unsurprising to read in Densmore's book how at first he felt like he was slipping into the void, nose-diving into the classic Bad Trip. Before Grant's helpless laughter pulled him out of it and he began ascending into the full-on lysergic rollercoaster sunshine moonstone acid trip. Afterwards he knew he was changed in some fundamental way. As he so eloquently puts it in his book, 'A crack had appeared in the façade of reality and I had peered through.' Afterwards, 'Nothing had changed yet everything had.'

Coincidentally or not, depending on your mind-blown headspace, man, it was just a few weeks later that John Densmore met Robby Krieger, another acid-virgin looking to take the big ride. Robby was a year younger than John but many more miles further down the road of his own journey from apprentice to astronaut. He may not have climbed aboard the psychedelic wagon train just yet, but Robby had been a pothead since he was 16, been sent to private school by his exasperated father and survived to tell the tale in the kind of soft-rolling, low-slung argot that sounded like the surf at Venice Beach rolling in and out again on an exceptionally calm early-hours morning. He also played the kind of far-out guitar that had clearly been touched by jazz yet would snake off into so many other hazy directions it was impossible to know where it had all come from originally. A bit like Robby himself, who just kind of appeared one day, beamed down as if by some bearded god-freak in the sky that fancied fucking with John's head just a little. Then maybe just a little bit more.

Robert Alan Krieger was born on 8 January 1946, in Los Angeles. The son of an aeronautical engineer who held several US government contracts, Robby grew up in a home steeped in classical music. A big favourite was *Peter and the Wolf.* Like every other teenager in Fifties America, however, it wasn't long before Robby had swapped the delights of Prokofiev's 'Children's Symphony' for the more illicit pleasures of Elvis Presley, Little Richard, Fats Domino and Chuck Berry.

A friend had an old acoustic guitar always lying around the place and whenever Robby visited he would find himself plucking away, trying to figure out how to make it work. It wasn't until he and his non-identical twin brother, Ron, were sent to private school, Menlo, near San Francisco – after he and Ron got busted for smoking pot – that Robby really got hooked on guitar. 'I was flunking out of school and spending too much time surfing' is how he later recalled it, somewhat disingenuously. He took up classical guitar at Menlo because of the rule that obliged students to spend three hours each night in their rooms studying. 'But if you had a guitar or something, you could do that.'

He became passionate about flamenco guitar, obsessing over the music of Sabicas, the self-styled King of the Flamenco Guitar, and the great Zambra Juan Serrano, whose intense demeanour and evocative single-note style Robby was particularly taken with. Receiving lessons from teachers at Menlo called Arnold Lessing and Frank Chin, 'I learned to play with my thumb under the neck.' He also eschewed the idea of using a pick, preferring to grow his fingernails long and use those instead. When he discovered Segovia, he approached him in the same, open-minded almost too innocent way.

After high school, Robby spent a year at the University of California at Santa Barbara, which he later described as 'keeping out of the army'. Bob Dylan was suddenly where it was at and Robby got himself a neck-mounted harmonica and began getting up and playing and singing on the local folk circuit. He also played occasionally with a jug band, the riotously named Back Bay Chamberpot Terriers. Robby got deep into the scene, digging Dave Van Ronk and the loose-fitting blues style of Spider John Koerner.

Robby didn't care what musical 'tradition' these players came out of. As he said to me, 'I just dug the good stuff.' After he saw Chuck Berry play at the Santa Monica Civic Auditorium, he went out the next day and bought himself a black Gibson SG. The classical acoustic was iced and Robby never looked back. 'I got to know some people who did rock'n'roll with jazz, and I thought I would make money playing music.'

Getting his kicks playing electric guitar for the first time, Robby absorbed any and every influence he came across, from the wild city boy blues of Albert King to the Gypsy polyrhythms of Django Reinhardt; from the hip jazz guitar stylings of Wes Montgomery to the tough, earth-powered blues of Muddy Waters. They all became jumping-off points for Robby, musical footprints he would follow without question, never thinking to stop for long anywhere while there were still places left to go. When the path led him to Indian classical music he kept right on going there too, playing along to Ravi Shankar's 1963 album, *Ragas & Talas*, using his flamenco finger-picking style on his SG to try and replicate the master's transcendental sitar.

Though he didn't know it, Robby had first breathed the same air as John at college, where the latter recalled him as the rich kid that drove his dad's big Plymouth and paid for petrol using a credit card: the first time John had ever seen anyone do that, let alone a frizzy-haired, spaced-out teenager who looked more like he'd stolen both the card and the car.

Because Robby came from money – his family lived in a big house in the swish Pacific Palisades part of West L.A. – John found him hard to figure at first, misinterpreting his quiet, surefooted demeanour as arrogance, even snobbery. But Robby was a gentle cat, used to being misread by others. He moved in his own space and time; John would come round like all the others, and he did.

It was John who turned Robby on to acid, but Robby who took it and ran with it and was soon the go-to guy for John and all his other friends that wanted to score. Robby would also bring around pot and sometimes a little Methedrine. For the quiet guy of the bunch he sure was fearless when it came to getting it on. Robby was a dude. He just didn't feel the pressing need to make a big deal of it.

In his book, John maintains that Robby did have an edge, just that you wouldn't see it at first. That Robby displayed that classic passive-aggressive quality which a lot of children of the wealthy have when vying for space with the less fortunate of their peers: too well-mannered to talk trash but steely sure of themselves and not about to be pushed into anything they didn't already want to do. It was this quality, more than any other, in fact, that would so enamour Robby Krieger to Jim Morrison, who quickly became used to riding roughshod over everyone else's feelings, yet could never find any real purchase with quiet, cool, hugely unimpressed Robby. Robby was like L.A. after dark, when the heat hasn't quite worn off but the light no longer blinds your eyes. Dark, sometimes dangerous, but dreamy too, part of the same undulating neon ooze of the Strip as it starts to settle into what it really is, not what Jim Morrison or anyone else, no matter how loud they shout or how much they kick against it, wants it to be.

If John, with his feet planted firmly on the ground, represented the element of earth in The Doors – of solidity, strength, indomitability – Robby would come to represent the element of air – of expansion, vibration, flexibility. Tellingly, Jim – who would provide the element of fire, of energy, dynamism, volatility – considered Robby his best friend in the band. So did John. 'Robby was my best friend, most of the way,' John would tell me. Ray, not surprisingly, said he didn't believe in 'childish concepts' like best friends. But that was only because Ray, who would represent the element of water – of cohesion, interconnection, fluidity – got cold-shouldered after Jim finally refused his offer of brotherhood and tutelage, to hang out more with Robby. Because it was Robby, more than the others, more than anybody, who saw Jim for what he really was – another spoiled boy with rich parents searching for a way to pay them back without admitting they were somehow responsible – and so he never expected anything more from him. Ever.

FIVE

Give This Man a Ride

In his autobiography, as in later life, Ray talks mindlessly about Jim being 'a satyr', being high on the spirit of Dionysus, of being in fact the earthly embodiment of the overripe old goat god, just as all the great ones had been, like Rimbaud, Modigliani, Neal Cassidy . . .

Yet when Ray Manzarek first met Jim Morrison at UCLA he found him something of a lost cause. An overweight self-absorbed stoner who rolled such beautiful joints Ray considered them, far more than the incoherent, patchwork student movies he made, Jim's real 'works of art'.

Garrulous, overeducated, supremely self-confident and already living with the beautiful, intelligent and cultured young woman who would one day become his wife, Ray was the alpha-male at UCLA, not Jim. As Robby Krieger would later put it, Ray was the 'big man on campus'. Jim was the screwball. 'We were all heads,' Ray would later say of his time at UCLA. 'Everyone was high. Everyone was giggling and laughing just having the grandest time.' Few though would have as grand a time of it as Ray Manzarek.

And yet his and Jim's paths to UCLA were not so very different. Both had arrived on the West Coast from distant parts of America – Ray from the Midwest, Jim from the Southeast. Each of them was accompanied by the love of his life: Dorothy with Ray, Mary with Jim. Both had a marked passion for and superior knowledge of film, literature and music. And both shared a deep and abiding ambition to somehow get more out of life than the professional careers their respective families still sought for them.

Where they differed were the ways in which they went about achieving this ill-defined yet ever-present goal. Ray saw his best chance of cutting loose being to take great strides at university, to get his MA in film studies and go on to become a big Hollywood director. No matter that so many of his favourite movies had been made largely outside the Hollywood paradigm, Ray always knew where the main chance lay.

Jim simply couldn't see that far ahead. Still thought he could cruise by on luck, though the fear of failure never left him. Still thought if he turned in too early he'd wet the bed and incur the wrath of the gods. Jim never wanted to sleep again; never wanted to get out of bed in the morning; never wanted to be in class anyway, yet never felt more abject than when one of his tutors stood him up in front of the rest of the class and accused him of being 'Opposed to everything this Department stands for.'

A later incarnation of the future Doors wild man might have laughed it off, taken it as a compliment even. But the 20-year-old Jimmy was mortified. It meant him taking the entire course again in order to ensure he got his BA, the very thing he had promised his parents he would do if they let him go to UCLA. To prove he was really a serious boy, and not the artsy-fartsy disappointment his father was beginning to consider him.

But Jim was about to find temporary solace in a new father figure, in the tall, bespectacled, all-knowing figure of UCLA's favourite son, Ray. Jim would eventually rebel against him too, of course, in an inevitable repeat of his relationship with his real father, getting in the disappointment early before things got too deep and out of his control. In the meantime, he had also acquired a mother figure, in the form of Mary Werbelow, who against her parents' wishes had decided to follow Jim down to Los Angeles when he started at UCLA in 1964.

Speaking to the *St. Petersburg Times* in 2005, Mary recalled how Jim had asked her to wear 'something floaty' when she arrived. 'He wanted me to look like an angel coming off the plane.'* But Mary being Mary, she decided she would rather not do that and simply drove herself nearly 3,000 miles instead, arriving in L.A. a week early in order to surprise him. By then Jim was living in a small pad on San Vicente Boulevard paid for by his parents. But Mary, determined not to be perceived as merely Jim's concubine, refused to stay there with him for long and found her own apartment nearby. She found a part-time job working as a clerk in a hospital X-ray department, and enrolled for art classes at L.A. City College, where she was adored by the other students, many of whom, when they met Jim, could not believe such a sweet girl was somehow tangled up with a guy like that.

---

* Copyright © *St. Petersburg Times*, 2005.

Even though she spent most of her free time with Jim, she resented what she saw as his attempts to absorb her identity in his. 'I just knew I had to be away from him. I needed to be by myself, to find my own identity.' Jim, though, saw these developments less as Mary's way of finding her own true identity and more as her simply abandoning him, the way his parents had. 'I really hurt him,' she confessed in 2005. 'It hurts me to say that [but] I really hurt him.'*

The fights between them got worse, with Jim now railing against what he saw as the injustice of the situation. He'd long since allowed the buzz-cut Mary had always insisted on to grow out, so that his hair was now becoming an unruly mop of curls, which he refused to comb. Now he seemed intent on shrugging off all her other influences. Just like everybody else at UCLA, Jim was now doing acid and smoking pot – something Mary never did. LSD-25, still legal, had been around the UCLA campus since 1963. Unlike most others at UCLA, though, Jim would spend hour after hour rolling his perfect joints; he would take two or three doses of LSD in one hit. Los Angeles in the early to mid-Sixties probably had more 'heads' per capita than any other city in the Western world. But few that could keep up with Jim. He could never get too high or stay high for too long. He was drinking heavily as well. The boy Mary had fallen in love with back in Clearwater had always had an edge. Liked a drink and a prank and always had the right bad words to say about everybody. But this guy was becoming something else, someone whose inner darkness

---

* Copyright © *St. Petersburg Times*, 2005.

now seemed to hover over him some days like a halo of flies.

Jim wanted to shock, to be shocked. One day he climbed to the top of one of the faculty buildings, stripped off his clothes and hurled them through the air. Another time he got drunk and pissed on the floor of the public library, exposing himself to several passing women. Anything he was told was wrong, he wanted to do. Making fun of wheelchair-bound soldiers outside the nearby army vets' hospital. Hanging out not with clean-cut high-achievers like Ray Manzarek but with the college's outsiders. Heavy cats like Dennis Jakob, whom Ray would later characterise as 'a Nietzschean wild man' and was nicknamed 'The Weasel' because of his hunched shoulders and scurrying gait. Dennis also had a penchant for depicting scenes from various 19th-century classics on the blackboard in different-coloured chalks. He would later claim, in his brief but colourful memoir, *Summer With Morrison*, to have aided Jim in the making of his ill-fated student movie, helping him edit 'about 40 separate images' down to 'nine great shots'.

Then there was Big John DeBella, the tough-nut son of a New York cop who claimed to have once been a longshoreman, knew how to hustle – he wore a special long coat with several inside pockets in order to steal books – and would describe in lurid detail his latest sexual escapades with his busty German girlfriend, Elke. And Phil O'Leno, who *was* serious about his film career and looked on Jim as his 'little brother', and who later claimed to have given Jim some of his own discarded footage for his student film, but who mostly spent time with Jim gobbling shrooms and chasing peyote, 'breaking through', as he puts it, and being 'shown by spirit guides the way around.' Phil was heavy but he was also reputed to have read the complete works of Carl Jung. He was no dummy. Another of Jim's uncharmed circle, Felix Venable, was not so smart and was widely considered the most abject of the group. Already 34 when he arrived at UCLA and on his way to full-blown alcoholism, he is credited by many with being the guy who taught Jim about the illicit pleasures of excess for its own sake. Jim romanticised Felix as being like Dean Moriarty in Kerouac's *On the Road*, the Peter Pan of the Beat Generation who simply refused to grow up and live in the straight world, not realising how pathetic that actually was. Felix would do speed, acid, pot and anything else you had all in one go, then empty a bottle of bourbon down his throat, and Jim loved him for it, began to emulate him. There were some strange cats at UCLA that year, including one who reportedly cut the heart out of his girlfriend in search of the soul of his mother. But Felix was the only one who would achieve the distinction of killing himself before he even got his degree, dead at 37 from cirrhosis of the liver.

Jim saw something in each of these people that he could relate to, felt comfortable being around, much more than he did the clean-cut, idealistic Manzarek. Yet it was Ray who would always be the most affable towards him. Who never really looked back at Jim the way Phil or Dennis or Big John did and saw what they saw: the mess he had befouled himself in. Ray only saw the light. Only wanted to see the light. Jim preferred the dark, felt at home there; where he didn't have to live up to anyone else's hopes and dreams. Where he could be excused anything.

And of course, though Mary had no hard evidence of it yet, she realised he must also be seeing other girls. After one particularly bad fight when he'd stormed out and simply didn't come back for days, Mary tracked him down to where she felt sure he probably was: the apartment of another girl named Mary, this one actually the girlfriend of the hapless Felix Venable. She banged on the door but when Jim's new girlfriend came to the door she swore Jim wasn't there. Mary knew better. Eventually, after she stood there calling him by name – 'Come out wherever you are!' – Jim sheepishly appeared from behind the door, naked but for a towel around his waist. Devastated, Mary ran to her car and drove off, accidentally hitting the garden fence as her car shrieked away from the kerb. This was 'the beginning of the end', she said.*

By the summer of 1965 it really was all over. Once Jim had left UCLA, he seemed to simply give up on all the extra-curricular trappings that had come with it, beginning with the San Vicente apartment, which his parents refused to continue paying for unless he got a job and Jim was far beyond getting a job. He begged Mary for another chance but she wasn't having any of it. Jim the eternal seeker was on a quest, he told her. Mary, as if to get her own back and prove she wasn't the uptight small-town Miss Clean, got herself a new, much better-paying job as a dancer at Gazzarri's, a hip new nightclub on Sunset run by Bill Gazzarri, who billed himself as the godfather of rock'n'roll and liked to dress up as a Chicago-style mobster. When Mary went on to become Gazzarri's Go-Go Girl of the Year, Jim, who knew Gazzarri's and would play there a year later with The Doors, was filled with a mixture of envy, despair and contempt.

---

* Copyright © *St. Petersburg Times*, 2005.

'I don't know if he ever really got over Mary,' Ray would tell me. 'She was a great girl and he really seemed to be in love with her. But that was also the summer Jim went through some kind of transformation – physical, mental, emotional, on every level – and I don't think any relationship he'd had could have survived that. Jim was about to start this whole new chapter in his life and I think he felt that on some deep level. But he still talked about Mary a lot. I mean, she still lived close by and who knows what might have happened with them in another life, some kind of parallel universe where The Doors never happened?'

Instead, the summer of 1965 found Jim Morrison freer of responsibility, of relationships and commitments and other people's ideas of what he should and shouldn't be doing, than he had ever been. What would he do with this newfound freedom?

He had no idea.

Ray Manzarek was first introduced to Jimmy Morrison by their mutual UCLA pal John DeBella. DeBella had acted as the nominal cameraman on Jim's end-of-term movie, which no one can now recall the title of or if it even had a title, and which none of the UCLA faculty staff took remotely seriously. Ray would later refer to it as Jim's missing 170 Project, describing it in his book as 'cinematic poetry . . . a juxtaposition of images that didn't really have any relationship to one another in a linear narrative form. But after five minutes went by it became a collective whole. A poetic piece.'

That was certainly one of way of putting it. Another might be to describe it as a jumbled mess with several less than original ideas strung together in the hope they might somehow amount to something, anything, at least in the context of the sort of self-consciously 'surrealist' idiom that would become eternally popular among first-year film students, post-Buñuel and Dalí.

The most striking scene – and the one the UCLA faculty found most objectionable – was shot in Jim's apartment and featured DeBella's girlfriend, the tall, well-built Elke, dressed in stockings and suspenders and stripped to her bra and pants, and a pair of black stilettoes, doing a Germanic bump and grind while perched atop Jim's big old fashioned American TV. As DeBella starts flipping channels with the 'lazy bones' remote, to his and Jim's obvious delight a World War Two movie comes on, complete with images of tanks, stormtroopers, explosions. Overjoyed, Jim told John to 'Leave it, leave it! It's perfect!' In another scene, Jim is shown smoking one of his 'works of art' joints. As he exhales deeply the film cuts to an atomic mushroom cloud. In his book, Ray breathlessly explains how the Russian director and film theorist Sergei Eisenstein did it first but how Jim's movie was 'in the tradition'. It's such an absurd claim it would be comforting to think Ray was sending the film up when he wrote that. More unsettling – though, sadly, more believable – to realise he actually meant it. Other scenes depict a bunch of college brats hanging around drinking beer and throwing darts at a female pinup. Dennis Jakob claimed the pinup in question was Mary and that the picture was deliberately turned upside down, to imply how deeply Jim now distrusted her. Yet the whole thing comes across as exactly what the university faculty decried it as: stoned student hogwash. Nothing they hadn't seen before, but they hoped their students had grown out of by the time they came to study at a place as steeped in the history of cinematography as UCLA.

Given Ray's more elevated position as a student of genuine promise, it's hard to imagine he ever saw Jim's stuttering attempts at cinematic art as anything other than embarrassingly amateurish. Yet with the benefit of the hindsight that unchallenged decades of refining the Jim Morrison myth had given him, Ray instead recalls in his book the many great films he and Jim both immersed themselves in during their time together at UCLA.

Like Ray, Jim had been bowled over by Camus's *Black Orpheus*, had dug especially Bergman's *The Seventh Seal*, relating on a personal level to the part where Death and the Knight play chess on the beach. Like Ray, Jim had swooned at Kurosawa's *Rashomon* and come out fighting after seeing Truffaut's *The 400 Blows*. And he had reached a new epiphany with the films of Josef von Sternberg. This latter most especially, but less for the dark, forbidding tones of his movies than for the knee-knocking performances of von Sternberg's central star and muse, Marlene Dietrich. Jim became besotted by Dietrich and would go to repeated viewings of *Blue Angel*, *Shanghai Express*, *Blonde Venus*, all the classic American and German expressionistic movies she'd made with Sternberg.

What Ray forgets to mention is that when Sternberg showed up at UCLA to lecture for a semester, Jim had planned to approach the great auteur with an idea to tape-record a series of interviews, but the old man was so dull that a hugely disillusioned Jimmy was one of the first to bail out.

When they later formed the band, writes Ray, it was all

about, 'How do we bring all of this good stuff into The Doors? How do we bring the drama? How do we bring the depth of emotion? How do we bring the pathos and the joy, the sorrow and the terror into rock'n'roll music? How do we bring the terror, indeed? *That's* what The Doors were all about.' In this, he was spot on, though. For Jim, as for Ray, the best cinema, wherever it came from, combined the best of all the arts. And the best films of all were the ones that made even more sense when you went to see them zonked out of your mind on the good strong weed that circulated so freely in Southern California, or best of all the acid that was still legally available. Scribbling in his notebooks, Jim would liken the movie camera to the all-seeing eye in the sky. Great cinema, he wrote, was the 'most totalitarian' of all the arts. It actually allowed you to play god. Great cinematic art, he wrote, lay in the tradition of 'ancient, popular wizardry . . . an evolving history of shadows'. And 'a belief in magic'.

When they started The Doors, Ray would later insist, they wanted to combine as many of the arts as possible too, music, art, theatre, even film and poetry, set design, painting, playing with different effects on the eyes, ears, body and mind. Yet what Jim really loved best was not about any one medium; at root it was simply about beholding the spectacle of great art made for the masses by the most elite of exquisite soloists. A viewpoint that would eventually drive Ray, the great populist, to extortionate levels of obeisance in his increasingly desperate defence of Jim's most self-destructive behaviour.

Cultured, comfortable, inquisitive Ray would look back on those early days of knowing Jimmy Morrison and recall the 'very nice apartment' he lived in, the bookshelves stacked with Greek and Roman classics – the former evolved from the song and dance ceremonies honouring Dionysus at Athens, the latter focused first on the military history of Rome, then turning later to poetry and comedies, histories and tragedies; with French symbolist poets such as Charles Baudelaire, Paul Verlaine and Arthur Rimbaud standing tall next to American literary highwaymen like Hemingway, Faulkner and Mailer; these peppered with true 20th-century heavyweights like Camus, Sartre, Joyce, even some Céline, whom not even Ray had heard of until then. And when the shelves and the cupboards were too full, in big messes across the floor lay contemporary miscreants – Burroughs, Kerouac, Ginsberg, Ferlinghetti, Corso . . . what didn't Jim have lurking there somewhere? It was better than a bookstore. Had he actually read them all? He had. He said. And Ray believed him. Why, there was even one wall completely covered in a slapdash collage of magazine and newspaper cuttings: pictures and text scissored in a frenzy then glued to the wall, from *Time*, *Vogue*, the *L.A. Times*, *Playboy*, local rags, stroke mags, pictures of sexy chicks, of hooded gangsters, football players, cheerleaders, musclemen, all splattered across the length and breadth of the wall overlapping onto the ceiling. What did it mean? Even Ray didn't know. Maybe Jim didn't either. It wasn't clearly defined enough to pontificate about it being some sort of surrealist juxtaposition. It was just . . . wild. Later, of course, looking back, Ray would cite it as merely further evidence of Jim's fast-flourishing genius. But at the time it looked more like drug-induced madness; a typical student's harem of garbage imagery and pot smoke slapstick.

When Ray started playing around town with Rick & The

Ravens, he naturally invited all his UCLA pals to come along, including Jim, the more the merrier. Jim would come to Ray's gigs, get drunk and high and keep shouting out for 'Louie Louie', a Simple Simon tune he'd lately become over-engaged with, stripping away at it in his overheated mind until it became his stoned mantra. At Ray's gigs, that was his thing, the guy who always shouted out for 'Louie Louie'. Ray tried to see the funny side but soon grew exasperated, having to explain away the boorish behaviour to his brothers, who took their gigs tremendously seriously, didn't appreciate having them spoiled by some stoned oaf from Ray's school. Finally, one night, they grabbed Jim, pulled him up onto the tiny stage of the Turkey Joint West, and told him to sing the damn song then. No messing. Partly to shut him up, like okay, let's see you do it, big mouth.

So Jim got up, high, drunk, doing his usual solo flight around the moon, and belted out 'Louie Louie' at the top of his voice. No rhyme, no reason. More like the bellow of a big wounded bear. And the crowd went nuts! Jim whooping, giving it his all, his first time ever on a stage singing and he loved it, man, fucking loved it! When afterwards the chicks all came around, he *really* loved it. Other stoned and drunken guys slapping his back, like this was somehow real. Far out, man! The Manzarek brothers though were not so easily impressed. Jim was not invited back for any further cameo appearances.

When, in June 1965, Ray graduated with a Masters Degree from UCLA, Jim was mailed his BA diploma, refusing – as with his high school graduation – to even show up at the ceremony. Instead, he chose to spend the afternoon with Dennis

Jakob, gathering his numerous ringed notebooks into a pile then feeding them one by one into the building's basement incinerator. When Dennis asked for just one page to hold on to, Jim smiled that stunned, lazy smile and drawled, 'Don't worry, I'll just make new ones.' The books were only 'Things I'd seen and heard,' he told Dennis. 'Especially things that have no meaning.' Dennis wasn't so sure but in they went, into the burner, anyway. Along with the Senior Thesis that helped him get his BA, which he had worked and reworked into something he titled *Notes on Vision*, heavily influenced, Dennis wrote later, by *The Book of the Damned* by Charles Fort, a decidedly bizarre almanac of UFO sightings, hostile weather and unexplained phenomena. Some of which Jim would eventually return to and re-describe in his poetry collection *The Lords: Notes on Vision*.

When Ray ran into Jim a few days later and asked what he was going to do with his degree, Jim announced he was going to New York, where he planned to hook up with Jonas Mekas, from *Film Culture*, the prestigious American film magazine started by Adolfas Mekas and his brother, Jonas, in 1954. Ray was impressed, and bid his odd-fellow friend a fond adieu. Six weeks later, however, they would meet again but under much different circumstances, after Jim had completed his butterfly act, shed his lumpy caterpillar carapace and emerged like a newborn consciousness onto a rainbow-lit plain so elevated only he and Ray might become one there. That was how Ray might like to have described it anyway.

In fact, the next 40 days and nights *were* to become something of a transformative experience for Jim. The moment when he ceased to be fat Jimmy, the weirdo at UCLA, and turned into Jim Morrison, lizard king rock star in waiting.

Without the UCLA cafeteria to load up on food – Jim had a student meal ticket and would feel if he ever missed a meal 'I was getting screwed' – and with no place to live and no money to spend, except on the usual cacophony of weed and acid and booze and dope, Jim began to shed nearly 20 pounds in weight.

Going from place to place every other night, sleeping on couches or floors or whatever was offered, soon lost its novelty value, though. When Dennis Jakob told him he could come and share his tiny one-bedroom place in Venice Beach, Jim didn't need to be asked twice. It was a tiny rooftop apartment on Brooks Street; so small there was no shower, just a hot-plate and a bed. But the rent was only $35 a month, and even Jim could find half of that every few weeks. In return he got to spend a lot of time smoking weed and tripping with Dennis and discussing the great literature of the world. And when he grew tired of that, he could sleep under a rug on Dennis's roof. No biggie, it was summer and a lot of dudes did that in Venice. Where once it had been muscle beach central, Venice was now strictly Boho, old rundown bungalows next to abandoned storefronts and cheap roadside cafes, dingy waterways and long alleys overhung with faded palms and long shadow, where time moved so slowly it felt like it was bent sideways.

In *Summer With Morrison*, Dennis describes the many conversations he and Jim had over these weeks. In particular, he describes turning Jim on to the philosophical ideas of Friedrich Wilhelm Nietzsche, the German philologist, philosopher, poet and composer, whose writing encompassed theories on religion, contemporary culture, science and music, but whose central theme was built around the idea of the Superman, or Übermensch, a combustible meeting of opposites that placed the Apollonian ideals of logic, harmony and forward thinking next to the Dionysian compulsion for disorder, emotion and intoxication, raising individual will and its ultimate power over the now surely outmoded idea of god. Indeed, one of Nietzsche's most controversial ideas was what he described as 'the death of God'.

What most interested Jim, though, as he read key Nietzschean works like *Beyond Good and Evil* and, most especially, *Birth of Tragedy in the Spirit of Music*, was the idea that in a fundamentally meaningless world there is no right or wrong. No past, no future one is beholden to. That there is only the now, and that each moment is there to be challenged, to be flagellated, to be exploded and rebuilt, torn down and revised, however one sees fit. That one should always strive for transcendence by whatever means available. That the strong and powerful individual is always greater and therefore much closer to the ultimate truths of the universe than the angry, frightened herd.

Jim really dug that whole trip, man. But then Jim was into a lot of weird shit even Dennis didn't get to hear about. At least, not at first.

There was a long, dimly lit footpath, called Speedway, near to Dennis's flat that connected his building to the beach. Danny says Jim spent several nights prowling along the Speedway as a peeping Tom, sneaking up fire escapes and peering through the corners of windows, at lovers, solo artists, night creatures of every stripe. He saw arguments, fights, kisses and caresses, people sleeping, masturbating, making love. He saw visions of himself as a younger and older man, alone in the darkness. When he returned to Dennis's apartment he would slip silently through his bedroom, out the window and up onto the roof, often without a word.

Dennis would sometimes follow Jimmy on his nocturnal ramblings, just to see what he was up to, a stalker trailing a peeping Tom. In his book, Dennis recalls how Jim would sit atop a fire escape 'for hours, watching, his eyes frozen on the panels of window glass . . . mesmerised'.

Other nights, with nothing better to do, they would read and talk and read again, sharing the tiny room together, Dennis on the bed, Jim on the couch. Jim held Dennis in especially high esteem as the only person he'd ever met that had actually read more books than him. Jim confided in Dennis that he didn't know yet what he wanted to do with his life. According to Dennis it came down to either writing lyrics for a rock band or writing cheap paperback novels. Jim cited *Billy the Kid* as a possibility for one of his novels. He related to the Kid, he said, because 'I'll never live to be 30.' But what wide-eyed stoner at that age didn't come out with tiresome drear like that? In that regard, Jim was no different to anyone else.

Jim told Dennis another tale that has never been proven and one suspects came from the same source as the dead-Indians ditty: about the time he hitchhiked from Florida down to Oxford, Mississippi, where he claimed he saw a white-haired William Faulkner sitting in the town square, smoking a pipe. Said he just watched the old man sitting there with friends, smoking his pipe and brandishing a walking cane. It sounds like a page from one of his proposed paperback novels. Or maybe it was true, one never knew with Jim, who acted out these fantasies with such delicate force he would never have doubted himself, so why should you?

Dennis recounts how Jim then decided he would like some sort of musical troupe, ostensibly a duo, featuring both him and Dennis, to perform Jim's own poetry, based on the influences of all the books he and Dennis had consumed. He even had a name for it: The Doors. Dennis would be the 'open' Door and Jim would be the 'closed'. Dennis also claims the inspiration for using the name The Doors came not merely from Huxley or Blake but from Thomas Wolfe's *Look Homeward Angel*, and his phrase about the 'unfound door'. But then Jim had said much the same thing some months before to an old pal from his Florida State days named Sam Kilman, when he came to stay for a few days at Jim's apartment in L.A. Sam, who at least played drums, had laughed it off, calling Jim's bluff: 'Yeah, and what would you do?' 'Sing,' said Jim. 'Can you sing?' asked Sam. 'Hell, no, I can't sing!' cried Jim. Then fell about laughing.

But the idea was obviously percolating in his mind. As it was for many a young dude Jim's age that fulsome summer of 1965. The Byrds' lush electric pop version of Dylan's 'Mr Tambourine Man' had topped the American charts in June. It may only have featured half the lyrics of Dylan's mind-melding original, but it did contain the most obvious reference yet to LSD in the verse: '*Take me for a trip upon your magic swirlin' ship / All my senses have been stripped / And my hands can't feel to grip / And my toes too numb to step / Wait only for my boot heels to be wanderin'* ...' Jim knew instantly what they were talking about. It was the first time he'd realised just what you could get away with in a modern rock song. When the Stones then followed it with one of the anti-establishment anthems of the Sixties, '(I Can't Get No) Satisfaction', which stayed at No. 1 the whole of July, he didn't need any more convincing. He would still be a poet, but he would be so before the widest possible audience. Including chicks. Suddenly his notebooks began to fill not just with smoke-ringed thoughts and tripped-out observations but with actual lyrics. Verses and choruses. Even titles. Most of which would eventually feature on the early Doors albums.

There was another aspect to Jim's 'transformation' in the summer of 1965, however, that has never been fully revealed before. His discovery of gay bars, specifically, and his tentative foray into gay culture, in general.

In his book, *Summer With Morrison*, Dennis Jakob writes that Jim was the first person to introduce him to gay bars. How Jim had spoken in fascinated tones about the 'tension' that builds up in a gay bar around closing time, as the patrons who haven't yet scored hurry their search to find a partner for the night. Jim was obviously speaking from experience, and Dennis was shocked.

Danny says that one night Jim took him and a pal named Vic to a bar on the Boardwalk at Venice West 'that was split right down the middle, with gay males on one side and lesbians on the other'. Danny then describes how Jim attracted a lot of obvious interest, but just stood there, eyes to the floor, impassive, not moving. Dennis and Vic wondered how far Jim expected them to take this 'experiment', but Jim gave no sign. Clearly, he had been here before, alone. What had happened on those occasions? With Dennis and Vic the evening merely petered out as Jim led them out the door again before closing time, and back to the familiar sanctity of Dennis's hovel. Whenever the subject was broached in the days to come, however, Jim would clam up.

Dennis speculates about what Jim was trying to prove but the answer seems obvious. Jim, who carried so much anger towards his mother, such contempt that would surface in the coming years towards women in general; Jim, who still shuddered at the prospect of standing before his father, having to explain himself. Jim, with his now lean and tanned body, and his ringlets and deep-set eyes and long eyelashes; Jim, the great thrill-seeker, always on the lookout for new and more daring adventures. Jim, the hot young Hollywood dropout looking for a place to spend the night. Dennis describes one night when he followed Jim on one of his peeping Tom expeditions: only to find Jim taking things a step further when he stood outside the house of the wife of a friend. She had seen Jim standing out in the street and beckoned him inside. When Dennis chanced a glimpse through the window, he saw Jim, quite impassive, sitting naked in a chair, before the woman led him, again quite impassively, into the bedroom. Might Jim have been the same with one of his wannabe suitors at the gay bar, on those nights he visited alone?

Sure, why not? It's much easier to imagine him accepting drinks, favours, money, from the wealthy older men in these bars than making a big deal about protecting his 'innocence'. Impassive Jim, eyes on the floor, being led quietly into the bedroom . . .

As the years sped by, there would be much speculation about Jim Morrison's 'true' sexual identity. In his excellent Morrison biography, *Life, Death, Legend,* the American author Stephen Davis writes of an unsavoury incident that would occur five years later, when a well-known Hollywood male hustler would try to blackmail Jim – an act of the utmost foolishness which Davis alleges resulted in said hustler being threatened with having his legs broken. The rumours would continue to fly around him, and still do. Most likely, though, is that Jim was simply attracted to both sexes. Attracted to any scene that promised forbidden fruit. As we shall see, he certainly had a propensity towards anal sex, even as his female partners protested. So much so, more than one of his future girlfriends would accuse him outright of being 'a fag'.

Danny Fields, the outspoken gay writer who would become an influential early publicist for The Doors, refutes the idea that Jim might have been gay, insisting that 'His first sexual attraction was to himself.' Speaking from his New York home, Danny says he 'never saw horniness' from Jim towards other men. 'I wasn't that much around him but I didn't see that.' That said, Jim's sexual aura 'was ritualistic . . . I think he would have done his utmost to not display any sexual [preference]. But he didn't do it with women either.'

Danny adds: 'I always liked to think that he had an affair with Tom Baker,' the Hollywood actor Jim would befriend after he became famous. 'And why not? Maybe someday someone will find a packet of letters with a blue silk ribbon, you know, like Jane Austen? Or poetry . . . I mean, I don't see why he wouldn't. But sex was different [back then].' Because it was still illegal in America, 'He'd still have to pretend to be seduced, or to pretend to have, you know, a . . . Brokeback Mountain [moment]. I think that's possible.'

In his book, Dennis Jakob also relates the time Jim met the

famously gay actor Sal Mineo in a Hollywood movie theatre. Again, Dennis says Jim just hung on in there, no obvious signals, no obvious acceptance, but no obvious discouragement either, just waiting for the other guy to make the first move, maybe. Mineo's interest was so 'intense', says Dennis, that he even invited him over to his house to pump him for information about Jim. Dennis insists it never went any further than that, though, but then there were a lot of things about Jim Dennis didn't know. A lot of things no one ever really knew.

Dennis concludes by insisting that he never saw Jim make a move towards him or any of their friends. Adding: 'I only heard the rumours.'

SIX

Swimming to the Moon

In the end Jim didn't go to New York to work for some film magazine and Ray didn't go looking for a job at some big movie studio in Hollywood. Any ambitions either of them really had were instead quietly deferred while they sat around, stoned, wondering how in hell they were going to do what it was they both now had a real hankering for. Becoming rock stars. Though neither of them would come right out and say it just yet.

Instead Ray kept tooling around with Rick & The Ravens in the vague hope that they would cause enough ripples to start a wave somewhere. Jim, meanwhile, would try out his 'I'm gonna start a band' rap on anyone stoned enough to listen but nobody ever took him seriously enough to put him on the spot and say, all right, then, let's do it.

That is until that now famous day in July 1965 when Jim was wandering along the beach in Venice and he happened to run into his know-better old college buddy, Ray. Their subsequent exchange has become a story nearly as oft told as that of the three bears. But then it beats most other rock origin stories into a leopard skin pillbox hat. For while Elvis arriving at Sam Phillips's Sun studios to make a record for his mother is sweet, and the story of 15-year-old Paul McCartney offering to tune the guitar of 16-year-old John Lennon at a village fete is filled with yearning, what occurred when Jim and Ray knelt down on the sand together that hot afternoon in 1965 resulted almost immediately in the songs that would form the backbone of The Doors' career, and in effect help reconfigure pop and rock throughout the late Sixties. The drama unfolded that quickly.

Initially, Jim and Ray had sat around chatting on the beach, catching up on all the things they'd said they were gonna do and hadn't, checking out the chicks – including one beautiful black girl Jim impetuously called out, 'Hello! I love you!' to but got no reaction from – scanning the far-off horizon through stoned-red morning eyes. When Jim suddenly announced in his drowsy Southern voice, 'I've been writing some songs.'

It was an apt moment for this kind of talk. The Beatles' sixth American album had just gone to No. 1 on 10 July. A month later the *Help!* album would replace it. By Christmas *Rubber Soul* would be released and pop would suddenly turn into rock. The Stones were hard on their heels. 'Satisfaction' was still No. 1 and Sunset Strip was crawling with new psychedelic groups all vying for your third-eye attention. Leading the way were Los Angeles-based bands like The Byrds, now being talked of as 'the American Beatles'; Love, who you either knew and dug special, baby, or you were nowhere with, man; The Seeds, who weren't as good as anyone else but had the grooviest-named frontman in Sky Saxon;

and most Hollyweird of all, the Mothers, led by some crazy cat with a Zapata moustache named Frank Zappa – can you dig it?

Ray asked Jim to sing him one of his songs but Jim demurred, getting his excuses in early, saying he didn't really have a singing voice. Ray responded by pointing out that Bob Dylan didn't have much of a voice either but his songs were pretty good. Jim gave him the silent treatment. Eyes down, body absolutely still. Ray kept wheedling, 'Come on, man, come on, man . . . only me . . .' Just the two of them out there. Who would know? Come on, man . . .

Slowly, hesitantly, Jim began uttering the words to 'Moonlight Drive'. Sitting upright on his knees, eyes closed, shy but not that shy once he got going. *'Let's swim to the moon, uh huh . . . Let's climb through the tide . . .'* Ray could hear the gently prancing music that went with it instantly, and began miming playing the piano. 'Oh, man, I love it! This is incredible! Do you have anything else?' Jim started another, called 'Summer's Almost Gone' . . . Then another called 'My Eyes Have Seen You' . . . Ray gave a little cry of joy. He liked the sound of that. '"My Eyes Have Seen You", baby! Do that one for me,' he said. Jim did.

Recalling that moment in his book, Ray likens Jim's voice on this occasion to Chet Baker's, which was soft and high, tremulous. A million miles from the drunken yowls of Jim's 'Louie Louie', that time at the Turkey Joint West. Ray thought he even heard a little bit of London pop in there, maybe? Mixed with some hot Latin. He began to imagine being in a band playing behind Jim, doing some jazz-rock. 'It had never been done before. Chet Baker cool into hot Latin rock, oh yes! Ray could hear everything, even the solos. 'Go, Ray,' said Jim, laughing.

And then Ray uttered the immortal line, since repeated and amplified a thousand times: 'We're gonna make a million dollars!' In his book Ray says he was joking when he said that, but one feels he doth protest too much. Ray says Jim replied, 'Ray, that's exactly what I had in mind.' And you can bet it was. The same thought that has entered every young man's mind whenever he has thought of starting a band, then as now.

What also struck Ray was how far removed this new, drastically trimmed Jim seemed from the fatso college kid. You could really see his face for the first time, see how surprisingly handsome it actually was, without the jowly fat to get in the way; see how lean his body now was. Ray thought he looked like a young Steve McQueen. When Ray asked how Jim lost all the weight, Jim replied, 'I just stopped eating.' He'd been taking so much acid and getting so high, he'd 'hardly eaten anything since we graduated'.

Ray invited Jim back for something to eat. Ray and Dorothy were now living in a place above a garage, part of a typical 'California bungalow', overlooking the beach. One bedroom: $75 a month. While they waited for Dorothy to come home from work they smoked a doobie and talked some more about the million-dollar group they were going to form. Ray already had it in his head that what the new band would play would be somewhere between jazz and rock, with some LSD thrown in, with Jim's poetry, which seemed to combine all those things, overlaid. Jack Kerouac meets John Coltrane. But Jim needed a lot of cajoling into being the singer, lots of ego stroking and coaxing and assurance. Ray, a couple of years older and wiser, as he saw it, than Jim, didn't mind that. He'd been through a similar trip with his younger brothers in the Ravens. This would be the same, only with much better end results.

It was now Jim offered up the name 'The Doors'. Ray recalls that they toyed jokingly with calling it Morrison and Manzarek, but laughed it off as 'too folky'. How about Jim & Ray, he said, thinking, well maybe . . . But Jim shot that down with 'Two guys from Venice.' Then Jim finally spilled and suggested the name he'd been thinking about all along. But Ray didn't like the idea of calling the band The Doors. For all his immersion in the emerging counter-culture, for all his expensive education, Ray just didn't get it.

Jim tried to explain, saying the name was 'an homage to William Blake', from *The Marriage of Heaven and Hell*, the line: 'If the doors of perception were cleansed everything would appear to man as it is, infinite.' The same passage that Aldous Huxley lifted the title from for his book on mescaline experimentation, *The Doors of Perception*, and that Jim had just reduced to The Doors. Ray got all that but was still unconvinced. The Doors . . . it sounded kind of . . . dull, didn't it? But then they got to talking about acid, what Ray would still refer to when we spoke nearly 50 years later as 'the sacrament', and how the best trips were the ones that unlocked the doors of your mind and allowed you to break on through, Ray, dig?

And that's when Ray nodded his head sagely, exhaled a huge plume of pot smoke, and gave his consent with the two words that denoted ultimate respect back then in that acid-blasted summer of 1965: 'Right on.'

By the time Dorothy came home from work that afternoon, Jim and Ray had the whole thing worked out. Or, at least, Ray did. Jim would move in with him and Dorothy right away – today! Far out, man. Okay! According to his book, Dorothy was cool with that, though one can't help wondering how easily the highly intelligent and well-organised Dorothy really took to the idea of having one of UCLA's more wayward former students doing his stoned thing under her small but hard-earned roof. Perhaps she was smart enough to realise it wouldn't last long. Strong enough to know she could always kick Jim out the moment he got too out of control. Maybe.

Jim only had one box of books left; the rest sent home to his parents, who were now living in San Diego. Other than an electric blanket and several pairs of socks, that's all he moved in with. And for a while, at least according to Ray, they lived in a sort of hippy idyll. Dorothy would go off to work each morning and Ray and Jim would spend the day together, hanging out at UCLA, in the basement practice rooms with their sound-baffled spaces, working Jim's poems and vocal melodies into actual songs, Jim learning to sing in his still thin, high voice, Ray in his element, directing musical traffic from his keyboards. 'Moonlight Drive', 'My Eyes Have Seen You', 'Summer's Almost Gone', 'End of the Night', 'I Looked at You', 'Crystal Ship', another called 'Go Insane' . . . none of it sounded like The Beatles or the Stones, or even Bob Dylan. There were major 7ths, B-flats, weird shit. Some sounding very European, balladic and stark; some still sounding how Ray imagined the Ravens might sound if they had the benefit of some properly tripped-out lyrics, like freak out, baby, hang on! Some of it worked straight away, some of it stubbornly refused to gel. But the ideas were all there. They knew they were on to something: Doors music would follow where bands like The Beatles and The Byrds were now going, beyond rock'n'roll's joyous puberty and full-tilt into its grievous, questioning adolescence. But where The Beatles and their disciples were aiming for was where The Doors would begin: where rock was first visited by night things.

To pay his way, Jim would steal steaks from the market for Dorothy to cook for dinner. Jim may have 'stopped eating' during his epiphanic summer metamorphosing on the roof at Dennis's, but he had never lost his craving for meat. If things were going wrong, he would announce, 'We need meat!' If there was ever something to celebrate, he would insist, 'Meat! Must eat meat!' Or if things were just dragging by, well, meat was the answer to that too. He got so used to stealing choice sirloin steaks he grew bored with their taste and began 'shopping' for fillet and rib eye. After all three had filled their stomachs on the juicy steaks, they would spend the rest of their evenings tripping, though Ray mainly tripped with Dorothy, while Jim tripped with whichever willing supplicant he could find to accompany him, otherwise alone. Wandering off into the night, as he had at Dennis's place, as he would always. For Ray such occasions were 'sacred', for Jim it was just who he was now. They wrote a new song about it, called 'Break On Through', taking acid and finding yourself on the other side of the rainbow – 'or its opposite', as Jim drawlingly put it.

In fact, it was this 'opposite' realm that Ray now began

to experience in earnest every time he tripped. Suddenly, the blissed-out vistas were replaced by a hellish terrain, full of fear and paranoia; total bummers that Dorothy would have to talk him down from. Ray knew he could not keep putting himself – or Dorothy – through this ordeal. Yet he held firm to the belief that acid, when it was good, was a place of deep wisdom, of radiance and truth, and he was not prepared to cease his explorations. There had to be another way.

Discussing his problems one day with Dick Block, the older, wiser-time dude who had signed Rick & The Ravens to Aura, Dick suggested Ray might like to try transcendental meditation. *Tran-scen . . . what?* Dick went to the shelves in his office and pulled out an album he had recently released through the larger World Pacific imprint: a two-disc recording of the lectures of Maharishi Mahesh Yogi. 'Listen to this,' Dick said. 'It might be what you're looking for.'

The very same Maharishi Mahesh Yogi who would, two years later, become 'spiritual advisor' to The Beatles, and later have them to stay with him at his retreat in Rishikesh, India, for several weeks. And who John Lennon, in a volte-face after rumours circulated that the Maharishi had made sexual advances to Mia Farrow, another of his celebrity converts, would subsequently write a scathing review of in the Beatles song 'Sexy Sadie'.

Ray was also sceptical at first. Listening to the record back home, 'I didn't really buy into the whole TM thing when I first came across it,' he told me. 'It sounded good. God and man and nature, pure contemplation. I just had no idea how you put it all together without the aid of some external force, you know?' How could something so simple lead him to the place of glorious wonderment that acid had? Most urgently, how could it remove the terror?

Ray would discover the answer after Dick told him of a new meditation class that was beginning nearby in which the teachings of the Maharishi – specifically, his form of mantra-based yogic meditation – would be passed on to willing initiates. So Ray, still searching for 'answers', went along, bringing Dorothy with him. He'd also tried to persuade Jim to come along, but Jim already had his personal mantras and didn't feel he needed any help whatsoever crossing the great divide. In fact, he invited the terrors, he said. He found them cleansing. Okay, man.

Meanwhile, over in the canyons, John Densmore was experiencing very similar forms of acid-induced heebie-jeebies as Ray – and was reaching out for the same cure. It was Robby Krieger who turned him on to the idea of transcendental meditation, and for much the same reasons. Robby liked to get as out there as possible, but he was no brain-dead loser who couldn't find his way back. He still wanted to go to those places that only existed in that state but not alone, riding roughshod over whatever unknown obstacles came his way. He wanted guidance, a helping hand, a joining mind to help him see through the multi-coloured lights, to give him a real chance at the truth, whatever it might really turn out to be.

Robby was at UCLA by then, ostensibly to major in physics but really so he could join their unique for the times Indian Music class, where he was able to study both sitar and the sarod, a fretless lute-like instrument, similar to the sitar but with a deeper, more introspective tone. He also took classes at Ravi Shankar's own Kinnara School. It was here that he first heard about the new Maharishi Mahesh Yogi meditation class, in West Hollywood. He decided to check it out – and take his freaked-out friend John with him.

Coincidence, karma, destiny, fate or just old-fashioned luck, however one might like to consider it, it's curious to note that the shared factor which finally brought the four members of The Doors together – the group that would stand for transcendence, for breaking through to the other side, for flipping the bird to straight, conventional society in order to lead its children to a more enlightened, acid-singed reality, the band whose very name was a not-so-oblique reference to the benefits of LSD – was that its principal musical authors were all victims of such unutterably 'bad trips' that they actively sought help.

As well as a shared interest in getting high and getting laid, Robby and John had also begun to play together in a loose conglomerate they jokingly christened 'The Psychedelic Rangers'. John and his pal Grant on drums and piano, Robby and his pal Bill on guitars. Just like The Doors they never did manage to find a bass player but that didn't really matter as they only managed a couple of actual gigs. They would jam in one of the big rooms at Robby's parents' place in Pacific Palisades. Their best-known original number was titled 'Paranoia' and was about having a bad acid trip, wow. Kind of folk rock, kind of rock, a sort of proto-West Coast sound without ever getting past the shambolic rehearsal stage – though they did make a 'psychedelic' 8mm film of themselves, tooling around in kimonos as their raggedy demo of 'Paranoid' blasted away in the foreground. But mainly they just tripped on out until John really couldn't take it any more and Robby promptly suggested they seek solace in the welcoming climes of the Maharishi's meditation classes.

It was at their second 'follow up' class, after they'd been given their special Sanskrit words to chant by themselves, that John met Ray. John recalls somewhat typically in his book how irritated he was at first by Ray, claiming he spent most of the time complaining loudly that he was getting 'No bliss!' from the sessions. 'As if he expected to become Buddha overnight.' In Ray's book, however, just as typically, he maintains that he and John bonded immediately over their shared love of John Coltrane. Getting into just how great John thought Elvin Jones was and how deeply influenced Ray was by McCoy Tyner. They parted that evening agreeing they should jam some time, man. John pointing out Robby, telling Ray, 'He plays great bottleneck.'

Ray wasn't on the lookout just then for a guitar player, though. He was still thinking of how to blend what he and Jim were doing into what his brothers were trying for in Rick & The Ravens. A good drummer, now, that was harder to find. Vince Thomas, the usual drummer in the Ravens, had only ever shown up whenever they had a gig. Rehearsing, writing, jamming, that wasn't his scene. But this Densmore, he seemed to have a little more going for him in that regard. Cat dug Elvin Jones, man, how bad could he be? So a few weeks later Ray phoned John and invited him to come down to his parents' garage, no less, where they were set up, and 'have a blow'.

John went along, met Ray's brothers, and in the corner, trying so hard not to be noticed John didn't even realise he was there until Ray made a big deal about introducing him, sat this other kid, Jim Morrison, dressed, like any other student then, in brown cords and a T-shirt

John set up and they rambled through 'Louie Louie', the surf bum anthem *du jour*, with Ray on vocals, Jim just out of shot, looking on, awkwardly. John couldn't figure out his deal. Decided maybe he was shy simply because he was the only one in the room who didn't actually play anything. But then Ray pulled out a sheaf of papers and told John to check out some of Jim's lyrics; how far out they were, man. John wasn't big into lyrics, but the first verse he read began: '*You know the day destroys the night / Night divides the day . . .*', the opening lines to what would soon become 'Break on Through (to the Other Side)', and even hard-to-impress John got excited. John remarked on how 'very percussive' the lines seemed to him. Excited, Ray said that's right, that he felt the same and already had a bass line for them on the keyboards. They began churning it out, Rick Manzarek strumming a bare-bones rhythm while little bro Jim blew away on his harp. The band kept going, vamping away, seeing where it took them. After what seemed a long interval the boy in brown eventually tiptoed over to the mike and ever so gingerly began to sing-speak the words in that still soft, high voice of his, eyes tight closed.

After that they jammed on some of the blues numbers the Ravens had got good at playing live – Muddy's 'I'm Your Doctor', Willie Dixon's 'Hoochie Coochie Man' – and Jim began to loosen up and get into it more, the voice growing louder and stronger, his eyes starting to open just a crack. They took a break, smoked one of Jim's tailor-made joints, then began again. It was fun. Felt good. Nothing too special, for John, but nice enough for him to agree to come back a few days later, when they did the whole thing again. Surf covers, blues and a sprinkling of these 'songs' Jim and Ray were shuffling around with. After a couple more sessions John realised it was the latter stuff that really interested him. The band really wasn't up to much but this stuff Ray and Jim kept coming up with, it was . . . different.

The only ones who weren't entirely convinced were the younger of the Manzarek brothers, Rick and Jim, who were beginning to feel their high-times party group was being hijacked by a lot of dope-smoking freakdom that wasn't doing anything to help get them paying gigs. In an effort to placate his brothers, and help them understand just how special what they had going now with Densmore and Morrison involved, Ray talked Dick Block into giving over three hours of recording time he'd earmarked for the next Ravens single to a special session to record the best of the original material the band was now coming up with.

The result was six tracks that have since gone down in legend as the original Doors demo, though in fact they were recorded with the idea of getting a deal for Rick & The Ravens, and comprised Jim Morrison on vocals, Ray Manzarek on keyboards and backing vocals, brothers Rick on guitar and Jim on harmonica, John Densmore on drums and Patricia 'Pat' Hansen (née Sullivan) from another local bar band, Patty and the Esquires, on bass guitar.

Playing the tape back at Ray's Ocean Drive pad later that night, Jim was delighted to hear his voice recorded for the first time, impressed less by the fact it was so good, which it wasn't, but that it didn't sound that bad, which it didn't. Ray was equally delighted, at the sheer quality of the material. As was John, whose only reservation was that you couldn't hear the drums as well as he'd envisaged. The only ones who were less than thrilled with the outcome with the two younger Manzarek brothers and bassist Hansen, who found it all much too pretentious.

When you listen to the original recording now, with its galloping piano, feeble vocals and overeager harmonica, although all six tracks – the jaunty, nursery rhyme-ish 'Hello, I Love You', the tiptoeing 'Summer's Almost Gone', cobwebby 'End of the Night', spaced-out 'Moonlight Drive', do-the-monkey 'My Eyes Have Seen You' and the aptly titled 'Go Insane' – would later resurface, albeit in far superior form, on subsequent Doors albums, with 'Hello, I Love You' actually becoming a million-selling No. 1 single, it's not hard to understand why the demo tape was rejected by every record company executive the band played it to. Why some even felt hostile towards it, throwing the band out of their offices in disgust.

In 1965 the American pop business was still run by major record labels based almost exclusively in New York. Los Angeles was still considered an outpost, at best, with only Columbia and Warner Bros of the majors really having a substantial base on the West Coast. In order to capture the imagination of their East Coast overlords, most A&R execs in L.A. were looking for Top 40 certs. As Kim Fowley, the maverick producer and purveyor in the Sixties of novelty hits such as 'Ally Oop' – credited to a made-up group, The Hollywood Argyles – would say, 'Art for art's sake, hit singles for fuck's sake.' And while L.A. acts like The Byrds were scoring contracts, they only did so because they brought with them guaranteed hits. New L.A.-based, album-oriented acts like Buffalo Springfield, Love and the Mothers were all still a year away from signing their own deals. For now, with their suddenly inopportune moniker – whatever they were supposed to be, these songs did not sound like they were meant to be played by a group called Rick & The Ravens – and clearly drug-hipped band members, Ray and Jim were practically laughed out of the room. Capitol, RCA, Decca, Dunhill, Reprise, Liberty . . . Most of these execs didn't even get past the first couple of tracks. A decision they would soon come to regret, perhaps, but then isn't that the story of the entire entertainment business in Hollywood? One man's meat being another's eat-shit.

By October 1965, with his disillusioned brothers now playing the told-you-so card – as far as Rick and Jim were concerned, this new, Morrison-focused configuration of the Ravens had ruined whatever slim chance they'd ever had of making it – Ray and Jim and John suddenly found themselves alone with their unwanted demo tape. Jim, of course, was loudly defiant, yelling at one executive who had simply flicked through the tape, grunting, 'Can't use it, can't use it', that that was okay. 'We don't wanna be *used* by anybody!'

They were left in a quandary though. Even Pat Hansen couldn't see the point in continuing and went back to her own band, where she married the singer, Chuck. With not much to hang on to, it was now Jim who suggested dropping the Ravens as a name – after all, Rick had gone and was definitely not coming back, he had made that clear – and replacing it with The Doors. John hardly needed the idea explaining to him. What concerned him more was where they were going to find good new players for the band.

Enter their knight in frizzy hair: Robby Krieger.

Robby had been staying away from the acid, though he still smoked copious amounts of dope, attending TM classes and playing guitar in another small-time college outfit named The Clouds. All the while, 'John was telling me about . . . this wild and crazy guy, Jim Morrison, who was going to be the lead singer even though he couldn't sing at the time.' When it turned out John's band needed a new guitar player, Robby didn't need too much persuading to come along and meet the 'crazy guy'.

With his sleepy face, far-off green eyes and flyaway tea-coloured hair, Robby appeared inscrutable to the others. Until they got to know him, they assumed he was either permanently stoned or simply disconnected from what the rest of them were feeling. In fact, the opposite was true. Robby was so into the music, he would become the musical *éminence grise* of The Doors, the secret x-factor who would provide them with their biggest hit and become the main musical touchstone to Jim Morrison's most out-there lyrical endeavours. He was a boy who had been born with the L.A. sun in his eyes and the sounds of the breaking waves forever in his head. He was a floater, but that didn't mean he didn't know where he was going or where he wanted to be. The kind of guy who would get on well with all the other members of The Doors while never quite becoming the best friend of any of them. Not even Jim, who now drifted apart from the avuncular attentions of Ray and more towards the less demanding, less loquacious and non-judgemental company of Robby, who never seemed to get freaked out about anything. Or didn't feel the need to show it off so much anyway.

Speaking to *Guitar World* magazine some 30 years later, Robby remembered thinking Jim seemed 'pretty normal. I didn't really get a sense that there was anything unusual about him until the end of our first rehearsal. Initially, everything was cool. Then this guy came looking for Jim. Something had gone wrong with a dope deal, and Jim just went nuts. Absolutely bananas! I thought, Jesus Christ, this guy's not normal.'

Robby's first impression of Ray was equally insightful. 'He was a major character,' he recalled. 'But Jim kind of kept him in his place. Jim was so out there that Ray's personality was overwhelmed – which, oddly enough, created a good balance.' But then Jim had that effect on everybody, Robby laughingly admitted. 'I couldn't hold a candle to Jim and Ray. But I had already gone through acid and I was onto meditation – so I had already mellowed out.'

Unable to use the family garage any more – that was still his brothers' haven – Ray persuaded his old college sidekick Hank Olguin to let them come over to his parents' place in Santa Monica and use their piano. As luck would have it, another of those big carved wooden uprights Ray had learned on back in Chicago.

According to Ray, the first song the nascent line-up attempted together was 'Moonlight Drive' – though Robby now insists it was a newer number Ray and Jim and John had been jamming around with called 'Indian Summer'. Whichever it was, one thing they all remember is that before they started Jim pulled out a 'big bomber' – a family-size version of one of his expertly rolled joints he loved to impress with – and insisted they all smoke it. That it would provide them all with 'some ammunition'. Ray and Robby got stuck into the joint, no problem. John hesitated then seemed to mentally shrug and say what the hell. Then started coughing. Jim smiled, 'Groovy', and Ray counted the song in.

Things seemed okay as they began to shuffle forward into the first couple of songs. Robby could certainly play guitar better than Rick. The turning point came, though, running through the chords of 'Moonlight Drive' for the first time. At the song's end, Robby, now super-stoned, pulled something from his guitar case and placed it on the ring finger of his left hand: the broken neck of a green beer bottle to use – literally – as a bottleneck for the guitar. The sound that began snaking out of his guitar made them all instantly freak – Jim, especially, who wanted Robby to do the ring finger bottleneck thing on every song. '*Every* song?' Robby sniggered, stoned and grooving. 'Yeah, man! Get it on!' cried Jim. So they did.

It didn't matter that they didn't have a bass player. With Ray handling the basic rhythm on his 1960 Fender Rhodes piano bass – ostensibly with the idea of making do until they could find a real bassist to replace Pat – both Robby and John realised early on that this other way of finding the rhythm had unforeseen advantages.

As John would recall for me in 2012, Pat 'was a good [bass] player but she made us sound like the Stones! Like a white blues band, like a regular thing. And then we just stumbled onto this keyboard bass and so that was it for us. We knew it'd make us different, and I knew it would leave more space for me to play freer. Although my responsibility was compounded because usually bass players and drummers have to work together getting down the groove and I had to do it alone. And when Ray did a solo with his right hand he'd get excited, like any soloist does, then his left hand would speed up. But, you know, I was up for it let me tell you . . . I didn't want to rein it in. I wanted it to go out further on the edge!'

Talking to *Guitar World* in 2005, Robby concurred, insisting that The Doors' sound 'was largely a result of the fact that Ray had to play really simple bass lines, which gave the music a hypnotic feel. And not having a bass player affected my guitar playing a lot. It made me play more bass notes to fill out the bottom. Not having a rhythm player also made me play differently to fill out the sound. And then, of course, I played lead, so I always felt like three players simultaneously.'

That afternoon they also worked their way steadily through 'End of the Night' – Jim's Céline-inspired paean to night crawling – 'Summer's Almost Gone', 'Indian Summer' and 'My Eyes Have Seen You'. Some worked instantly, others didn't seem to work at all. They would have to keep trying and they did. 'We are gonna go all the way with this,' declared Ray, during another joint break. 'I can feel it.'

They all could. All the way to Venice Beach and back. *Get it on . . .*

SEVEN

Sexy Motherfucker in Black Pants

At the end of 1965, just after his 22nd birthday, Jim Morrison wrote a letter home to his father, a kind of end-of-year summary in which he explained how hard he had tried to get a job in the movie industry following his graduation from UCLA but that it was nigh-on impossible. How it had left him poverty-stricken and sleeping on a friend's rooftop. There was, however, a ray of hope on the horizon, in the shape of the very talented musical friends he had made and how they had now started a band, in which Jim was the singer. He ended by asking, respectfully, if his father could see his way to extending his son a loan. Just to get the band on its feet, and how he would pay him back once they'd 'made it'.

Speaking with Jerry Hopkin for his superb 1991 book, *The Lizard King*, Jim's brother, Andy, well recalled his father's reaction: 'Dad wrote back and said he'd paid for college and Jim never did anything musically before in his life, never showed any musical ability, and "now you're telling me after I paid for four years of college you're starting a band! I think it's a

95

crock!" Jim never took kindly to criticism and he never wrote again.'

Instead Jim took out his frustrations on his other 'father' – Ray Manzarek. As Robby Krieger would relate, 'He fucked their house up – trashed it on more than one occasion – and took advantage of them in many ways.' He even began to doubt The Doors. As Robby would tell me, 'Jim was the kind of guy who would subconsciously try to sabotage anything that we were trying to do. Even from the earliest days. I remember the second rehearsal we had – over at my parents' house – and Jim doesn't show up. That was the second rehearsal. Where is he? Where is he? Made some phone calls. Found out he was in jail, out in the desert, out in Bryce, California. He'd took a trip with a couple of his buddies and got in a fight with some bikers and got thrown in jail. That was our second rehearsal. It was all downhill after that . . .'

Most of Jim's sudden disappearances were down to the same thing. He'd simply found something better to do that night, often involving Felix Venable, whom he still looked up to as the ultimate night tripper. Not all of these adventures ended well, though. Early in January 1966, on another of Jim's impromptu 'road trips', heading off to the desert in search of peyote, this time with Felix Venable and Phil O'Leno, it led to a bizarre situation in which Felix and Jim were later investigated for the murder of O'Leno.

It had been nearly five in the morning when Jim phoned a girl he'd recently been seeing named Carol Winters. Calling from a phone booth out on the highway, he said the three of them had been mooching around a golf course tripping, but now they were lost and exhausted and could Carol drive over and rescue them? By the time Carol had picked them up and driven them back to Phil's parents' place they were all raring to go again and decided to 'borrow' one of the O'Lenos' cars and drive out to the desert in search of peyote and UFOs. Or something, it didn't really matter. Jim just wanted to drive. As they headed out of town Jim pulled the car to a screeching halt while he jumped out and French-kissed a beautiful Mexican-American girl he'd spotted on a street corner, the morning sun streaming through her dress. That was the last anybody saw of them for the next 48 hours.

In the intriguing Frank Lisciandro memoir, *Feast of Friends*, O'Leno recalls that Venable had scored some pure LSD-25 reputedly direct from a Sandoz laboratory batch, and that the three of them had dropped it in a motel somewhere out near the California–Arizona state line. At which point Phil decided his destiny lay further down the road into Arizona and then on into Mexico. While Jim and Felix decided it would be better to turn around and hitchhike back home.

According to O'Leno, Jim would later claim that some miles down the road he and Felix had been set upon by a truckload of passing rednecks, who gave them 'a pretty good beating'. In fact, Jim later said it was a car full of Mexican-American guys – friends of the girl he had kissed – that had followed them down the highway, in search of vengeance. Bedraggled, bruised and bloodied by the time they finally got back to Venice Beach, rather than confess to the prosaic truth – that they had been the victims of a beating because of some thoughtless act of Jim's – he and Felix concocted a story in which they had been transformed out in the desert into reckless, cold-hearted killers, murdering Phil and burying him by the dry banks of an old riverbed. Not even the credulous Ray believed them, though. Jim was always coming up with these preposterous stories that no one was ever sure were true. But, in an ironic twist, when O'Leno failed to return or send word of his whereabouts for weeks, his worried father, a powerful attorney, somehow located the girl Jim had kissed and convinced her to press charges for assault. When he was arrested two weeks later, police wasted no time in questioning him about the disappearance of Phil O'Leno and reports that he had claimed to have murdered him. Utterly freaked out, Jim told them what had really happened but the cops didn't believe him. Fortunately for Jim, Phil reappeared back in Los Angeles the same week, and the charges were dropped.

Jim came out of the police cell dazed but weirdly inspired. The tale of the hitchhiker killer on the road became one he would revisit several times throughout his career.

It was the kind of behaviour the rest of The Doors had already resigned themselves to putting up with. They knew they wouldn't be the musical force on the scene they needed to be without Jim's strange, druggy charisma, without his sepulchral words and intonated voice. At the same time, they knew Jim needed them just as much. That without their smouldering music, with its bruising, gothic rhythms and snaking, indelicate melodies, Jim would be back to being the notebook-toting roof-dweller.

'Yeah and, you know, I think we all realised that and that's the reason we did stick together,' agreed Robby. 'If the music wasn't great, we wouldn't have. After that second rehearsal, that would have been it. But we knew we had something, and that was better than anything we'd heard, and we wanted people to hear it and we would go to any lengths.'

And they really would.

With Jim still staying at Ray and Dorothy's, it was the keyboard player who bore the brunt of his behaviour. But he did so, cheerfully enough, in the hope of making that million dollars he still saw as theirs for the taking on those nights when Jim did surrender himself to The Doors. Whatever else he did, Jim was constantly writing, not always songs, but enough scraps of lyrics and verses for Ray to be able to fuse them into the kind of 'music noir' The Doors were now building together.

John tended to look up to Jim and his weird pals like Dennis Jakob and Felix Venable, as they were a couple of years older, still a big deal when you're only 20. John got that Jim was a deep reader and didn't really get half the references he would casually include in his generally stoned ramblings, chain-smoking the immaculate joints he would roll one after the other. The rest of his behaviour he dealt with by simply thrashing at his drums. It was hardly in the same league as the musical dialogue between Elvin Jones and John Coltrane, but John was determined to take it as close to that flame as he could, learning to give Jim space when he wanted to take off into some stoned monologue mid-song, his drums chattering percussively behind, around and with him.

In the meantime, they began to find gigs, to begin with the same sort of seven-day weekend parties where the crowd didn't come to see the band but to dance to it. That was okay; the band used them to essentially rehearse. Encouraged by how quickly their novice frontman took to showing off in front of a crowd, his reedy voice growing stronger with each lung-bursting performance, the band began to musically space out, to surf the waves of energy that were beginning to go back and forth between them and the crowd.

They thought they'd made it when a talent scout from Columbia named Billy James decided to do something crazy and sign them. Billy was a failed actor who had become a publicist at Columbia in New York, before moving on to A&R. Billy was no musician but he was young and hip enough to get along with Bob Dylan, at a time when Dylan refused to talk to anyone else at the label. Moving out to the West Coast offices in 1965, Billy had performed a similar role for The Byrds, writing the sleeve notes to their debut album, *Mr. Tambourine Man*, and establishing his presence in L.A. as one of the few young record label gunslingers who really dug the scene coming together on the Strip.

Billy's office had been one of the last places Ray and Jim had managed to talk their way into with their six-track demotape. They'd seen a picture of Billy in *Cashbox* magazine, saw he had a beard and figured he was 'hip'. They were right. Like every other label guy who'd sat through the tape, Billy didn't jump for joy at the music. But he liked the look of these guys. They wore the same psychedelic garb as other L.A. street freaks but they clearly had a little more going for them intellectually.

'I guess they appealed to the snob in me,' he later joked. 'Because they were UCLA graduates and I thought, "Great, here are some intellectual types getting involved with rock'n'roll."'

Billy offered them a deal on the spot – a six-month contract to record four sides' worth of music, with a guarantee from the label to release two of them. Jim was ecstatic. Ray even more so when James arranged the 'gift' of a free Vox organ. In reality no big deal as Columbia owned Vox at the time, but Ray took it as a good omen. Red and black, with the keys inverted so that the whites were black and vice versa, and the chrome legs formed into a 'Z'. 'I said, "All right! A Vox organ! Like the Dave Clark Five!"'

The enthusiasm was short-lived, however, when it tran-spired that none of the house producers at Columbia liked the demo enough to want to work with the band. By the start of 1966, with some months left on their contract but clearly nothing happening for them at the label, The Doors consid-ered themselves unsigned again.

Their real break came at the end of February, when they landed a gig at one of the hip new young clubs on Sunset Strip: a dive named the London Fog. With Swinging London and The Beatles now epitomising everything that was cool and far out about the Sixties, an L.A. club with 'London' in its name was sending out a very clear message: this is where it is at, baby. In reality, however, the Fog, as it was known, was a dirty, dark little cavern, owned by one Jesse James, that barely anybody went to. Situated next door to the much better-liked Galaxy club and less than a hundred yards from the Whisky A Go-Go, then the most popular, cool nightspot in Hollywood, other than its name there was very little that was cool about the Fog. The stage stood ten feet high – above the wooden, indoor shack that served as the toilets – which the band had to climb a ladder to get to.

Offered the job as the regular house band, for $40 a night, playing Thursday through Sunday doing five sets a night, starting at 9 p.m. and finishing at 2 a.m., when the club closed, the place was so bad the rest of the band hesitated over taking the gig. But Jim was adamant. It would be great. They would get a lot of exposure. And that's exactly what happened. Eventually.

Where the Fog gigs really worked in The Doors' favour, though, was in the opportunity they offered Jim to learn his stagecraft. Unlike the private parties they had played so far, where they could goof off and no one knew or cared as long as they kept bashing out 'Louie Louie', the Fog residency was all about repertoire, about performance. It may have been a dive but it was a dive with a name and, as such, it would become Jim Morrison's, and The Doors', first real proving ground.

Playing five sets a night, four nights a week, the band not only got tighter; they were now able to stretch out fully and experiment with their own material. For the first few weeks barely anybody came to the shows anyway so whatever they did, it didn't really matter. To fill up the time, they began taking newer material and extemporising around it, making new two-minute ballads like 'The End' into lengthy Indian ragas. There was another new tune still in its infancy which Robby had written – after Jim had castigated the others for not coming up with some material of their own to help him and Ray out – called 'Light My Fire'. They had the bossa nova rhythm, the swirling Bach-like filigree intro, and Jim's deceptively innocent-sounding swoon. Now though it stretched to seven, eight, 12 minutes a go. The songs would not only thin out into endless improvisations; new songs would start to emerge from the quagmire of the fourth-set-in jams,

Jim ranting his made-up-on-the-spot lyrics to them. Hence 'When the Music's Over', which came into being over several nights.

The group's becoming musically bolder and more competent with each set also allowed Jim to find himself onstage as a performer. Still insecure about his voice, the great imposter, as he saw it, standing mostly with his back to the crowd for the first few gigs, Jim would throw himself around largely in an effort to deflect attention away from the fact he was never going to be a musician. Other groups, real musicians, who came by to check them out, didn't get it. 'Jimmy's antics were considered extreme even then,' recalled Mirandi Babitz, whose fashionable new clothing store on Sunset Jim had begun to visit. 'It made him so nervous he had to get totally looped . . . I used to wonder what was holding him up.'

It was Mirandi's sister, Eve Babitz, though, who would take the full measure of the young pretender. 'He had the freshness and humility of someone who had been fat all his life and now was suddenly a morning glory,' she later wrote. 'I met Jim and propositioned him in three minutes even before he so much as opened his mouth to sing.' This had been at an early London Fog gig, 'where there were only about seven people in the room anyway. "Take me home," I demurely offered when we were introduced.'

Eve, who says she wasn't speaking to her sister at the time, 'because I hated her husband', only found out later that Jim had been visiting Mirandi's store. 'She sold leather clothes. Other rock stars came in there [too].' The night Eve met Jim, 'he was wearing this suede grey outfit – leather sewn together with white lanyards . . . I promised I'd get him LSD and I didn't do it. He told me he'd lost all that weight by taking LSD. Well, I mean, it will keep you from eating.'

His disappointment lasted only as long as it took for him to figure out who Eve actually was: the daughter of Sol Babitz, first violinist for the L.A. Philharmonic and a Fulbright scholar who once got into a brawl over the correct way to play the dotted notes in Bach; her mother was Mae, a stunningly beautiful artist in her own right; her godfather was Igor Stravinsky. When she was growing up, family friends included Charlie Chaplin, Jelly Roll Morton, Greta Garbo – and Aldous and Laura Huxley. Jim could not let that one go!

At 19, Eve had been the subject of a notorious Marcel Duchamp photograph in which she is pictured playing chess, completely nude, against the great conceptualist. Since then she had glided effortlessly through art and music circles. Later in life she would arrange for Frank Zappa to meet Salvador Dalí, put Steve Martin in his first white suit, discover Brett Easton Ellis and write a series of shameless and amusing L.A. novels and memoirs of her own, including, famously, one titled *L.A. Woman*.

A dreadful fire in 1997 – the result of ash from her cigar falling onto her dress – left her with the lower half of the 'body of a mermaid', as she drolly puts it. Since then she has lived in Hollywood largely as a recluse. But she is happy to share her memories of Jim Morrison, if less of The Doors – she tinkles with laugher as she describes them as 'awful, I mean, *really*'.

She didn't even like the name The Doors, she says, and tried to get Jim to change it 'before it was too late'. As she once wrote: 'I dragged Jim into bed . . . and tried to dissuade him; it was so corny naming yourself after something Aldous

Huxley wrote.' She described sleeping with Jim as 'like being in bed with Michelangelo's David, only with blue eyes. His skin was so white, his muscles were so pure, he was so innocent. The last time I saw him with no shirt on, at a party up in Coldwater [in 1971], his body was so ravaged by scars, toxins and puffy pudginess, I wanted to kill him.'

These, though, were still Jim's 'Young Lion' days and Eve, though a year younger, found herself acting as cultural chaperone. 'I took him over to see my father play in Pasadena,' she recalls in her teasing voice. 'My father was a baroque musician. He was a musicologist. He had this weird little group of like harpsichord and, you know. And they were playing at Cal Tech for the old ladies. I dragged Jim upstairs and he watched my father. Dressed in this outfit.' She laughs. 'I don't know what [the old ladies] thought. But he loved it! The whole thing. He wanted to meet my father but I said, no. You can't do this. And to his dying day he was pissed off because I didn't introduce him to my father.'

Other female fans also began to congregate around Jim during the long London Fog residency, which eventually stretched into May. There was the go-go girl. Then one of the dancers from the TV show *Shindig*. He also had a fling with Pamela Zarubica, then working as a cleaner at the Whisky, whom Frank Zappa would later take on tour as one of several young women that performed under the name Suzy Creamcheese. 'It was wonderful,' Zarubica told Jerry Hopkin. 'He didn't know much about what was going on and neither did I.' In fact, Jim's lack of sophistication in the sack got him into trouble with one conquest, Gay Blair, who bawled him out for being 'the worst' lover she'd ever had. Jim was so infuriated he smashed a lamp then pinned her down and ripped her clothes off, before spitting in her face. Then made it up by taking her to Barney's Beanery and being 'so lovey dovey'.

One girl, in particular, though, a too-cute redhead with huge green eyes, cinnamon freckles and creamy white skin, named Pamela Courson, was about to change the course of Jim Morrison's life in a way no other woman, after his mother, could ever do.

Pamela was a 19-year-old student studying art at Los Angeles City College. Born in Weed, California, a tiny town (motto: 'Weed like to welcome you!') ten miles north of Mount Shasta, the second-tallest volcano in the Cascade Range and once regarded as a holy place by Native Americans, Pamela Susan Courson came from a military family. Like Jim's dad, her father, Columbus 'Corky' Courson, was a Commander and former pilot in the US Navy. Unlike the Morrisons, Corky had left the service behind and become a teacher, then Principal, at Orange High, where Pam was also a student. But if the Courson family did not move around as much as the Morrisons, they were equally estranged from their surroundings, mixing uneasily within the small-town community. Embarrassingly for her father, Pam was far from being an A-grade student, saying she hated school and getting in trouble for truancy. Things did not improve during her time at Orange High School and she was just 16 when she and a friend left home and rented a cheap apartment in West Hollywood.

She and a friend had wandered into the London Fog on an otherwise uneventful night in April. The place was even less packed than usual. But even in a crowd Pamela would have stood out. Slim, boyish figure, just the way Jim liked them, but with a heightened sense of Hollywood chic, dressed to the nines in hippy couture, all pretty handmade shifts, sexy cut-down tops, teeny-weeny miniskirts, exotic and elfin. Her dominating character, hard-as-nails interior and river-deep psychological problems were completely undetectable beneath her beguiling aura of life-affirming warmth and bright, incense-burning nights.

During a break that night, John Densmore had been the first to try his luck, going over and inviting himself to sit at the same table as Pamela and her friend. Ray and Dorothy, seated at an adjoining table, looked on amused as John gave it his best shot. Jim, standing at the bar chatting to Jesse, the owner, paid no attention.

John thought his luck was in but when he went to look for Pam at the end of the night she was already gone. Two days later, however, she and her friend were back – and John resumed his courtship, joining them again between sets and putting on the charm. And just as before she was gone again before the end of the final set – a pattern that continued right through that fateful week. Except now Pam started to come to the club on her own, and she and John would sit in a booth together, more private, intimate, while they talked between sets. Until, on the fourth night, Jim slipped into the booth alongside Pam, bit her neck and that was it. Their eyes remained locked for so long neither of them even noticed John getting up and walking away. They spent their first night together.

Jim later rhapsodised about the experience, saying it was the first time he'd ever really *made love*. This time it really wasn't just about the sex, Jim getting turned on by the fact that Pam was born in the same month as him – December – that her father was in the US Navy like his, and, most far out of all, mama, that the place where she came from was steeped in occult Red Indian rites. When Pam told him of the old Indian legend of the Lizard People, who had lived there originally, in a mystical underground city, Jim almost came in his pants.

They would both continue to see other lovers over the next few weeks, until they took the plunge and actually moved in together. But, as Ray would tell me, years later, 'She was his and he was hers. It was the start and end of everything – for both of them.'

It was just two weeks later that the start of something else came to an end. 'Guys this is gonna be your last weekend,' Ray recalls Jesse James telling them. 'I've got to get a new band in here. You're not drawing flies.' Jesse gave them a fighting chance of finding a new gig, giving them two weeks' notice. But when Jim managed to start a bar brawl the very next night to which Jesse was forced to call the cops, that was it, they were told not to come back. The band was abject. Ray, in particular, thought they'd never find another gig as good. Not one on the Strip. Which is when Jim's philandering came in useful again. Ronnie Horan was blonde and beautiful but she was no groupie. She worked at the Whisky A Go-Go, doing promotion and helping book bands. Jim had been working on her to come and check out The Doors, to see if he could get them into the Whisky too. As luck would have it, Ronnie had come, without fanfare, to see their earlier set that final night and was impressed enough by what she saw to wheedle her bosses at the Whisky into giving them a shot. The band was good, said Ronnie, but it was Jim's 'major star quality' that sealed the deal – at least for her.

Just to make sure, though, when the band auditioned for the Whisky's owner, Elmore Valentine, 48 hours later – romping hopefully through three of their newest songs, 'Break On Through', 'Light My Fire' and 'Crystal Ship – Ronnie secretly arranged for some of her friends to phone Valentine and ask for 'that sexy motherfucker in the black pants'.

Yet when Ronnie drove over to see them the next day with the great news that they'd got the gig, Jim put on his best poker face and told her they'd get back to her. They would need to think it over. Frantic, Ray nearly killed him. 'I didn't want her to think we were easy,' Jim drawled. They needn't have worried. By the end of that week not only were The Doors the new house band at the Whisky, but Jim was also living at Ronnie's, who'd agreed to become the band's de facto manager – at least while they remained at the Whisky. Unlike the liaison with Pamela Courson, though, this was not an affair that inspired either party to any great declarations of love. Ronnie's main memory, she later told Jerry Hopkin, was of Jim lolling about her apartment all day, rolling one enormous fat joint after another, smoking himself into an engorged oblivion.

It was that kind of summer. Bob Dylan was in the charts with his single 'Rainy Day Women', with its pay-off line, *'Everybody must get stoned!'* The Beach Boys – a kind of Californian photosynthetic opposite of the menacing L.A. noir sound The Doors were perfecting – were revolutionising pop with their enormous hit, 'Good Vibrations' ('Oom, bop, bop, excitation!'), The Mamas & The Papas, though not an actual

L.A. -based group, were nevertheless living their Hollywood highs with another of the summer's major anthems, 'Monday, Monday' ('Feels so good to me!'), and as well as The Doors the Whisky was now playing host to a veritable menagerie of wilfully out-there new groups, from Zappa and the Mothers, to Van Morrison and Them – with whom Jim got up and sang 'Gloria'. From the Buffalo Springfield to Love, The Byrds, Captain Beefheart and his Magic Band, even Smoky Robinson and the Miracles, just as they were riding the charts with 'Going to A Go-Go'. The scene at the Whisky in the summer of 1966 epitomised a fast-paced cultural melting pot where the music business was midway through its transformation from single-oriented pop to album-oriented rock. It also coincided with what became known as the Sunset Strip curfew riots, aka the 'hippy riots'. Local residents, infuriated with the sight and sound of several hundred hippy freaks spilling out onto the street outside the Whisky and similar clubs each night, had managed to push through new bylaws that restricted movement along the Strip after 10 p.m. When the freaks protested, the law moved in, truncheons and batons swinging, resulting in dozens of needless arrests and many more injuries. (Buffalo Springfield would immortalise the scene with their breakthrough hit, 'For What It's Worth', often mistaken for an anti-war protest song but in fact a direct commentary on the 1966 riots outside the Whisky.)

But if The Doors were the house band at the forefront of an increasingly radical scene, their next move was so beyond the realms of what was considered right on, even by the new chemically enhanced social and musical culture of the summer of 1966, that it nearly ended their career overnight.

It began, as so many of their stories did in those days, with Jim being so out of it on acid he couldn't function. Having missed the first set one night – Ray filling in at the keyboards with his remarkably accurate copycat Morrison voice – Elmore Valentine reminded them he wasn't paying for a trip and told them to find Jim or not bother coming back. When they did, though, he was crawling around on his hands and knees drooling and mumbling about '10,000 mikes, 10,000 mikes . . .' He had swallowed 10,000 microdots worth of LSD. Enough to send most grown men to a psychiatric ward, assuming it hadn't killed them first. Jim though was Jim and the only thing that really bothered Ray and the guys as they tried to get him on his feet was how he was going finish a set back at the club. In the end, they could only hope for the best. At the very least, he would be there with them onstage, thus fulfilling their contractual obligation to Valentine.

'We were going great, the last thing we wanted was to blow it because our great shamanic frontman had partaken too heartily of the blessed sacrament,' as Ray told me in his typically heady apologia. Practically carrying Jim back to the Whisky, when Elmore began ranting at Jim for being late he reached up and grabbed the startled club owner by either side of his head and kissed him on the mouth. That shut him up, though not for long.

By now The Doors' live set had evolved way beyond the limited musical ambitions of their weeks at the Fog. Some of the jams they'd used to fill out their endless sets – the longest and most frequent of which they'd labelled 'Latin Shit No. 1' and 'Latin Shit No. 2' – had evolved into full-blown future classics like 'Light My Fire' and 'Break On Through', both of which betrayed Ray's and John's recent fetishisation of the *Getz/Gilberto* bossa nova album, and increasingly 'When the Music's Over', built off the back of Herbie Hancock's 'Watermelon Man' riff.

Tonight, though, they would unveil – albeit unwittingly – a new magnum opus. Originally begun as minor three-minute ballad – 'a short goodbye love song to Mary [Werbelow]' was how Ray put it – 'The End' had grown through repeated performances into a lengthy Indian raga, but just like a traditional raga, one seemingly without climax or end. Even as Jim would launch into his roaring *'Ride the snake!'* mantra, the band would eventually merely blink out. And when he then added the long, *'Fuck! Fuck! Fuck! Fuck! Fuck!'* rant to the finale, although the swearing nearly drove Valentine and his club manager, Phil Tanzini, crazy – the club's go-go dancers twirling ridiculously in an effort to try and dance to the tirade emanating from the stage – the crowds always erupted at the end, partly through shock perhaps, but always with applause and whistling and calls for more.

That was all about to change as the monumentally tripped-out Jim Morrison held on to the mike for balance and launched into a stream of consciousness that ended with him adding a new piece of theatre to the finale of 'The End' that nearly proved to be just that.

As if channelling his recurring hitchhiker fantasies, Jim began to intone something about the killer waking before dawn, putting on his boots and, thrillingly, taking *'a face from the ancient gallery'*, walking down the hall to his parents' bedroom, where he goes inside and utters the soon to be immortal lines: *'Father . . . Yes, son . . . I want to kill you . . . Mother . . . I want to . . . FUCK YOU!'*

The number came clamouring to its end, but this time there was no eruption of stoned applause; instead hoots from some in the crowd, shocked silence from others. Even the go-go dancers ceased to move a muscle. The only person in the club who knew exactly what to do was Phil Tanzini, who followed the band into the dressing room, went berserk, yelling that they must be out of their fucking minds. He didn't wait for an answer, just told them to get their things and get the fuck out. Now! Pronto. Go. They were fired. They would never play the Whisky again.

Fortunately for Jim Morrison and The Doors, there was already a new saviour waiting in the wings to carry them off to safety. Not another uptight club owner, or another drug freak or groupie. Nothing like that. But a dapper-looking gentleman from New York with no particular interest in rock'n'roll, but an unfailingly keen sense for what he now calls 'music that's on the edge'.

His name was Jac Holzman and though nobody in The Doors had yet heard of him, he was about to make all their dreams come true – even as Jim was making their worst nightmares come true too.

EIGHT

Driver, Where You Taking Us?

Jac Holzman was nearly 35, had run his own record label, Elektra, for over 15 years, had recently signed Love – whose debut album he also produced – and had absolutely no interest whatsoever in signing another psychedelic rock band. But when Love's leader, Arthur Lee, hipped him to these new cats, The Doors, Jac felt obliged to at least give them the once over. When it turned out the two bands were appearing the same night at the Whisky in the summer of 1966, Jac felt he had no choice anyway. But his head was gone. A perennial New Yorker in those days, he'd arrived on the red-eye into LAX at 11 p.m. – 2 a.m. NY time. By the time he'd driven to the Whisky, stood through Love's senses-blurring set, then watched The Doors, he'd been awake for nearly 24 hours and travelled nearly 2,500 miles, and was in no mood to mess around.

Predictably then, as he later recalled, 'Morrison made no impression whatsoever. I was more drawn to the classical [influences] of keyboardist Ray Manzarek, and was attracted to the leanness of the music. The lead singer seemed reclusive and tentative, as if preserving himself. There was nothing that tagged him as special, but there was a subtle invitation to "play", if you were willing to do so on his terms. It was only later that I sensed Jim's "game".'

Speaking now for the first time in years ('I get asked all the time to speak about The Doors. I say, read my book, *Follow the Music*!'), Holzman recalls being so underwhelmed he had virtually made up his mind not to pursue any interest, when, just as he was leaving mid-set, Ronnie Haran stopped him and insisted he come back the following night. Jim was acting up, she said, refusing to put on a show for the record company 'suit' Arthur Lee had told him was in the audience. Which is how Holzman found himself back at the Whisky the following night, watching The Doors all over again. But still no eureka moment. Just a band bashing out a terse form of blues with vague classical and jazz leanings. Nevertheless, everyone he talked to in L.A. seemed to have a bead on The Doors. When Barry Friedman, a genuinely out-there record producer and former Beatles publicist who had recently begun managing one of L.A.'s hottest new bands, Buffalo Springfield (and who would soon be appointed Elektra's West Coast head of A&R), started babbling about them too, Holzman went back to the Whisky the next night – and the next.

Says Jac now: 'The question I ask myself when I look at any artist is: is this music something I haven't heard before? Well, it wasn't the first two or three nights but it was the last night, where suddenly all the Doors songs that had been hidden while Jim . . . Jim loved to do sets that involved long blues. Now I didn't need Jim Morrison to do that. I had the Butterfield Blues Band to do that. What I wanted was something odd but interesting that people could get, viscerally. Sometimes there are songs that are like Rosetta Stones, and once I heard [their version of] "Whisky Bar (The Alabama Song)", I got the rest of it. Everything just filled in. The gaps just filled in. And I went back and listened to the songs again and I heard the stuff that I had glossed over before and didn't get.' Because The Doors 'had taken something that was so off the wall' – a 1927 Bertolt Brecht poem set to music by Kurt Weill – 'and converted it into a song that could appear on a rock album', Holzman finally got it, what the rest of their monochromatic, mock-Weimar cabaret sound was all about. This was rock but with a major difference. Where every other major band in 1966 was extolling a wide-eyed gambol through the psychedelic prism of love-love-love, The Doors appeared as the antithesis to all that, the dark angel come to eat its own children. Fuck its own mother; kill its own father.

A calculated risk-taker whose modus operandi had always been to ponder long then, once his decision had been made, move fast, Holzman approached the band in their dressing room at the Whisky that same night. 'When I heard that fourth night I knew this was a great band,' he says. 'I wanted to be where nobody else was yet. The beauty of being an independent is you make your mind up and you just go for it.'

According to Ray, Jac made them an offer on the spot: $2,500 upfront (less than he gave Love and others, they later discovered) against a 5 per cent royalty and with Elektra holding on to the song publishing. 'Like a Brill Building deal,' Ray dismissively described it in his memoir, a claim Holzman bristles at. 'I offered what was slightly on the generous side of a standard deal in 1966 for an unproven group,' he wrote in *Follow the Music*, adding that Elektra would advance all recording costs plus $5,000 cash to the band against a 5 per cent royalty with a separate advance against publishing, 'of which The Doors would own 75 per cent and Elektra 25 per cent'. He added that 'as a show of faith' he committed to a three-album deal.

In truth, the band could not believe their luck. Whatever claims they might have later made, The Doors had been turned down by every meaningful record company on the West Coast, their only deal with Columbia had petered out, and though they didn't know it yet they were mere days away from being fired – again – from the only steady gig they had. If Jac Holzman had walked into their dressing room wearing a Santa Clause outfit and carrying a sackful of cash, he could not have made a more welcoming impression. Nevertheless, true to form, Jim urged the others to play it cool. With his smart dark clothes and elegant New York talk, Holzman presented himself to Jim as yet another father figure and he was not going to be won over that easily. As a result, Holzman would recall, he was forced to go 'through the agony of a summer trying to nurse them toward signing [the deal], which did not occur until several months later'.

Billy James at Columbia told them to sign to Elektra without delay. But Billy was on his way to working at Elektra's soon-to-be-opened Los Angeles office. Ronnie Haran told them to get a good lawyer, suggesting they use hers – but they turned down the offer. This caused bad blood and Jim was forced to move out of Ronnie's apartment. As he was leaving, he told her, 'I'll be dead in two years.' But Jim was always saying stuff like that.

In the end they followed the advice of Robby's father, Stu Krieger, who put them together with the deliciously named Max Fink, a big-cigar and bigger-desk Hollywood attorney who looked like he knew his way around the blood-smeared back alleys of L.A. as well as he did its glitzy, tits-first front offices. Max Fink ate out-of-town New York suits like Jac Holzman for breakfast – or told The Doors he did – and set about his work with relish. Jac, in his customary hurry to get the act signed and set up to record, was forced to think again when Max came back to him with practically every page of the contract covered in red ink in which he'd noted his various questions, amendments and straight deletions – it looked like the deal might never get done. But the wily Max drafted a letter of agreement that everybody signed on 20 August, allowing The Doors and Elektra to proceed with recording an album, but delaying any long-term legal obligations until the contract was finally agreed in November.

Any other record company chief would have walked away. Fortunately for The Doors, Jac Holzman was not any other record company chief. The eldest son of a Park Avenue doctor, Jac was a super-smart boy who studied Descartes at college, and who would bring his gift for minute analysis and almost geometrical calculation to all his future dealings, philosophically and in business. Jac was 19 when he started Elektra – named after the mythological Greek princess, Electra (with the 'c' replaced by a 'k' – 'To make it seem more intriguing'), who plotted revenge against her mother, Clytemnestra, for murdering her father, King Agamemnon. Within a few years, Jac had grown the label from a tiny mail order company run from his St John's College dorm to a storefront Greenwich

Village operation where he delivered his ten-inch LPs – Elektra didn't do singles – personally to other stores on the back of a second-hand motor scooter. (He would carry old parking tickets and place them on the scooter's tiny mirror in order to fool traffic cops and park wherever he liked.)

To begin with Elektra specialised in specific folk idioms, bringing out limited-edition runs of LPs by Cynthia Gooding (*Turkish and Spanish Folk Songs*, 1953) and Theodore Bikel (*Israeli Folk Songs*, 1955) – what would today be described as world music. The label also released homegrown American folk stars like Ed McCurdy, whose anti-war classic, 'Last Night I Had the Strangest Dream', would eventually be recorded in 76 languages.

The big difference between Elektra and the leading independent label in the 1950s, Atlantic, was that the Ertegun brothers, who had started their label just three years before Elektra, were expansionist. Quality music was what drove their label, but they were on a mission from day one to turn their vanity label into a major player in the mainstream market. They produced singles as well as albums, looked to create a worldwide network of distribution outlets and aimed to have hits. Holzman was coming from the other direction. Small was beautiful, and Elektra would remain essentially a boutique label right up until it signed The Doors. Releasing records with limited runs, Elektra did not create music for the mass market, but concentrated instead on making their LPs deluxe propositions: each came with its own booklet – unheard of until then – featuring the work of top photographers of the day like George Pickow and, later, Pompeo Posar, with detailed, evocative liner notes by star writers such as Studs

Terkel and, down the line, Shel Silverstein. If Atlantic was for hip swingers, Elektra was for the knowledgeable elite.

One of Holzman's most significant early signings had been that of Josh White, the country blues singer who first came to prominence in the 1930s with 'race records' intended solely for the rural black population. He became one of the first black artists to successfully cross over to a white audience with his Depression-era hit, 'One Meat Ball', which became the first million-selling record by a black artist. From there he was able to launch a lucrative career in the 1940s working in supper clubs and cabaret. He also used his more elevated position to become a leading voice against social injustice suffered by blacks in America. So successful were his various speeches and interviews he was targeted as a communist sympathiser and, in 1950, called before a hearing of the House Un-American Activities Commission, leading to a virtual ban on his records and live appearances.

By the time Holzman met him, playing backrooms in Greenwich Village in the mid-Fifties, White's career was in stasis. Jac, an iron-willed young man who resented any outside involvement in his decisions, business or musical, decided to make the point by signing White for a series of albums in the late Fifties that would redraw the lines of both White's career and that of Elektra Records. White's first album, produced by Holzman in 1955, also happened to be Elektra's last ten-inch release, *The Story of John Henry*. White's second, *Josh at Midnight*, in 1956, became Elektra's first 12-inch release, and would go on to become one of the label's biggest sellers up to that point.

'Having someone like Josh White on the label said

something beyond just the music,' Holzman explains. 'It raised the stature of the artist and the label. I don't want to be where everybody else is, in the centre. Because by the time you make an album from the centre, the centre has moved on and then you're stuck with this record. I don't want anything that anybody else is doing. I wanted people to think of Elektra as different to the others.'

Well, they certainly did that. By the time he met The Doors, ten years later, Holzman's Elektra had expanded to become one of the leading independent record labels in the world. An electronics expert, Jac had commissioned a series of sound effects LPs with a view to then licensing the various tracks – a car crashing; a window breaking; a radio signal; a machine grinding its gears; anything and everything – to TV and film companies for use in their shows, movies, commercials. They proved to be among the most consistently lucrative releases for Elektra throughout the Sixties. In 1964, he also started a subsidiary label, dubbed Nonesuch Records, whose remit – to produce 'fine records at the same price as a trade paperback [book]' – saw the label focusing initially on licensing European recordings of baroque and chamber music, which Nonesuch made available in distinctive new LPs for half the price of normal albums. Ray Manzarek would later claim it was the Nonesuch catalogue that had really attracted The Doors to Holzman.

By 1966, however, Holzman had bigger fish to fry. Having successfully ridden the folk revival of the early Sixties, releasing the first albums of groundbreaking new folk artists like Judy Collins, Phil Ochs and Tom Paxton, Jac had narrowly missed out on signing L.A.'s The Byrds – the first successful folk-rock hybrid group – been out-manoeuvred trying to sign New York's the Lovin' Spoonful – another destined-to-be-huge, proto-folk-rock outfit that Jac had nurtured then had snatched from him when he discovered a previous production deal the band had not told him they'd signed. However, he had managed to sign the Paul Butterfield Blues Band, whose eponymous 1965 debut is now ranked by *Downbeat* as one of the Top 50 blues albums of all time, and by *Rolling Stone* as one of the Top 500 rock albums.

Now his full focus was on Southern California. 'I had given up on New York because of the Lovin' Spoonful incident, and because everybody in New York was going to hear everything and I didn't want to be in a bidding war against Columbia. That was not a winner,' he says now. 'I mean, there were record companies out [in L.A.] but remember the Los Angeles offices or the away-from-the centre offices, either in London or Los Angeles, don't get paid as much attention to. So when stuff is sent back to New York for consideration, they don't take it seriously. They don't get back right away.'

Jac decided he and Elektra would be on the spot to pounce quickly. Hence, what he calls his '20-minute deal' with Love. 'That's all it took to sign them.' Holzman felt sure The Doors would come around eventually, though. 'Well, it wasn't happening fast for them,' he says. 'They had been rejected by every label in town. Columbia threw them off the label. That's what made it easy for me, because I knew the key to signing the band was to say, "I'm going to give you a home and you and I are going to be working together for three albums that I promise I will release."'

Holzman was looking to expand Elektra's New York-based

operation down to the West Coast, specifically L.A., where he planned to open an office, and when it became clear that would also serve as a de facto office for The Doors, the band could not pretend to be aloof any longer. The deal was signed at the start of August. Three weeks later The Doors were ensconced in Sunset Sound Recorders, a bare-knuckles recording facility in Hollywood – purpose-built by Walt Disney in 1958 to record the soundtracks to Disney classics like *Bedknobs and Broomsticks*, *Mary Poppins* and *101 Dalmatians* – which would now become the go-to studio for all Elektra's West Coast artists until it built its own studio.

Originally, Holzman had considered producing The Doors' album himself, as he had done for Love. But he had second thoughts after meeting Jim and turned the job over to his right-hand man at Elektra, the producer Paul A. Rothchild. 'I loved the studio, but I thought Paul knew more than I did about how to do this kind of band,' says Jac. 'He had a lot to learn as a producer but he had deep musical knowledge. And you're talking about a band where the guys were all very smart and frequently about different things. Ray and Jim were super-smart and you needed a guy who was as well-read as they were and Paul was that. So I thought he was the ideal person. I thought he could really whip them into shape.'

At 31, Paul Rothchild was just old enough to exert authority over the group, just young enough to be hip to their trip. A classically trained musician who had grown up in New Jersey, where he had been groomed for success by his mother, who had sung with the Metropolitan Opera, Paul had trained in the Fifties under the tutelage of the great conductor Bruno Walter. Swept up by the folk revival, he found himself in

Cambridge, Massachusetts, on the board of Club 47, the small but significant folk club in the Harvard Square area of Cambridge where Joan Baez gave her very first concert, barefoot, in 1958. The next few years found Rothchild working as a Boston-area record distributor, while also trying to make his mark as a producer. In 1962 he talked some Harvard student friends, The Charles River Valley Boys, into letting him produce their second album, *Bluegrass and Old Timey Music*, released on Prestige Records, where Paul was working. This was followed, in 1964, by a second album with the Valley Boys, *Blue Grass Get Together*, but by then Bob Dylan had taken folk into the rock arena and Rothchild had relocated to New York, where he first hooked up with Jac Holzman and produced his first albums for Elektra

Clad in regulation skintight jeans, even tighter T-shirt or often as not no shirt at all, his long hair tied in a ponytail to distract attention from the fact that he was already going bald on top, Rothchild would come striding through the studio door, avoiding all eye contact until he was settled behind the console, where he would snap open his briefcase. 'The briefcase was famous,' Jac recalled. 'It held everything he might possibly need: pitch pipe, the latest gadgets, cigarettes, whatever drug was up for the evening.'

Paul was a loner, seriously focused, as self-absorbed as any artist, even Morrison and The Doors. 'He could do a "Hey man" to the artist, though he didn't say "Hey man" to me,' as Holzman put it. His only drawback: he was a perfectionist. A year before, and against Holzman's better judgement, Rothchild had insisted his original production of the debut Paul Butterfield Blues Band album be scrapped because it 'didn't sound quite right'. He re-recorded the whole thing, and though the album had a huge impact, when the original was finally released nearly 30 years later, critics, including Jac, lamented it had not been released in 1965 as originally intended.

Since then, he'd co-produced – with Holzman's longer-serving production lieutenant Mark Abramson – the second Butterfield album, *East–West*, another neo-blues classic that pre-figured some of the acid-flayed, improvisatory blues The Doors were also now meddling with, and worked directly with Holzman on the production on the startling debut album by the latest Elektra signing, Tim Buckley. The latter was re-corded in only three days at Sunset Sound just prior to the arrival of The Doors in August 1966.

Only snag: Paul just didn't see it. After Butterfield and Buckley and the other great artists like Tom Paxton he had worked with for Elektra, being brought in to hold the hands of what Rothchild then thought of as little more than a rowdy club act seemed beneath him. Besides, he had already decided who he wanted to work with next: a Canadian psychedelic outfit named The Paupers. But Jac disagreed, thought The Paupers 'a crappy band . . . not a band that was an Elektra signing', and put his foot down about The Doors. (Holzman's view was later vindicated when The Paupers' debut 1967 album, released on MGM–Verve, promptly sank without trace.)

Plus, Paul owed Jac big – and gave in when Jac reminded him of it. Rothchild had just got out of prison after serving eight months of a two-year sentence for possession of mari-juana. And not just a pocket full of spliffs but several suitcases full of the stuff, which he later swore had just turned up on his doorstep one morning, the act, he suggested, of a disgruntled musician he had crossed. It seemed a tall story, but though the cops didn't believe him, most crucially Jac did. And while Paul had been incarcerated, Holzman had offered his wife part-time work at the label, to help her meet the bills.

'I had been very supportive of [Paul] when he went to jail and took care of his family,' says Jac. 'I kept Paul on half-salary and . . . gave [his wife] some work a couple of days a week.' So when Paul initially baulked at producing The Doors, 'I finally said to him, "Look, you're the only guy who can do this band that I trust." Paul was very smart and knew how to adjust to the temperament of the artist for the most part. He could become a martinet, and if he was a martinet he was kind of miserable to be around. No, he was not impressed by The Doors. But I said, basically, "You kind of owe me. I stayed by you and now I'm asking you to stick by me on something I feel is going to be very important." He said, "Put it that way, absolutely." There was no discussion after that.'

First, though, Rothchild insisted he work with the band at some serious pre-production rehearsals, 'Because,' says Jac, 'the songs had not been shaped by the addition of anybody else's intelligence. They had been shaped totally by themselves. The arrangements and the way things went, were a lot Paul Rothchild.' The prime example was 'Light My Fire', which the stickler-for-detail producer sculpted from the musical miasma of its sprawling live incarnation into something with real shape and gravitas. 'So as [Paul] got into it he realised how good the music was. And we talked about how long they should be in the rehearsal studio and we figured ten days maximum, because we didn't want to get them totally there. We wanted them to put the last 20 per cent of energy and whatever magic was going to come directly into the songs in the studio. The fact they were in the studio doing it would give them a boost. [Paul] was on board by that time. And then as we were putting the album together he got it. Because there were these certain magic moments, when he would turn and say, "God this is great!" And they occurred in many, many different songs.'

Even though they were there with Rothchild and his usual sidekick, the engineer Bruce Botnick, for less than a week, The Doors 'owned Studio B' at Sunset Sound. At the end of every session the doors would be double-locked so their sound could not be altered. Often a studio will be broken down for other acts to use after a session is over. Not with The Doors, though. Dropping in on the sessions, Holzman was already convinced this was precious cargo.

'It was for Elektra Records so I knew it was going be different,' says Botnick now, speaking from his home in Los Angeles. 'I had already recorded Tim Buckley's first album with Paul. This was the first album he did when he got out of jail, because he had been busted for pot, which in those days was a pretty bad thing. He told me he was lucky that he didn't get raped in the prison. He said some massive black guy took pity on him and protected him. Until Jac was able to finally get him out of jail.'

While Rothchild had the 'vision thing' – converting what was at the time an extremely functional four-track facility into a late-night netherworld where Jim and the band could let their spirits fly, even as he obliged them to do different takes, try it more this way, less that way, teasing the best performances out of them, his joints competing with Jim's for perfection – the 23-year-old Botnick's job was to be Mr Fixit, getting the set-up right, keeping the tape rolling, placing bafflers and mikes, helping Paul fly the faders, coming up with the little extras that might make the difference.

'Jim was in the vocal booth. The guys were in the studio itself. It's ten feet apart at the most. They could see one another. I always kept the lights dark in the studio for certain acts. You know, they needed to have that. Down to screwing in some red light bulbs in the studio that glowed like that.

'At that time I was still working for the studio,' he recalls, 'and in the early morning, I was recording radio commercials. For muffler companies and things like that. Then around lunchtime I would be doing a children's album for Disney. Or doing a jazz project. And I loved doing all these things at the same time, because I would get something from one and I would try to put it into the next one then put it into the next one. It was just constantly feeding and it's a good, very healthy atmosphere. Or we'd do Mexican Week. We'd do everything from Herb Alpert and the Tijuana Brass, perhaps, to totally indigenous [music] with harps and everything. And it was the greatest learning experience I've ever had! I brought some of that into The Doors and I brought it into Love, for *Forever Changes.*'

The first day the band arrived in the studio, Bruce recalls, 'they had everything down. They had pretty much the first two albums ready to go. The thought that Paul had and which I agreed [with] is that we were to be invisible – to allow them to capture their performance, to capture the magic of The

Doors as you went to hear them.' He adds: 'They were totally different than anything else I was recording. I was recording the Beach Boys, the Turtles, the Ventures and a lot of pop music as well – and [The Doors] were totally different, it was the beginning of that era of American Sixties music.'

Bassist Larry Knechtel, from the top L.A.-based session outfit, The Wrecking Crew, who playing on dozens of hit records throughout the Sixties, was hired to play on six of the album's eventual 11 tracks, with Ray handling the others on his keyboard bass. Only three of the studio's four tracks were actually used – drums and bass on one, guitar and keyboards on another, and Jim's vocals on the third – with the fourth track kept back for overdubs.

Apart from the album's two cornerstone tracks – the seven-minute-plus 'Light My Fire' and the nearly 12-minute 'The End' – most of the tracks were less than three minutes long. But then, in truth, despite regularly being hailed since as one of the all-time great rock debuts, the first Doors album was a mixed bag of disposable Sixties pop and a truly gothic form of rock, with layers of Indian raga, jazz stylings and neo-classical pretensions. So that while tracks like the rousing, call-to-arms opener, 'Break On Through (to the Other Side)' and the genuinely spaced-out 'Crystal Ship', with its, for the times, outlandish opening couplet, *'Before you slip into / Un-con-scious-ness . . .'*, suggested a very different, far more advanced, into-the-night type of rock band than any seen before, certainly out on the West Coast, others like 'Soul Kitchen' – inspired by the band's fondness for a cheap and cheerful Venice Beach joint, called Olivia's, that sold soul food – and 'Twentieth Century Fox' – a droolingly stoned play on words, geddit? – are so wincingly à la mode they would have struggled to get on the first Monkees album, also being made that summer.

While the painfully peacocking 'I Looked at You' sounds like a Rick & The Ravens throwback, tracks like 'End of the Night' – another self-consciously spooky interlude with only its Céline-inspired title to guide it – and the deliriously vacuous 'Take It As It Comes' – even if the organ solo, as Ray claims, was lifted from J. S. Bach – sound like what they are, side salads for the real steaks on the plate: 'Light My Fire', with its grandiose Bach-fugue intro and swirling instrumental middle section inspired by John Coltrane's 'Olé', and 'The End', the only truly riveting musical journey into the mystic they make, which, fittingly, closes the album.

Given the inclusion also of two cover songs – their admittedly inspired live reading of 'Alabama Song (Whisky Bar)' – and Jim's thinly veiled reference to his growing obsession with anal sex, Willie Dixon's 'Back Door Man' (every groupie on Sunset was now privately complaining about how Jim was pestering them for it) – it seems strange that they didn't consider including some of the other tracks they already had completed, specifically, the truly trippy 'Moonlight Drive' and the equally ethereal 'Indian Summer' – or at the very least, if they were looking for a hit, 'Hello, I Love You'. All of which were recorded during the sessions – and would be included on future Doors albums – but passed over when it came to the final sequencing of their debut.

According to Robby Krieger, the beautiful 'Indian Summer', though it would not be released for another four years, was the first song the band ever fully completed, with

'Moonlight Drive' coming after. But Paul Rothchild had decided they needed more upbeat numbers so 'Indian Summer' got nixed in favour of 'Back Door Man', and the original version they cut of 'Moonlight Drive' they simply didn't think was good enough. (Listening to the cut on the contemporary re-mastered CD version of the album, released after Rothchild's death in 1995, it's hard to disagree.)

'Every day we got something great,' Rothchild would later tell Jerry Hopkins. 'Jim was out of control on some days, but that was just another aspect of that phenomenon: the Jim Morrison spirit! Because we were recording when Jim was at one of his most insane points, when he was deep into acid.' They would try various different songs, do a few takes, then move on to another. They even tried having a go at 'The End' on the first night but it just wasn't happening. So they got it on the second night instead, said Rothchild.

In fact, the recording of 'The End', which would eventually roll out to almost 12 minutes in length – unheard of for a rock song at that time – precipitated one of the most oft-told, yet always exaggerated stories from the making of the first Doors album. According to legend, the band was two-thirds of the way through playing the track, just after Jim had turned his onstage announcement of wanting to fuck his mother into an incoherent yowl, and as he began to dervish around the studio he noticed – oh, the insult! – that Bruce Botnick was watching a small black-and-white TV tuned to a baseball game, which Jim, absolutely furious, smashed to the floor before picking it up and hurling it through the studio glass into the control room, where Botnick and Rothchild sat shocked.

Speaking now, however, Botnick sighs and claims it was

a far less dramatic moment. 'I don't know why I did this but I had this Sony TV, a little one, on a stool looking into the control room.' The Los Angeles Dodgers were playing the St Louis Cardinals with the baseball legend Sandy Koufax pitching. As far as Bruce, who had no idea who The Doors were, or thought they were, was concerned, he'd simply brought the TV in to work with him to catch the game – with the sound off. 'And in [Jim's] flying around he knocked it off. It did not explode. It did not catch on fire. He did not pick it up and throw it through the glass as Ray Manzarek said that he did. None of that happened. But he knocked it off and yes it went on the floor, and the tape continued. In between takes I walked out into the studio and got it and turned it off. And then we did a second take. "The End" comprises two takes and we edited it together – the first half and the second half. For the performance aspect we made the cut. Because everything that happened on that album was based on performance.'

The other flashpoint story from those sessions that has since gone down in history has also been exaggerated, according to Botnick: the one in which a fiercely tripping Jim – on the same night they completed splicing the two best performances of 'The End' together – returned alone to Sunset Sound and trashed the studio, throwing ashtray-sand over the floor and emptying a fire extinguisher into the mixing console.

According to Botnick, though, this was not merely an act of acid-crazed petulance but a genuine attempt, albeit with lid flapping open, to avert what Morrison saw as a disaster. 'The way that Sunset Sound studios was, it was an old garage [that had] been converted. It was absorption, brick, absorption, brick ... But inside each brick was a light and that's where I screwed the red light bulbs.' After everyone had left the studio that night, Jim had 'gone across the street to the Blessed Sacrament, a Catholic Church, and he had an epiphany over there. He came back to the studio and the gate was locked. He climbed over the gate, got in but he couldn't get in the control room. That was locked. But the studio was open and the red lights were on and he thought it was on fire so he grabbed a fire extinguisher and knocked over the ashtrays that were full of sand and tried to put out the fire.'

Recalling the incident at the time, however, Rothchild said he'd received a phone call from the chick Jim had left the session with, saying Jim had jumped out of her car and was headed back to the studio. When Paul got there Jim was shoeless and shirtless, almost naked. When Paul asked him what the fuck, he just grinned that slow-burn grin and said, 'I want to record.' Paul talked him down and they retired to Jim's pad, and spent the rest of the night digging the Stones, Donovan, Howlin' Wolf . . . Paul finally escaped around dawn. As he walked through the door of his Laurel Canyon home his phone was ringing. It was studio owner, Tutti Camarata, apoplectic with rage, saying the studio had been trashed: fire extinguisher foam all over the mixing console, sand from a stand-up ashtray hurled across the room. Also a pair of Jim's old stinky boots . . . Did Paul know who they belonged to? Paul said he did not. Then wearily told him to send the bill to Elektra.

PART TWO
UNLOCKED

NINE

Suck My Mama

According to Bruce Botnick, the first Doors album – simply titled *The Doors* – took just five days to make, from start to finish. 'Because it was performance, capturing performance, editing, doing overdubs if we needed to double his voice or whatever. But it took five days.'

It would take five months, though, for Elektra to finally release the album. This was almost entirely down to the fact that Holzman didn't even know if Elektra would have The Doors under contract until November, when after interminable contractual wrangling Max Fink finally agreed the deal with the company. Jim and Ray had pushed at that point for the album to be released immediately, so that it was in time for Christmas. But Jac, the wise old label head, knew better and tried to talk them into allowing Elektra to hold back release until the New Year.

Ray and the rest of the band acquiesced, realising they had no choice in the matter anyway. But Jim threw a tantrum and needed to be talked down. As Holzman later wrote, even then Jim and the other three members of The Doors were 'really two entities: Ray Manzarek–Robby Krieger–John Densmore, and Jim Morrison, separate and apart'. Jim was now living in a $9-a-night room at The Tropicana ('The Trop', as Jim called it): the rundown West Hollywood motel where the black-tiled pool had no water and the guests festered alongside each other, sharing their drugs and cheap wine bottles, bed-hopping and stealing from each other, the kind of low-rent dive where all the musicians that hadn't yet made it stayed, the actors out on loan, dogs without a bone, all scavenging after each other, hoping someone's luck might change and, when it did, would carry the rest of them along too. Sure. This, though, while the other three Doors still lived in either the comfort of their parents' house (John and Robby) or with their live-in partners out by the Beach (Robby and Dorothy). There was Jim and there were The Others. Holzman got this immediately and discerned early on that the key to working successfully with The Doors would be to always keep Jim happy.

Speaking now, Jac recalls he told Jim, 'We've got something very special here and I don't want it to get lost in pre-Christmas, and this is what I'll do if you agree to that.' His first move was to book The Doors into their first New York shows, a month-long residency at Ondine's, the ultra-fashionable East Side discotheque on East 59th Street that had lately become *the* hangout for the Andy Warhol Factory crowd and satellite hangers-on like Mick Jagger, Bob Dylan and the Velvet Underground. Jim, who read all the music and film magazines, gazing at all the celebrity pictures in *Vogue* and *Time* as avidly as any fan, was aware that the status a residency at Ondine's would confer on The Doors would help them become part of that scene.

Jac also painted Jim a picture of the kind of campaign Elektra would build around the album when it was finally released in the New Year. 'I said, "We'll have more time to prepare for you and I'll release no other album that month, which means you've got Elektra working 100 per cent on your album for the first month. And by the way I have this idea about putting a billboard up on Sunset Strip . . ." Well, that caught Jim. He loved that idea. He said, "Where'd you come up with that?"'

True to his word, Holzman didn't release any other album in January 1967, got his Elektra staff so cranked up on *The Doors* they could talk of nothing else right through the Christmas holidays, then added the promised cherry of making The Doors the first rock band ever to feature on one of Hollywood's giant billboards overlooking the Strip.

By then, though, The Doors were starting to feel a sense of entitlement that very soon would outgrow a dozen billboards on Sunset Boulevard. Their November 1966 residency in New York had seen to that. Before Jim and The Doors took over the joint, Ondine's had belonged to the Warhol crowd. When it opened in 1965, Edie Sedgwick became one of its first celebrity patrons, showering the dozens of guests she brought with her each night in endless bottles of champagne, endless vials of speed, orgies of fun, fun, fun. And sex, lots of sex. The first place in New York where the prettiest girls wore the shortest mini-skirts, though they weren't called that yet. When the 18-year-old Marisa Berenson, then the world's highest-paid teenage model, went there she was immediately spotted by Gerard Malanga – the college dropout poet-actor-scenester who had latterly become Warhol's most outré assistant, appearing in five of Andy's celebrated 'art movies' before he was 22 – and who insisted Andy screen-test her for his next planned movie, *Chelsea Girls*. Marisa had other ideas but that was okay. Gerard was already starring in his own movie anyway, the reels constantly rolling in his head. Some said he was the real star of the early Velvet Underground shows, the band Andy managed and built his Exploding Plastic Inevitable (EPI) multimedia experiences around, standing there in his leather trousers and brandishing a whip, dancing like a cross between Nureyev and Twiggy.

Warhol later recalled walking into Ondine's with his entourage the first night The Doors played there. 'Gerard took one look at Jim Morrison in leather pants just like his and he flipped. "He stole my look!" he screamed, outraged.' It was true. When Warhol's EPI, as it was dubbed, set up at The Trip in Los Angeles, in May, Jim had been there to see them do it and had been so impressed by Malanga's macho, crotch-bulging, leather-trousered presence, dancing in a Marlon Brando T-shirt, lifting toy barbells and pretending to shoot up with lighted candles, he immediately set about appropriating the look for his own purposes.

It was another of Jim's acquisitions from the EPI, though, that would later cause him the most trouble: the German actress and model Nico. Born in Cologne, in 1938, Christa Päffgen had been 'discovered' as a model when she was 16 by the photographer Herbert Tobias, who nicknamed her 'Nico' after his friend the filmmaker Nikos Papatakis. Her career had immediately taken off: the face of Coco Chanel at 17; by 20, a well-travelled actress with parts in Alberto Lattuada's *La Tempesta* and Rudolph Maté's *For the First Time*, and, most famously, in 1959, while visiting Cinecittà studios in Rome, where Federico Fellini was shooting *La Dolce Vita*, she so intoxicated the renowned director he immediately wrote in a small part for her – playing herself. In 1962, she'd given birth to a son, Christian Aaron 'Ari' Päffgen, whose father was the French screen star Alain Delon.

When she arrived at the Factory in 1965, as the new girlfriend of the Rolling Stones' guitarist Brian Jones, the homosexual Warhol was equally smitten by the tall, ice-blonde dominatrix, with the voice of a doomed siren, her heavy German accent inflected with narcoleptic traces of English, Spanish and French. He was beside himself with glee at the prospect of casting such an obvious bird-of-paradise-lost in his deeply transgressive movies. Nico had been taking 'method' acting lessons at Lee Strasberg's class, had appeared on the cover of the jazz pianist Bill Evans's 1962 album, *Moon Beams*, and had starred, two years earlier, in Jacques Poitrenaud's *Strip-Tease* – for which she had also sung the title song of the soundtrack, written by Serge Gainsbourg. Becoming a leading light of Andy Warhol's Factory scene was merely the next step towards her own supernova-bursting superstardom, she felt sure.

When Warhol decided to push her to the front of the Velvet Underground, insisting they write some songs especially for her to sing, the singer, Lou Reed, was at first affronted, then mollified when the two began sleeping together. What Jim Morrison saw the first time the EPI performed at The Trip – a tiny venue also owned by the Whisky's Elmore Valentine – was a rock band as just one element in a much greater theatrical performance, combining art, film, lights, music . . . exactly the kind of concept he and Ray had raved about constructing for The Doors in their early Venice Beach daze. The band, all in shades, played almost without moving as Warhol's films were projected across them, interspersed with full-spectrum psychedelic lights, while Gerard Malanga lashed his whip, improvising dance moves to 'illustrate' the songs. And fronting the whole spectacle, Nico – no shades, just those deep swimming pool eyes defying the gaze. A living Warhol sculpture dressed in a white leather catsuit, Nico had only sung three songs, but Jim had not been able to take his own heavily tripped-out eyes off her.

Yet despite the largely apocryphal tales of people fainting during the shows while others became so spaced out they didn't even bother going home, just slept on the floor and kept going the next night and the next, the show closed on the fourth night after local cops moved in to shut down the club, reacting to the endless reports of drug dealers operating openly inside and complaints about couples having sex in the street outside. In truth, it was probably for the best. While future Velvet Underground classics like the heart-pounding 'I'm Waiting for the Man' and the psychotic 'Run, Run, Run' were recognisably accurate portrayals of New York's rancid underbelly, paeans almost to Lower East Side sensibilities, in L.A., where the sun always shone and the local freak scene was predicated more on weed and wine and LSD-25 – on reaching for the stars, man, inviting the universe and its vast mysteries to seep into our souls, man – this shit just didn't play. Or, as Cher put it, after walking out on the much-hyped opening show at The Trip – along with the crème de la crème of West Hollywood scenesters like Warren Beatty,

Jack Nicholson, Roger Vadim, Jane and Peter Fonda, Dennis Hopper, Natalie Wood, Michelle and John Phillips, and Julie Christie – 'It will replace nothing, except maybe suicide.'

When the EPI entourage was forced to take an extended break while they waited to begin the next leg of their West Coast tour in San Francisco, Jim had begun a brief but blitz-krieged affair with Nico that would be rekindled – and nearly burn them both alive – again and again over the coming year. When he discovered Nico was staying at John Phillip Law's concrete 'Castle', in Los Feliz, south of the Santa Monica Mountains, waiting for Warhol's *Chelsea Girls*, which she starred in as herself, he drove straight over to see her – and stayed. And how.

'He spent that whole night sort of dancing for her,' says Danny Fields. 'It was like one of those birds in New Guinea. He was just climbing around the roof naked and standing on the edge of the precipice. Then he would come down, he would beat her up. And I mean not violently. Shove her around and pull her hair. And then go back up. I presume they ended up doing it though he was so stoned, I don't know. I can't visual-ise it. I think they saw each other a few more times but one is more aware of the first time with people.'

'I see her as kind of an equal,' Jim would tell Ray. But Ray didn't believe him. Even then, for Ray, Jim simply had no equal. This girl would soon vanish like all the others. Ray hoped. But things never did happen quite so easily for Jim, who now ditched West Coast thrift-store cool for Green-wich Village chic. Before leaving for New York, he'd been to Mirandi Babitz's far-out new store on Sunset and ordered a bespoke leather suit with a zip-less sailor front on the trousers.

Très butch, this would be Jim's hip new look for the next two years, until he ditched it for good, disgusted by the copyists, the Steppenwolfs and Iggy Pops, the imitators and backdoor fakers. Out of love with himself, just as his millions of followers were leaping exultantly through the doors he'd unlocked.

By the time The Doors arrived in New York six months later, Jim Morrison's new leather pants and shirt open to the navel were an established part of his act – and an immediate hit with all the women at Doors shows, who were now starting to outnumber the men. On their first night in New York, Jim had taken the beautiful black groupie Devon Wilson – a future lover of Hendrix, who would write 'Dolly Dagger' for her – back to the band's hotel. Word was already out on The Doors though, with Elektra – the hot and happening label that had already brought us the Butterfield Blues Band and Love that year – pushing The Doors as 'the American Rolling Stones'. This was a masterly piece of PR equating the recent hit Stones album, *Aftermath* – a glowering, almost gothic work that had been a turning point for the Stones: their first to feature only original material; their first recorded entirely in America; their first to make a clear distinction between singles and albums – with the crazy, head-spinning trip The Doors were about to take you on.

Ray Manzarek: 'As Jim once said, "We perform a musical séance. Not to *raise* the dead, but to palliate the dead, to ease the pain and the suffering of the dead and the living." And, in doing that, we dove into areas that were deeply, deeply Freudian, and psychologically deeply Jungian at the same time. So we were a merging of both Freud and Jung, which might seem impossible but it happened onstage, and really upset the establishment. There was just something about the power in the music, and that insane sexuality of Jim Morrison, that drove the establishment right over the edge.'

One convert, though she would never have described herself as being in any way part of the establishment, was a 39-year-old former model, Gloria Stavers. Then editor of *16* magazine, at the time the biggest-circulation teen music magazine in America, Stavers had once been Lenny Bruce's girlfriend, had had a well-publicised affair with the baseball legend Mickey Mantle, and was said to have helped, through her patronage, turn Herman's Hermits into bigger stars in America than both The Beatles and the Stones. Gloria liked to photograph the bands herself, inviting them over to her New York loft apartment, where if all went well the session would conclude in her bedroom. When the freelance writer turned ad hoc Elektra publicist Danny Fields arranged for Jim and The Doors to spend an afternoon being shot at Gloria's apartment, the band was quickly dismissed while Gloria got down to her real work, photographing – then seducing – Jim.

Fields was one of the new hip young gunslingers that helped define the mid-Sixties New York spirit. One week he was a pop writer for *Datebook*, asking singers what their favourite colour was, the next he was sitting at the feet of The Beatles' publicist, Derek Taylor, learning everything there was to know about how to hype a rock'n'roll band. The week after that he'd be hanging out with 'the early Warhol scene, which was a mixture of people from Harvard and others I knew in New York'. In the autumn of 1966 he found himself doing PR for an all-girl group called The UFOs. 'They got a booking at the Whisky in L.A. I rang [Ronnie Haran], who did the club's publicity, and told her they were going out and asked if she could look after them, get them press and so on. And I asked if there was anything I could do in return and she said, "Yes, as a matter of fact I have a group coming to New York . . .'"

The group was The Doors. Picking them up from the airport, Danny took one look at Jim Morrison and knew exactly what he should do. Call Gloria. According to Fields, speaking from his home in New York, Gloria Stavers was 'one of the most brilliant people who ever lived, invented *16* magazine singlehandedly. I mean, there was the publisher and the paper and the ink but she invented it. She used to boast of her blowjobs. That she could give the best blowjobs in town. And she was giving [Jim] a blowjob – and she loved her skill and was proud of it – and she swears he vanished; he dematerialised and was sitting on the other side of the room. Now I attribute this to feminine folly, or the girl got carried away. But she was no girl! Hello, she'd been around the block big time, like with important people. You know, quite an arsenal there. Okay, so then he came back on the other side of the room and there he was, sort of smirking. Okay. Yes, Gloria, I'm sure that was wonderful!' He laughs. 'She says it straight-faced, you know, you didn't go into it. She was a very spiritual person.' However implausible Jim's dematerialisation mid-blowjob may be, the fact is when *The Doors* was released in January 1967, it would be Jim's image on the cover of *16* that month, under the heading: *Morrison is Magic!*

Andy Warhol, meanwhile, who became as love-struck at the 22-year-old Morrison visage as Nico (who also showed up at Ondine's to begin their fiery liaison again), plotting to get Jim to star in his next movie project, simply called *Fuck*, begged Jim to let him film him having sex with Nico. When Jim laughed in his face and told him to fuck off, Andy wheedled: would he at least allow him to film Nico giving Jim a blowjob? 'Fuck off, Andy,' Jim smiled. 'No.' Jim, though, was not above considering the outer reaches of his star potential, certainly in Warhol terms if nothing else, and now seriously considered changing his name to James Phoenix, going so far as to request that Elektra alter his credits on the forthcoming Doors album sleeve. The rest of the band assumed he wanted to sound more like a Warholian rock star, but secretly Jim was more concerned that his growing reputation for debauchery might eventually impinge on his estranged father's career in the US military. When the others talked him out of it – 'It just sounded dumb, even for a warrior poet,' explained Ray disingenuously – he settled instead for merely being an orphan.

Back in L.A. for Christmas, when Elektra requested biographical information from the four band members so that they could assemble a press package in readiness for the album's release in January, Jim claimed his whole family was dead. He went along with the rest, fairly standard stuff for 1966, like: who are your favourite singers? 'Frank Sinatra and Elvis Presley.' He added that his favourite colour was 'turquoise' and his favourite food 'meat'.

When asked for his personal philosophy, however, Jim couldn't help himself and gave it both barrels: 'You could say it's an accident that I was ideally suited for the work I am doing,' he began earnestly. 'It's the feeling of a bowstring being pulled back for 22 years and suddenly being let go. I am primarily an American; second a Californian; third, a Los Angeles resident. I've always been attracted to ideas that were about revolt against authority. I like ideas about the breaking away or overthrowing of established order. I am interested in anything about revolt, disorder, chaos – especially activity that seems to have no meaning.'

Elektra, though, had its own ideas about the 'meaning' some people might take from Doors songs, and to the band's dismay decided unilaterally to edit the first single from the album, 'Break On Through (to the Other Side)', so that the line, '*She gets high*', which Jim sings four times, on the single version scanned as, '*She gets . . . she gets . . . she gets . . . she gets . . .*' This became the version they were forced to mime to in their first ever television appearance, on *Shebang*, on 1 January 1967. You can see the frustration in Jim's wincingly subdued performance, barely bothering to move his lips, eyes wide shut, as he stands there, all gussied up for the cameras in fawn-coloured trousers tapered at the ankles, black shirt and dark hunting jacket, but with an attitude as sullen as a teenage punk-girl forced to wear a pretty dress for the prom. A performance that stands in marked contrast to the film clip which Jac Holzman commissioned Mark Abramson to shoot: a suitably noir-ish colour clip defined by its stark black tones, no one but a snarling Jim seen for the first minute, and then only the heavily silhouetted form of Ray Manzarek stooped over his keyboards, the priest at his lectern, Robby not getting a look in until the song is almost over. Yet it was this dark, somnambulant quality – the antithesis of the bright Californian mien of The Byrds and the Beach Boys – that helped define The Doors as different. Special. So that when the clip aired on the L.A. Channel Nine show *Boss City*, it resulted in the band's first serious plays on local radio.

None of this, though, gave the single the impetus it needed to 'go national', as the saying went; that is, give The Doors their first recognisable countrywide hit. Jac Holzman, though, insists that was not his plan anyway. 'I was not a person who made singles. I felt that singles should be calling cards for albums, because that was a greater impact of the artist. A hit single tells you a lot about the song and nothing about the artist, or not much about the artist. I've always felt that way.' Nevertheless, if Elektra was going to get involved in the singles market, which Jac knew it had to if it wished to promote The Doors to the potential audience that awaited them, he insisted that at the very least the 'calling card' should be of a standard that said more than I-love-you. The result, he says, was that while 'Break On Through' was not a hit, it demonstrated 'a level of intellect not usually heard in rock bands'.

The Doors, though, would never be seen as a singles-reliant act. Unlike The Beatles and the Stones, who'd begun that way, then evolved into album-oriented groups, The Doors would always be about the albums, recording epic rock suites double-digit minutes long before Led Zeppelin or Pink Floyd or even Jimi Hendrix had considered it viable. The Doors may or may not have been the beginning of rock as art, but they were about to become the most authentic, most successful end product of that idea.

Holzman claims it was for this reason that he deliberately avoided releasing an edited version of 'Light My Fire' as the first single from the album. 'I didn't want to go with "Light My Fire" and not have it happen and I didn't think we knew enough about how to promote singles [yet]. We learned a lot on "Break On Through". The other thing I was counting on was the crush of interest from FM radio forcing AM radio [to play it], and that takes a little time. So I bought two to three months, meanwhile, the album is selling 10,000 copies a month in Southern California, which was a lot of records back then. Then we grafted it onto the state and the album began selling across the country because of FM play. So I had all of that stuff going for us', long before 'Light My Fire' was eventually released. 'Because [of] the impulse hearing on FM where the stuff sounded good and you could hear it in stereo, which you couldn't do on AM radio, made a difference. That was the avant-garde. Once you get the avant-garde [the rest of] that stuff flows down.'

The Doors hadn't made any money yet, the living wage their $5,000 advance from Elektra had helped provide them with barely augmented by the low-tide fees they were picking up for live performances. But Jim had promised Pamela Courson that once the money did come in, as they both fervently dreamed it would, they would live together in their own little place in Laurel Canyon, every hippy couple's desire in those dreamy, incense-lit days. By the mid-Sixties what had been a rundown, overgrown semi-wilderness had been transformed by musicians looking for cheap places to hang out and get high; to play their music beneath the bird of paradise plants, thickets of pepper trees and pines, and reinvent themselves as the love generation. The place where the Elektra Records exec, Barry Friedman, would famously phone all his neighbours and get them to drop the needle on the new Stones album, all at the same time, until the Canyon rang out with their groovacious sounds.

It was here, in a green, one-bedroom, wooden shack, that

The Morrison family, circa 1950. L-R: Anne Morrison, George S. Morrison,
Andy Morrison, Clara Morrison, Jim Morrison. (Sipa Press/REX)

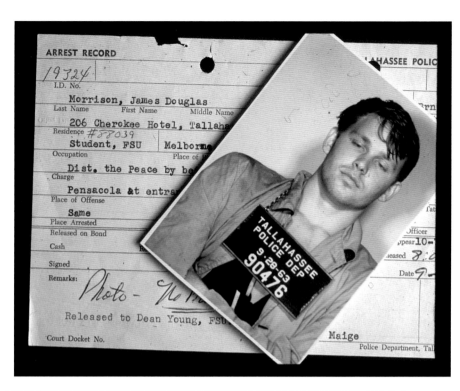

From Tallahassee to Miami, in just seven years. Jim Morrison, outlaw.
(*Top:* Collection of the Museum of Florida History/PA Images; *Below*: Kypros/REX)

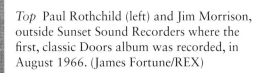

Top Paul Rothchild (left) and Jim Morrison, outside Sunset Sound Recorders where the first, classic Doors album was recorded, in August 1966. (James Fortune/REX)

Middle In the recording studio with Bruce Botnick (right) and Paul Rothchild (middle). (James Fortune/REX)

Below Hanging out backstage, 1968. (Getty Images)

The guru and his disciples, San Francisco, 1968. (Getty Images)

Top right New teen sensations The Doors
light America's fire, 1967. (Getty Images)

Below right An early TV appearance,
circa 1967. (Getty Images)

Above and right Let the ceremony begin . . . Jim and The Doors beckon
you to join them on their dark journey, 1967. (Getty Images)

Above Onstage at Steve Paul's The Scene nightclub, New York, 1967. (Getty Images)

Left Jim, alone, surrounded by people. Recording of Strange Days, Sunset Sound, September 1967. (Globe Photos Inc/REX)

Jim and Pam now set up home – high up in the Canyon, where the rent was cheap, on the street Jim later immortalised in song as 'Love Street'. Jerry Hopkins, who knew them well, recalls now how 'Jim called her his "cosmic mate" and I believe he meant it, although neither of them even came close to exclusivity; they had their secrets and they respected – or ignored – them, just as most "committed" couples do. Why did he stay with her? You're asking me to guess. I suspect it was not because she was some sort of family substitute, but because she was so much like him, a mirror image with tits. I also think she may have reminded him of his mother.' A point the astute Eve Babitz also made when she wrote: 'A friend of mine once said, "You can say anything about a woman a man marries, but I'll tell you one thing – it's always his mother."'

It was Eve's sister, Mirandi, who got a close-up view of the relationship in those early days, when she and her then boyfriend and fellow clothes designer, Clem, stayed with the newly made couple. In Jac Holzman's book, *Follow the Music*, she recalls the endless fights between the two, then the making up, then the fighting again. 'I don't think Jim was ever the greatest guy. I think he was a morose, depressed, moody, violent person.' According to Eve, though, Jim had finally met his match in Pam. 'Whereas all he had previously brought to the moment was morbid romantic excess, he now had someone looking at him and saying, "Well, are you going to drive off this cliff, or what?"' Jac in his book describes them as 'Hurricane Jim and Cyclone Pam', recalling one occasion when 'Pam has thrown all Jim's books out the window. She has shredded his clothes. She has scrawled FAG on the mirror. Jim has put a knife to her throat. The two of them have dropped acid and are playing chicken on the railroad track . . . Again and again.'

On those nights when things got too much, Jim would simply take off, checking in back at The Trop or swinging by to visit one of his growing army of girlfriends. For all her self-knowledge and insight into the increasing malaise surrounding Morrison, Eve Babitz, for one, could never resist his call. 'If the phone rang at night [and] there was a long pause after I said hello, I knew it was Jim. He and I had a lot of ESP in some kind of laser-twisted, wish fulfilment kind of way. I always wished he were there, and every so often he zoomed in.'

Another California-beautiful, Hollyweird-crazy chick Jim now zoomed in on was also named Pam – Pamela Ann Miller, aka Miss Pamela, aka Pamela Des Barres (as she became better-known in the mid-Seventies after marrying the rock singer Michael Des Barres). Miss P, as she would also soon become known, sometimes babysat for Frank and Gail Zappa, who also had a house in the Canyon. By the end of the Sixties, she would be widely recognised as one of the upper-echelon groupies on the L.A. scene – at a time when the term 'groupie' had yet to acquire the stigma there is about it now. Groupies then were, as Elton John sang in 'Tiny Dancer', the song he and the lyricist Bernie Taupin wrote specifically about Pamela, the *'Blue jean baby / L.A. lady / Seamstress for the band'* – the beautiful angel with a broken wing every music man dreamed of and wrote songs about, before the tide of cynicism that arrived with bones-into-dust Seventies bands like Led Zeppelin killed such faraway notions at birth.

Just as Elton's song suggests, Pamela Miller would make

handmade shirts for her boyfriends, and 'was too romantic for one-night stands'. If she was with you, it was 'for the
whole tour – at least, locally!' Remembered now by Alice
Cooper as 'a smiling open-faced girl who looked like Ginger
Rogers' with her strawberry blonde hair, freckles and goofy,
flower-child smile, Pamela was the epitome of the California
Girl the Beach Boys had earlier eulogised. Although she was
still only 18 when she met Jim Morrison, her conquests would
later include Iron Butterfly's singer, Darryl De Loach, Noel
Redding of the Jimi Hendrix Experience, Chris Hillman of
The Byrds and the actor turned country rock singer Brandon
de Wilde. She would also meet and spend time with the Rod
Stewart-incarnation Jeff Beck Group. To name a few.

As a first-hand witness to the L.A. scene of the time, they
don't come any more insightful than Miss Pamela. Speaking
now from her little casita near the Boardwalk in Venice, dec-
orated with paintings of Elvis and James Dean and a huge
photographic portrait of Walt Whitman, just a bike ride
away from the apartment building where Jim used to sleep
on the roof, she laments how 'mythologised' that world has
now become to those who weren't there, 'to a degree where
[it's] almost become unreal. Like, people imagine Jim as that
picture of him with the beads – that famous image from
16 magazine – and also the various images of him onstage,
clutching the microphone when he was young and beautiful –
as opposed to how he later became.'

Pamela first saw The Doors play Bido Lido's, another tiny
club on the Strip, in September 1966. 'It was a new band that
I hadn't heard of and I always wanted to see any new band
that was in town. At that time I was indulging in this strange

drug that was short-lived called Trimar that I got from [some-one who used to work in the] hospital during the day and he must have gotten a sniff of it somehow and he started smug-gling it out of the hospital and selling it on the street for ten dollars a vial. But I was very close with him, so he just gave me quart jars of it. I later found out that it was liquid PCP. It was terrible stuff. At the time, I wasn't even smoking pot yet. What it did to you was that everything got huge and glorified and shimmering and throbbing, so the Doors stood out even more that evening,' she laughs.

She would go and see The Doors several more times over the following months. Her main impression was that they were 'very edgy because of Jim; he was doing things that white boys weren't doing in California. He was literally almost having sex with the mike stand, rolling around . . . Mick Jagger was doing some of those things, but L.A. boys were not. It was a much more laid-back, almost countrified scene at that point, musically, and Jim was just pulling all the stops out and cutting loose and letting go. He sort of became the music, and let it just go through him from head to toe and whatever happened inside him, he just let it come out. I don't think he knew what he was doing, part of the time. I just loved them. Jim was someone you wanted to touch. He would lay down on the floor and you could just go right up to the stage and caress him, touch his hair. He didn't notice. He was in thrall. He was wrapped up in his music . . . his muse, his words . . . he didn't notice. He was just out there. He was a poet. To him, the music part of it was a side note.'

It was a few months after the Bido Lido's gig that Pamela met Jim for the first time. 'I was staying with a friend of mine in Laurel Canyon; I spent a lot of time up there. It's the house behind the Canyon store with the big picture window. All kinds of stuff went on in there, but I was visiting there one afternoon – I was waking up, I'd spent the night – and I heard the Doors record being played, and it hadn't been released yet. I'd seen them play many times already, and I wondered who had it, and I was high enough to just go in and see who it was. I went down these rock stairs, a long bunch of steps, and I peeked in through these Dutch doors – the top was open – and it was Jim. He was playing his own record and he was digging through the refrigerator, singing along with "The End". I just went, "Ooh, my God!"'

She was so surprised she ran back upstairs, told her friend what – who – she had just seen downstairs. 'She said, "Are you kidding? Go be a neighbour! Go say hello." I wasn't high enough, so I sniffed some more of this crazy Trimar stuff, and I went back down there and he kicked the door open for me. He used to always growl this, "Get it on . . ."' She does an impression of his a low, raspy voice. 'He always used to say that, that was one of his phrases that he used a lot. So I went in there and got it on. I had just learned how to do a back bend, so I proceeded to go into a back bend for Jim. I was so high . . .' As she was mid-bend, she saw another pretty red-haired girl named Pam coming in. Uh oh. 'She looked down at me and said, "Get the fuck out of my house!" He was just in the corner, going, "Get it on! Suck my mama!" He said that a lot, too. "Suck my mama!"'

That infectious happy-go-lucky laugh again. 'I scrambled up and said, "Oh, sorry!" and I offered her some Trimar. She said, "No", and I went running back up to where I was.

A few minutes later I heard a big commotion down there and she was yelling and screaming and there were these crashes and these crazy noises and pretty soon he knocked on the door. He wanted to know what I was sniffing. He was interested. I invited him in and he spent a bunch of time with us girls. There was my friend staying there and we just snorted this stuff and rolled around and laughed and made out and all this. He invited me to see him play the next day at the Hullabaloo Club.' She adds how later when she went back downstairs, she saw what Pamela had been throwing at Jim. 'It was these Doors demos that were all over the steps. She was throwing them at his head when he was coming up. She was going, "Don't you dare go up there!" She was intense.'

Over the next few years, though they could never be friends, Pamela Miller formed a strong, more favourable impression of Pamela Courson. 'She was a fiery, wild-spirited, free-spirited, intense girl, who never gets enough credit for being his equal. She was his equal.' She pauses, then adds: 'It was a tempestuous relationship, but he never left her. It was a karmic link that was not going to be severed, except by death. That's how I saw it.'

But not before Miss P had her own little tryst with Jim. Accepting his invitation to join him at the Hullabaloo club, she recalls how he had led her up 'this rickety ladder, up to this place where there was this old equipment in there and we laid down on my muskrat jacket and we just started making out. Now God knows how long we made out for. In those days, we didn't have full sex or anything. I was a virgin at the time. So we were just making out and making out, and we heard "Light My Fire" starting to play. That's how The Doors already were starting to get him onstage. They didn't know where he was half the time, so they would start playing the song and he would just show up from wherever he was. He went, "Whoa . . .""

Pam had brought her quart jar of Trimar along and 'we were so high on this stuff', Jim was disoriented, nearly fell down the ladder. 'It's short-lived, though; it only lasts a few minutes unless you keep inhaling it. So he clambered down the ladder and went on stage, and I was so high, I just followed him, and I was onstage with them, just right at the edge of the stage where he was. He was already clutching the microphone and I was going, "Whoa . . ." Then a roadie came and gently took me off. We met afterwards and that's when he drove my car all over Hollywood and threw away the Trimar.'

Though they never did become lovers, they did become friends for a while. 'He was easy to talk with. He was a very sweet guy in those days. He did change, but in the very early days, he read me poems out of his poetry book and was very caring and he didn't want me to get all fucked up on this weird drug.' Mainly, she recalls, 'the conversations I had with him were about his poetry and how he believed that the musical thing – the rock thing – was a very temporary thing for him. He basically said that it was a lark. He was almost, in a way, putting it over on people because he was going through the motions. But believe me, it didn't look like it.

'I think he got caught up in it. But I think it had a lot to do with the words he was saying and the feeling those evoked in him, because he did say that this was temporary. He always carried his poetry book with him, he was always writing and he said that [The Doors] was really a short term thing because he was really a poet and everyone would know it someday and this was really just a side thing.'

Or so he hoped.

TEN

Young Lions

Danny Fields claims it was he that first brought the commercial potential of 'Light My Fire' to the attention of Jac Holzman. 'I was the first person outside the company that thought 'Light My Fire' should be a single,' he told the writer Giovanni Dadomo in 1977. 'They'd already released another one but it was 'Light My Fire' that made all the difference, that made the company from a small, classy company into a force in the marketplace.'

Speaking now, Holzman insists 'Light My Fire' had always been in his thoughts, pointing out that the full seven-minute version from the album was already being played on the new, longer-format stereo FM stations. 'It was already a hit on FM. That's what I was counting on. I was counting on FM radio to force AM radio to play it.' The problem was AM had strict rules about 'needle-time' – the duration they would allow a record to run between commercials: no shorter than 2 minutes 45 seconds, no longer than 3 minutes. So Jac asked Paul to go back into the studio and cut an edited version that would fit. Paul was sceptical. Jac told him to get on with it.

He did what was required and cut nearly five minutes' worth of the lengthy solos Ray and Robby had spent so long perfecting. The result was the defining hit song of the summer of love. And nobody, not even Jac Holzman, could have predicted that.

One thing that most definitely was not Holzman's idea was the acquisition by The Doors of their first managers: Salvatore Bonafede, an old school Italian-American East Coast mover-and-shaker who had previously managed Dion and the Belmonts, and his partner, Asher Dann, a Beverly Hills real estate broker and regular patron of the Whisky, looking to get in on the crazy, go-go scene then enveloping L.A.– Sal and Ash to their friends, among whom The Doors would never quite be counted.

'Let's just talk about these guys,' says Holzman, still smarting all these years later. 'These were managers not experienced in music and without the connections in music. And I personally thought they were a little on the crude side.' What really hurt, though, he admits, was 'the boys had gone on ahead and done it without talking to me. And that really hurt. I knew what that was about. They got talked into something. They knew that they had to have a manager of some kind to keep things going. They signed up with these guys and then they found out what I suspected all along. That these were not people that a band of that quality should be associated with. That's a personal opinion, it's not a legal opinion.'

In fact, the band had not needed much persuading at all. Max Fink had put the deal together, seeing in Bonafede a hardnosed music biz pro that would get the band working and cut the best deals for them, while Dann was the typical Hollywood schmoozer seen as the perfect foil to keep Crazy Jimmy in check. To add insult to injury, as far as Holzman was concerned, no sooner had the band signed with them than Sal and Asher did everything in their power to try and get The Doors out of their Elektra deal – and back with Columbia.

Says Jac: 'The way actually Bonafede and Asher Dann would have come off, is that they could get out of the Elektra contract and move to Columbia and get a giant advance. Because then they would get a piece of that. They had no piece of the [Elektra] recording contract.'

Holzman mentally gave the band six months to right the boat, while at the same time preparing himself for the worst. He knew his contract with the band was cast-iron. He also knew from hard-won experience that a contract in the music business was not worth the paper it was printed on if both sides simply refused to work together. The immediate impact of the new B&D management structure on The Doors, however, was largely positive. Overnight they went from being a ramshackle club act, living haphazardly from one week to the next, to a professional working band with a diary rapidly filling up with work.

The band's only real stipulation, made at Jim's instigation, was that the band be an equal four-part democracy, with all songwriting credits split equally and credited simply to The Doors; and that all decisions pertaining to their music and business had to be unanimous before they could be acted on. It seemed like the perfect all-for-one strategy to bind them against whatever vicissitudes having a major record company and management behind them might bring. If everything else failed, they would have each other. A decision they would all later regret, in one way or another.

Meanwhile, with both 'Break On Through (to the Other Side)' and *The Doors* now on release, and Sal and Asher working their mojo, the start of 1967 found the band appearing in San Francisco for the first of two weekends at Bill Graham's famous Fillmore, opening on bills headlined by The Young Rascals the first weekend, the Grateful Dead the second. Between times they found time to attend – as spectators – the first Great Human Be-In, before 20,000 people at Polo Field, in Golden Gate Park, where they got their first exposure to the very different San Francisco scene: a free-flowing psychedelic festival featuring music from the Dead, the Airplane and the Quicksilver Messenger Service, and spoken-word performances from Allen Ginsberg, Gary Snyder, Timothy Leary, Lawrence Ferlinghetti and Michael McClure. A strange mixture of weed, acid, Zen, poetics and anti-war protests, the whole deal 'policed' by apparently tame Hell's Angels. It was here that Jim coined his memorable phrase about seeing The Doors as 'erotic politicians'. As he explained enigmatically in an interview shortly afterwards, 'The city is looking for a ritual to join its fragments.' The Doors, he whispered, 'are looking for such a ritual too'. What he called 'an electric wedding'.

A week later The Doors were back in New York for their second residency at Ondine's. This time, though, the Lower East Side was ready for them, led once again by the dynamic duo of Danny Fields and Gloria Stavers, who unwittingly pulled off the biggest publicity coup of the year when they arranged for the distinguished New York photographer Joel Brodsky to do a session with the band.

Born and raised in Brooklyn, Brodsky was a 27-year-old Syracuse University graduate who had started off in in a camera shop acquiring the cameras he would take into his budding career as a photographer. After a spell in the army, he'd worked as an assistant to one of New York's top fashion photographers. Then in 1964 he opened his own studio, where his striking photographs of local folk music figures brought him to the attention of Elektra and others. He'd already done one session with The Doors on their previous visit to NY, a shot from which adorned the back cover of *The Doors*, a technically advanced for the time quadruple exposure combining portraits of the individual group members that would later be nominated for a Grammy. Now, though, with Danny and Gloria to guide him, he would take the most iconic shots of his – and The Doors' – career. 'I never actually heard him listen to the music he shot,' said his son-in-law, Sid Holt, a former managing editor of *Rolling Stone*. 'He didn't particularly like the Doors.'

Maybe so but it was Brodsky's shots – an extended series of black-and-white pictures of a shirtless Jim posing with a string of beads around his muscled neck, his hair a halo of waterfall curls, his face expressionless as the moon, arms outstretched in the most striking shots of all, in mock crucifixion pose. Now known as the 'Young Lion' shots, they remain to this day the defining image of Jim Morrison, and therefore The Doors.

Quoted in an article in the *Washington Post* following his death in 2007, Brodsky recalled, 'The Doors were among the

brighter groups I'd shot at that point. They had a visual ori-
entation and seemed to understand the potential of a good
photo session.' Although the rest of the band bridled at again
being asked to leave once the group pictures were done so
that the photographer could concentrate on the real money
shots, of Morrison alone, the rock god at his most exalted yet
intimate, 'The others understood that Jim was the sex symbol
and an important visual focus for the band.' Nerdy, big-bird
Ray, goofy, frizzy-haired Robby and nervous, pinch-faced
John could hardly argue.

As usual, Jim had been drinking throughout the day and
was 'pretty loose' by the time Brodsky began suggesting poses.
The 'American Poet' shot, as Brodsky called it, was one of the
last to be taken. And while the singer's 'equilibrium wasn't
too terrific' he was 'great to photograph because he had a very
interesting look'.

When, a week later, the *Village Voice* ran the iconic
Christ-like shot of Jim, arms stretched in supplication, in the
showpiece article by the staff writer Howard Smith, under the
heading 'New Teen Idol', Brodsky found himself inundated
with 'something like ten thousand requests for the picture'.
'You know, Morrison never really looked that way again,' he
reflected, 'and those pictures have become a big part of The
Doors' legend. I think I got him at his peak.'

He did that. 'Oh, Brodsky was the genius photographer,'
says Danny Fields now. 'Gloria Stavers was just coming off
The Monkees and Paul Revere & The Raiders, you know?
Both of whom I respect and admire tremendously. But she
was always looking for something deep and dark, and she
saw that right away [in Brodsky's new shots of Morrison].

Was it farfetched at all? I mean, it sounds like a *Mad Men* thing but when you have pros executing a marketing idea, it's gonna be covered. And we had that one covered. The basic and the main element of it was not the [piece written by] Howard Smith [in] the *Village Voice*. It was that picture. Gloria Stavers and I just engineered that. Like, this picture will work. It's like Dionysian. Is it a boy, is it a girl, what is it? What kind if beauty is this?'

After New York there were more shows on the West Coast, their fame and with it their sense of entitlement growing with each performance. Jim decides the next time they play in San Francisco, capital of flower power and home to a genuine 'scene' in a way L.A. could never be, he will wear all-black, in defiant contrast to the now obligatory multi-coloured garb of most Bay Area bands. Some look askance at his 'negative' attitude, but the band notice there are more people showing up in imitation black leathers, their hair and stoned faces a soporific celebration of the Jim Morrison look. *The Doors* was now selling upwards of 10,000 copies a week on the West Coast, even if it was still barely registering anywhere else other than New York. The band seemed pleased with the way things were going. But they hid their feelings from Jim, for whom nothing ever happened fast enough. 'Look at The Beatles, whoosh!' he'd say. Ignorant of the fact that it had taken The Beatles years of toil to finally find their overnight success.

Appearing as special guests at Gazzarri's, at the end of February, as part of the celebrations that marked the venue's move further up the Strip to the Whisky, what should have been a triumphant homecoming for The Doors turned into an under-par, acid-flayed night for Jim. Jim affected not to notice this was the same joint where Mary Werbelow had just won go-go dancer of the year, but by the time he staggered onto the stage he was drunk and tripping, slurring his words, lost in everything but music it seemed, standing hunched over with his back to the audience for much of the time, as if amazed to find a band standing alongside him doing their best to raise the energy levels he was singlehandedly draining. Two weeks earlier he'd been arrested for public drunkenness after foolishly sounding off to some cops outside the Whisky.

Pamela Courson, who had lately started wearing a ring on her wedding finger and referring to herself as Mrs Morrison, now came to every show she could, increasingly bedevilled by the knowledge that each gig offered her 'husband' a thousand opportunities to leave the show with someone else. On this occasion she was accompanied by Tom Baker, a stage actor from New York who had recently worked with Norman Mailer on the short-lived Off Broadway production of his novel *The Deer Park*.

Like Jim, Tom was a good-looking, fucked-up boy from a military family whose talent was only matched by his unquenchable thirst for booze, drugs and 'good times'. Recognising a fellow traveller, Morrison would recommend Baker for a part in Warhol's latest 'art' movie, *I, a Man*, (bizarrely co-starring the same Valerie Solanas who a year later would try to shoot Warhol dead), one of the several movies Andy was still trying to wheedle Jim into appearing naked in. Standing with Pam at Gazzarri's, watching Jim do his slo-mo run through a set that had been bringing down the house everywhere else it had played that year but now appeared little more than a feeble sham – at least on this occasion to the singer – Baker later recalled: 'While stumbling through a song he let out a deep-throated roar, a bloodcurdling scream, really, and it startled me, as though someone had snapped a wet towel against my bare skin . . . Pam kept telling me I was seeing him at far from his best. I replied that he was a good guy, but he should keep his day job.' Pam must have agreed. The next time The Doors left town she began a very public affair with Baker, payback, perhaps, for Jim's own barely concealed infidelities. Or just Pam proving anything Jim could do she could do better. As Jerry Hopkins put it, Jim's 'mirror image with tits'.

Fortunately for The Doors, the review that followed in the *L.A. Times* – their first in the paper – was not nearly so finely attuned to them: 'The Doors wield a rock'n'roll beat with continuous jazz improvisation to produce an intense, highly emotional sound,' it began. Though their reviewer, Francine Grace, certainly got it right when she wrote: 'Trying to avoid the "hard straight sound" of many rock groups, The Doors aim for "dramatic impact" in their music.' It's unclear, however, how much this is a testament to her powers of observation, or how much it reflects the fact that the band had grown accomplished at compensating for Jim on those nights when he singularly failed to hold his own.

The following month The Doors were back for their third, and final, residency at Ondine's, three weeks of shows that would see them playing three sets a night, five nights a week. The quality of the shows differed each night, each set, each number sometimes, depending on the condition Jim was in. Livid with rage at Pam's affair with Tom Baker, cut to the quick by what he saw as more than a betrayal but an actual execution, it was the most mixed-up he'd felt about any woman since Mary. And it was this energy that helped fuel some of his most intense performances with The Doors. The band was also reaching a new, dizzying peak, in a hurry to include new works-in-progress into the set like 'People are Strange', a new, more finessed version of 'Moonlight Drive' and, most especially, what looked to be a sequel to 'The End', a whale song of environmental despair called 'When the Music's Over'. Like its witchy precursor, it would stretch and contort some nights to ten, 15 minutes, sometimes even longer as the mood took them, Jim improvising more poetry over the top, adding new lines, new verses, new worlds each time they performed it, the rafters of the tiny club's ceiling seeming to enclose his head in a wooden crown, the band hypnotized over their instruments like medieval monks in rapture at their illuminations.

Bruce Botnick recalls his friend Fred, who later became a major executive at Fox Films, catching the band on a good night at Ondine's. 'He said it was a moment that he'll never forget. Totally changed his life.'

Reviewing the opening night at Ondine's, Richard Goldstein wrote glowingly in the *Village Voice* of the band beginning quietly, Ray lighting a stick of incense on his keyboards, as Jim seemed to glide from the shadows onto the stage. 'Morrison twitched and pouted and a cluster of girls gathered to watch every nuance in his lips,' he wrote avidly. Before concluding: 'Whatever the words, you will discern a deep streak of violent – sometimes Oedipal – sexuality. And since sex is what hard rock is all about, The Doors are a stunning success.' Reviewing the same show, but from its own unique perspective, the trade magazine *Billboard* awarded

The Doors its highest accolade when summing up: 'They are definitely top chart contenders.'

With Elektra getting ready to release the new, AM radio-friendly, edited-down version of 'Light My Fire' as their next single, the band were also expected to make the most of their off-time in New York too: more photo sessions, more interviews than ever before. And of course, for Jim at least, more drink, more drugs and more women. Standing at the bar each night between sets, he'd throw back double shots of vodka and orange while gobbling up every pill, powder and potion the various hangers-on were only too eager to pass his way ('Take this,' says one beautiful Chinese girl, palming him some 'black bombers', high-quality speed, 'I can see you're a stranger in town'). In his black leather suit, his tea-coloured hair falling in angelic ringlets about his, for once, cleanly shaven face, he looked exactly as he did in the recently published Joel Brodsky 'Young Lion' shots, nailed to the cross of his own doomed beauty.

Watching close by most nights was Andy Warhol, still as obsessively in thrall to Morrison as when he first clapped eyes on him six months before. Still desperate for Jim to appear in one of his films, naked and surrounded by Andy's Factory 'girls', some of whom are not girls at all, nor even good facsimiles. One of whom, Nico, is so ball-achingly beautiful Jim will soon resume his affair with her.

Warhol, never normally shy about introducing himself to the rich and famous, the beautiful and the damned, just couldn't bring himself to approach Jim on these late, louche nights at Ondine's, not now the rest of New York had woken up to the narcotic delights of Morrison and The Doors. He was too scared of what might happen if he distracted the rock star from the attentions he was receiving. One night it might be the chick with the singer's cock in her hand while her friend unbuttons her cheesecloth blouse so Jim can drunkenly fondle her breasts. Another night it might be because Jim was too busy allowing himself to be spirited away by the female photographer that had been shooting him all afternoon. The one named Linda who always got her way with the musicians she fancied, and who would later claim the ultimate groupie prize by marrying a Beatle. 'Oh gee,' Andy would sigh, his go-to response to any situation in which he found himself reeling. 'Oh, gee. I guess I'll talk to Jim later . . .'

But later never comes, not on this trip anyway. For despite The Doors' giving some of the most powerful performances of their short career, Jim Morrison's offstage life is already going to hell. He may have still looked like an angel from some decadent rock heaven, but inside he was fighting just to keep his head above the dark waters he now found himself in, caught between his own idealised vision of himself as a hedonistic poet and artist, the latest, maybe greatest, guardian of rock's philosopher's stone, and the more realistic expectations of a record company, Elektra, that is about to enjoy the biggest record-sales success of its existence in 'Light My Fire', which will soon be on its way to becoming the biggest hit of the biggest summer in rock. Ever.

Some nights Jim would be so beyond hope the rest of the band simply left him there, clutching the bar rail at Ondine's, while they hailed cabs and found something better to do, like have a late dinner with their own girlfriends, catch a movie on TV, or simply go back to the hotel and grab some shuteye.

Not Jim. Standing at the bar in Ondine's only partly conscious, as he got his cock squeezed and his ego massaged to orgasm, he knocked back the booze and Quaaludes – downers – which he increasingly seemed to favour over acid and speed, dimly aware that his fast-track ascent towards rock god status had now begun in earnest – and, along with it, his personal descent into the quagmire that accompanies such a journey in the summer of 1967. Torn apart by his pain over the wayward behaviour of Pam, the obvious distaste of his band mates, particularly John, who had stopped looking up to Jim after helping pick him up off the floor one time too many, Jim was running wild in New York. But not free. Not any more. Or not for much longer anyway.

Standing at the bar at Ondine's, with people either too scared to approach him or too hard to keep away, eventually he would black out, at which point he would be carried to a cab and driven back to the apartment on 45th Street where he was temporarily staying, apart from the rest of the band, safe in their hotel. Jim and all his new best friends. Most mornings he awoke to find at least one, sometimes two or three groupies sharing his bed. Chicks whose names he didn't know or would never bother to learn. According to legend, one night at around 4 a.m., while drunk and tripping, he decided, stupidly, to pay a visit to the New York apartment of Jac Holzman, pounding on the door to be let in while Jack and his young family hid inside, fearing for their lives. Speaking now, though, Jac says that's simply not true. The fact that the story, clearly apocryphal, seems so plausible says a great deal about just how out of control Jim then was.

Meanwhile, the rest of The Doors could only look on and

wonder what if. As John Densmore ruefully remarked when we spoke about it in 2012, 'You know, self-destruction and creativity don't *have* to come in the same package. Picasso lived to be 90. But in Jim they came together so I had to accept it. We all had to. That was the card we were dealt as a band.' Or as Robby Krieger put it, 'With Jim, it wasn't always easy. It was worth it because of the stuff that we got. But it would have been a lot easier if he'd been just a *normal* genius. You know?'

But no one else wanted Jim to be a 'normal genius'. They just wanted what they got: Jim Phoenix, ready to go down in flames. Danny Fields laughs as he recalls trying to get Jim to come to the Elektra office for more press interviews the day after he spent the night with Linda Eastman (soon to be Linda McCartney). He and another Elektra executive, Steve Harris, had spotted the couple leaving Ondine's the previous night, 'arm in arm. And we call after him, "Jim, don't forget you have an interview tomorrow at the office at one o'clock."' But Jim did forget and the following afternoon, when Jim didn't show, they finally got him on the phone, to remind him. Jim's response: 'Oh, man, that babe . . . I can't come, man. She exhausted me. She had me. We were like upside down and sideways and climbing over the couch, and then her [four-year-old] daughter walked in the room while we were in like a vertical 69. And [Linda] said, "Ah, Heather, go back to bed, your mommy's busy."'

Even Ray began to get in on the act. So that while John and Robby may have considered Jim 'the card we were dealt', Ray began to polish his spiel, lauding Jim's worst excesses as simply part of the greater journey – the bigger, better trip – the whole band was now embarked on. As he put it to me, some months before he died, his deep baritone booming down the line from his home in the Napa Valley, 'We would make our own rules. Because we have ingested LSD, we have opened the doors of perception. And we have seen that we are the equal, and perhaps better, of any generation that ever existed – that we could do *anything*. And we were so fuelled with life and potential and possibilities that we were bursting at the seams, mentally and certainly semen-wise, we were bursting with life.'

Okay, Ray. If you say so, man.

The rest of April was taken up with more shows back in California. With 'Light My Fire' now being played by AM as well as FM stations, Holzman, still under pressure from B&D to show what they could do, took a leaf out of the majors' book and surreptitiously hired a band of young girls to go to the shows and show as much voluble support as possible, screaming and even throwing underwear on stage, as though they were at a Monkees concert.

'Well, we had a disadvantage,' says Holzman now. Elektra had no experience in trying to market and sell hit singles. 'We were the right label to husband their music toward the world. But we may not have gotten every last sale because we didn't control our own distribution at the time. Columbia did and Columbia's distribution was terrific. Columbia could probably milk more sales out of a record than anybody. We did *really* well – as well as any independent out there. And the only other independents that counted were A&M and Atlantic, ah, Warner Brothers.' But they still felt the need to 'pull ourselves together'.

With 'Light My Fire' starting to gain traction, state by state, by the early summer of 1967 both Elektra and B&D were agreed at least on one thing: this could be The Doors' big break; the kind that comes just once in a band's lifetime. A cash-dash they would be fools not to capitalise on; not least by coming up with a convincing follow-up as soon as possible. To that end, the same month The Doors were being flown back and forth between coasts to perform in a series of one-night stands, back in L.A. the band had been rushed back into Sunset Sound studios, the featureless four-track bunker they'd recorded their first album in, where under pressure they recorded the first two tracks of what would become their next single and B-side: 'People are Strange' and 'Unhappy Girl'. They also attempted an early sketch of 'When the Music's Over', but abandoned it when Jim insisted it could only be captured live, while he was in the zone. Right in it. And he just wasn't. Yet.

With the 'Light My Fire' single now beginning to pick up pace on the national chart, there was no time to lose, though, and the band was sent back out on the road to promote it. Again, how good the shows were all depended on what mood Jim was in. When he was riding high – literally, in some cases, as he began a new stage move that entailed using the lip of the stage as a tightrope, resulting in at least one nasty fall during a show with Jefferson Airplane at Santa Monica Pier, in April, when he crashed eight feet down – he was on top of the world. Recalling his first sight of Morrison in full kinetic swing at the Avalon Ballroom in San Francisco on 12 May, one of their new roadies, a smart young kid named Bill Siddons, describes now how it 'took me to places I never imagined, and I realised,

"Oh my god!", I mean, you know, I'd seen concerts but absolutely *nothing* like this. This was . . . it created movies in my head. You know, it prodded me at the base of my spine and made me wonder what everything meant. You experience it and go, '*Holy shit! Okay!*' I walked out of there going, 'Okay, this is important. Whatever this is, this is important.' I didn't quite understand it but I certainly knew its power.'

Others, who had caught Jim on a bad night or day, privately took the opposite view and were damned if they were gonna help this asshole out. One such was the powerful promoter Bill Graham, who had done so much to help the band out in the early months of 1967, putting them on high-profile bills at the Fillmore and generally spreading the word (to the point of introducing them onstage more than once). When a clearly baked Jim began twirling his microphone cord around the heads of the audience during a Fillmore show in June, Graham made the mistake of trying to take control personally, going out onstage to stop Jim – who then 'accidentally' let go of the mike, which swung and hit Graham straight in the head, nearly knocking him out.

'Are you out of your fucking mind?' Graham exploded in the dressing room afterwards. But Jim just gave him his usual bullshit Cheshire cat smile, insisted it was 'just an accident' and that it wouldn't happen again. The rest of the band, mortified, crept off across the street to the Avalon Ballroom to check out a funky new chick singer named Janis Joplin. Graham, who knew there were 'bucks in those schmucks', continued to work with The Doors, but his personal relationship with Jim was soured. Another father figure Jim had successfully punished for caring too much.

According to the American writer Stephen Davis, in his excellent Morrison biography, *Jim Morrison: Life, Death, Legend*, another early adversary was Lou Adler, the celebrated songwriter-producer who had managed Jan & Dean and produced Sam Cooke, The Mamas & The Papas and several others. According to Davis, Adler 'had a long memory of being dissed by Morrison', after Adler had turned down the original Doors demo, during his time running his own boutique West Coast label, Dunhill, when Adler became one of the principal organisers of what was shaping up to be the first really big open-air rock festival, Monterey Pop. Everybody knew the three-day event, held over the weekend of 16–18 June, at the Country Fairgrounds in Monterey, California, was going to be important. And so it proved, introducing to America's mainstream public such startling new performers as Jimi Hendrix, who was introduced onstage by the Stones' Brian Jones; The Who, who had the misfortune to have to follow him but still came away with their career in America advanced several notches; Janis Joplin and her band, Big Brother and the Holding Company, who Columbia signed on the basis of this performance; and several others already riding the crest of a wave like Jefferson Airplane, Otis Redding and The Mamas & The Papas. Yet despite several high-profile no-shows and last-minute cancellations, including, it is now said, the Beach Boys, The Kinks and Donovan, try as Sal and Asher at B&D and even Jac and Steve at Elektra might, they could not sway the festival committee to letting them have The Doors on too – this despite 'Light My Fire' fast becoming the radio hit of the summer.

Speaking now, Jac Holzman insists he has 'no idea why

they didn't get to Monterey. The only thing I know is I couldn't believe it. But we were at Monterey in the sense that ['Light My Fire'] was a No. 1 on the West Coast at that time. AM radio was driving everybody nuts [playing it]. I mean, someone in another band said, "If I hear that song one more time . . ." But Paul Simon, who was a member of the steering committee, said, "You know, we just missed it. We didn't get it. I apologise." I said, "These things happen."'

Jim would eventually get his revenge, of course – but on all the wrong people.

When The Doors arrived back in New York in June – just days before the Monterey Pop weekend – they came on a down yet somehow managed to get almost as much publicity for not doing Monterey as if they'd been there. Almost. As Robby Krieger would sigh, when I brought it up, nearly half a century later, 'When Monterey Pop was happening we were stuck at the Scene club in New York for three weeks.' But to miss out on Monterey, which took place in their own Californian backyard, and is now regarded as one of the most historic events in rock history, that must have hurt more than a little? 'Oh yeah,' he said, tremulously. 'We were just . . . it was all new to us. If I had realised that fact I probably would have really been mad. But we didn't know Monterey Pop was gonna become a huge, iconic concert. We had no clue.'

As a result, despite their burgeoning success, The Doors had spent the summer of love largely in New York, playing the Village Theater on Second Avenue (very soon to be renamed the Fillmore East when the legendary promoter Bill Graham bought it) and other smaller, nondescript venues. For all that, the media spotlight still somehow found them and, when it did, lingered much longer than it should have.

Life magazine's critic Albert Goldman was so stunned by what he saw when he caught the band's performance in New York that summer, he switched virtually overnight from writing about jazz to covering the emerging rock scene. 'A Doors concert is really a public meeting called by us for a special kind of dramatic discussion and entertainment,' Jim told him straight-faced. The audience 'go home and interact with their reality, then I get it all back by interacting with that reality'. Goldman, who would later become famous for his witheringly salacious biographies of Elvis Presley and John Lennon, wrote it all down and presented it in *Life* as tablets brought down from the rock mountain by the new Moses of music.

Less impressed was Gloria Stavers, whom Jim now treated as he eventually did everyone that went out of their way to help him.

Danny Fields recounts one striking incident: 'Here's a wonderful story. This has never been printed, I think. [Jim and Gloria] had been separated for a few months. She lived on First Avenue and 63rd Street, you know, Upper East . . . Okay. Phone rings. It's him. "Hey." Cos I know that's what he would have said. She'd say, "Where have you been? Where are you?" She gets right down to it. And he'd say, '"At the Chelsea, room blah, blah, blah. Come over." And she would get in a taxi, which is a long ride, to 23rd Street and Eighth Avenue from First Avenue and 63rd Street.

'She went to the room and the door was ajar. Okay?? She knocked, nevertheless. "Jim? Jim?" And it's spooky. Women, no, anyone, do not like to walk into rooms where you go knock-knock and there's no answer, right? So she walked in. "Jim?" Found a light and switched it on and gingerly walked over to the bathroom and looked in. Because don't forget Lenny Bruce had died on the toilet seat and she had bad memories of that. So, okay, totally gritting her teeth and clenching her fist, she walked over to the closet and sort of opened that, and thought the worst that can happen is he can go, "Boo!" Or the best that can happen is that he'll be dead. Or the other way around! [Laughs] I don't know, whatever. But you know, this woman has seen it all. But she's afraid. Like, what? I spoke to him like a half-hour ago. "Um . . . Jim?"

'So she says, "Fuck this!" and she stomped out, got in a cab, went all the way home and don't you know the phone was ringing when she walked in. And he said, "Hi. Heh, heh, heh!" She said, 'Where the fuck were you?' He said, "I was there!" He said, "You were way off." She said, "I was in your room! I looked everywhere!" And he said, "Not under the bed . . ."

'Now . . . what a gentleman! You do this to your lover? To a grown woman, who may make you a star? Who is one of the most respected and brilliant people in the world? "You didn't look, not under the bed, ha, ha!" And that was it. She slammed down the phone and said, "Fuck you!" Never spoke to him again. Like, "What the fuck? You make a fool of me like this? To physically transport me and make me fearful and scared and opening doors in dark rooms", and she's horny, presumably. She's picturing in her mind getting, you know, that thing in her mouth . . .'

Where did Danny think that mean-spiritedness come from, though? He doesn't skip a beat. 'I think it came from being a fat kid. Who was being worshipped.' He also points to Jim's exceptionally high IQ. 'Which is very important about him. He was *extremely* smart. He was one of the smartest people I ever knew. And that's saying . . . I don't go out of my way to know smart people but he was smart. And a step ahead was important to him. To be smart and leading this little whatever it is we're engaged in.'

ELEVEN

Winter of Love

When 'Light My Fire' reached No. 1 nationally on the US chart for the first time on 25 July 1967, it was both the start of something and the end. The same week they made their first appearance on the biggest nationally broadcast TV pop show of the era, Dick Clark's *American Bandstand*. It was a banner moment for The Doors. Not only did they get to mime to their new No. 1 single, but they were also able to preface it with the B-side, and one of the other most evocative tracks from their album, 'The Crystal Ship'. It was America's first opportunity to get a good look at the newborn, home-grown star close up, as the 37-year-old Clark unsuccessfully tried engaging him in conversation between the two songs. Asked why he thinks the San Francisco scene has assumed such importance in recent times, Jim deadpans: 'The west is the best.' Leaving Clark to add the big smile for the cameras. He fares even less well when asking Ray Manzarek how he would 'characterise' The Doors' music, as a possibly stoned Ray goes into a toe-curling spiel about 'being on the inside of the music' and therefore being unable to answer the question as that must come from 'outside'. The real message though was contained in Clark's pay-off line, after 'Light My Fire', before the show goes to a commercial break: 'That has to be the biggest, most fantastically successful group in the coming year – The Doors!'

It was the start of mass acceptance, worldwide fame, big money, all the things Ray and Jim had fantasised about, smoking one work of art joint after another back on Venice Beach two years before. It was also the end of The Doors being safe to be whoever they wanted to be, whatever they thought they might be, safe within the almost claustrophobic L.A. scene. It was also now that Jim Morrison, college crazy, hippy beachcomber maverick, began his transformation into the Lizard King – the alternate, take-no-prisoners, no-one-here-gets-out-alive rock consciousness that would ultimately both build his legend and deprive him of his senses, until all that was left was a bloated body floating in a bathtub, relieved only by the myths that have continued to grow around the dead king ever since.

The success of 'Light My Fire' coincided with the band's new, distinctly edgier image. Just six months before, their promo shots had depicted them as a sort of older-brother version of The Monkees, looking breezy in mod-style suits, their longish hair neatly styled. Now with their first album smoking up the charts, they emerged onto the covers of magazines as the epitome of a darker, more mysterious kind of cool. 'Light My Fire', with Jim's neo-Gothic croon and Ray's ghostly, cathedral-like organ, spoke of murkier climes than those offered by The Beatles' brand of polychromatic pop. If *Sgt. Pepper* was the emblematic symbol of pop's rising from gutter-level singsong to symphonic high art, *The Doors* gave the lie to such positivism, drawing on the growing feeling of us-against-them that pervaded a generation of young Americans then in fear of the draft to Vietnam, or in protest against what it saw as the overarching dead hand of a society where long hair was now a symbol of angry defiance, of deep questioning, of bloody revolution.

On the surface then, The Doors seemed to be on message like no other band of the moment. Yet, as Manzarek would admit to me, looking back all those years later, 'There really were no plans. We were excited that our record was doing so well but that wasn't what was driving us forward. It was the thought of what we might do *next*. Suddenly it felt like we could do *anything* . . .'

Their next album, *Strange Days* would be aptly named. The first track they recorded, a song Jim and Robby had written together called 'People are Strange', had been the result of 'a bad trip' Jim had needed Robby to talk him down from at five one morning, at the tiny hilltop villa in Laurel Canyon where Robby now lived. 'He was talking about killing himself and all this stuff,' Krieger recalled, his voice fragile, almost ghostly as he whispered down the line from a hotel room in Miami, where he was on a promo tour in 2012 for yet another new Doors compilation, 'and so we decided to take a walk up to the top of Laurel Canyon. Like, "Let's go up and watch the sun come up." And when the sun came up he suddenly got this idea about the fact that when *you're* strange then people are strange. The whole idea just popped into his head. "Oh, I got an idea for a song!" You know, and half an hour later we had it.'

Not all such occasions ended so harmoniously though. Jim loved Robby, yet hated him too for having written 'Light My Fire'. Everywhere Jim went that summer people were slapping his back, thanking him for writing a song he'd struggled to learn the lyrics of, to get the metre right when he recorded it, seeing it as almost a throwaway. Not any more, though. And that fucked with his head, along with all the other things that would fuck with his head from here on in. The only way he could deal with it was to let it out, and to hell with the consequences. Janis Joplin certainly got that impression when Jim suddenly forced her face down into his crotch while sitting next to him at a party in L.A. one night during the *Strange Days* sessions. She thought that motherfucker knew exactly what he was doing. When he tried to laugh it off, she broke a bottle of Southern Comfort over his head and called him an asshole. 'I *am* an asshole!' he hollered after her, as she stomped off, giving him the finger.

It was a relief when the sessions were called to a halt while the band returned to the road to promote their huge summer hit. Though being away from his familiar Hollywood haunts could present their own strange-day circumstances for the fast-rising Lizard King. Back in New York for more shows in July, Jim resumed his impossible affair with his psychic and spiritual opposite, Nico, ice queen of New York's most celebrated yet least famous band, the Velvet Underground. According to rock orthodoxy, the Velvet Underground and their followers – in particular, the Velvets' vituperative singer, Lou Reed – despised everything The Doors stood for. When just four years later Reed heard of Morrison's death, he sneered: 'He died in a *bathtub*? How *fabulous* . . .'

Yet Morrison appeared blissfully unaware of either Reed or his still unknown outfit of, as he would have seen it, Broadway dropouts and Bowery freaks. The Doors were now riding high, selling more records per week than the Velvets would manage in their entire career together, and when Jim saw Nico again during the band's week of shows at Steve Paul's Scene club in Manhattan, he simply had to have her. At one of their earlier shows that week, Jim and Asher Dann had got into an onstage brawl when the hapless manager, like Bill Graham before him, freaked out when he saw Jim whipping the mike so close to the audience's faces you could almost feel the air rush by.

Already convinced that Sal Bonafede was a member of the Mafia – 'It was ridiculous but he was convinced that Sal was one of those guys,' recalls their tour manager, Vince Treanor, now – Jim freaked out, convinced that when Asher told Sal what had happened there would be a price to pay. Then he saw Nico again. Nico would make it better. For Jim, it was yin meets yang; sun fucks moon. A coming together as significant to the rock universe, as chaotically elemental, as the first time Adam spied Eve standing naked beneath the apple tree.

They had met before, made love before, Jim before he was famous, just another Hollywood honey for Nico, reclining on her ice throne, to toy with. But not heavy like this. Pamela may have been Jim's 'equal', his 'cosmic mate', but Nico offered something else. She had her own solo album, *Chelsea Girl*, coming out that autumn, full of songs by former lovers like Jackson Browne, Tim Hardin and Bob Dylan. Now she was trying to write songs of her own but she was struggling. But English was not Nico's first language. Neither was American.

185

She could communicate with Jim just fine though. Jim loved her straight-to-the-waist platinum blonde hair and her thick Berlin accent; loved that she was part of Warhol's coterie, that she had spent time in Europe with Fellini, that she was older than him and in control. Something no other girlfriend, including and especially Pamela, had ever been when Jim was around.

Nico, so cold and aloof, usually, even began to tell friends she was in love with Jim. Of course, they didn't believe her. Why would they? Nico was always in love. Nico never loved anybody. She came and went as she pleased. Men were just there always, scurrying around her like mice. Yet Nico really did love Jim, in her own peculiar way. Because of her crystal beauty, her metallic accent, others made fun, said she didn't have a heart like other women. But Nico now gave her heart and soul to Jim. She loved him so much she told friends it terrified her. Jim could do whatever he wanted with Nico, she said, and then shuddered. Two inches taller than Jim, broader shoulders, bigger legs and hips, she was also the first woman he'd ever been with that had borne a child. Jim, who was into mother love, who had that whole Oedipus thing going on in his songs, had never experienced it for real like this before.

When Nico sat on Jim's face, which is what she liked doing best, he almost suffocated in her livery sweet labia and blonde pubic fur. That's what he told friends. When Jim fucked Nico in the arse, which is what he liked to do the best, and then whipped her with his new conch belt, she looked at him pityingly. As if to say, 'Is that it?'

Nico would become Jim's blood sister. She could relate to his Oedipal fantasies. Although she never knew her own father, a Nazi soldier in the war, shot in the head by a French sniper, she described her own parents as being in 'a father–daughter relationship' because of their age difference. At Monterey, where Nico taunted Brian Jones for his relentless obsession with the right clothes, she later said she thought what he really needed was a good mother. It was the same for Jim, she later decided.

Nico was strong, physically and mentally. Jim was used to crazy women, groupies, hangers-on. Even Pamela was crazy, with her flaming red hair and her refusal to play by Jim's rules. Nico was more than that though. She knew the movies, could talk about art, she understood poetry and music. She knew how to sit on a man's face and fuck his brains right out of his head. Nico, Jim declared, was simply the cleverest, most interesting, sophisticated woman he had ever known. While for Nico, Jim was the happiest, least complicated young stag she had ever lain with. When Nico turned up for one of their early trysts still bearing a black eye given to her by Brian Jones, instead of being repelled or outraged, Jim begged her to tell him everything the doomed Stone had ever done to her, said to her, taking it all in, revelling in the detail like a dreamy, masochistic fan.

When Jim returned to Los Angeles to resume recording on *Strange Days*, Nico followed him. He knew he couldn't simply hide her at the Tropicana, knew he couldn't simply install her in her own wooden shack in the Canyon – the very idea of Nico assuming the earth mother role up there in the purple brush was so absurd it made him shake with laughter and dread. So instead they returned to John Philip Law's magic 'Castle' in Los Feliz.

Jim offered to help Nico write some songs, she fell to her knees and buried her face in his crotch. For inspiration he took her out in his car, the radio blasting 'Light My Fire' and – Jim's current favourite – Aretha's 'Respect', as they drove for miles out to the Indian canyons of Palm Springs, then the next day to the strangely shaped shrub and burnt bush of Joshua Tree National Monument, right on through the following night to Death Valley, where they dropped some especially strong acid Jim had been given by another of his acolytes and lay back in their seats, tracing all the incoming UFOs in the sky.

There was nothing they could not share, it seemed. Jim even told Nico about all his other girlfriends, including Pam, even about his thing for red hair. The very next day, Nico dyed her own hair a pale strawberry red. 'He had this fetish for shanties with red hair,' Nico would shrug. 'Shanties' being Nico's broken English for chicks. 'You know – Irish shanties,' she explained. 'I was so in love with Jim that I made my own hair red. I wanted to please his taste . . . like a teenager or something.'

When Jim saw what Nico had done to her beautiful silver-blonde hair he burst into tears. But when Nico asked Jim to propose marriage to her he laughed so hard he fell off the bed. Furious, humiliated, she drew back her fist and hit him square in the face. Jim, still laughing, got off the floor and hit her back. Hard. After that, Jim and Nico began to fight a lot, mostly when they were drunk and high. But often when they were simply having sex. Not like Nico used to fight with Brian Jones, though. Jim would never beat Nico up. They were 'punch buddies', he said. They simply 'enjoyed the sensation,' Nico said. 'But we make love in the gentle way, you know?' Yes. Her sitting on his face. Him fucking her in the arse.

One night, tired of fucking and fighting, tired of being drunk, of being tripped out but in that snug way lovers get when they are re-entering the Earth's atmosphere, Jim and Nico lay there on the bed watching the TV news together. In Oakland, more than 5,000 Black Panthers were parading in public. The newsman said they had served more than 200,000 free breakfasts to poor black children. But the Panthers also had guns and rifles, he added. The police had been called and fighting had broken out. Twenty-eight Panthers would be killed by the cops, another 65 badly wounded. Then the TV news moved on to the war in Vietnam. The body count of American soldiers, mostly poor white trash and uneducated blacks, was now escalating out of control. 'We are living in hell,' Jim told Nico. She simply nodded. Then asked when he would write some of those songs he'd promised for her.

Jim, who never did learn to play an instrument, could at least offer Nico some of the words scratched down in the endless notebooks and journals he still liked to carry round with him, the eternal student of life on some arts-funded American vacation. Nico, who could not really play either, just learned how to get some ghoulish wheezing out of an old harmonium the Velvet Underground's John Cale – another former lover – had bought her, swore that nothing Jim wrote for her ever ended up on any of her solo albums. Yet one only has to listen to tracks from what was to be her next solo album, *The Marble Index*, recorded the following year, to detect an undeniable Morrison flavour of languid, trance-like tracks like 'Lawn of Dawns' and 'Evening of Light'. There is no credit for

Morrison among any of the liner notes though, despite Nico's later confession that Jim had become her 'soul brother', who had given her 'permission to become a writer. Jim believed I could do it. I had his authority.' The album, ironically, would also be released on Elektra. According to Jac in his book, the first time Nico arrived at his office, she casually announced, 'I like to sleep with dead men . . .'

Jim and Nico, hanging out at the 'Castle', making love on the parapet above the pool in full view of other guests like Dennis Hopper and Peter Fonda, snorting hilltops of dentist-quality coke with the writer Terry Southern, as they worked on the script for what would become *Easy Rider*. These post-Beats, Fifties scene-makers, all of whom regarded Jim as a punk, with his big hit song and his leather trousers, his cherubic baby-doll looks and corkscrew hair, could not figure out how someone like him could be fucking that lubricious German cunt Nico, when none of them had the moxy to do so, had the nerve to even go up and say hi.

The only one of that crowd to make any connection at all with Jim and Nico was the writer Michael McClure – and then only with Jim, who had really dug McClure's new play, *The Beard*. Jim told Michael how he too was really a poet, not just a rock star. Nico would sit there impatiently smoking, deeply unimpressed with the so-called poet, living at the Castle while he worked on his novel, he told them, about a cocaine dealer. Nico bored, far away, waiting for him to stop talking and leave. Jim lapped it up, though, this literary, salon talk. Jim saw McClure as the person he wanted to be: a 'real' poet, someone worth getting to know. Jim even told him he should come down to the studio the next time The Doors were in the studio at Sunset Sound working on their new album. McClure promised he would.

The only other visitor to Jim and Nico's unfeathered nest at the 'Castle' had been Danny Fields, also in town. A visit he remembers now as 'The day I kidnapped him.' Jim, drunk beyond belief, stoned on whatever cocktail of drugs he had to hand that day, had kept talking of going for a drive. Panicked at the prospect of Jim driving – 'I was afraid he would drive off a cliff into the canyon or something. Then I'd be fired for having him drive off a cliff in my presence!' – Danny 'took the keys out of the ignition [so] he couldn't get anywhere'. The trouble was, 'We were in the middle of nowhere' and Jim threw a fit. 'It wasn't malicious,' protests Danny. 'He was so stoned – and I was working for the company.'

For Jim, who was already beginning to resent the 'Young Lion' portraits that had become so ubiquitous in the American teen press, detesting the idea that they should portray him as anything other then the streetwise poet and acid visionary he saw himself as, this was the last straw in his relationship with Danny. 'Can you imagine him being at the end of the strings of a puppeteer, which is really what I had done to him? And this is him. This is *him*. He didn't need any other reason to hate me for ever other than that. And he asked Jac Holzman to fire me right after that.'

Most disturbing for Jim, however, was the little gift the band left for him to find during Danny's stay, after he and Nico had returned from another of their little trips into never-never land, this time with Danny accompanying them. 'Somehow they tracked him,' Danny says. 'And at the house we were staying at, we came back one afternoon and all the chairs in this baronial dining room had been put on the table. Neatly, in a row. Just to say someone [had been] here. And on the table was a still [of Nico] from the *Chelsea Girls* [movie] and [written on it] it said: "Jim, get back here or your ass is grass." Signed Ray, Robby and then the name of one of his managers. And that was left. I used to have it. What an artefact but I can never find it now. They were there looking for him. This must have been an amazing charabanc. What a day! We've found out where he is . . .'

Jim read the runes but said nothing. For the next few days, after Danny eventually left, he and Nico were left alone to their thing. Night and day, fucking and fighting; screaming and laughing; Jim crying sometimes; Nico coughing so hard he thought she might be fitting. Jim and Nico going at it so hard the neighbours began to get antsy, avoiding them whenever they were outside together, asking to move rooms so they could get away from the endless nameless noise, pestering John Philip Law to know for how much longer the charming young couple would be staying . . .

Then suddenly it was over. Not when Jim or Nico decided, but when Pam decided. Once Pam had found out where Jim was and who he was with, she began a new affair of her own with 'a real life Count': an 18-year-old French aristocrat named Jean de Breteuil with apparently permanent access to high-quality heroin, which Pam also now began 'experimenting' with. Breteuil was a full-time dilettante, part of the new international jet set whose circle included another occasional lover, Talitha Getty, wife of the oil tycoon John Paul Getty Jnr, whom the 1966 *Guinness Book of Records* had just named the world's richest living citizen, worth an estimated

$1.2 billion. Keith Richards later recalled how John Paul and Talitha always 'had the best and finest opium'. While Marianne Faithfull, then Mick Jagger's girlfriend, would recall how Breteuil used his easy access to money and drugs to reinvent himself 'as dealer to the stars'.

She knew what the Francophile Jim's reaction would be when he found out and began thinking about it, in those frozen hours he was always most terrified of right before dawn, during the coldest, darkest moments of the night-day. To turn the screw, she began telling mutual friends she was also fucking 'Castle'-owner John Philip Law, something the actor, currently enjoying huge success of his own as the co-star with Jane Fonda of *Barbarella*, loudly denied. He had been on a few dates with Pam, he admitted to Jim, but that was all. And, anyway, he'd stopped when he realised it was just Pam's way of getting back at Jim.

Jim pretended not to care. Told Nico it was nothing. Then early one morning, while Nico was still passed out, Jim got in his car and drove back to L.A. and Pamela – as he always did eventually, as he always would. Not even leaving a note behind. When Nico discovered the truth, utterly distraught but not in the least surprised, maintaining the same icy front that had seen her through the end of so many affairs, she flew back to New York, where she dyed her hair an even darker shade of red.

It wasn't until September, just as Jim's affair with Nico was reaching its nadir, that work began again in earnest on the second Doors album, *Strange Days*. By then, with both 'Light My Fire' and *The Doors* having topped the US charts, the pressure was really on for them to come up with another hit. Yet Elektra and Paul Rothchild did their best to shield the band from outside interference. According to John Densmore, speaking to me for *Classic Rock* magazine in 2012, 'despite the pressure, I would say that was our most fun recording. First of all, we had written both albums before we even went in the studio – 30 or 40 songs. But the first album we were a little intimidated by the studio. It wasn't our turf. We had to learn how to make records. I would say by the second album we were more relaxed and we started using the studio as the fifth Door. I think we had an early copy of *Sgt. Pepper* and we were really turned on to experimenting with the studio and doing backward piano tracks and having a lot of fun.'

Some tracks came easier than others. 'My Eyes Have Seen You' dated back to the original demo that had won them their deal with Elektra the year before, but was made more frantic with this telling, sounding more like the Stones, with barrel-house piano and tequila-sunset-drenched guitars. The title track came with a suitably disconnected lead vocal, fear and mystery and the chase to catch the new dawn. 'Moonlight Drive', the very first thing Jim had ever sung for Ray, but never properly captured on tape well enough to make the first album, now came alive in the new, recently refurbished studio at Sunset Sound, helped not a little by the use of the new Moog synthesisers, invented by Robert Moog, that had just arrived on the market – and of course a suitably far-out new solo from Robby, the broken neck of a real Gallo wine bottle snug on his ring finger. 'We were constantly breaking bottles and filing off the end so he could use it for a slide,' Bruce Botnick recalls. Everything was now working better, it seemed, the months on the road having taken the band to another level from the ramshackle college gang he'd encountered in the studio the previous year.

'The second album was very adventurous,' says Bruce. 'When I was recording The Turtles, they gave me a monaural reference acetate of *Sgt. Pepper*. It was a good four months before the album ever came out. I had to give it back to them of course. But I played it for The Doors. I think we must have listened to it six, eight times. And we realised that we were given freedom to experiment. Just by listening to that album. We didn't copy anything on that album. Nothing. Not stylistically or technically, anything. But it just was like – there's another door to walk through, because [The Beatles] had done it and shown us the way. That was a big influence. Otherwise I think that *Strange Days* would have been closer in approach to the first album.'

The other big difference, says Bruce, was that Sunset Sound had recently been upgraded to an eight-track facility. 'Getting four more tracks, made it so that we could really take our time . . . I mean, Paul . . . In those days fuzz-tones were coming into favour and wah-wah pedals, and Paul to his everlasting credit refused to allow Robby to do any of that. He wanted The Doors to be The Doors. He recognized that. That they had something unique and they had a sound and they weren't to be [like] everybody [else].'

A prime example, he says, is 'When the Music's Over', 'when Robby has his big solo and there's two guitars going and they're very fuzzy? Well, it wasn't a fuzz-tone. It was me reacting to the moment and taking the signal out of one fader through a pre-miked amp into another fader.' He would 'turn one up against the other until I got the tubes in the console to glow real bright purple until we got that sound, and we recorded it. That's how that happened. So we were creating everything.

'On "Horse Latitudes", that whole opening was like something from Pierre Boulez's experimental electronic music lab in Paris or from the soundtrack for *Forbidden Planet*. I played the hiss into the echo chamber, recorded it back and manually rolled it through the machine, creating up and down speeds, playing that back into the chamber and recording that onto a track of the eight-track. So I built all this stuff. It was all created on the spot, so we didn't have anything from the outside world.

'They had written this music and [it was] very cinematic in my head . . . recording the album I saw it cinematically. I don't know why. They say, don't think, it's dangerous, and in most creative incidents it really holds true. So I was inspired by what they were doing and I think this all came together without anybody saying, well, let's do this, let's do that. It just came together. And most of the time with them, that's the way it was. It just happened. Everybody being in the room at the same time and somebody hearing this or hearing that and just going there . . .'

One thought that never intruded, Bruce insists, was that they had to come up with a follow-up to their big hit. Nevertheless, even Jim Morrison could not ignore the clamour for more success, from both the record company – and inside his own head. He still did acid whenever the fancy took him, still smoked and toked and did what the hell. But alcohol was now his preferred stress-buster and it was now he first began to hit the bottle in earnest. All the while they continued gigging, too, adding to the pressure, allowing them no rest, fitting in weekend gigs between late-night sessions in the studio.

When Michael McClure took up Jim's offer to visit during these sessions, he was amazed by the newly installed latest eight-track facility at Sunset Sound. By how Paul Rothchild would turn the lights down low, burn incense and light candles, and allow the band to smoke weed and drink freely – anything to capture the right mood for each song. The only thing they actually stopped short of doing was dropping acid while they worked.

'No, no, no, no, no!' gasped Manzarek, aghast at the very idea, when I suggested it. 'LSD was a sacred sacrament that was to be taken on the beach at Venice, under the warmth of the sun, with our father the sun and our mother the ocean close by, and you realised how divine you were. It wasn't a drug for entertainment. You could smoke a joint and play your music, as most musicians did at the time. But as far as taking LSD, that had to be done in a natural setting. It was for opening the doors of perception. Perceiving why we're alive on this planet, where we've come from, where we're going. Answering those basic human questions that all people have asked themselves. Then bringing that information back and getting into your rehearsal studio, getting into the recording studio, creating your music, creating your songs, creating your words. That's where all of that came out. You didn't do it on LSD. LSD was your foundation. Psychedelics were your foundation on which to build.'

Consequently, said Ray, 'Each song [had] its own sound. The first album was The Doors live at the Whisky A Go-Go. That's essentially what it is. The aural spectrum is the same.

But on *Strange Days*, The Doors begin to show their versatility. That's what it's all about. My god, I played an entire song backwards! I wrote out the chord changes for 'Unhappy Girl', then started at the bottom right-hand side of the page and moved to the left and up the page . . . and I'm thinking, oh god, let me be on the beat. [When I'd finished] I went back into the studio to a round of applause. It was a great sound but it was insane. It was *totally* insane! It was youth having no idea of its limitations . . .'

And very little idea of its responsibilities either – certainly as far as Jim was concerned. When it came time to record the album's pivotal track, the ten-minute eco-anthem, 'When the Music's Over', Jim had absolutely insisted the whole track be sung and played live in the studio, rather than broken down into its constituent parts. Live, 'When the Music's Over' now rivalled 'The End' as the band's most climactic moment. First aired publicly during a stint at the Matrix club, in San Francisco, back in March, Jim would break the piece up with two different poems, 'Who Scared You' and 'Everything Will be Reported (At Night Your Dreams Will be Recorded)'. But it all depended on the moment. No matter how great the new eight-track equipment was, Jim wanted this one kept raw and alive.

The band acquiesced then sat there for more than 12 hours waiting for him to show up. He never did. Instead, he phoned the studio at 3 a.m. and spoke to Robby. 'We're in trouble here,' he told him. He and Pam were tripping on strong acid and wanted Robby to drive them to nearby Griffith Park, where they could 'cool out'. John threw down his drumsticks in disgust but Robby wearily agreed. When he dropped them off at Pam's again at daylight he reminded Jim he was due back in the studio at noon. Once again, however, Morrison didn't show up. They sent out people to find him but again no go. The band eventually hung on until nearly three o'clock the following morning, when they decided they could wait no longer. They recorded the music with Ray singing lead.

When Jim finally showed – at noon the following day, 48 wasted hours after he was supposed to, John Densmore had it out with him. Densmore was always the band member most likely to question Morrison's quasi-philosophical standpoint during his lifetime; becoming ever more frustrated at the increasingly overindulgent antics of the only guy in the band who couldn't actually play an instrument. It was never Morrison's art that Densmore wanted to rein in, he says, simply his self-destructive behaviour. 'Musically, I wanted it to go out further on the edge! I was a jazz buff before The Doors. I even was a snob about rock. I mean, I knew about Elvis and Little Richard, loved it. But I came from a sort of improvisational, experimental background, so I loved exploring the edge.' John just didn't want to waste time. 'Jim knew I disapproved of his self-destruction, that's for sure. More than anyone else in the band, he could feel my vibe . . .' Rothchild eventually broke it up by suggesting they simply get to work. Jim began whining about having to overdub a vocal that was always a product of his imagination at any given moment. But the track was recorded and Ray insisted he would simply cue him in. To everyone's astonishment and no little relief, a riled-up yet secretly repentant Morrison nailed what would become the album's finest moment on the second take.

It was Robby's turn to need some extra help, however,

when it came to recording his solo for 'You're Lost, Little Girl', the first song the guitarist ever wrote, back when The Doors were still a bar band. Much as he agonised over it he simply could not get it down. Again, Paul Rothchild provided the remedy when he turned Robby on to some super-strength black hash, imported from London, then threw everybody else out of the studio and recorded Robby playing in the dark. When the producer then suggested getting a hooker in to give Jim a blowjob while he did the vocal, things did not go so well, though. 'We went with a later take,' Densmore concluded diplomatically, when recounting the story for me in a 2012 *Classic Rock* interview. A few nights later Grace Slick, of the Jefferson Airplane, showed up while the band was in the middle of recording 'Horse Latitudes', Morrison's 16-line poem set to Manzarek's *musique concrète*-style musical vortex. Recording yet again in pitch darkness, save for the candles and incense and the glowing ends of several joints, and amid an entourage of whooping and screaming freaks and followers, the Jefferson Airplane singer went back to San Francisco saying The Doors had scared the living daylights out of her.

Finally, with the album still unmixed but at least in the can, the band were sent back out on the road. On 2 September, The Doors played with Jim in full black-leather outfit in Asbury Park, New Jersey, where an 18-year-old Bruce Springsteen was in the audience. When they performed 'When the Music's Over' at the Village Theater in Manhattan the following night, Albert Goldman again wrote of it as 'an incredible moment'. Charged up by their sudden, overweening commercial success, buoyed by the confidence completing their new album had given them, The Doors were on a roll. Jim was already working on new material that would not see the light of day until the following year, raw anti-Vietnam anthems-in-the-making like 'The Unknown Soldier' and 'Five To One', while the band and Elektra did what they could to keep him focused enough to finish the second album first.

By the time The Doors made their fateful appearance performing 'Light My Fire' live on the *Ed Sullivan Show*, on 17 September – complete with Jim's broken promise to Sullivan not to sing the line, '*Girl, we couldn't get much higher*', which Sullivan reacted so angrily to, informing the singer that The Doors would never do the show again, to which Jim sardonically replied, 'Hey, man, we just *did* the Ed Sullivan Show' – advance orders for *Strange Days* were already topping half a million. Elektra rush-released the first single, the delightful 'People are Strange' – and watched as it skimmed the US Top 10 then vanished without trace. 'Light My Fire', meanwhile, was still nailed onto the charts more than six months after its release, even returning to the charts early the following year with the release of the hit José Feliciano cover version.

Determined, however, to ram home the fact that The Doors stood for more than mere pop stardom, at Morrison's insistence the band then put its foot down and vetoed the album cover originally suggested for *Strange Days* – another group shot, similar to the one that adorned *The Doors*. Jim explained to the *L.A. Free Press*: 'I hated the cover of our first album.' For the new album, he'd told Elektra, 'Put a chick on it. Let's have a dandelion . . .'

What he actually told Elektra was that he wanted the band in a room surrounded by a pack of dogs. When their art director, Bill Harvey, asked him why, he shrugged: 'Because dog is god spelled backwards.' With Bill trying to keep a straight face, a compromise was finally reached with the now famous scene of half a dozen carnival freaks, comprising a midget, a juggler, two acrobats, a strongman and a musician, while on the reverse is the extraordinary sight of the 'surreal' fashion icon Zazel Wild, wearing a flowing kaftan, regarding the midget coolly from her doorway at Sniffen Court, off East 38th Street in New York, where the pictures were taken. Elektra thought the shots too weird even for The Doors but Jim loved them. The only sign that this was the new album from The Doors came with the glancing shot of a Doors' poster, placed at a slant on the back of the sleeve, with the strap *Strange Days* slapped across the foot of the poster. Other than that, you either knew what you were looking at or you were from the wrong planet.

When the album was released just weeks later, it was raved over rapturously by a rock media already primed to receive anything their new favourite group did next. The first time *Crawdaddy*'s editor, Paul Williams – then the doyen of serious rock writing – heard the album he told Jac Holzman: 'It just felt like everybody involved would be in jail in six months. It was so revolutionary-sounding.' In just their second issue, newcomers *Rolling Stone* ran a more garbled version of Williams's view, concluding that 'what Morrison is doing is about 3000-years old fashioned and very contemporary in approach'. Yeah, baby.

The Doors' audience, however, made up, as it was now, of furry freaks and pop fans, damaged heads and hot-to-trot hotties, remained unsure, even somewhat baffled. With no comparable anthem to 'Light My Fire' to bring them all together, the album tiptoed rather than raced to the top of the US charts, eventually stopping off at No. 3. In the UK, where the first Doors album had been a minor commercial hit but a major critical success, *Strange Days* came and went in a flash, without getting anywhere even near the charts. For years after, no one could recall anything about *Strange Days* other than its strange cover.

TWELVE
Jimbo Rising

Looking back now, all three of The Doors I later spoke to agreed that *Strange Days* was a watershed moment in the band's story. That it was, arguably, their finest, purest moment. 'Well, I'm surprised that you think that because very few people realise that,' said Robby, when I interviewed him for *Classic Rock* magazine in 2012. 'But I think you're right. I think it is one of our best albums. And we thought so too at the time. We loved it. You know, we took our time making it and really, really liked how it came out. The record company did too. Jack Holzman played it for Paul Simon. And Paul Simon, after listening to the record, said, "The Doors are the best band in the United States." *Strange Days* was really the four of us working together kind of on the same path. After that, things got kind of . . .' He tailed off, into another mumble. By the time I got to speak to Robby Krieger for the first time, in 2012, he had reached a place beyond acceptance. It was far too late for regrets, his off-kilter slow-talk seemed to suggest. The past was simply a place that ran on its own fumes. Watcha gonna do, huh? And yet he seemed genuinely disappointed still at what the relative failure of *Strange Days* signified in The Doors' story. The band at their peak, with everything so right, yet already starting to be so wrong.

As if to live up to their somewhat neglected new album's title, The Doors spent the final weeks of 1967 imprisoned on the road, living out a strange dream that was already turning into a nightmare. Their tour schedule had grown so out of control that they were often playing auditoriums on the West Coast one night, only to be sent flying across country back to New York to play some club – a hangover from their days before they'd hit it big which their inexperienced management team had not the foresight to renegotiate – leaving all four band members exhausted, disoriented, flat and, in Jim Morrison's case all too often, simply unconscious. When John Densmore's new girlfriend, Julia Brose, asked to be introduced to Jim, the drummer merely pointed at a figure curled up under a bench at the airport, where he was sleeping off his latest drunken binge. Two rubbish bins had been strategically placed in front of him to discourage the multitude of teenage fans that now routinely followed the band everywhere. 'There he is,' Stephen Davis later reported John telling her with barely concealed loathing. 'That's our famous lead singer.'

Twenty-two concerts in October alone were followed by 13 in November, shows of all sizes and variations. One night they would be playing to a thousand studious onlookers at the Bushnell arts centre in Hartford, Connecticut, at the next show they would be 2,500 miles across the country appearing at the Long Beach Men's Gymnasium in California, the kind of club-plus gigs a band plays before it goes to No. 1. Not *after.* Then a few days later back across to New York for a packed stand-up date in a college. Then a sit-down Playhouse Theater in New York, a psychedelic Ballroom in Washington, then back to Sacramento to 3,000 screaming hippy chicks and their frazzled main squeezes at the Convention Center, the sort of place the Stones or the Beach Boys would play.

'I always used to joke and say, after "Light My Fire" it was all downhill from there,' Robby said when we discussed those days. 'But it kind of was. Except for *Strange Days*. That was probably us at our best, when it was still fun.' The band certainly felt they had achieved something special, as did even the hard-nosed Paul Rothchild, who later considered it the best album he made with The Doors. 'We were confident it was going to be bigger than anything The Beatles had done,' he told Jerry Hopkins. But there was no single.' And despite Elektra taking advance orders of 500,000, 'The record died on us.'

Though not before the band's new super-smart lawyer, Abe Somer, had threatened Jac Holzman with the band's going on strike if Elektra didn't raise its royalty rate, which Jac, still fighting to hold on to the band and ward off B&D, eventually did, raising it to 7 per cent. The new album may not have lit up the charts as they had all hoped it would, but it was still a sizeable hit and The Doors were hotter than ever. Paul Newman talked of having them write the title song for his next movie, *Cool Hand Luke*, which would feature a hip soundtrack based on jazz and rock. But Jim didn't see Newman as the kind of cool number he could relate to any longer, equating him more with the old school Ed Sullivan generation. And Jim had already laughed in the face of Sullivan when old Ed vowed The Doors would never be invited onto his show again. (Which they were not, though Sullivan relented enough, in order to boost his own ratings, to repeat the 'Light My Fire' clip in the summer of 1968, when The Doors were No. 1 again.)

Ray Manzarek had a good chuckle at that one. 'That line in "When the Music's Over" that Jim sings: "*Cancel my subscription to the resurrection / Send my credentials to the house of detention*" – I think that was almost his way of saying, "Okay, I already see what this whole fame trip is about, and I won't let you make me play by those rules." That's Jim using The Doors to look into the future right there . . .'

On tour, each night was different: either very, very good, or very, very bad. Mostly, they were good. The band were still riding their success, yet were refreshed by the material from the new album, which now became the focus of their shows: the swirly candy-coloured organ on 'Strange Days' that framed Jim's portentous lyrics in a suitably carnivalesque way, Jim moaning like a sheep-killing dog, '*Strange days / Have found us . . .*'; the gloom offset by the joyful interplay between Robby's wino guitar and John's feathery percussion on 'Moonlight Drive'; the sheer youthful exuberance of tracks like 'Love Me Two Times', Jim's young voice still full of its honeyed purr, or flailing wildly on 'When the Music's Over', exhorting audiences across America to want the world and 'want it now!'; the treacly way he softly delivered *coups-de-grâce* one moment, then yelled and swore and declaimed loudly on 'Horse Latitudes', the mystic invocation that had so startled Bill Siddons the first time he saw Jim cast its spell. There were also even newer numbers, songs that had not originally sprung from the pot-filled air of Venice Beach or rehearsals at

Robby's parents' house: newly politicised anti-Vietnam rants like 'Five to One', or the section in 'Back Door Man' where Jim began to ramble, 'I want to tell you about Texas radio and the big beat . . .' These were exciting, if often unnerving, times for Jim and The Doors. Good times. Flaming days and deep-cut nights. All this, though they could not know it then, a far cry from the growling out-of-control drunk that came to dominate and eventually destroy Doors shows over the coming years; the band still able to make albums that would cast their own tawdry spell, still find their poet-singer holding on grimly to whatever self-respect he had left, but evoke none of the fragile beauty of the voice on *Strange Days*. A long way further down the road than any of them, including Jim, had even known you could go. To where Jim would become Jimbo, as Paul Rothchild tersely nicknamed this bible-black alter ego.

The first real sign of the gathering gloom came on 9 December 1967, the day after Jim's 24th birthday. At the gig the night before, at a college in Troy, in upstate New York, the crowd had singularly failed to be impressed by the band's posturing and a drunk Jim was so down he declined to take the short plane ride back into Manhattan and forced a driver to drive him the 150 miles or so.

The following day, a cold, snow-filled Saturday, The Doors had driven to New Haven, to the local hockey rink. At one of their first arena shows, the band were nevertheless depressed to discover the promoter had sold less than half the 5,000 tickets allocated. Jim began drinking heavily during an early dinner and carried on in the improvised dressing room before the show. As usual there were chicks hanging around backstage and as usual Jim began 'playing' with one, as the tour manager, Vince Treanor, puts it now. Vince had been hired by B&D to try and bring a new level of professionalism to the band's touring schedule, which was now almost constant. A slightly older, former organ builder, who knew more about road equipment than anyone in the band did, Treanor was to be a level head among the growing madness. Between them, Vince and the 19-year-old Bill Siddons were now doing all the donkey work *and* all the handholding.

Jim had invited the girl into the band's dressing room, but the rest of the band had soon left them to it, after 'getting tired of watching Jim play with this girl'. The next thing they knew, some kid was running down the backstage corridor to find the band and tell them, 'Your lead singer's been Maced by a cop!' Vince and Bill and the rest of the band ran to the dressing room, where they found Jim, his face a scarred red rash of pain, his eyes closed but streaming with noxious tears. It took a while to figure out what had gone on. Eventually two stories emerged. The popular one, which would live down the ages was that Jim had been making out with these two chicks in the shower stalls, man. When this uptight black cop got in his face and told him to quit it. But Jim told the cop to 'Go fuck yourself', man. Right on. And that's when the cop grabbed his can of Chemical Mace and sprayed it right into Jim's face. Jim collapsed, man, screaming and gasping. The chicks freaked out and split.

According to Vince Treanor, though, the truth was both more prosaic and more horrible. There had only been one girl and Jim had simply been canoodling with her on a couch in the dressing room. The cop had no right to be there and when he ordered Jim and the girl out of the room Jim understand-ably took offence. This was his dressing room, he explained. He was the singer of the band. It was the cop who should mind his business and leave. But the cop didn't like being spoken back to and simply reached for his Mace and blasted Jim in the face – an outrageous thing to do in the circumstances, as the singer posed no physical threat.

'The cop had no excuse to say that Jim had attacked him. He was bigger, stronger and taller than Jim,' Treanor later wrote. When he and Bill and the rest of the band found out what had happened, 'Phone calls started to fly. The cop called his station, the Musicians Union representative called their attorney, and the promoter called the police chief, who was relaxing at home. Then he called his lawyer.'

Mayhem ensued as the dressing room began filling up with people from both sides of the freak–straight divide: the show's organisers panicking at the prospect of having to cancel the show; the local police authorities confounded by the idea that this group of young oddballs and freaks might be able to bring a lawsuit against them; and everything compounded by the fact that two reporters from *Life* magazine, sent to cover the 'hottest new group in America', now on the verge of a much bigger scoop, were also in highly visible attendance, asking questions, taking pictures.

By the time Jim's eyes had been sufficiently flushed for him to see again, and some burn cream found to tend his blistered face, the police chief had arrived flanked by more uniformed officers and several other 'well-dressed men', as Vince puts it. Speaking now from his home in Singapore, Vince Treanor says he remembers it as if it were yesterday. How the whole room turned on the now sweating cop for causing such a scene, yelling and screaming at him. How as the scene eventually calmed down the police chief made a show to everybody of apologising to Jim, 'hoping that he understood what a terrible mistake had been made and [that] disciplinary action would follow'.

The chief also made a point of getting the young black cop who had fired the Mace into Jim's face to apologise to him too, but Jim, still drunk and now bristling with righteous indignation, refused to shake the cop's outstretched hand. 'Okay, man,' Jim mumbled then turned his back on him. The rest of the room heaved a giant sigh of relief in the hoped-for assumption that that would be the end of it. That the show could now go on, and that both sides, freaks and straights, longhairs and cops, could go back to simply mistrusting each other. Like before.

The show finally began, half an hour late but with Jim and the band in surprisingly sprightly form. Ray and Robby would both later recall for me how freaked out they still felt though, as Ray lit his ceremonial incense stick and Jim began prowling the stage like a bear with one leg in a steel trap. Nevertheless, they moved through several numbers without any further incident, save for Jim's even more exuberant than usual screeches and cries during 'When the Music's Over' and 'Break On Through (to the Other Side)'. All the while, though, the extra cops and plainclothes men that had arrived with the police chief stayed and watched from the wings, their faces unmoving, their eyes never once leaving Jim.

And then it happened. During 'Back Door Man', at one of those now familiar crossroads in the music which Jim used to either extemporise on his work-in-progress poetry or simply unleash a stream of consciousness babble-on that may or may not lead one night to another 'Horse Latitudes' or even, if the gods were feeling wicked enough, another 'The End'. Tonight though in frozen cold New Haven, Jim, his eyes still stinging from the chemical spray, his red face burning so hot no matter how much beer and whisky he pours down his scorched throat he can't relieve the pain, comes up with a new twist on an increasingly old tale. He decides to tell the audience – his people – all about the cop who just Maced him backstage for the heinous crime of making out with a girl.

'Hey, you want to hear a story?' he called out, that playful half-smile on his face that the rest of the band knew spelled trouble. 'It's a true story. It happened right here right . . .' He stopped and looked around, drunk, confused still, and in a voice off mike but audible to the front rows, pleaded: 'Where is this?'

'New Haven!' came several cries from the audience.

'Yeah, right here in New Haven . . .'

And then he spilled it, the whole deal. The sweet chick. The bad cop. 'A little man in blue . . .' The Mace. '. . . and his hand came up and ssshhhttt!, right in my face, man, and I went blind'.

The crowd, primed for rebellion – revolution, man, go crazy, fuckers, yeah! – begin to call out, the indignation of the congregation as the preacher begins to spout the gospel. Jim waved them down. Then told them straight: 'The whole world hates me. Nobody loves me, the whole fucking world hates me!'

At which point the already agitated cops side-stage could

take no more. Ordering the house lights be put back on, two of them strode across the stage and arrested Jim on the spot. Sitting at his keyboards, digging the scene something special, like one of his Marlon Brando or Jimmy Dean movies, Ray Manzarek revels in the sheer theatricality of it. Years later, he was still cheerleading Jim on as he told the story again, for the millionth time.

'I mean, my god,' he gushed, 'Jim Morrison should have been up there running for *political office*. Jim Morrison is the son of the *admiral*. He is the well-born young man, white Anglo-Saxon Protestant, who is *heir to the throne*. He should have been a well-behaved young *Republican*, except he's not, he's in The Doors and he's *totally misbehaving*.

'And proof of that,' Ray went on, 'is the captain – Captain Kelly, the classic Irish cop – who arrested him onstage in New Haven, he said to Jim: "You've gone too far, young man! You've gone too far!" And I thought, it's *perfect*. He has broken no law, other than the law of civil restraint – *and he had gone too far*. Into a land where no so-called rock star had gone before.' He broke into laughter. 'Into an unknown place, and they were arresting him for that very reason.'

The crowd, now robbed of their show and outraged at living proof of The Man coming down hard on one of their own, could take no more. Fights broke out as people started to leave. Others refused and tried ripping up chairs, loose floorings, anything they could prise free to hurl at the stage. As Jim is dragged offstage by the two cops, one on each arm. The other three band members watching him in shocked silence for a moment, before slowly following. No one knows what has just happened. Except maybe the cops, who drag

Jim along the hall, the first two propping him up while another two begin beating him savagely, one punching him from behind in the back and kidneys while the other swings his meaty fists into Jim's already messed-up face, his body bouncing back and forth between them.

Vince Treanor, who had somehow managed to barge his way through – 'I have no idea where Bill was' – to see what was happening, recalls the cops then dragging Jim, 'who was in pretty bad shape', back through the dressing-room area and out through a door into the icy car park. In the struggle to get him inside one of the squad cars, Jim fell face first onto the ground, 'and at least two of the cops kicked him more than once.'

When the reporting team from *Life* arrived on the scene just in time to take shots of what was happening, the cops went into overdrive and arrested them too for 'disturbing the peace'. By now, though, more members of The Doors' touring team had made their through to find out what was happening, where they were taking Jim. More than 80 members of the audience had also now gathered to add to the melee. What Vince calls 'a parade of cars' then made its way speedily to the local New Haven police station, where Jim Morrison, lead singer of The Doors, was charged with 'breach of peace, resisting arrest and indecent or immoral exhibition', becoming the first rock star in history to be arrested on stage.

'That was horrible,' Robby told me. 'We didn't know what the hell was gonna happen. They beat the hell out of him.' A rapidly sobering-up Jim was fingerprinted, his mugshots were taken (again) and he was placed on a bail bond of $1,500. It was 2 a.m. before the cops finally took the cuffs off him and released him into the care of Bill Siddons. The next morning it was announced that Jim would stand trial in January and the story became national news across America. Thus was born Jim Morrison, rock star martyr; a role he would continue to play right up to and beyond the grave. The role, in fact, he still enjoys today.

This was something the razor-sharp Jac Holzman also seized on. Scanning the acres of newsprint generated by the story not just in *Crawdaddy* and the fledgling *Rolling Stone*, but in *Life* and both the L.A. and the New York editions of the *Times*, hearing it talked about on the radio and discussed on the television news, Jac, ever the wily record man, as he recalls in his memoir, *Follow the Music*, quickly realised that New Haven was 'a defining moment in pop history: Jim Morrison, the first rock star to be busted while performing'. It was, in fact, the very thing to 're-legitimise The Doors as a counter-culture group'. Having gained and then lost the immense pop audience in the wake of the enormous success of 'Light My Fire' and its less spectacular follow-up, 'People are Strange', The Doors had clearly failed to replenish their hardcore following among the freaks and hippies now buying record amounts of albums by the Rolling Stones and The Beatles, Bob Dylan and Jimi Hendrix. The arrest in New Haven though – played out as our hippy hero Jim, our freedom-fighting poet, duking it out toe to toe with the 'little men in blue' – was just too goddamn much. He quickly ordered Paul Rothchild to get ready to begin work on the next Doors album as soon as Christmas was out of the way. When advance sales for it, sight unseen, immediately 'shot up to three-quarters of a million units', he knew he was on the right path. Easy. At least, that's how it appeared in Jac's world.

In the world of The Doors though, nothing they did from now on would ever be quite so easy again.

As the year wound uneasily to its close several new things were happening at once, all of them suddenly thrown into even greater focus after the PR martyrdom of New Haven. Jim, as always, hovered between angel and devil, working feverishly when he was straight enough on completing what he intended to be his grand poetic statement, a sweeping monologue in various stages, set to whatever improvised maelstrom The Doors were able to concoct on any given night. It had been coming together in fractions over several months, dating back to their San Francisco Be-In experiences earlier in the year, Jim slipping the words into passages of 'Light My Fire' or 'Back Door Man' or just standing there some nights sleep-talking into the mike as the band tuned up. After one spectacularly bad show opening for Simon & Garfunkel in Queen's, in the summer, Jim had got so wasted in an Irish bar he didn't bother to go home, just stayed on drinking right through the next day too, treating the patrons to lines from his new Homeric epic, as he saw it. Another time he ended up on Paul Rothchild's couch, where he began reciting a new poem he'd been working on for months, he said, called 'Celebration of the Lizard'.

Now in the dying weeks of 1967 it had begun to assume a pivotal role in The Doors' concerts, stretching some nights to nearly 20 minutes long. After the iconoclastic and confrontational 'The End' and the biblical warnings of 'When the Music's Over', this new poem was to be the ultimate piece of

Doors theatre. Full of all the by now familiar Morrison imagery of snakes and lizards and waking up in strange places, dreams and nightmares all interwoven, along with the familial death sentences, this time 'the body of his mother, rotting in the summer ground', along with snatches of lyrics that went right back to The Doors' earliest fumblings, 'the game called "go insane".'

On those nights when it did not go well, either because Jim was too far gone to put the words together luminously enough or in the case of one show where The Doors had been booked into a high-school dance as last-minute replacements for the Four Seasons, and the audience simply didn't get it and began wandering off, Jim really did 'go insane', stomping the mike stand so hard into the stage it broke and a new one had to be hastily found from somewhere.

Jim's plan, he kept explaining, though no one else in the band gave the idea much more play than an indulgent nod of their heads or a half-smile – Jim was always going on about his plans for *something* – was that 'Celebration of the Lizard' should form the entire second side of their next album. Although a rough studio draft of the piece, less than half the length of the crazed live version, would eventually surface on one of the numerous Doors compilations and YouTube links that now proliferate, in the event only a very small section of it would make it onto record in his lifetime, and then only after Paul Rothchild had forced them to refine the piece and pull it into a more recognisable song shape, retitled 'Not to Touch the Earth'. Indeed, only the 'Wake Up!' section would survive into the band's later live performances, with lines from the demo subsequently cut and pasted onto the posthumously released *An American Prayer* album.

For now, though, this was where Jim was at, even as the band's audiences were still yelling for 'Light My Fire' and Paul Rothchild and Jac Holzman saw an opportunity for The Doors to come back with their most commercially successful album yet. Even as – especially so, in fact – Salvatore Bonafede and Asher Dann came to Jim in the dead of night with a new, decidedly reptilian plan of their own: for Jim to leave The Doors behind and start afresh as a solo artist.

Why not? On paper it made sense. The way Sal and Asher saw it, Jim was the star of The Doors, far more than, say, Mick Jagger was the star of the Stones or Lennon was the star of The Beatles. The Stones also had Brian Jones, The Beatles also had McCartney. Who did The Doors have other than Jim? Owlish Ray? Rickety Robby? Come on, man, be fucking serious. The same dark logic would be put in front of Janis Joplin just a few months later about her band, Big Brother and the Holding Company, and Janis saw it made even darker sense and quit on the spot, going solo overnight. The late Sixties were all about grabbing it while you can, no one having the faintest idea that any of this – the sex, the drugs, the bread, the fame – would last longer than the time it took to come down off your latest trip. Bands – big hit-making bands – broke up all the time. Jimi Hendrix would also soon dissolve the Experience; Jeff Beck would sack his entire group, leaving Rod Stewart to become an even bigger solo star. Bob Dylan ditched his whole audience by going electric.

What was Jim waiting for? There would never be a better time, they argued. Jim was the one being interviewed by Albert

Goldman in *New York* magazine, had been the big splash in *Life* following New Haven, was the one being slavishly photographed for *Vogue*. *Crawdaddy*, the thinking dude's rockzine, loved Morrison. *16*, the one the little girls understood, loved him even more. Jim had it all. What did he need The Doors for any more? Not only were they holding him back with their nerdy looks and creepy music, but they were getting three-quarters of the dough, when Jim could have it all! In fact, under the new solo deal Sal and Asher would put together with Columbia, still hovering to pounce since foolishly letting The Doors slip through their fingers just the year before, Jim, Sal and Asher would all be ten times richer! What wasn't there to love? C'mon, Jim, what d'ya say? Have another drink and think about it, huh? C'mon, baby, let the good times roll . . .

But Jim didn't dig that idea *at all*. Jim, the new anti-establishment hero who had faced down the cops in New Haven, who had told Ed Sullivan where to go when he tried to censor his song, who stood up on stage night after night telling the people the unvarnished truth, man, who wanted the whole fucking world and wanted it *now*, nearly shat himself when Sal and Asher got him on his own and began talking about the future. For one thing, as Vince Treanor recalls now with a chuckle, 'Jim was convinced that Sal Bonafede was in with the Mafia, and that if he didn't behave he'd have him rubbed out, you know, Mafia style.'

Mainly, though, Jim the great shaman shrunk back into being a little lost boy needing constant reassurance at the idea going it alone. He may have hated John, who didn't tolerate his bullshit, may have put up with Ray, who talked the talk but never once walked the walk the way Jim did, may have been jealous of Robby, who didn't feel the need to come down from the mountain with tablets of stone the way Jim felt obliged to but could write better songs than any of them, but he needed them in a way business guys like Sal and Asher would never understand. The other three guys in The Doors really knew who Jim was when he wasn't wearing leather pants and giving the come-on to some overeager chick or hyped-up young head. Knew who Jim was when he was fucked up for days, the phone hidden under the bed in some cheap motel room, knew the Jim who didn't shower for weeks, had whisky puke all over his face and bats flying out of his hair. Knew the Jim that existed before he lost the weight and gained the acid-gravitas, and who had become super-skilled at turning his midnight ramblings into coherent, chart-friendly songs that kept the whole shebang on the road.

But Jim was too scared to say no to Sal and Asher. Not to their faces. So he ran to Ray and Robby and John and told them all about the wicked men who had tried to steal him away from them, then demanded to know what they were going to do about it? Already feeling beaten down by all the crazy roadwork they were doing, all the TV shows and one night stands fitted round recording dates, but sensing this was just how it went when you were a successful Top 10 band, when your dreams were actually coming true, even as the nightmares began to unfold, Ray and Robby and John had not seriously considered firing their managers. Their grumbles were the same complaints of any hardworking band in America in 1967. This, though, amounted to treachery, as they saw it. Something would have to be done, and soon. But there was a contract, they knew they wouldn't be able to just walk away from that. So they turned to their other father figure, Jac Holzman.

He recalls: 'When Robby came to me one night in the studio and said, "Can we get an advance against $50,000?" I said, "Of course you can. Do you wanna tell me what it's for?" He said, "We have to pay off Bonafede and Dann." And I said, "Come by in the morning and I'll have the cheque ready for you."' As he put it in his book, 'I never wrote a cheque with greater pleasure.' The Doors were now crucial to Elektra's long-term prospects, 'a band that could make a string of great albums'. Removing B&D would make things immeasurably simpler for Jac to make that dream a reality. It would not be straightforward, and The Doors would have to pay and pay again for the privilege of reneging on a deal they had been only too delighted to sign when they were penniless and unknown. And a suitable replacement would have to be found, one who could manage but not lead; could work with Jim but not get in his way. Could keep the other band members happy but do as he was told. The sort of manager than simply did not exist. Nevertheless, one would have to be found. Or made.

In the meantime, the last few weeks of the year were taken up by a handful of gigs, all in California, and a general celebration not of the lizard but of the astonishing success The Doors had enjoyed in their inaugural year as a professional recording group. Ray, in particular, saw this moment as an auspicious one and married Dorothy Fujikawa, four days before Christmas Day, at L.A.'s City Hall. It was a ceremony typical of Ray's charmingly conflicted thinking. Like Jim, Ray liked to see himself as more than just a high-profile player in a pop group. He was an artist, an outrider of the Aquarian Age. What did such petty rules as held back the lowing herd mean to one such as him? Why, nothing! At the same time, his love for Dorothy, his impending tax bills and his burning desire to 'get it made legal' made him yearn for marriage to his college sweetheart. At the same time, as he later wrote in *Light My Fire*, 'We didn't want to do a traditional wedding with formality and whiteness of the bride.' Nor did they fancy standing on the beach or up in the hills or indeed anything where many guests were invited and big words were said followed by a forced revelry.

So instead they simply booked a lunchtime slot at City Hall and invited Jim and Pamela along as best man and maid of honour. Jim and Pam were 'a fine couple', wrote Ray. 'And I really needed Jim's support in this extreme moment of truth.' Afterwards they all went for lunch at a nearby Mexican joint and drank margaritas, *por favor*. The following night, a Friday, The Doors played the first of two shows with the Grateful Dead at the 4,000-capacity Shrine Exposition Hall, in downtown L.A. Only 2,000 people showed up but the band made up for that by putting on – whisper it – something very closely resembling a true homecoming show. Even Jim was on his bestworst behaviour. Halfway through the show Ray brought Dorothy onto the stage and Jim introduced them as 'Mr and Mrs Ray Manzarek!' The couple kissed and the audience whistled and applauded. The following night, halfway through the show, the cops invaded the stage – not again! – and shut down the show. The fault this time though was not Jim's but to do with various city ordinances the promoters had not complied with. At least, that's what the cops said. Ray felt it was more to do with the law taking 'the opportunity to hassle the hippies'.

One of the final Doors shows of 1967, however, ended on a more surreal note. Having recorded blistering performances of both 'Light My Fire' and 'Moonlight Drive' live for the Jonathan Winters TV show on Christmas Eve, The Doors interrupted their second of three shows at the Winterland Ballroom, in San Francisco, on 28 December, in order to wheel a TV set onstage, so they could watch themselves. They had been halfway through 'Back Door Man' when the Winters show started. They simply stopped playing, downing tools, as it were, and walked over to the side of the stage the set was on, and gazed at themselves on TV.

Ray Manzarek laughed when I reminded him of it years later. 'Yeah, we had the audience watching us, while we watched us – onstage and on TV.' When it was finished Ray simply walked over and switched the TV off. Then went back to his keyboards and counted them all in again.

THIRTEEN
Dog without a Bone

Sal Bonafede and Asher Dann did not go quickly or quietly. For a while, at the start of 1968, it looked like they might not go at all. In legal terms, they had broken their contract with The Doors, on paper had done nothing except fulfil their obligations, and spectacularly so. The two Doors albums had both gone gold in the US, and become significant hits in other parts of the world (though not, as yet, Britain, where *The Doors* barely scraped the Top 40 while *Strange Days*, despite rave reviews, disappeared without trace). Meanwhile, 'Light My Fire' was the only million-seller single by a new group in 1967. By the end of the year, by Ray Manzarek's reckoning, their share of combined record sales and publishing royalties enabled the four members of The Doors each to walk away with around $50,000 – around $350,000 in today's money, or around £210,000. There were other perks too: when 'Light My Fire' went to No. 1 Jac Holzman told the band they could have anything they liked as a gift. Robby and Ray opted for expensive new tape decks. John asked for and got a thoroughbred horse. Jim, that emblem of possession-less free spiritedness, got a Gulfstream aqua blue Ford Mustang Shelby GT 500 with all-black interior, known as the King of the Road.

What then did The Doors have to complain about? Apart from the fact B&D had offered to make Jim Morrison an even bigger, richer star as a solo artist, but that the singer was needlessly afraid Sal was in the Mafia and would have him 'rubbed out' if he failed to comply? When it was next revealed that another Hollywood powerbroker had offered Jim a $250,000 'advance', a Rolls-Royce and a house in Beverly Hills, in order for him to break his ties with The Doors and Elektra and start him off on his own solo career, The Doors' case for mismanagement became even more undermined. Big, successful rock groups were breaking up and reconfiguring into supergroups all the time in the late Sixties.

As far as Sal and Asher saw it, says Vince Treanor now, from his home in South Korea, 'They had brought The Doors to public knowledge and fame and they felt they were guiding them along the right path. But the guys were told, you *will* have this news event, you *will* have these photo events, *you* will have these different things. They were just told to do it. There was no "Would you like to do it?" Or "Do you think we should?" That was the real basis of the problem. But as far as [Sal and Asher] were concerned, they put those boys on top. There was never an argument, never disagreement or anything like that, just this undercurrent of too much control.'

On another day in court, the judge might easily have told The Doors to quit bitching and get on with their work, just be thankful they still had a contract with B&D. Fortunately for The Doors they found their case being treated sympathetically

225

by a judge well versed in the entertainment business, who recognised that a contract was worth no more than the paper it was written on if one side was so unhappy it was unwilling to work with the other. In the end, the judge decreed the contract null and void. Sal and Asher were awarded $50,000 in compensation and a share in royalties on all future Doors recordings, plus all their commissions and fees due. The Doors were free to do what they wanted. At a price that was climbing steadily higher with every move they now made.

The early months of 1968 were similarly confused, the band apparently on a winning streak while privately floundering. Two shows at the Carousel Theater in West Covina, California, were booked for 19 and 20 January. Jim was amazing the first night, bounding with energy after a three-week lay-off from the road; the second night out for the count as he struggled to beat an almighty hangover. Backstage at a Doors show was no longer a happy place, with the two sides now clearly defined: Jim alone on the one hand, the big boozer who still liked to drop acid occasionally, chain-smoke anything that he could roll and light, and never get out of bed before 3 p.m.; the other three opposite him, non-drinkers, meditators, musicologists, whose only drive was to perform to the utmost of their abilities, who didn't need to 'challenge' authority or fuck anything in a skirt, whose moods did not ebb and flow like the tides of the moon. They had to hand it to him that he didn't abandon them when he could. They must have resented him for it too though – knowing he was not a Janis Joplin, not an Eric Clapton or a Jimi Hendrix; could not have carried the show alone; could not have created new material with the meaning he invested in it, personally, without The Doors to alchemise it into musical silver and gold.

They were complicit in other ways too. Jim may have been the overindulged child, but the other three also liked having things done just the way they wanted; were easy with none of the 'uptight' obligations Sal and Asher had imposed on them. Which is why when really big-name rock managers presented themselves to The Doors in early 1968 as the natural heirs to the shaky B&D throne, heavy biz cats like Bill Graham, who Vince Treanor rightly characterises as 'one of the pioneers of the theatrical rock performance', Ray and Robby and John were just as happy to deny them access as Jim was. It didn't matter that these people might boost their career; all four Doors were so intimidated by their presence they shrank from the idea. Like a dysfunctional family that refuses professional help because it means throwing open the blinds on problems they consider too dark to face.

So it was that the new Doors manager – the 19-year-old Bill Siddons, upgraded overnight from his gig as surfer-dude-with-brain road manager to Doors office overlord – would not be a manager at all, but a facilitator. According to Bruce Botnick, 'There was just something about [Bill], about his smarts, about dealing with other people, being able to talk to them, with hall managers . . . getting things done without any drama, and being able to handle Jim. And they just went, you know what? We don't want a manager, or managers, *per se*, to tell us what to do, and to take a large portion of our performance monies. Hire him.' Jac Holzman offers a similar uncomplicated view: 'They had other people hanging around but Siddons was a good choice. He was a kid but he was wise beyond his years. He was very smart and he was very good to work with. He was hired to keep things together. Not as a conventional manager because the band realised they would have to make the choices themselves. He would present the choices. They would sit and discuss them. He would make his recommendation and they'd vote on them.'

John Densmore, however, writing in his 1990 memoir, *Riders on the Storm*, claimed there were doubts over the wisdom of appointing someone so young and inexperienced right from the start. 'Bill [Siddons] was a great guy . . . but Jim was destroying himself, and who was going to stop it?' According to Vince Treanor, though, 'The one key factor, in 22-point type, was HE WILL DO WHAT WE TELL HIM. And the best of the best of the best were vying to become The Doors' manager, making all sorts of concessions to the usual fees and percentages and all sorts of things. To become part of that Doors organisation. But they chose Bill *because* he was 19 years old, *because* he was a kid.

'They promised to get him out of the draft, which they did. And he was beholden to them, in that sense. But his contract was, when we say jump, you simply say how high. That was the final and most critical point. They could control Bill where they couldn't control some of the big boys that were gunning for the job. They did not want to replace Sal and Asher with somebody that might be worse.'

In the end, it proved a recipe for disaster, says Vince. 'Bill made a lot of enemies [including] the one guy who broke his back to help The Doors to success and that was Bill Graham. Once Bill [Siddons] got to be the manager of the group he treated Bill [Graham] like he was just another puppy dog in the street. And I felt shame over a thing like that but that's the way he was. Bill [Siddons] did and said a lot of things that alienated a lot of people. And eventually it caught up with him.'

Bill Siddons was a bright, good-looking, level-headed boy then attending California State University, in Long Beach. After his high school buddy Rich started helping with The Doors' equipment, he dragged Bill to a Doors show in San Francisco in May 1967, just as 'Light My Fire' was starting its ascent to the top of the American charts. Blown away by what he saw, when helping out Rich for a couple of weeks turned into the offer of a full-time gig, Bill didn't have to think twice.

A hard man to pin down who rarely speaks about The Doors these days, Bill Siddons still lives in Los Angeles, where he is now one of the most respected rock managers in the business. Back in 1968, though, being thrown into the deep end like that, becoming manager of what was at that moment the biggest American group in the world, he says the only way he could deal with it was by simply taking things as they came.

'Whatever you threw at me, I figured out how to handle. And that was what made it possible for me to succeed, because when crazy stuff happened, it didn't make me crazy. It just made me go, okay, I know where we're going. I know we've got to get to this show or make the studio happen, or whatever it was. I had some idea of what needed to really happen and then I started steering things towards doing that. I was raised a middle child with a five-years-older sister and a five-years-younger brother and a kind of crazy father, so I had to learn to mediate. And with The Doors there was a lot of mediating because they were *very* different personas.'

It wasn't until he began working directly for The Doors in his new day-to-day capacity, Bill says, that he discovered how much people in a band like The Doors 'could want to kill each other!' Bill was instantly caught in the middle. 'John was holding on very tightly to the things that made life predictable and stable, and Jim was trying to break everything. So it was two very different personas and to a large degree Ray was the business guy more than Robby and John. He was the one who knew where we were going and so it was . . . most of the strife in the band was really just about how hard it was to plan your life, control anything, have shows that worked, etc., because Jim was such . . .' He pauses and allows himself a small, ironic chuckle. '. . . an extraordinary person.'

He goes on: 'There wasn't that much yelling and screaming and melodrama, because they were all adults. It's just Jim was impossible to control and that made it emotionally really challenging for everybody, because the unpredictability of what would happen today was very hard to deal with, especially for John. I think Robby and Ray coped a little better than John. John took it more personally. But they all did. They all had . . . ah . . . they all knew they were holding on to the tail of the tiger and, well, we roll with it. We see what happens.'

With more control over their business affairs at least, The Doors instructed Bill to find them an office and rehearsal space, which he did immediately, renovating an old antiques store at 8512 Santa Monica Boulevard in West Hollywood. Upstairs was the office, run by Kathy Lisciandro, wife to Jim's and Ray's UCLA buddy Frank, and with Siddons installed 'to take calls, book gigs, deal with Elektra, then sit down with us every Friday and talk it through', as Ray put it. While down-stairs was where 'the art' took place. The Doors also asked Bill to formalise their new financial arrangements, paying themselves equal salaries of a few thousand dollars a month, then splitting end-of-year profits after deducting expenses. Bill would also be on a good salary, but not commission. The new Doors office would also come to serve as another of Jim's im-promptu crash pads on those nights when he was too wasted to make it back to Pamela's or one of his other girlfriends. Or he couldn't remember where he was supposed to be staying, the Alta Cienega, around the corner, or the Tropicana, up the street, or the Beverly Terrace, also just up the street. Or he just couldn't be woken from his stupor, so his friends would leave him to sleep it off on the office couch.

Not far from the Doors office was the Phone Booth, a top-less bar. There was also a bar called the Extension, both of which Jim would go to. Soon the new Doors office became a target hangout for every deadbeat who'd ever sat on a barstool next to Jim or passed him a joint at the Whisky. Freaks began showing up every day: characters like Cigar Pain, who wanted to be Jim so badly he would shove lit cigars down his throat to make his voice more gravelly, chicks like Crazy Nancy, who would show up at all hours on the off-chance of meeting Jim, even broke in a couple of times and slept there – Bill han-dled Nancy with special care. Others even more weirded out would randomly show up so that Bill or Kathy would simply call the cops. Other times real-life Jim girls would come by, chicks he had fucked once or twice then forgotten about. The semi-famous Plaster Casters tried to get in once but neither Jim nor The Doors were interested in having moulds made of their erect penises. Until one day Bill had finally had enough and had iron gates fitted outside the office entrance.

The new Doors office was also conveniently just a walk away from Elektra's own new premises, at 962 North La Cienega Boulevard, just south of Santa Monica Boulevard. Eighteen months before, just as he was readying his staff for the release of the first Doors album, Jac had paid $69,000 for 'a nondescript building and some land in the heart of West Hollywood'. By 1967, as the first monies from The Doors and 'Light My Fire' began rolling in, Elektra was buying contiguous lots in order to build its own studio. By the time the company had tricked it out, says Holzman in *Follow the Music*, it had cost $120,000 (almost $1,000,000 in today's money). 'I didn't care,' wrote Jac. 'It was the fulfilment of a dream.'

Seated like a guard at the gates of heaven was Suzanne Helms, a married woman unimpressed by longhaired rock and rollers; she would make them wait for their appointments like anybody else, on a wooden bench in reception. Even Jim, whom she would berate for not sitting up straight: 'He liked to hunch his shoulders,' she recalled, 'and I hate that.' Mostly, Jim would do as he was told, settled in a chair in front of the little refrigerator drinking a beer and reading one of his heavyweight books, *The Red and the Black* by Stendhal, one visitor recalls.

But then drunk Jim would turn up at Elektra sometimes too and terrorise the secretaries, or start an argument with one of The Doors, there would be pushing and shoving, raised voices. Drinks would be spilled on people's desks. When Jim poured a malted drink all over Mrs Helms's typewriter, she was furious with him and complained to Jac. He told her to buy a new typewriter and charge it to Morrison's royalties. Another observer swears Jim wore the same clothes every time he visited – for a year. Jim's shambolic appearances at Elektra became such a regular occurrence that when staff arrived for work one morning and found Jim unconscious, collapsed in the bushes outside, they just ignored him. Sure enough, he eventually came to, promptly dusted himself down and went on his way again.

According to Robby Krieger, though, there was often a serious purpose behind Jim's always being at Elektra or the Doors office. 'The music was all he lived for. A lot of times he was at the office when we weren't. He'd even live there some-times, because that was his whole life. We all had lives other than The Doors, but he didn't, and he kind of resented that. He felt like he was living it 24 hours a day, and we weren't. And he was right.'

By the time The Doors were ready to go into the studio again with Paul Rothchild and Bruce Botnick, in February, Jim Morrison's life was an ever more complicated, ever more drunken mess; the balance between Jim and Jimbo increas-ingly tilting to the latter. 'They were enjoying the fruits of their labours,' says Bruce Botnick dryly. 'They were start-ing to get money. Jim was actually enjoying his celebrity, I think, to the point of getting polluted all the time. You know, drinking lots of booze and taking . . . you know, if somebody came up to him and said, "Hey, Jim, take this", he'd open his mouth and – bam! – not knowing what it was. So you never knew who was going to walk into the studio, whether it was Jim or Jimbo – the one who went crazy.'

As far as Jim was concerned, though, he had everything under control. He had 'dodged a bullet' by narrowly avoiding marrying Pam, who, inspired by Ray and Dorothy's nuptials, such as they were, had used a New Year's Eve Doors show in Denver to obtain a Colorado marriage licence, which she filled out for both Jim and her – but which Jim pointedly failed to have legally endorsed or properly registered. Pam still returned to L.A. convinced she was Mrs Morrison, even if she had neither the ring nor the marriage certificate to prove it. To keep her cool, though, Jim agreed to Pam's great new idea about 'lending' her the money to open her own La Cienega fashion boutique, which she named Themis – after the ancient Greek goddess known as the personification of 'divine law'. Certainly there would be nothing ordinary about Pam's new shop. She would stock it, she told Jim, with her own taste in far-out trippy gear, snakeskin leathers, ostrich feathers, Afghan coats, Indian trinkets, fiery beads, moon crystals, blood incense, floaty dresses. And she would travel the world to unearth such luxuries. To Morocco, Paris, London, India . . . buying handmade clothing, rugs, jewellery. And Jim would pay for it – or else. Jim duly instructed his new office to allow Pam access to his bank account. He had his divine orders. It was later estimated by his office that Pam eventually sank around $250,000 (nearly $2,000,000 today) of Jim's money into the shop over the next few years. But while it became a cool Hollywood hangout – Miles Davis went there, as did several other high-profile musicians, including the wives of the other Doors, whom Pam would take great delight in overcharging – the shop never once turned a profit.

Meanwhile, Jim was spending so much time fucking other

people, he was just glad Pam had something to take her mind off things. There were the usual groupies, of course, the one-offs whose names he never even asked for. And the more upscale numbers like Eve Babitz, whom he would still call on occasionally, even though he knew he'd have to be on his best behaviour. 'He knew in his worst blackouts to put my diaphragm in and take my contact lenses out', as Eve amusingly put it. And then there were girls like Judy Huddleston, neither full-blown groupie nor old and smart enough for him to feel he had to play fair with.

Judy was a pretty 18-year-old girl from Newport Beach, Orange County, who would drive with her girlfriend Linda up Sunset Boulevard every weekend to seek out bands. Her parents had recently divorced and she was in her final year at high school, studying art, living with her mother alone, just the two of them. Soon she would enrol at the Chouinard Art Institute, in L.A. (now known as the California Institute of the Arts), where the breakthrough American artist Ed Ruscha had studied.

Judy and Linda had managed to say hello long enough at the Whisky one night to Bill Siddons and his pal Rich, along with Robby Krieger's twin brother, Ronnie, for Judy to feel confident enough to try talking her way into getting backstage at a Doors show at the Shrine in L.A. the previous Christmas. Unable to get near Jim because of all the other girls surrounding him, Judy had hung on a little longer in the parking lot afterwards on the off-chance that Jim might wander by. Stoned on grass, she thought she was imagining it at first when Jim actually appeared – surrounded by the same gaggle of eager chicks, all of whom crowded into his blue Mustang.

But there was an exchange and Jim told Judy to follow in her car. One thing led to another and within a couple of hours Judy was alone with Jim in his squat little motel room at the Alta Cienega. Jim had been so sweet, so vulnerable almost, taking it slowly, playfully, a tender lover. When the next morning Judy asked him about the other Doors, he told her: 'The other guys in the band are like brothers, you know, brothers . . . I mean, I like them, we work well together, but we're not really alike.' It was a Sunday morning, Christmas Eve, and Judy was sure she would see Jim again soon.

The next time they met, again at his motel room, in January, after Judy had taken a chance and just shown up at the Alta Cienega one afternoon, Jim had been surprised, but pleased. He had to run an errand, told her to wait for him in his room. Then when he returned he kissed her passionately, pulled off her clothes and his, in a tremendous hurry suddenly, and threw her down on the bed. And then raped her. Anally.

She recalls the scene in her astonishing memoir, *Love Him Madly*. They were on the bed, naked, about to make love, but this time there was something different about Jim, something menacing. 'Have you ever been fucked in the ass?' he demanded. 'I want to fuck you in the ass.'

Alarmed, she pretended to be aloof, told him she had but that she hadn't liked it. 'I don't really want to. Don't, okay?' Jim ignored her. She wrote: '"I want to," he hissed, hollowing me to the marrow. He had snapped. Jim's eyes looked black, blazing with hatred or defiance. I was afraid he was going to hit me, slap me, shake me. He pinned down my arms, flat against the bed. I was watching a movie I was acting in, but he was directing. He seemed so crazy that I realized he could kill me. And something died, dropped out of me. The surroundings blurred, my boundaries were lost, and nothing was left but his brutal need driving out of control, until I realized he was raping me.'

Judy then describes 'lashing out for survival' and yelling for Jim to stop, which he reluctantly did. She lay there stunned while Jim went to take a shower, whistling as he went. When Pam turned up a little later Jim taunted her about having another girl in the room and refused to let her in. Pam called Jim by her pet name for him, 'Sapphire', which only made Judy squirm more. Pam pleaded to be let in. Jim just continued taunting her. Eventually he told Judy to lock herself in the bathroom while he dealt with Pam. Judy heard angry voices, then the door slamming as they went off somewhere together. When Judy crept out she noticed her own blood, 'bright on the clean bedspread, and hoped it would make a nice conversation piece when they returned'. She never told anyone what had happened. 'I was too ashamed.'

It's a disturbing memory Judy says she still remembers every detail of, all these years later. Now a lecturer at California State University in Monterey Bay, she spent years in therapy getting over the battle scars, physical, mental, emotional, that the Sixties left on her – and many other young women of her generation.

She begins by pointing out how powerfully attractive the 24-year-old Jim Morrison was, how almost impossible to resist: 'Just his physical presence. I mean he didn't pretend he wasn't a rock star. But if he wasn't you'd still go, "Oh", when you saw him. Particularly a woman would go, "Wow, who is that?" He could sometimes cover it up. He could try to look anonymous but it was a little hard. He definitely had something that made him . . . you just gravitated toward him.'

Judy feels strongly that his rape of her was about more than just being an oversexed, overindulged rock star. She thinks Jim was 'a borderline personality, or that thing that everybody is now – bipolar! I think he was probably a borderline, and once he did too much alcohol he was . . . it really, really fucked him up. I've heard stories . . . He got to be mean to me but I heard he would get really, really mean [with others] . . . Like that rape in the beginning, it was almost like he was possessed. It wasn't at all like a normal mood swing. It was like, what the hell was that? It wasn't a normal change of consciousness. It was like really extreme. I don't know what the mental diagnosis was but it wasn't that he was just a little neurotic. He had a real thing there and I think the alcohol or whatever drugs, though he was more of an alcoholic, that that could push him into probably what I would call psychotic episodes. Not that he wasn't also an asshole. But there were underlying things, yeah . . . that's the thing that you can't forget. It's like a weird domination.'

Judy says the fact that he raped her anally was also significant. 'I believe there was a problem with Pam on that, that she resented. But I'm not the authority on that. But I think that was like the possessive ownership god only knows [thing] . . . There was definitely rage in it, let's put it that way.

'And the other thing, I don't know if it comes through, but it was very desperate. So even though it was like a command to do that, it was like, if you don't, I'll die! It was like really so desperately needy that that was almost scary. So that urgency – I mean, beyond urgency! – where is that coming from? I don't know if there's a latent homosexual thing to it. To me it seemed like a real act of aggression. I own you. This is all for me. It's not for you. I win. You don't.'

At one point in her book, when Judy assumes Jim is bisexual, he reacts angrily. 'He rolls his eyes like, "How could you possibly think such thing?" It's like, well, because it's sort of common and that's happening. I think I had another boyfriend who said, "Oh, for sure, he's [Jim's] been with other guys." You just kind of go, oh, never mind. But Jim was very defensive . . .'

The question of whether Jim Morrison was gay has never gone away – whether he was either closeted at a time when homosexuality was still illegal in America – hence also his aggression towards women, or perhaps he was just bisexual, still then a verboten subject among even the most liberal-minded of people, unless of course they were bi or gay too. This may have been another reason he was so drawn to the arts. He could be more his true self. By 1968, he was certainly becoming a gay icon, in his tight black leather trousers, ruffled white master-of-the-hall shirt, pouty mouth and kissy waterfall curls. Some nights Ray would see Jim posing fitfully not just for the screaming girls in the audience, but focusing his whole persona on some handsome young stud in the front row too. Other times he would stand in front of Robby as he was soloing and pretend to jerk him off, forming his left hand into a broken circle. 'Jim was the beautiful boy,' as Ray put it to me disingenuously. 'He offered all possibilities to all people with eyes open enough to see them.'

As Pamela Des Barres points out, 'In those days, everyone was experimenting. Supposedly Mick Jagger slept with [men].

It doesn't mean he was bisexual or gay in any way; people were experimenting in the Sixties with drugs, with sex, with spiritual things, with religion . . . everything. We were expanding ourselves. I'm not in the least bisexual and I had a couple of girl experiences, and if Jim did, he was either really, really drunk, or experimenting.' Sexual experimentation was more than just accepted, she says. 'It was *expected* in our culture.' She laughs. 'Everybody was doing it. In our sphere, in our reality, in the trippy hippy, peace and love, flower child love-in days, yes, everybody was experimenting with it, and doing it didn't at all mean that you were bisexual. I think we all are to a degree, but that's another whole story. . .'

Pamela Courson certainly thought she knew what Jim was. 'Why do you think she was in a bad mood all the time?' says Eve Babitz. Pam hated anal sex yet that was all Jim seemed to want to do. After another big bust-up, she went into his wardrobe and took one of his new tailor-made waistcoats and wrote 'FAGGOT' in big letters across the front. Eve Babitz later wrote of Pam rampaging through Rodeo Drive's most expensive appointment-only stores, 'Yves Saint Laurent, Rive Gauche, piling her arms higher and higher with more stuff, muttering under her breath, "He owes it to me, he owes it to me, he owes it to me."'

If Jim relied on women, from his disapproving, shaming mother to his disapproving, shaming girlfriend, Pamela, and every groupie-stop between, that didn't stop him wanting to mess with them whenever he could, to draw outside the lines and throw darts at them. Lately Jim had even begun to use 'Back Door Man' as a way of defiantly projecting those fantasies in public. Taking the usual emphasis away from the line, '*The men don't know, but the little girls understand*' and obliterating it with his own insinuating improvisation, 'Come on, baby, be my man. *Be my man! You understand! Yeeaaahhhh!*'

'Music is so erotic,' Jim told one interviewer. 'One of its functions is a purgation of emotion, which we see every night when we play. To call our music "orgasmic" means we can move people to a kind of emotional orgasm through music and words. A concert only clicks when the musicians and audience reach a kind of united experience. For me it's stirring, satisfying . . .'

Offstage, however, Jim's men friends now outnumbered his women companions. Lately he had become fixated on Elvis Presley and Frank Sinatra, the singing alpha-males of their respective generations. Like every young American boy growing up in the 1950s, the legend of Elvis loomed large in Jim's mind. The controversy, the outrage, the attempts at censorship – they were Jim's first glimpse of just how exciting, righteous even, it could be bending the rules so far back upon themselves that the world of rights and wrongs, of old folks telling young folks what to do, began to break. Sinatra was a more recently acquired taste. Jim's dad had liked Sinatra. That meant he was off Jim's radar completely – until he got to be a singer himself, and began to understand just how incredibly powerful yet sweet Sinatra's voice was. Two of Frank's big hits in 1966, 'Strangers in the Night' and 'That's Life', showed Jim just how indelibly Sinatra could imprint his vocal on a song, going from fierce yet sexy growl one moment, to coal-fire warmth and reassurance the next. Jim began to unconsciously mimic Frank's low-slung crooning style, most obviously on tracks like 'People are Strange' and 'Light My Fire'. It is said that every time Sinatra heard 'Light My Fire' on the radio, he was so convinced Jim was deliberately ripping off his style, he snapped, 'We ought to let that guy have an accident.' (What Frank thought of his daughter Nancy's later cover of the song is not known but can be easily guessed.)

Now, though, Jim was taking his emulation of the two men he still saw as 'the true greats' a step further by surrounding himself with his very own entourage.

Frank had bodyguards, yes-men, and regular payroll friends like Pat Henry, the comedian who used to open Frank's Las Vegas shows, George Schlatter, who would secretly fill a vodka bottle with water in order to keep up with Frank, Leo Durocher, Frank's broad-shouldered PR man and minder, Brad Dexter, a TV actor who had become part of the inner circle after saving Sinatra from drowning on a Hawaiian vacation, and several others. For all of them Sinatra was The Boss, and they lived under the protective spell of Il Padrone at the Las Vegas home Frank named The Compound. Similarly Presley surrounded himself with good old boys like his high school friend Red West, a Texan musician, Sonny West, who'd written hits for Buddy Holly, Billy Smith, who stuck with Elvis from start to finish, and several others, all sequestered at Elvis's version of The Compound – Graceland, the eyesore mansion with the white-columned portico that Elvis turned into his own Memphis palace.

Jim now aspired to do the same with his own good buddies, forming a coterie of likeminded 'free spirits' silently sworn to protect and serve him; to laugh at his jokes and egg him on in his most reckless and stupid moments. Though in

Jim's case there would never be a Compound or Graceland for them to congregate in, only a series of cheap motel rooms and titty bars, apartment floors and Doors-sponsored travel expenses. Self-consciously in the way dudes like Paul Ferrara, another UCLA moth drawn to The Doors' flame, initially as their official photographer ($275 a week, plus 15 per cent royalty on all the posters and tour books that would feature his pix, plus any side money he could make selling his Doors shots to magazines), but in reality more as one of Jim's regular drinking buddies. Trailing after Paul came Babe Hill, yet another UCLA underachiever now shacked up in a small shed at the back of Paul's beach pad.

When Paul expanded his role into Doors film archivist, Babe became Paul's assistant, operating the Nagra tape recorder for sound. Mainly, though, Babe was bagman, car boot loader and hangout artist. Jim valued his company most for the fact that Babe could drink even him under the table. No trouble. Prior to this Babe had been married to Diane, with whom he'd fathered two little girls. Babe left them, according to Paul in his book, because 'he wanted to learn about LSD. He was ready to turn on.'

Others, like Frank Lisciandro, whose wife, Kathy, worked front of office for The Doors, had known both Jim and Ray long before The Doors' success and had his own career as a photographer and filmmaker to think about, were a far less corrosive influence but still could not prevent themselves becoming enablers to Jim's endless moods and drunken misadventures.

'I was *not* one of Jim Morrison's "drinking buddies",' Lisciandro insisted in a 2002 interview, drawing a distinction it was hard for anyone else to divine. 'Babe Hill and I went to bars and clubs with Jim because we were his friends and that's what friends do, they hang together. We didn't lead him to bars; we didn't encourage him to drink. He went to bars and clubs because he was young and he enjoyed it. He drank because he was an alcoholic. There were many nights that either Babe or I, or both of us, carried Jim to his car and drove him wherever he was staying, and put him to bed. It's what friends do for each other; they look out for each other. I won't claim that we protected him or that we kept him out of trouble. Jim did what he wanted to do. But when there was trouble, Babe and I did what we could to get Jim out of its way. And that is the absolute truth.'

And there was Tom Baker, the one friend of Jim's that Danny Fields now says he feels Jim might have consummated a homosexual relationship with. 'There were these rumours about Morrison and Tom Baker.' He says that if there were 'any nominees for what men I would go with' Jim perhaps having had sex with, Tom Baker 'would be the one'. Certainly Baker was another who liked to think he could match Jim, drink for drink, line for line, toke for toke. And like Jim he would die too young of a heroin overdose, in 1982, his stiffened body eventually found by cops in a shitty flophouse on New York's Lower East Side.

Jim and Tom and Babe were of Irish-Scots descent. Paul and Frank were both Italian-American. That was a lot of hot blood boiling over on the Strip the nights they would be out there raising hell, which was most nights in 1968. Ferrara recalls a typical occasion in his fascinating memoir of the period, *Flash Of Eden*. At the opening night of a Blood,

Sweat & Tears show at The Troubadour, they were sitting in the balcony: Jim and Pam, and Paul and his new girlfriend, Georgia, and Babe and Tom. Already plastered, Jim started causing such a ruckus, yelling 'Yeah! Yeah!' at the top of his voice, screaming almost, that the club called in security to have him removed. When they lifted him out of his seat by his hair, Ferrara writes: 'We were all embarrassed for him but tried to act like we didn't know him so we weren't ejected also.' So much for looking out for Jim.

As Bruce Botnick puts it, '[Jim] wasn't drinking his own Kool-Aid, let's put it that way. But I mean, you're spending time with the Andy Warhol crowd in New York. He's getting introduced to all kinds of exotic intellectual things. It's gotta change your thinking. Especially if you're chemically enhanced or you're drinking a lot. It's just a wonderful, fun world, you know? But then after a while it gets to be too much. And later on, that became too much.'

Like the night Tom Baker had taken them to a party in the San Fernando Valley, where Jim played pool with Janis Joplin, the latter another of Baker's occasional 'squeezes'. Next thing they are found fighting in the front seat of a Mercedes, Janis hitting Jim over the head with her empty Southern Comfort bottle, Jim grabbing her by the hair and not letting go. The Animals' singer, Eric Burdon, another party-hearty figure then on the Hollywood rock scene, recalls seeing Jim getting up onstage at the Whisky with some small-time young band and taking over, reciting poetry, before descending into a vile drunken rant: 'You've all had your revolution, and it's all over. And there'll never be another revolution, cos you're all niggers.' He looked out at the shocked crowd and repeated the line: 'You're all niggers!' No one applauded. A deeply un-comfortable silence fell over the club. Until an old black cop, moonlighting that night as club security, came out and told him, 'I'll give you niggers, you son of a bitch. Get off the fucking stage!' The cops were called, and they dragged him outside, but he escaped and ran off, bouncing off the bonnets of cars. Robby later bemoaned the fact that Jim was always getting into trouble with cops. 'I'm amazed he never got shot by a cop, because he used to taunt them so.'

Or the time Jim, drunk out of his mind again, insisted on putting Babe and Paul and a chick named Violet, 'one of our cocaine queens', into his Mustang and racing the 'blue lady' so fast down Sunset that Babe cried out, 'We're going to die!' The car skidded up onto someone's lawn and collided with a tree, at which point a drunk Jim crawled from the wreckage to find he'd crashed into the back garden of the Beverly Hills Police Department. 'So we sent Violet in and she called a cab and we left,' Babe later told Frank Lisciandro. 'The cops never even knew we were involved.

But Jim would pull others into his orbit too. Visited on tour in Las Vegas for a magazine article by the *New York Times* journalist Bob Grover, Jim had instigated a brawl in the parking lot with the venue's security guards after cupping his hand around a cigarette pretending to smoke it like a joint, and was knocked down by a blow to the head. When the cops arrived they arrested Jim on the spot for vagrancy, public drunkenness and failure to possess sufficient identification. They also arrested his 'accomplice', Grover. In his subsequent article, headed 'A Hell of a Way to Peddle Poems', Grover wrote of Jim's uncanny ability to attract trouble wherever he

Right Boy, you couldn't get much higher. Jim onstage in April 1968. Toronto, Canada. (Getty Images)

Below September 1969, Frankfurt, Germany. (Getty Images)

Morrison on stage in 1968 after his 'execution' during 'The Unknown Soldier'.
(Getty Images)

Top far left and top left Give this man
a ride. Jim looking his best, circa 1968.
(*Top far left:* PA Images; *Top left:* Peter
Sanders/REX)

Left New Haven, December 1967.
Cops getting ready to pounce.
(Everett Collection/REX)

Above Pamela Des
Barres (bottom,
centre) and The
GTOs (Girls Together
Outrageously) LA,
1969. (Getty Images)

Right A young
pre-Warhol Nico
performs on TV in the
early sixties.
(Getty Images)

Hollywood Bowl, 1968. (Everett Collection/REX)

Left Navel gazing. Jim performs at the Northern California Folk-Rock Festival at Family Park, Santa Clara County Fairgrounds on May 19, 1968 in California, USA. (Getty Images)

Below On the only Doors tour of Europe, August 1968. (Getty Images)

Left Stoned immaculate. Jim before the fall. 1968. (Araldo Di Crollalanza/REX)

Below Jim Morrison and Pamela Courson, Los Angeles, 1970. 'She was his equal,' says Pamela Des Barres. (Getty Images)

The Doors perform, circa 1970. (Getty Images)

went now: 'His charisma was such that your ordinary up-holder of the established order could be infuriated merely by the sight of Morrison strolling down the street – . . . that invisible something about him that silently suggested revolution, disorder, chaos.'

Whatever it was, it was about to cause Jim and everyone around him, most especially The Doors, a whole lot of trouble. 'Jim attracted the lowest of the low, like flies on garbage,' says Vince Treanor. 'Jim asked for everything he got. He surrounded himself with people who were nothing more than sycophants. As long as he had money in his pocket, was paying the bar tab or the restaurant tab or the travel fees or whatever the hell was going on, they were there. But the minute Jim ran out of money in his pocket that was the end of it, they all went home. Gee whiz, the party's over, Jim's broke for the night.

'And I hated that and so did the other guys [in The Doors]. They realised it was people from the outside who were doing this, who were creating this myth, that were creating this god. Putting Jim up on the ivory tower, which was cracking while they did it.'

Sometimes they would even try and muscle in on Jim's songs. In *Flash Of Eden*, Paul Ferrara recalls one night at the beach cabin he shared with Georgia and Babe, when Jim spent the night with them tripping, seeing in the dawn making music and singing, just crazy shit off the tops of their heads, acid babble mostly, but how Jim suddenly got inspired, reached out for the purple light, and began running around on the sand, coming up with bits that later found themselves in The Doors' song 'Waiting for the Sun'. Jim was so high on the moment, the sun, no longer keeping them waiting, rising like a bubbling stew in the sheet metal sky, that he thanked Paul for his inspiration for the melody, which Jim could hear clear as bells under the moment where he began to shriek about 'First flash of Eden!'

When, sometime later, the band came to record the track, which they would not yet use, simply borrowing its title for their next album, and Jim tried to clue them in on Paul's co-writing credit, Robby nearly bit his head off. Robby had seen Jim try to pull this shit too many times. Jim who couldn't play a lick telling the band where the music came from, the melody, how he'd already had the whole thing worked out in his charred mind weeks ago, man, you should've been there, baby . . .

Jim tried to insist but Robby put his foot down, insisted that he had replaced Paul's melody with one of his own. Jim, who could never remember exactly what had gone on with the music, not really understanding anything about it, finally acquiesced. Leaving Paul to bitch about it for years after.

FOURTEEN

Out on the Perimeter

By May 1968, The Doors had completed work on their third album, *Waiting for the Sun*. To Jac Holzman's immense relief, it would be their grooviest and most commercial yet, complete with the belated follow-up to 'Light My Fire', the rather whimsical 'Hello, I Love You', which became the second Doors single to race to No. 1 in America later that summer – and their second gold record. As far as Jim Morrison was concerned, though, *Waiting for the Sun* was a bitter disappointment, an embarrassment, signalling the end of The Doors as a viable vehicle for his boundless talents.

His biggest disappointment came from the almost unanimous decision not to devote one side of the album to 'Celebration of the Lizard', Jim's latest and, he felt sure, greatest masterwork. When the band tried working through it in the studio for Paul Rothchild, though, the producer shook his head, rolled another work of art and tried to decide how best to tell them there was no way he was going to let them put it on the album. Jac Holzman had been very clear in his instructions to Rothchild before the sessions began. The Doors were in the headlines, but they'd never really followed up the massive success of 'Light My Fire'. Elektra, so long the bastion of singles-free artistic freedom, now had too much invested in the new, more commercial era the success of The Doors had singlehandedly ushered in for them as a company. Jim's and the band's artistic choices were to be respected wherever possible, but the bottom line was Jac needed a hit. No more fucking around. With advance sales for whatever album The Doors released next tipping half a million, he knew it was now or never.

The rest of The Doors seemed to agree. Any doubts they might have privately harboured were banished by Jim's increasingly irresponsible behaviour in and out of the studio. Using the loss of his beloved 'Celebration . . .' piece as his excuse, Jim began treating the studio as just another place for his entourage to hang in. Jim and the guys, Paul, Babe, Tom, whoever, would turn up drunk and stoned, downers now replacing acid as the zonk of choice. Paul Rothchild would tolerate it for as long as the band remained productive then yell at them to get the hell out, the friends of the band standing around pretending not to notice but quietly seething. 'Some heavy, heavy scenes,' said Robby. Sometimes it was cool. Like when Paul Ferrara and Babe Hill showed up in their latest guise as documentary filmmakers. Through Jim they had somehow swung a deal with Bill Siddons to make a movie of The Doors and been given $20,000 and as much access as the others could stand to film them for the next six months. Mostly it was none. One time Jim and the gang turned up with all these chicks, straight from some party, to no one's amusement other than Jim's. Rothchild called time on the session and left them to it. Another time Jac Holzman recalls seeing an unconscious Morrison with piss running down the front of his jeans, as he lay huddled on the studio floor.

Paul Rothchild complained about never knowing which Jim Morrison was going to turn up: the forward-thinking poet determined to create great art or the monstrous drunk whose ego was so out of control he viewed the rest of the band almost as an appendage. 'In the *Strange Days* period Jim was more interested in psychedelics than, you know, getting wasted,' Robby told me. 'I mean, he still might not show up if he was on too much acid but he was still just one part of this bigger . . . thing.' By *Waiting for the Sun*, though, 'he was really in big trouble'.

'By that time, Jim was being taken advantage of by various hangers-on,' Robby would recall in a *Guitar World* interview. 'He would bring them to the studio and Rothchild would go crazy – all these drunken assholes would be hanging around, fucking in the echo chamber and pissing in the closets. It was a mess. Jim would drink with anybody because we wouldn't drink with him. He would take on all these assholes, who used him: "Hey, we're hanging with Jimbo." And they wouldn't care how fucked up he got – they'd leave him on somebody's doorstep in his own puke.'

The result was, with some notable exceptions, the thinnest-sounding album The Doors would release. Without the sprawling 17-minute-plus epic, 'Celebration of the Lizard', to fill it, The Doors were forced to reach deep into their kit bag and dig out songs they had never intended to record, including two, 'Hello, I Love You' and 'Summer's Almost Gone', from their original Rick & The Ravens demo. It was Jac Holzman's ten-year-old son, Adam, who reminded his dad of 'Hello, I Love You'. 'Jim was terrific with my son,' says Jac now. Just weeks before, on Adam's birthday, Jim had turned up unexpectedly at the Holzmans' Los Angeles home, 'clutching an erratically wrapped present for my musically inclined son. He came in, sat quietly with Adam, and showed him how to play the kalimba, an African thumb piano. They sat there for an hour, fully absorbed – two children in their own world.'

Nevertheless, Jim was mortified at the idea of renovating what had been one of the first songs he'd ever written and played with the band. It was a straight rip-off of The Kinks' riff to 'All Day and All of the Night', a US Top 10 hit just months before 'Hello, I Love You' was written, but Robby Krieger later claimed the song's 'vibe' was taken from Cream's 1968 hit, 'Sunshine of Your Love', but nobody believed him. In fact, Densmore later told me, 'At the start of that song, in the studio, Robby said, like, "Why don't you turn the beat around like Ginger Baker does in 'Sunshine of Your Love'?" And I did. I kind of copped a little offbeat thing that he did. Everybody's listening to everybody else and doing it or whatever . . .' (The British courts, however, would later find in favour of a claim made against the song by the publishers of The Kinks' song, awarding them all royalties from all sales of the 'Hello, I Love You' single in the UK.)

Adam, who had always loved the demo, didn't know that though and so Jac called Paul Rothchild in the studio and asked him to record a new, up-to-date version. Jim was appalled at the suggestion, seeing it as adding insult to the injury of bumping 'Celebration of the Lizard' from the record. But when Paul told Jac the band didn't want to do it, that it wasn't just Jim, that they all felt they had gone past that kind of pop fluff now, Jac said to record it anyway and if it didn't work he would 'eat the studio costs'. Once again, Holzman was right. But that didn't make Jim feel any less wrong about it, especially when his cronies ragged him about it.

Speaking to me about it more than 40 years later, however, Ray had reconciled himself to the notion completely, as though he and Jim had actually planned it. 'Isn't it wonderful?' he chuckled. 'It's Jim running up to this little black girl, the 16-year-old girl, the café-au-lait figure, the Nubian princess walking along the beach in Venice that we both saw [in 1965]. This was an actual incident, and he said, "I'm going to talk to her." I said, "No, you're not, man." That girl with those nubile breasts and those *legs* as long as . . . she had six-foot legs, for god's sake! What a gorgeous Nubian princess! Café-au-lait-coloured and just sashaying down the beach, just entering her fullness, her ripeness, her womanhood! But she was only 16. I said, "Do not talk to her! That's all we need, child molestation!" He said, "She's not a child." I said, "I know she's not! But legally she's still a child!" And two or three days later Jim came to me and said, "Remember that girl?" I said, "Of course." He said, "I wrote this song for her. And this is what I wanted to say to her. 'Hello, I love you . . .'". And that's where it comes from. So the line in there, "Do you hope to make her see you, fool? Do you hope to pluck this dusky jewel?" that was really . . . that's telling us that it's . . . this gorgeous café-au-lait creature.'

'Summer's Almost Gone' was another resuscitation from the original six-track demo, never intended for release, now repurposed as album filler; the kind of Sixties pop whimsy, written two years before at the height of the success of folky groups like The Mamas & The Papas and the Lovin' Spoonful, that was a musical state of mind now abandoned by The Beatles and the Beach Boys, who had moved on to more grandiloquent pop statements.

'We Could be So Good Together' was another desperate addition to the track listing. Originally recorded at the *Strange Days* sessions (and listed as on the album on very early pressings of the sleeve) but rightly dropped for being too plain-clothed, despite the Thelonious Monk reference – a brief musical quote from Monk's 'Straight No Chaser', about halfway through, superfluous and trite – this was The Doors working at half-speed, Jim's vocal throwaway and showy.

But at least these were genuinely old tracks, there simply to bolster the rivetingly new. There was less excuse for wince-inducing tracks like 'Wintertime Love', so utterly of its moment it even has a harpsichord on it, all candy-coloured miniskirts and beatific smiles and a happy carnival of love-love-love. Not so irksome but still only half trying was 'Love Street', a self-conscious stab at the kind of baroque pop that defined some of the best work by Love. In the hands of the more noir-ish Doors, though, it sounds more like a nursery rhyme.

The padding continues with 'Spanish Caravan', Robby's hazy, uncredited take on Isaac Albéniz's classical masterpiece 'Asturias', a technical challenge for any guitarist, but in this context, with Jim crooning along like a languid Torero slowly twirling his cape, so pretentious it's almost a send-up; the sort of faux rock-classical nonsense that would become the house music of Seventies wine bars.

The half of the *Waiting for the Sun* album that was originally supposed to complement 'Celebration of the Lizard' is much better though, beginning with 'Not to Touch the Earth', the only section of 'Celebration . . .' to survive the cull: nearly four minutes of avant-rock that demonstrated once more just how far removed from the mainstream Morrison's lyrics and The Doors' music could be when allowed to. With its giddy rhythms, gaunt guitars and mock-opera keyboards, Jim finally engaged in his declamations of outlaws living by the side of lakes, preachers' daughters 'in love with the snake', and its enigmatic pay-off line, *'I am the lizard king / I can do anything'*, one can only feel sympathy for the singer's plight, permitted only to demonstrate one small, if vivid, aspect of what he then saw as his greatest lyrical feat yet. Listening now to the full nearly 20-minute live renditions of 'Celebration of the Lizard' that exist on the internet, one can only lament the decision to prevent The Doors from fully realising this magnum opus in the studio. If Jim really did wish to see himself as more of a poet than a rock musician, this was surely the right place to start. When one also considers how well received his posthumous 'spoken word' Doors collaboration, *American Prayer*, would be, how also the section that begins *'Way back deep into the brain'* is superseded by the same funky, tribal-drum motif that the band would finesse further for much of *American Prayer*, one can only wonder how the musical career of The Doors might have panned out differently had they chosen to go with it, not chop it into its more 'accessible' bite-size.

Rothchild and Holzman tried to placate Jim by allowing

the first single from the album to be The Doors' very own anti-war protest song, 'The Unknown Soldier' – one of the other musical highlights from the album, a taut shuffle that climaxes with the sound of a firing squad marching to its date with destiny, tolling bells, and Jim ranting over the top of the band freaking out. The first Paul knew of it was when Jim had pulled out a ragged note from his leather pants, as he lay drunk on a couch. Then retched into a wastepaper basket. Elektra even greenlighted a budget for the band to make a promotional film, in imitation of their new stage act, wherein Robby 'executes' a tied to a stake Jim by firing his guitar at him like a rifle. But Jim still came away horribly disillusioned. (The 'Unknown Soldier' promo film would later be shown at art gatherings but pointedly not on commercial television, where the scene of Jim's suspiciously ketchup-like blood dripping onto an 'innocent' bouquet of flowers – deep for the time, but rather too much like another of Ray's UCLA student movies – was deemed unnecessarily provocative at a time when American troops in Vietnam were being flown back in body bags by their thousands. Top 40 AM radio took a similar view, preferring to play the new version of 'Light My Fire' by José Feliciano then on its way to the top of the charts.) Inevitably then, the 'Unknown Soldier' single was not a hit; any kudos gained from it with the hip rock press swiftly dissipated when 'Hello, I Love You' then followed, becoming the big pop hit of the summer.

The other real grade-A number on *Waiting for the Sun* was the track that closed side two, 'Five to One'. A real tour-de-force on an album otherwise almost unbearably light on musical muscle, and an even more devastating anti-war statement than the more literal 'The Unknown Soldier', with needle-sharp Morrison lyrics and sardonic vocals, at least partly inspired by the 19th-century poem 'Now the Day is Over' by the Victorian polymath Sabine Baring-Gold, transposing its opening verse, *'Now the day is over / Night is drawing nigh / Shadows of the evening / Steal across the sky'* into his own 20th-century iteration, *'Your ballroom days are over baby / Night is drawing near / Shadows of the evening / crawl across the years'.* While for the nominal chorus Jim dips into Dylan Thomas's back pocket, and his vignette 'The Fight' from *Portrait of the Artist as a Young Dog*, where the main character reads from a poem titled 'Warp' and five things (designated by Thomas as 'tears', 'suns' and 'inscrutable spears in the head') are made into one. Or as Jim growls with almost sexual malice: *'One in five / No one here gets out alive . . .'* It makes for a towering, juddering end to the album and would soon become another major highlight of the still evolving Doors live performance – as well as becoming a favourite of all the 'grunts' in Nam now tripping out to The Doors, the Stones and Jimi Hendrix on a regular, fuck-you basis.

What nobody appreciated was the deep irony in Jim Morrison going to such extravagant lengths to protest against the war in Vietnam, when his father had, not inadvertently, played such a significant role in starting the war. Steve was serving as operations officer on the aircraft carrier *Midway* in 1963 when he was given command of the carrier *Bonhomme Richard*. The first act as captain he was obliged to make in November that year was to announce over the ship's broadcast system the assassination of President John F. Kennedy. Nine months later, he was overseeing naval operations in the Gulf of Tonkin when, on 2 August 1964, the US destroyer *Maddox* opened fire on three – communist-controlled – North Vietnamese torpedo boats, which it had identified as approaching enemy vessels. What happened next has remained open to debate among conspiracy theorists and military historians alike – a second 'engagement' was recorded 48 hours later but later denounced – but the political outcome was the passing by U.S. Congress of the Gulf of Tonkin Resolution, which granted President Lyndon B. Johnson the authority to 'assist' any Southeast Asian country whose government was considered to be under threat of 'communist aggression' – thereby sparking the commencement of open warfare against North Vietnam. Yes, the singer who would just four years later pen 'The Unknown Soldier' – with its creepy 'Hut-hut-hut' marching drum middle-eight – was the son of the USN commander who effectively kick-started the Vietnam war by firing on three North Korean torpedo boats. (In a further irony, Admiral Morrison, as he would become in 1968, later claimed not to have been remotely aware of his son's public protests at the time he was making them, as by then he was too involved in guiding American troop movements in Vietnam, though he did confess to finding it strange to see his son's image – one representing a moral culture defiantly at odds with his own precepts of service and duty – on the bedroom walls of his friends' teenage children.)

Did Jim Morrison know any of these things about his father? It seems highly unlikely, given the top-secret nature of his father's career. As Bruce Botnick points out, the subject of Vietnam was on everyone's minds, not least because of the shadow of the draft that hung over every healthy American male between the ages of 18 and 25. 'They were always paying attention to what was happening and what had happened, and what might happen. And there were always discussions amongst us about what was going on.' He adds, 'I had just escaped having to go in, with my bad back. I'm a 1Y, which meant that unless it was all-out war in the world I wouldn't be drafted and have to go and fight. Then I got married and President Kennedy, in his infinite wisdom, had passed a law that men who were married and reached a certain age [wouldn't be called up].' And the band had just helped pay Bill Siddons's legal fees to help get him out of the draft. 'And of course,' says Bruce, 'dramatically, Jim loved throwing himself on the ground, where he was shot at the stake for speaking his mind. You know, he loved that whole thing, the theatre of it all.'

Given the paucity of more truly top-drawer new material, it seems odd, even lax, that they never finished recording the track the album was to be named after. Instead we would have to wait another two years for that little gem to surface. For now, the third Doors album was rounded out by two slender but no less evocative tracks: 'My Wild Love', a swampy blues, complete with voodoo chanting, handclapping; part Red Indian war dance, part gumbo stew gospel psych-out. (Jim originally saw it as a folksy thing with banjo. The band demurred. Robby suggested a cappella version as a compromise. Jim went for it. Just then Jac walked in. He took part too.) And the wonderfully understated 'Yes, the River Knows', a woozy, rippling jazz blues full of yearning where all four Doors excel themselves, gently ebbing and flowing like a warm pool of blood. Perhaps in that spirit they also tried their hands at recording a contemporary version of Albinoni's *Adagio*, which never made the finished album either, perhaps because that really was pushing the credulity of listeners – at least, by 1968 standards – beyond their tolerance. (Though again a more polished version would surface a decade later on *An American Prayer*.)

Recording of the new album had taken place over two periods in February and March, with a break in the middle for the band to complete a string of East Coast shows that many now regard as The Doors at their very peak. Already previewing new material from the album, including the full 'Celebration of the Lizard' set piece, the new shows were also the first to feature the new bit of business they had built around 'The Unknown Soldier', with Jim dropping 'dead' at John's rim-shot. Ray would hold one arm aloft, bunching his hand into a fist, grab the top of his amp, dropping it on cue, making it sound like a shot ringing out in the indoor sky

New dicks on the rock press block *Rolling Stone*, out to make a name for themselves, went out of their way to send up this latest piece of theatre, headlining their review of the show: 'Much Ado about Nothing, or, Humpty Morrison's Great Fall'. But according to Vince Treanor, then as now one of the band's harshest critics, 'The best I ever saw The Doors was their performances of March 1968. Anybody that followed the group around the east part of the United States in that period would have to say that those had to be the best.'

He recalls sitting backstage at the newly opened Fillmore East, after the second of two spellbinding Doors shows there in March, with Bill Siddons and the band and a couple of other crew members, laughing and joking and toasting their good fortune until dawn, drinking champagne and eating spaghetti, 'talking about the [recent] performances, the different locations, how each had grown on the other. The final show in Fillmore East had to be the epitome of the height of The Doors' career. It had to be the best. There was no show that [was] ever better than those three shows.'

Others tell stories of being on the band's tour bus when it stopped somewhere for a meal break. And how Jim went into a store that sold bait: cages of crickets and whatnot. Jim bought the lot and set them free. They were all over the parking lot. But he meant well and no one was hurt. Everybody was soon back on the bus and smiling, watching the crickets bounce off the windshield as the bus rode off down the highway again.

Things, however, would change once the touring began in earnest after the album was finished. At a show on Long Island, in April, Jim was so drunk he couldn't hold it together onstage at all. Bill tried to smooth things over in the dressing room afterwards but John was beside himself with rage. 'I can't do this!' he yelled. 'I'm going home!' When Bill later checked the tab with the barman he discovered Jim had drunk 26 Vodka Oranges between 4 p.m., when he arrived at the venue, and 8 p.m., when the band went on.

On another famous occasion in New York around this time, Jim ended up with Paul Ferrara at Steve Paul's basement nightclub The Scene, where Jimi Hendrix was doing a late set. Jim was so drunk he got up and tried to join in with Jimi onstage, singing, but then he started falling over. He grabbed Jimi and the two began to topple. Not cool. The roadies got nervous, moved in, then fans started trying to pull Jim away from the stage but Jim was now hanging on to Jimi's leg. Bad scene. Finally Paul jumped in and got Jim out of there, told him whatever he needed to hear to get him back to the limo then the hotel. Jim was unconscious by the time they got back to the hotel, so Paul put him to bed, then finally went back to the club.

'People came to see him [Jim] get crazy, and he did,' Ferrara would later claim. But Elektra disagreed. As Jac would later say, 'Morrison was extremely well-read, thoughtful, funny, and an absolute devil.' Fearing their hot property was about to self-destruct, Jac Holzman appointed the label's general manager, Steve Harris, to join the band on the road as their new 'day-to-day guy': in effect, Elektra's spy on the road. As Harris put it, 'As long as Morrison was behaving I stayed in the background.' At a show in Boston a few days later, Harris came up with the novel idea of matching Jim drink for drink, drug for drug, in order to try and gauge when the singer had had enough. When Jim realised what he was doing he raged at him, 'Don't ever tell me what to do!' But when a kid offered Jim some acid a couple of hours before the show, Jim declined and after the show thanked Steve for 'keeping me straight'.

According to Jac Holzman now, 'I was able to take it in my stride. Remember I am their record company. I'm not their pal. I had a responsibility and that was to help their career as much as I can. And yes I would come to sessions and I'd do a lot of stuff.' One thing he studiously avoided though, he says: 'I just did not hang out with them, because I thought that they thought – and Jim especially – that they might be able to co-opt me, and I never wanted that to be the case. Besides, sometimes you have to say hard things to an artist.'

He would balance the stories that came to him on an almost daily basis of Jim's latest outrages with the conviction that he was, at heart, a serious artist. 'I think he was a seeker. He had great curiosity. He loved films and he knew films well, and that was the point where he and I had a very strong intellectual relationship, because I had seen just about every movie ever made. I lived in movie theatres when I wasn't working. So we had that in common but I think in some ways he hungered for . . . he loved blues and he hungered for the blues life and being on the road and getting the girls and getting all that stuff. But I think he was a serious person. And he was also childlike. He was a very good observer and his observations I found frequently to be fascinating.'

Jim was now surrounded by people all wanting to 'help' him. Closest was Ferrara and his pal Babe Hill, there ostensibly to film and photograph the band, but mostly as an adjunct to whatever madness Jim was currently getting into. 'The dolls were literally fucking me to get in line to fuck Jim,' Ferrara recalls in his book.

Paul even helped Jim out when he wasn't there. Later, during a brief spell when Ferrara wasn't brought along for one of the band's road trips, he spent the night over at Pam's apartment. 'I felt guilty but it was like a duty fuck,' he writes in *Flash Of Eden*. He recalls that when Jim got back into town Pam told him all about it; that she'd fucked his good friend. Jim asked if it was true and Paul explained that it was *Pam* that had seduced *him*. Jim said he understood. He recalls the singer being strangely quiet on the subject afterwards, and not being able to work out why.

Passing the chicks around – that was just *normal*, baby.

263

What free love was all about, right, man? Having cats like Paul and Babe around on the road could have its real uses though. As well as filming some of the priceless material that is still used in countless recycled Doors films, documentaries, videos and DVDs, they provided extra bodies at a time when most road crews could be counted on one hand. Paul would sometimes go with Bill Siddons to the production office at the end of the night to pick up the fee, sometimes as much as $50,000 in cash. They would carry the money in plastic carrier bags and stash it in the boots of the two station wagons they were all travelling in. Once when Jim's mother came to a concert Paul had to lie and tell her Jim was busy and couldn't see her – because Jim simply refused to see her. She was 'sad when I told her', recalled Ferrara. Not as 'sad' as she was though when Jim, spotting his mother in the wings during the performance, looked right at her as he screamed, 'Mother! I want to FUCK YOU! YEEAAAHHHH!!!', during the juddering climax of 'The End'.

Paul also shot the album cover to *Waiting for the Sun*. He'd wanted to shoot a sunrise but it was impossible on the West Coast so they shot a sunset instead, in Malibu, at the top of the canyon, Paul standing on top of his car, some shiny boards in front of the band to reflect the setting sun back onto their faces. Faking the dawn. An apposite image for an album that was as twisted and contrived as some of it was uplifting.

Mostly, though, Jim's entourage were there to prop him up, a job no one in The Doors felt obliged to do any longer. Back in L.A., in May, while the band finished up the album with Paul Rothchild, Jim was on the loose again in what Eve Babitz later characterised as 'That Elektra–Barney's–Alta

Cienega Triangle'. Deciding Jim needed someone to watch over him off the road even more than on it, on the advice of Paul Rothchild Elektra hired the musician Bob Neuwirth, whom Rothchild later described as 'the only guy I knew who could outdrink Morrison, out-hip him'. Paul had first met Bob on the Boston folk scene, had stayed close as Neuwirth became a player on New York's Greenwich Village folk scene, befriending Bob Dylan, whom Neuwirth performed a similar 'professional buddy' service for, under the aegis of Dylan's wily manager, Albert Grossman. With Rothchild's help, Bob and Jim moved into adjoining rooms in the Landmark Hotel, a deliberately unhip joint in more suburban north Hollywood. Overnight, though, according to Neuwirth in *Follow the Music*, 'It became Action Central ... like a zoo.' Jim lived by night, diving in the pool, drunk, waking everybody up, yelling from the balcony, out of his mind. A loaded Janis Joplin would swing by on a whim, as would folk singers new in town like Leonard Cohen, various out-of-work actors and, of course, all Jim's usual gang of reprobates. What Bob calls 'really zoney'. Jim knew what Bob's gig was and hated feeling 'tricked' into things. At the same time, says Bob, Jim knew what he was doing, what effect his deeds had on the room. And he played up to it.

Looming on the horizon was the biggest show yet for The Doors: their first arena headliner at the Hollywood Bowl, on 5 July, for which the already sold-out ticket sales alone would gross them over $35,000 – just under a quarter of a million dollars in today's money. With 'Hello, I Love You' following in the footsteps of 'Light My Fire' the summer before, rocketing towards No. 1, and the *Waiting for the Sun* album ready for release the week after the show, the Hollywood Bowl was the big one for Jim and The Doors. History in the making, so whatever you do, don't blow it, okay Jimbo?

Holzman recalls the night of the show being completely 'over the top, the crowd crawling over cops and beefy security guards to try and get backstage'. Rothchild and Botnick had been instructed by Holzman to bring in mobile recording equipment. 'I knew it would be special, he says. Mark Abramson, who'd done such a great job on the 'Break On Through (to the Other Side)' promo clip, was brought in to oversee the filming of the concert, with Paul Ferrara and Frank Lisciandro doing the actual shooting. Four cameras: one a master shot in the centre of the seating area that Paul operated; Frank with his close-up camera at the foot of the stage; plus two other UCLA grads, David Thompson on a handheld camera, filming from the stage, and Steve Wax operating a high-speed camera for quick-shot extras. (Also helping out with the gear was Ferrara's beach bum pal, Harrison Ford, then an aspiring actor getting by as a carpenter. 'When it was over,' Ford later laughingly recalled, 'I was one step away from joining a Jesuit monastery. I thought it was cool, I thought it was hip, but I couldn't keep up with those guys. It was too much.')

Just before the show, Jim, who was using a room at the Alta Cienega, across the street from The Doors' office, as his informal warm-up room, played host to Mick Jagger, another sign of the new superstar status of The Doors. No longer one-hit wonders, the 'American Rolling Stones' were now serious players in a world Jagger then presided over. It was no co-incidence that a photograph of Morrison would appear on the wall in one of the scenes of the new movie Jagger was then filming, *Performance*, the disturbing for the times thriller written by an occultist and former Aleister Crowley *protégé*, Donald Cammell, about a reclusive rock star struggling with identity crisis and sexual malice who detonates his career to return in altered form as a murderous gangster.

Jagger sat close with Jim, ignoring everyone else in the room. Jim tried not to show it but was in awe of the Stones' main man. Jim couldn't believe it when Mick told him he'd just finished mixing the new Stones album, *Beggars Banquet*, in London 48 hours before, and flown in especially for the Bowl show. The Stones hadn't toured America since 1966 and their next tour later that year would be of arenas. Mick wanted to see how Morrison and The Doors handled playing in front of 10,000 people. But Jim didn't know the answer to that one – yet. When Mick asked Jim if he meditated before a show, he burst out laughing. 'No, man! I leave that to John and Robby!' All the while, though Jim never mentioned it, the folk singer Tim Hardin was trying to find a vein to shoot some smack in the bathroom. There was some desultory talk about how when they were both growing up – Jagger was only a few months older than Morrison – it had been cowboys and cops that were the heroes but now it was guys like them – rock stars! The kind of guys the cowboys and cops would have gunned down. Richie Havens was there too but otherwise excluded from this touching scene. Instead, he filmed the encounter with one of the first video cameras on the market. Havens later claimed he lost the footage – but recalled in his 1999 memoir, *They Can't Hide Us Anymore*, that Jim was 'Bombed out of his brain. In complete escape from the world that wouldn't let him be himself.'

According to legend, after Jagger left, Jim swallowed a tab of acid. When John found out he was furious. 'John loved to go out there and do it,' says Bruce Botnick. 'He wanted to do the best show possible, at all times. And he got frustrated when Jim was inebriated or stoned and inebriated, and after a while it really got him.' Looking at the raw footage now, years later it's clear just how 'off' Morrison really is, his eyes struggling to focus, a stoned smile never far from his glassy face. As if taking their spaced-out cue from him, the performance from the band never really gets off the ground either. Robby's guitar is out of tune a lot of the time, despite the endless fiddling around with it, and the crowd seems subdued, not at all the ravening monster they were later reported to have been. Quiet, in fact almost solemn, between numbers as Jim holds on to the mike for dear life, exhorting them to 'Wake up!' as he stands there his eyes tight shut, the beautiful moonlight-blue waistcoat with the gold braid Pam had brought back from the flea markets of Marrakesh for him to wear, and the suggestive Conch belt that reflected the stage lights right back into the eyes of the audience, thinly disguising the fact that his consciousness lies somewhere very far away from wakefulness.

When the show was over, Mick Jagger and his girlfriend skipped the after-show party. The Stone alone had found The Doors 'boring'. As had many younger members of the crowd, there to hear 'Hello, I Love You' and 'Light My Fire' blasted to the high heavens by a red-blooded rock band operating on full power. Not a woozy cabaret act strung out on too many late nights and not enough fun.

Jim, still tripping, retired to his motel room at around

dawn. Accompanying him was January Jansen, one of the laidback dudes Jim had met in San Francisco, who resembled Jim a little with his schoolboy good looks and long tangled curls. He also shared Jim's taste for fast women, slow days, good food and badass whisky – and the kind of drugs that were so powerful they sent you to places you were never coming back from. A designer who had put together some snakeskin suits for Jim, January was another of the singer's VIP guests for the Bowl show. As soon as they were alone in the room, Jim asked him, 'Did you bring what I asked?', referring to the powerful mescaline he had requested January bring to him especially for the show. Speaking to Frank Lisciandro for his own fascinating 1991 memoir, *Feast of Friends*, Jansen recalled placing '17 caps of mescaline sulphide needle crystals' into a pint of orange juice, then stirring the same dose into a second pint of orange. Then the two men drank their respective pints down – and waited to see what would happen. According to Jansen, 'Three days later, we were still peaking.' Eventually, Jansen began throwing up blood. Jim told him, 'It's all right. You just had too much blood in you.'

Two weeks later, after a show in Honolulu, Jim announced he was having a nervous breakdown and that he wanted to quit The Doors. Not even Ray believed him. Told him he was just drinking too much, drugging too much. That he needed to cool out, man. *Waiting for the Sun* was out now and despite the so-so reviews it was headed for No. 1. Number fucking one, baby! Walk *that* parapet naked, crazy man!

A week later, The Doors performed at the Singer Bowl, at Flushing Meadows, New Jersey, another giant arena where

The Who would be the opening act. It would become another notorious stopover in The Doors' steeply unravelling story. Jim, drunk, high, but oh so low on self-esteem, can't believe his bloodshot eyes when he shuffles onto the stage and sees it is ringed by cops, the stage actually barricaded against the audience. The band managed to nurse him through the hits, the place packed with kids screaming for their favourite songs from the radio. But Jim was still freaking out about the barricades, and he began baiting the cops, yelling at the audience to smash the barricades, to get up there on stage with him, why not? Fuck the police! Only the crowd can't, the cops won't let them, so people start to overheat, become frenzied, and that's when the broken wooden seats, torn from the ground, begin to fly, followed by the bottles and glasses, anything the crowd, now seething, can get their hands on.

'Jim was digging his power to incite riots' is how Paul Ferrara, there filming the whole thing on a new 16mm Moviola camera, would later explain it. But that wasn't how it looked to the cops – or the rest of The Doors. Except maybe Ray, who grinned devilishly from behind his keyboards, the ringmaster, hugging himself with glee almost at the sight of his dancing bear thrilling the maddened crowd.

'Ray would just kind of let it happen onstage,' says Bruce Botnick. 'He would sort of fan the flame a little bit. You know, see how far [they] could push it, because he enjoyed the spectacle as well, and the crowd going nuts . . . you got 10,000 people giving you love at the same time, there's no woman or man or anything on the planet that can match that. So if the situation kind of grew a little bit, Ray wasn't the one to go over to Jim and say, "Hey, you've got to stop", because

Jim always used the word "no" as "yes". Don't do this? Oh, okay, I'll do it, sure!'

Then things got really heavy. As Jac Holzman recalls in his memoir, Jim began making a lot of heavy eye contact with a Hispanic girl in the front row. Then during a break in the mayhem, as the band yell at each other trying to decide what to play next to cool things down, Jim directed his attention directly to the Hispanic girl. Grabbing his crotch, he snarls, 'Mexican whore, come suck my prick.' Then notices she has a boyfriend. Shit! Complete mayhem now breaks out as her boyfriend throws a big heavy chair at the singer. Cue pandemonium as the audience breaks the place up while the cops wade in and start breaking heads.

Then suddenly Jim leapt up into the air – and crashed to the ground. Jim dancing through the metaphorical flames, the panicked cops trying to get him off the stage but he won't move. Then cops can't even lift him. He has willed himself onto the stage. Eventually, Bill Siddons ran over and just grabbed Jim and carried him off like a dead body. Leaving kids behind the stage to start attacking it with broken wood. People are hurt, equipment is destroyed. When the audience is finally dragged out, Vince Treanor would tell Jac, 'There was just wood, like enormous tooth picks . . . just shredded wood wherever you looked.'

Afterwards, back in the dressing room, as Paul Ferrara kept filming, Jim tried to comfort one young female member of the audience who had sustained a bloody head injury, almost being knocked out by flying wood. The girl, despite blood dripping down her face, is clearly charmed. Jim, less obviously, looks rather concerned. But by what: the poor wounded bloodied girl or the dozens of cops waiting outside to bring their own comfort to him?

Back in L.A. a few days later, Judy Huddleston, who hadn't seen Jim for months, decided to drop by Bill's office, on the pretext of giving Bill 'a marijuana pill – THC'. But really in case they might run into Jim. Judy was in luck. He was arriving just as she and Linda had given up and were leaving. Bill had been nice but not encouraging. There are so many other chicks, he told her. Don't waste your time. But then he saw Jim, just to say hi and bye, but he recognised her and she went away hopeful. A few days later her phone rang at 5 a.m. It was Jim begging her to come to his hotel, the Beverly Terrace, a no-big-deal hotel in West Hollywood.

They made love, sweetly and passionately, but the following morning Jim went out to get passport shots done. The Doors would be leaving in a few days for their first trip to Europe, he explained, and there was still a lot of stuff to do. While Jim was gone, Judy, still a wide-eyed teenager, still hoping against hope, rummaged through the bedside drawers and found a note from Pam: 'Jim, I'm off for England. Hurry over. I love you. Pam.' Then when Judy went to take a shower she looked down and saw 'a bloodstained bikini bottom lying on the turquoise blue tiles. This was almost more sickening than Pam's note.'

When he returned they made love again but this time the menacing Jim returned.

'What are you?' he demanded. But she didn't know what he meant. 'You're a cunt!'

He repeated the question until she gave the right answer: 'A cunt.'

'Whose cunt?' he yelled. 'Mine, my own,' she answered. 'No!' he cried. 'You're mine! You're my cunt!'

He repeated the question until finally she got it.

'What are you?'

'A cunt.'

'Whose cunt?'

'I'm yours. I'm your cunt!'

Later when they went out for dinner he talked about his upcoming trip to Britain. He said he wanted to meet The Beatles. Judy said sure, why not? 'What if they just laugh at me?' said Jim.

When she asked about Pam, he dismissed it: 'Pam? Oh, I don't know – she doesn't really understand me . . . We've been together off and on for a few years. It's not really anything. I love her and everything, but it's never what I want. I don't know. I guess I'm just not ready. For anyone . . . I just don't want to be alone.'

There would be further collisions between the two over the next two years. The night he showed up drunk at Judy's door in the early hours. The time he came back drunk from Mexico, just showed up at her door in West Hollywood where she now lived with a new friend, Kathy.

Once, when she asked him if he was bisexual, he freaked out. 'I'm hopelessly heterosexual!' Lost his cool. Then a little later in the same conversation, he spelled out his latest mission: 'What I want to do is start a new religion . . . But first I want to be a movie star.'

At one of their last meetings, thoroughly miserable, Judy asked Jim again about Pam. He responded: 'She's always giving me trouble. She's always disturbing me – on purpose.'

He added, guiltily: 'I mean, she's been everything to me. She's been my mother, my sister, and my daughter, my friend and lover. Every time we start to live together I'm optimistic . . . Maybe I'm too idealistic but it never works out.' He sighed. 'I love her. I'm just not *in* love with her.'

Judy knew the feeling.

FIFTEEN

Hit Me, Babe

'The singer is American superstar Jim Morrison, leader of a Californian rock'n'roll band called The Doors. Through his music, Morrison comments on society as he sees it. He speaks for a generation who has spilt their dissent onto the streets of the world. For them he is poet, prophet and politician . . . The Doors' message is uncompromisingly loud. Please do not adjust your sets.'

So begins *The Doors are Open*, the 60-minute Granada TV documentary made about The Doors' brief trip to London in September 1968, at the start of their first – and as it turned out only – European tour. Knowingly or not, The Doors' arrival in Britain was seen by many of the fans who were now buying *Waiting for the Sun* and 'Hello, I Love You', their two biggest hits yet outside America, as a cathartic moment for what was now roundly known as the counter-cultural revolution. Just four days before, America had witnessed the bloodiest evidence yet of what was now described in the mainstream media as the biggest threat to law and order since the days of the old Wild West.

The trouble centred on the 1968 Democratic National Convention. With confidence in the Lyndon B. Johnson administration and its continued war in Vietnam at an all-time low following the massive losses sustained in the Tet Offensive that year, Vice President Hubert H. Humphrey and Senator Edmund S. Muskie were nominated for President and Vice President, respectively. Coming just two months after the assassination of the Democrats' first-choice candidate, the sainted Robert F. Kennedy, and on the back of deep political unrest that ranged from the arrival of Russian tanks on the streets of Prague, just days before, to the killing of Dr Martin Luther King, in April, violent student protests on the streets of Paris, mass demonstrations in London and running battles between longhairs and straights – young people and police – in more than 100 American cities, the Convention became a gathering point for America's most serious protests yet. They were led by the National Mobilization Committee to End the War in Vietnam and the self-styled Youth International Party (Yippies), who had deliberately organised a music festival the same weekend, knowing it would almost certainly spark a clash of ideologies if nothing else. Things quickly got heated when Chicago's Mayor Daley insisted to reporters that 'No thousands will come to our city and take over our streets, our city, our convention.'

Except, of course, they did exactly that and more than 10,000 demonstrators were met head-on by over 23,000 police and National Guardsmen. The spark that lit the fuse for mass rioting was the lowering of the American flag by freaks in Grant Park. When armed cops broke through the crowd and began beating people, the demonstrators responded with food, rocks and slabs of concrete. As the protesters began chanting, 'Hell no, we won't go!' and 'Pigs are whores!', the police used so much tear gas on them it eventually made its way to the Hilton Hotel, where it disturbed Hubert Humphrey in his shower. When the whole thing was broadcast live on national television, and recordings were endlessly replayed over the coming days, it looked to some like the coming of Armageddon, the crowd now chanting, 'The whole world is watching! The whole world is watching!' Nevertheless, when it was over, opinion polls showed that the vast majority of Americans supported the Mayor's tactics. It was later said that the Chicago riots all but sealed the presidency for Richard Nixon.

None of which interested Jim Morrison at all. When asked on camera in *The Doors are Open* if he considered The Doors a political group or whether that was just an image the media wanted to tie them into because of 'what's happening in the States at the moment?' Jim demurs, closing his eyes as if about to sing: 'I'd say, foremost . . . we're . . . uh . . . musicians and writers . . . the music can't help reflecting . . . things happened round you too . . .' Ray, meanwhile, is espousing his philosophy as succinctly as he ever would. Asked if there is any difference between art rock and commercial pop, he explains earnestly: 'In the new age, in the sort of new age that we're hoping for, is the thing where there won't be any separation. Where the artists, the people who are the greatest artists, will be the most commercially successful too.' Good old Ray, still chasing that million bucks.

None of which really gets reflected in the rest of the film, which intercuts footage of The Doors onstage with news film footage of the Vietnam War and various American politicians spouting their usual rhetoric. But with London then steeped in Che chic – the grooviest cats greeting each other by bumping fists and uttering the word 'Che', as in Guevara, the Cuban revolutionary who had been killed in battle aiding Bolivian rebels the year before – The Doors played along with their bolted-on role as American cultural revolutionaries here to fight the good fight.

There were so many requests for interviews with the man the *Melody Maker* now built up as 'Like Jagger . . . in skin-tight leather trousers [and] a poet of some stature . . . his audiences know he isn't kidding' that a press conference at the ICA, on The Mall, was arranged to try and satiate demand. They also cemented their reputation among the nation's pop fans with a live performance of 'Hello, I Love You' on *Top of the Pops*, which Jim considered a joke, and two stunning shows at the Roundhouse in North London. With Jefferson Airplane along for the tour as co-headliners, and the cream of London's rock royalty in the audience – Paul McCartney, George Harrison, Mick Jagger, Keith Richards, various members of Cream and Traffic – as well as the British film stars Terence Stamp and Julie Christie, for the first time since the East Coast bonanza six months earlier Jim put on really good shows. His senses for once largely unclouded by too much booze or too many uppers and downers, the crazy man persona no longer in evidence and the deadbeat loner who barely moved still some way in the distance, Jim Morrison was remarkably present in the moment, with the band, encouraged, coming on stronger than ever behind him. The Granada TV crew certainly got their money's worth.

Interviewed by the *NME*, Jim commented, 'I think I enjoyed the Roundhouse more than any other date for years.' He had anticipated a certain amount of hostility 'towards an American group'. Instead, 'they were probably the most informed, receptive audience I've ever seen in my life.' Speaking in 2012, John Densmore told me: 'We played "Light My Fire" and everybody got up and danced. Then we'd always do "The End" as an encore and everybody would always file out quietly like they'd been bludgeoned or something. Really, I thought, oh . . . they're taking the music home, inside, rather than dispersing it in clapping, and so maybe that's even better.' He offered a small chuckle.

Things began to assume a more familiar pattern, however, once The Doors and the Airplane departed for their continental European shows. Grace Slick had a soft spot for Jim ever since meeting him when Jefferson Airplane were recording their breakthrough album, *Surrealistic Pillow*, in L.A., a few weeks after The Doors had finished recording their debut. Staying at the Tropicana, the same cheap motel Jim was still a part-time resident of, she and the band came back from the studio one night to find a naked Jim on all fours, howling like a dog on their balcony. Grace found this 'both fascinating and frightening . . . He kept up the dog act even after Paul Kantner stepped over him to get to his room.'

Now seeing him work up close, seeing how he handled the adulation offstage, seeing him do his thing without yet seeing him deliberately trying to blow it, Grace decided that Jim was simply one of those far-out new cats who simply 'inhabited two places at once'. That she never heard him utter a banal word. That he was, in fact, extraordinary – and that she must have him.

In her marvellous 1999 memoir, *Somebody to Love*, Slick recalls being nervous when she knocked on his hotel room door. Jim had not 'hustled' her. She was 'the perpetrator'. It was while both bands were on tour in Europe, though she says she can no longer remember which city exactly, only that there was a plate of fresh strawberries on his bed. That they played around with them until they were smeared all over the bed. She describes the sex that followed as like 'making love to a floating art form with eyes'. That compared with the dark lord that inhabited The Doors' stage, Jim was 'surprisingly gentle'. He took his time, did it slow. Afterwards, Grace got dressed quickly and left. They were both supposedly in relationships and she didn't want to get 'caught' by anyone else on the tour finding her there. Jim just lay there with his eyes closed, naked on the bed, spent. He asked her obliquely, 'Why wouldn't you come back?' as if halfway through a conversation only he was having. Grace replied, 'Only if I'm asked.' Jim never did ask, though.

Instead, whatever sweet memories she would have of Jim Morrison were about to become blighted by the incident that marked the real turning point in the relationship between Jim and the rest of The Doors. Booked to perform at the 2,000-capacity Concertgebouw, in Amsterdam, on Sunday, 15 September, with the Airplane opening, members of both bands took the opportunity to spend the afternoon strolling around the city, checking out its pretty canals, it picturesque squares – and it's famous 'coffee shops', where marijuana, along with the tie-dyed clobber and multi-coloured beads, was sold legally. It reminded Grace and the guys from the Airplane of their hometown, San Francisco. 'The buildings were painted the same way,' said Grace, 'in the psychedelic sense . . . The business of having the door frames yellow, the doors red. The frames around the windows were blue . . . bongs in all four corners of the room . . .'

As the gaggle of musicians wandered around, they were recognised but not hassled. Jim led them, 'swigging on a bottle like a gunfighter', as Airplane's guitarist, Paul Kantner, later put it. 'All the way down this street they were offering us drugs of all kinds,' Grace Slick recalled. 'And we'd say, "Thank you very much." Put it in your pocket. "I'll have maybe a little of that later." Maybe I'll have a little drag off of this and then walk away. But you don't take everything you're given otherwise you would be dead. Jim, on the other hand, took everything that was given to him, on the spot.' She later reckoned that Jim probably ate the best part of an ounce of hash, not to mention several unspecified pills.

But Jim was Jim. This was how he rolled. And nobody from the Airplane thought any more about it until halfway through their set at the Concertgebouw that night. Jim – who had spent the hours leading up to the show carousing with some American sailors in Amsterdam's notoriously hardcore harbour – came staggering up the centre aisle, clambered onto the stage and started trying to dance with Grace, just as they were zipping through 'Plastic Fantastic Lover', one of their highlights. Grace pushed him away, but as the song speeded towards it bang-crash finale, Jim began swirling around faster and faster. 'He looked like a pinwheel,' said Grace. The band started playing even faster, 'because had had invaded our turf without asking,' said Kantner.

Faster *and* faster, until Jim, still trying to keep up, finally collapsed, unable to catch his breath. The audience assumed it was all part of the act. They'd read in advance of The Doors' wild man, who flung himself around in shamanic ritual. They cheered as the utterly zonked singer was dragged into the wings, where he promptly threw up then blacked out again. The local Elektra PR, Evert Wilbrink, went into full-on emergency mode and immediately rang for an ambulance. The rest of The Doors looked down at their singer, bowed and broken and unable to perform – again – with familiar disgust. Then went onstage, as scheduled. A brief explanation was offered – that sadly Jim Morrison was too 'ill' to perform that night, and that everyone could have their money back, if they so desired, but in the meantime, the band would continue, with Ray handling lead vocals. The audience stayed, the band played on, and Ray's imitation of Jim was so good nobody in the crowd – who had never seen The Doors with Jim anyway – really missed him.

'I didn't like Ray Manzarek because Ray seemed totally happy with the fact that Jim couldn't make it, and decided that he would be singing,' says Evert Wilbrink now, speaking from his office in Nashville. The ambulance whisked Jim to Wilhelmina, the hospital nearest to the venue. Wilbrink stayed to watch the show, then followed – alone. He stayed by Jim's side for the next 24 hours, fearful that he might die, or have done some permanent damage. 'You have to understand that he had taken big chunks of hash and swallowed it with a lot of whisky. That's what he told me the next day.

We had some strong hashish at the time [in Amsterdam]. Red Lebanese mixed with opiates, temple ball . . . that was just knocking you out . . . The doctor visited him in the afternoon and Jim goes, "Man, I've gotta leave the hospital. I've gotta go to Copenhagen." And the doctor goes, "I would rather have you here for a couple of days because it's better for your health." And then Jim says, "Well, I can deal with stuff. I had pneumonia once and the next day I was onstage; my body recuperates really, really well." Then the doctor said, "Well, let's sign you out tomorrow.'"

None of the rest of The Doors came by the hospital. It was left instead to Bill Siddons and Vince Treanor to organise the band's flight to their next stopover in Copenhagen, arranging for Jim to travel alone the following day. Only Evert stayed with him. 'I was sitting next to Jim's bed, talking about literature and paintings and stuff . . . I heard that he was a rowdy guy, but I didn't get that impression. I thought he was a very shy guy, and that his bullying father had sort of dented his personality. That's how I felt about it . . . that onstage he was a different personality.'

The morning he was discharged from hospital Jim took a cab back to the hotel, packed his things, then took another cab to the airport for the brief hop to Copenhagen. On the way, some people say they sighted him making a stop-off at the Rijksmuseum, to take a first-hand look at the Rembrandts. 'Now I've always said to people, "That's impossible",' says Evert. 'But I wouldn't be surprised if it was true. I think he was mesmerised by the Rembrandt idea.'

The show in Denmark was not a good one. John couldn't wait to tell Jim how easily The Doors had managed without him in Amsterdam, and Jim felt the audience was unresponsive and began taunting them. The band argued over which songs they would play, with Jim leaning on the easier-to-sing blues and the band pushing for more imaginative selections. Parts of new tunes like 'Wild Child' and 'Touch Me' were aired, as was an exquisite 'When the Music's Over', but when it finally was, Jim sloped off to be alone, surrounded by people in the dressing room, still feeling sick from his overdose – though no one dared call it that in front of him – and now with a new paranoia about his place in the band. Just weeks before, when he'd told them he was leaving, they more or less begged him to stay. Now they felt strong enough to do whole shows without him.

The following morning they taped six songs for Danish TV, at Gladsaxe studio, with Jim propped up on a barstool and the band set up on a giant American flag. The air-conditioned studio was so cold they all kept their jackets on. The performances were similarly frozen, brittle, aloof. It might have been the sterile TV studio, or the fact it was only ten in the morning. Or it might have been something else. As John would later put it to me, 'How did you adjust to a guy who couldn't play a note, yet could bring so much good to the cause – yet at the same time increasingly brings all this trouble too?'

Looking at the show now, what's most fascinating is how close the cameras get to Morrison's face, expecting it to catch every grimace, every pause, every half-smile, yet finding that it only really captures the Morrison mask. That studied, aloof, self-absorbed façade, out of which even the eyes conceal, or try to, their real intentions. The best moment comes on the

'Texas Radio' vamp, when Jim recites one of his more lucid poems as the band loosely extemporise around him, Jim directing his gaze straight into the camera as he declares: '*No eternal reward will forgive us now for wasting the dawn*' – the kind of thing that a just a few years later Patti Smith, another self-styled rock-poet and avowed Doors fan, would build her whole act around. Then, just as Jim appears to be losing the thread, Robby comes chiming in with the riff to 'Love Me Two Times'. 'Out of fear he would ramble onto something else,' sniggered Robby.

When the band returned to L.A., Jim and Pam stopped off in London, where they had rented a luxury flat in the heart of Belgravia. Jim loved the fact that London – unlike L.A.– was a city best experienced on foot. He would spend hours every day exploring the antiquarian bookshops of Cecil Court, in particular Watkins, with its rare and exotic collection of occult books, eating in Chinatown, going with Pam to Portobello Road market, buying antiques and hippy paraphernalia, digging the bands playing for free beneath the arches of the elevated motorway. Naturally, he thought Poets' Corner in Westminster Abbey was 'a gas'. And, of course, London was an easy city to score high-quality drugs in, so Pam was happy too. She was growing increasingly fond of heroin, while Jim was now indulging in the delights of cocaine. It certainly helped him concentrate as he stayed up all night, writing in his endless journals and scribbling verses of imagistic poetry.

Jim finally got his wish and got to meet The Beatles, when George Harrison invited him and Pam to visit them at Abbey Road studios, where they were making what would become the double LP that would be known as *The White Album*. There is an apocryphal tale that John Lennon invited Jim to help out with the backing vocals to 'Happiness is a Warm Gun', on the verse that begins, '*I need a fix cos I'm going down . . .*' It's not true, but given Jim's immediate future one can see why the story persists.

Jim and Pam were joined for their last week in London by the Beat poet Michael McClure, immortalised as Pat McLear in Jack Kerouac's 1962 *roman-à-clef*, *Big Sur*, about an alcoholic writer for whom the novelty of success has worn off, leaving only delirious episodes and withdrawal-driven nightmares. Morrison and McClure had been a two-hander waiting to happen ever since Jim had met Mike at the San Francisco Be-In nearly two years before and been flattered that a real-life poet might be interested in his work. Having successfully transcended his Beat credentials – now considered way too old, daddio – to become a revered figure in the Haight-Ashbury radical hippy scene, dubbed 'the Prince of the San Francisco Scene', by the Sixties' chronicler Barry Miles, McClure identified Morrison's surging fame as a means of getting his own work to a larger audience.

Jim had invited Mike to London to discuss starring in a film version of McClure's then notorious play *The Beard* – a fictional encounter in some other, more far-out realm between Billy the Kid and Jean Harlow that was shut down in San Francisco and Los Angeles for its 'lewd' content, before finally gaining an extended run in New York, where it became a *cause célèbre*, winning the Obie theatre awards – given by the *Village Voice* for best Off Broadway production – for Best Director and Best Actress. But McClure brought with him the manuscript of his latest novel, *The Adept*, which he sold to Jim as 'a mystical novel . . . about an anarchist Sixties idealist coke dealer, who is also a motorcycle rider', based on real-life people McClure said he knew in California. Jim was enchanted and immediately decided he would play this character instead – if they could get anyone in the movie business interested. They couldn't. The pair were sent packing by the Hollywood producer Elliott Kastner, in London to begin promotion for his next big movie, *Where Eagles Dare*, who told them it was too much like *Easy Rider*.

When Jim and Pam arrived back in L.A. on 20 October, it was straight back to business for The Doors. Jac Holzman was determined to repeat the 'one-two punch' he'd achieved with *The Doors* and *Strange Days* – that is, getting a swift follow-up out in the wake of the former's giant success –with *Waiting for the Sun*, still riding high in the US charts, and had booked The Doors to begin sessions on their next album at Elektra's own brand-new Hollywood studios, in mid-November. There would be ten days of rehearsals at their own place, followed by eight big moneymaking shows in eight Midwestern cities, heartland rock crowds, loud and proud, there to have a good time, baby, which Jim and The Doors sleepwalked through, except for one show in Phoenix, where a bored Jim deliberately tried to incite another riot by cajoling hundreds of teenagers to try and breach the stage. It was very nearly the Singer Bowl all over again, with Jim threatened with arrest afterwards for obscene language and lewd behaviour. After that The Doors just wanted him to cool the fuck out and sing the songs. They couldn't decide if they preferred him subdued to the point of somnambulance or so fired up he threatened to wreck everything. Then it was to be straight into the studio with the same Rothchild–Botnick team while the band were still hot from the road, to be followed by the fourth Doors album in the New Year, just six months after *Waiting for the Sun*, accompanied by their biggest headlining tour yet.

It sounded like a great plan. Only snag: The Doors had no new material. Worse, their singer was about to take a prolonged leave of absence – in mind if not entirely in body – that would extend eventually until his death three years later. Coming back to L.A.– coming back to reality after the romantic dreams of London – and being expected to start rehearsals with The Doors the very next day had plunged Jim into a depression that would never lift again. Pam had started in on him virtually as soon as the plane had landed at LAX. He'd been having trouble pissing and a doctor now diagnosed NSU – non-specific urethritis, a venereal disease related to gonorrhoea. Pam went ballistic, accusing Jim of getting the clap from all the fags he had fucked on the side in Europe. Well, he was on his own with this one, she decided. A week later Pam was back in London – with her latest flame, the Hollywood actor Christopher Jones, then on a career high with his latest hit movie, *Wild in the Streets*. Jim, meanwhile, took up with a pretty, blonde, bespectacled journalist named Anne Moore. He was sick of crazy chicks, he said. He wanted someone he could *talk* to . . .

Meanwhile, now sequestered at Elektra's new studio, an eight-track home-from-home, from its paisley-patterned walls to its eastern mysticism vibe, The Doors nevertheless struggled to make the ambience work for them as they started for the first time virtually from scratch, digging for ideas as the producer, Paul Rothchild, and engineer, Bruce Botnick, looked on despairingly.

'It's very common that an act when they're out on the road, they can't write,' says Botnick now. 'After they've been exposed to all the candy dangling from the tree, they don't think about those kinds of things any more. Not like they used to – and don't forget that's when Jim was totally bored . . . you know, they were locked in the studio. That's all we could do. That album took a *long* time to do. There were serious creative arguments.' The arguments were mainly between 'Paul and I', Bruce admits. 'I didn't agree with the strings and horns.'

Indeed, it would be the 'strings and horns' that became the defining feature of the album The Doors would decide to call *The Soft Parade*, after its final track, Jim's Brechtian declamation against 'petitioning the lord with prayer', the band adorning it with the kind of decorous, musical verbosity that would characterise the new progressive rock coming out of Britain in the shape of orchestrated jazz-rock snobs like Yes and Soft Machine.

At the time it sounded like The Doors were simply trying to keep up with the groundbreaking work The Beatles had just achieved with *The White Album*, or the monumental breakthrough of Jimi Hendrix's *Electric Ladyland* – both double albums, just released, that redefined what could be done within a so-called rock context, redrawing the maps and virtually daring everyone else to follow. In fact, says Botnick, the meandering, almost painfully ponderous material on *The Soft Parade* was the result of 'desperation. Because

Jim was . . . he was drunk all the time. He was trying to hide from all the pain that he was experiencing. There was no way intellectually he could deal with it and feel good. I'm not a psychiatrist. I can't answer that. But I know he was in a lot of pain.'

And the results were Rothchild's way of trying to compensate for the lack of strong new ideas? 'Yeah, and he wanted to keep the ball rolling. That's when it got down to the time of taking over 100 takes of something because he wanted to get perfection. I'm not condemning Paul here or trying to paint him in a bad light. It was an untenable situation and he did the best he could at the time. I mean, this was the number one group and we needed an album.' And there was one other key factor, says Bruce: 'He wanted to be known as a great producer.'

It was Rothchild who had come up with the idea of bringing in orchestral and jazz musicians to fill out the sound and try for something 'new'. Unfortunately, he was at least one album too late. The Doors hadn't come up with anything radically new since the rejection of 'Celebration of the Lizard' eight months before. In his own charming, self-deluding vanity, though, the producer had convinced himself he could carry the weight for The Doors. But, says Bruce, in 'trying to save the ship' the resulting sessions turned into 'drudgery' for everyone else, with Rothchild insisting on dozens, sometimes hundreds of retakes and overdubs in order to try and mould the indistinct sketches the band was noodling around with into something even vaguely coherent, let alone the grand musical statement Rothchild had been hoping for this time around.

'It was drudgery,' sighs Bruce. 'They'd come in and have to play over and over and over and over and over. And then overdub Jim and then, having to deal with him, you know? It was tough. It was hard. It was hard emotionally. It was hard intellectually. It was an affront to our pride. They didn't really have any pop songs.' 'Touch Me', the only obvious hit on the album – a yo-yoing organ riff lifted almost wholesale from the 'Break On Through' organ intro – as usual came from Robby, Bruce points out. As for the rest, 'I just didn't like the arrangements and the way that the orchestra was done at that time . . . that album, and I've said it many times before, it's not a favourite of mine, by any means. There's a couple songs on there that are, but that's about it.'

Bruce was not the only one having problems finding the heartbeat of *The Soft Parade*. When Jac Holzman heard some early tracks, he was aghast. He argued with Rothchild to shift focus away from the orchestrations, to get the band back to its roots. But Paul, who had also begun getting heavily into cocaine and was becoming even more of a martinet in the studio, if that were possible, stood firm.

'It was about a 15-minute heated argument,' Jac recalls now. 'Because [Paul] was doing too many takes. He was grinding them into the ground. It had nothing to do with the musical approach. Adding strings and horns was not new for us. We did it on Love's *Forever Changes*. It was the fact that Paul was going for such perfection he was squeezing the performances dry. I mean, he was saying, "This is what I need", on and on and on. And the band were frustrated, but they were tolerant of it because he was Paul and he had been right pretty much all along.'

The end results remain extremely discomforting to sit through. With tension among the band members and their production team spilling over into arguments and snide remarks, there were few highlights. 'Shaman's Blues' was a good title for an average blues-jazz jam with Jim riffing to no real purpose over the top. Tracks like 'Do It' and 'Runnin' Blue' were execrable, throwaway, 'please listen to me children' space-fillers of the kind any brain-dead club act would come up with. 'Easy Ride' sounded like a minor Tom Jones B-side. Even Robby's 'Touch Me' – which became the album's undeserving Top 10 hit – seemed infused with desperation, originally titled 'Hit Me', after a fight Robby had had with his girlfriend, Lynne. The only track that didn't quickly outstay its welcome was the swamp-blues funk of 'Wild Child' – which was the only track Rothchild didn't smother in over-produced coke-infused mush.

The only real moment of levity to occur throughout the tortuous sessions, recalled Robby, was when one of the numerous Morrison clones now routinely occupying the streets outside the studio somehow circumnavigated security and burst into the studio, demanding to know why they had written 'Celebration of the Lizard' about him. 'He was yelling, "How did you know that I'm the Lizard King, goddamn it! That's me. You wrote a song about me!" And he smacked Ray right in the eye because he thought Ray was Jim. Ray had his glasses on and they just crumpled. It was a mess.'

Talking to me in 2012, John Densmore said his main memory of *The Soft Parade* was of 'a lot of shit, strings and horns'. Though from this distance he did insist that, ultimately, 'we enjoyed making it. Ray and I had talked about fooling around with a bigger sound before we ever went in the studio, and so it was an experiment we needed to go through.'

Taking up the theme and running with it in his customary, deliberately over-the-top fashion, as if the more he blustered the more what he was saying might sound plausible, Ray told me: 'We were going into a totally different place. Ultimately it's the beginning of the realisation that The Doors [are] a group that has a great deal of possibilities built into it. Robby Krieger is a flamenco guitar player, for god's sake. John Densmore is a jazz drummer; a marching band drummer. The keyboard player can play classical and he can play blues and he can play some jazz. And Jim Morrison is a French symbolist, American Gothic, Southern Gothic poet, filled with all kinds of possibilities.' Barely pausing for breath he continued, 'And interestingly at the time, rock'n'roll for us had broken all categories. No categories applied any longer to rock'n'roll. My god, The Beatles were exploring, the Stones were, everybody was exploring. *Anything* was possible. *Anything* could be realised, as an outgrowth of the generation who came of age in the summer of love.'

Unfortunately, Jim must have missed the memo. He was so insanely bored with the whole process he began spending less and less time in the studio and more and more time hanging out with his cronies in West Hollywood, picking up boyish-looking chicks on the Strip and taking them home with him where he would only fuck them on condition they would let him do it anally. Otherwise, he was having trouble getting it up now. Eric Burdon, then living in a rented Bel Air villa while recording the final Animals album, *Love Is*, at Sunset Sound, recalls Jim and a parade of groupies coming to

293

visit – then staying for days on end, sleeping on the floor. For the next few days he had to tiptoe over Jim's half-naked body. Finally, Eric told Jac Holzman in *Follow the Music*, he had had enough. Grabbing his .44 Magnum, he put one round in, went downstairs and played a version of Russian roulette, aiming the gun at Jim and his chicks and clicking until finally – on the fourth pull of the trigger – a shot rang out, and the bullet 'ricocheted around the room upstairs about five times and then disappeared through the roof'. Jim and gals took off, pulling on their clothes as they ran . . .

Then, out of the blue, Pam phoned Jim from London late one night. She was in trouble, she said. Jones had left her and she had fallen in with Jean de Breteuil, the 'real-life Count', then hanging out with Keith Richards and his paramour, Anita Pallenberg, supplying them with his high-grade heroin and taking full advantage of all the fabulous connections being the new 'best friend' of the second most famous Rolling Stone could afford you in the London of 1968. Pam wasn't just 'dabbling' in smack now. She was a junkie, strung out and broke and forced to fuck the Count for her daily fix. Mostly, she needed money, but Jim was the only sucker big enough to still give it to her. He listened to her pitiful voice and booked himself on the next flight to London. But when he got there Pam was nowhere to be found. Jim ended up having to beg the Count for her address. Then when Jim found her, Pam refused to have anything to do with him. She was over whatever 'bump' she'd been struggling with when she'd phoned, withdrawing from smack. Now she was high again and didn't need Jim. According to Stephen Davis, They had a loud, very public row in the Bag O'Nails, the hip London club frequented by all the rock stars *du jour*. She threw her drink into Jim's face and he burst into tears. Then she stormed out.

'Let him cry,' Pam told a friend. 'He likes it.'

A few days later they were reunited, as Pam sobered up long enough to realise her best chance of junkie survival lay in returning with Jim to L.A. It was coming up to Christmas and London was just too fucking cold. But if Jim thought he was flying back to something more closely resembling sanity, he was sorely mistaken. In his absence the rest of The Doors had taken a decision that would more surely drive a stake through the heart of whatever collective consciousness still existed between the band than any of Jim's more *outré* shenanigans. They had agreed to allow Elektra to license 'Light My Fire' for use in a new TV commercial for Buick cars, with the ad altering the words to the song so that they now went, '*Come on Buick, light my fire . . .*'

Jim was apoplectic with rage. Beside himself with the scale of their betrayal, he couldn't calm down long enough to figure out what hurt most: the affront to his artistic credibility – equating such a deal with prostituting himself before the great god Mammon – or the fact the others had agreed to it without consulting him first.

According to Jac Holzman, the whole thing began when GM Motors offered $80,000 – over half a million dollars in today's money – to use 'Light My Fire' in a new TV commercial for their latest Buick. In *Follow the Music*, Jac explains that the split would have given $60,000 to The Doors, $20,000 to Elektra. When the offer was put to Manzarek, Densmore and Krieger by Bill Siddons, they all wanted to go for it. But under normal band rules no decision could have been taken without all four members voting on it. But Jim had gone to London without bothering to let anyone know where he was or how long he would be gone.

Says Bill Siddons: 'Jim had disappeared on us and nobody could find him and so therefore we couldn't get an answer, and Robby said, "Well, I wrote the song, I guess I'll answer." And he said he wanted to do it.' No big deal. A decision was needed immediately or the offer was going to be withdrawn and so the band gave it.

When Jim returned to L.A. and was told about the deal, though, he turned it into a very big deal indeed. He phoned Jac, who was in New York, in a shit fit. Jac talked him down, told Jim he'd donate Elektra's $20,000 to a film scholarship at UCLA if The Doors put up the same amount, which would still leave them $40,000 to share, $10,000 each. Jac reminded Jim that he and Ray had spoken in the past about having The Doors doing something to support film students at UCLA, in which case this would be an appropriate gesture, would it not?

Jim seemed momentarily placated. The commercial was filmed and began broadcasting. At which point, Jim lost it, began calling the band's lawyers, unilaterally ordering them to threaten Buick with a lawsuit if they didn't cease broadcasting the commercial. But when the lawyers checked with the rest of the band, the other three guys shrugged and pleaded that it was too late. Jim became petulant and said if the ad went ahead he would take his quarter-share and buy a lot of Buicks and smash them on Santa Monica Boulevard in protest. Eventually, Elektra and the rest of The Doors blinked first and

Jim got his way. The ad was eventually only aired in parts of the Southern states and the Midwest, where the yokels were too stoopid to care anyway. Or so the received wisdom of the music biz went. So they told Jim. But things would never be the same between Jim and the other three again.

'From that day forward the band was different,' says Siddons. 'Because he did not feel that his partners had his side, you know? He couldn't understand how they could decide to do that anyway, and he couldn't understand how the basic rule of The Doors – which is, we all vote – could be betrayed. I could understand it because I was dealing with Holzman, who was saying, "It's gonna go away unless we do it, and I think it's a big positive for The Doors' career. It's the first time a major corporation has used contemporary music." Jac felt strongly we should do it. And Jac had a big influence on the guys. Their whole life had changed because of Jac. The issue from Jim's perspective was, it doesn't matter what's right and wrong. It matters that my partners did something that we've never done before. They said yes without my vote and that's not okay. So he felt betrayed, and I understood it.'

Frustrated at the loss of income, insulted over the challenge to his ownership of a song Jim had practically nothing to do with writing, save for coming up with the second verse, Robby broke ranks and insisted that from here on in, any new songs recorded by The Doors would no longer simply be credited to the whole band. *The Soft Parade* would be the first Doors album to credit the songs directly to the band member who wrote them – in this case, as it transpired, that being mainly Robby. 'And that was a fundamental shift in the way that the relationship worked,' says Siddons.

Jim said he was fine with that. Just don't ever do anything behind his back again – geddit? Then he slammed out of the room and went in search of his next high. Or low. It was anybody's guess. The others said nothing. Not yet anyway . . .

PART THREE
Broken

SIXTEEN

The Thin Raft

1969 was supposed to be the year The Doors became more than just the 'American Rolling Stones'. This was to be the year they finally caught up with The Beatles. Instead, 1969 would become The Doors' *annus horribilis*. The year the whole shithouse went up in flames, as Jim would memorably put it. The start of a really bad trip . . .

Despite the ragged end to 1968, with recording on *The Soft Parade* still groaning fitfully on, and relations between Jim and the other three Doors similarly stalled, the first single from the album, 'Touch Me', raced into the US Top 10, peaking at No. 3. It would be the last time any Doors single went Top 10 in America but nobody knew that yet of course. Instead, despite the tangles and confusions, the resentments and short fuses, the band seemed set fair for another all-conquering year, at least in terms of chart success and ticket sales.

The New Year got off to a flying start with their first headline appearance at New York's Madison Square Garden on 24 January. All 20,000 tickets had sold out in advance. It was hard to imagine a more auspicious start to the coming year.

As they had at a pre-Christmas show at the L.A. Forum, the band also featured a bass guitarist onstage with them, Harvey Brooks, 24 years old and a tasteful player schooled in jazz but lately the bassist of choice for everyone from Bob Dylan – whose *Highway 61 Revisited* album and consequent single, 'Like a Rolling Stone', Brooks had played on – to Mama Cass Elliot and The Electric Flag. Brooks had been brought in by Paul Rothchild to add oomph to the sessions for *The Soft Parade* and had been hired to give The Doors' big showcase concert at the Garden added lustre. There was also a mini orchestra onstage for the night.

The Forum show, though, had been a downer, the crowd bored by the selections the band chose to play from *The Soft Parade* – a soporific 'Tell All the People', a righteous 'Wild Child', which somehow failed to ignite, a rousing 'Touch Me', their latest hit – the teenagers who made up the majority of the 18,000-strong crowd calling out repeatedly for 'Light My Fire', until the band finally gave in and did it for them, then had to endure the crowd shouting for them to play it again. An exasperated but defiant Jim finally called the band to a premature halt, then crouched down and asked the kids in the front rows what it was they really wanted. When they came back with 'Light My Fire' – again! – he stood and yelled, 'Is everybody in?' – the rest of the band exchanged glances, fearing the worst – followed by, even louder into the mike: 'Let the ceremony begin!' He then, rather magnificently, if wincingly painfully for the band, brought the show to a close by reciting the whole 20-minute 'Celebration of the Lizard' set piece without any musical support form the band, changing the words as he went along to whatever came to his angry, fevered mind. Ray, Robby and John had left the stage before he ended, the crowd eventually no longer heckling or even laughing but simply stunned into silence. There was no encore. Watching from the side was Pam, with Jim's younger brother, Andy. For once not even know-all Pam knew how to describe what had just happened.

The Garden in New York, however, would be an event of an entirely different character. Even Jim couldn't fail to be impressed by the grandeur of his surroundings, and the band heaved a collective sigh of relief as he appeared focused and completely into the whole thing, throwing his leather jacket into the crowd, then laughing and joking with them. Jiving on a whole new set of lyrics over the intro to 'Break On Through', 'Fat cats! Dead rats! Suckin' on a soldier's sperm . . . Crap, that's crap!' Only he's not being mean and twisted, he is being playful. 'You are life!' he announced grandly at one point, addressing one half of the arena. 'You are death!' he told the other side with a devilish grin. Then without skipping a beat, he told them all as one, 'I straddle the fence – and my balls hurt!'

The only dicey moment occurred during the 'execution' in 'The Unknown Soldier', when Jim hurled himself to the ground so hard and with such a loud bang that John Densmore thought he'd actually knocked himself out. 'I stood up from my seat and looked down at him over the drums. He didn't move,' John recalled in his memoir. 'The audience was so stunned it didn't know whether to keep quiet or applaud. . .'

There was a party after the show over at the swish Plaza Hotel in Manhattan, where Jim had his own suite, having arrived a few days earlier with yet another old UCLA chum, Alain Ronay. Word came back in the early hours that gate receipts for the Garden show had topped $125,000, almost $1,000,000 in today's terms, with The Doors walking away with a profit of over $50,000 (around $350,000), making them one of the highest-paid acts in the business. Jim toasted the band's success with vintage champagne and high-grade coke, followed by the more serious business of some exquisitely ancient single-malt whisky, which made him over-talkative for once and friends suddenly with the whole world, chain-smoking and getting down with the heavy Big Apple scenesters.

The following afternoon, after he'd come to, Jim played host in his suite to an attractive red-haired young woman named Patricia Kennealy, then the 22-year-old editor-in-chief of *Jazz and Pop* magazine. Jim had agreed to be interviewed by the striking young woman from Brooklyn while the rest of the band took off for a photo session. Jim was growing a beard and had had enough of simpering for music magazine photographers. Besides, this chick from *Jazz and Pop*, whom he had been introduced to briefly the night before after the Garden show, there was something about her . . .

Recalling the meeting in her enthralling 1992 memoir, *Strange Days: My Life with and without Jim Morrison*, Kennealy writes: 'He is bigger than I had thought, taller too, dressed in last night's concert clothes of unbleached white linen peasant shirt, black jeans and black leather boots. His brown hair is a little lighter than it looks onstage or in photographs, a deep rich brown with no red in it, shoulder-length and shaggy. The eyes are blue, and there is a depth in them, none of that shallow empty washed look blue eyes can so often have. The voice is soft, the smile frequent and charming, the grin devastating.'

Jim, normally so bored giving interviews now, became drawn into the conversation, which eventually went on for more than two hours. But then this was no normal Q&A with some chick from a pop 'zine. Jim found himself discussing mysticism, shamanism, mythology, music, literature, ancient Celtic arts . . . As Patricia got up to leave, Jim touched her arm and asked, 'Who *are* you?' Patricia told Jim who she was. And he immediately suggested they stay in touch, meet up again soon, very soon. It would be the start of the last meaningful relationship with a woman Jim Morrison would ever have. And it was as if they both knew it.

Back in L.A. in February it was another frustrating month in the studio. As an antidote to the suffocating atmosphere engendered by Rothchild's preoccupation with his intricately layered production of strings and horns, the band got drunk in a Mexican restaurant one evening, went back into the studio that night and began jamming on easy-to-remember numbers like 'Love Me Tender' and 'Mystery Train' by Elvis, and a long, rambling, improvised jam that quickly evolved into a Jim rant about 'the death of rock'n'roll'. This had become a recurring theme for Jim over the preceding weeks, telling one interviewer that he felt the band might soon 'retire to an island . . . to get back its vitality'. Now, with the band also letting off steam, chuntering away on an endless boogie, Jim growling and scatting over the top, their feelings were laid bare. 'I got a few things on my chest I gotta get them off. Now listen, listen . . . I don't wanna hear no talk about no revolution . . . the only thing I'm interested in, I wanna have a good time . . . let's roll!'

It was meant to be a fun track, a laugh for all concerned; in fact it was one of the most depressing tracks the band would ever record. Like being forced to spend the night on a park bench with a talkative drunk. When Paul Rothchild sat through the 45-minute tape the next morning he 'accidentally' erased all but the first 15 minutes or so. Suitably discouraged, the band never mentioned it again, though Jim would occasionally tell reporters about it, qualifying his words though by adding how he doubted anyone would ever hear it. (The truncated tape eventually resurfaced on one of the many Doors reissues and box sets in the 1990s, titled 'Rock is Dead'.)

Jim now seemed to carry that fatalism with him wherever he went. In his book, Jac Holzman recalls the stories that would come back to him. Jim now had his own corner booth at the Whisky, so there would be no one at his back, and the girls would come and fawn over him, Elmore Valentine, the Whisky's manager, would make a fuss, all that business of three years before about firing The Doors conveniently forgotten. Then once Jim was drunk enough he'd be standing up again yelling about 'fucking niggers'. The chicks would coo into his ear, try and stroke him down, but he would stand up and pour beer over the girls' heads. Then come on all sad and sorry afterwards.

One night, chatting friendlily with Pamela Des Barres, now making it herself as one of Frank Zappa's all-girl group, The GTOs, originally known self-mockingly as the Laurel Canyon Ballet Company, until the night they turned up at Zappa's hill cabin naked except for bibs and giant nappies, their hair up in pigtails and all sucking lollipops. A delighted Frank insisted they dance onstage with the Mothers of Invention that night – and that they change their name to The GTOs. GTO stood for many things: Girls Together Outrageously, Girls Together Only, Girls Together Occasionally, Girls Together Often, and any number of similar phrases. 'The GTOs would get dressed up every night to go dancing, cos there was safety in numbers,' says Gail Zappa. 'They wore these wild outfits [and] they would also get in the Whisky free so they could dance. Cos for a while, they *were* the entertainment . . .' There were Miss Pamela, Miss Christine, Miss Cinderella, Miss Mercy and Miss Lucy (plus, at different intervals, Miss Sandra and/ or Sparky). Having proved themselves by appearing onstage at several Mothers of Invention shows as dancers and/or backing vocalists, in November 1968 Zappa put them on a weekly retainer of $35 each. As Alice Cooper recalls, 'People just got off on them. They were a trip . . .' Not Jim, as Pamela now recalls: 'One night we were all at the Whisky – me and The GTOs – and Jim wandered in.' He'd recently let his beard grow, seemed less bothered by how cool his clothes were – or weren't –and appeared far from the chiselled rock god he'd appeared to be on the TV some weeks before, promoting 'Touch Me'. By now, says Pamela, Jim 'basically lived there [at the Whisky]. And by this point he'd become a terrible alcoholic. It was not so much drugs with him, it was alcohol. Jim just came and sat with us. He would sit with whoever was there whom he'd recognize. He was blotto, you know? Just drunk. He sat there with us and we were all there hanging out and all of a sudden he just hauled off and threw a drink in Miss Lucy's face. He just picked it up and threw it right in her face. She went, "Rude!" She was very upset and outspoken, and then he hauled off and slapped me across the face. Really hard for no reason!'

Pamela goes out of her way, though, to try and explain the context of Morrison's appalling behaviour. 'But at the same time, his mystique was growing and I don't know if you read it, but feel free to quote it if you want to, I almost enjoyed it, because it was such an anomaly and such a weird thing, and such a trip. I was offended at the time, but later I went, "Wow, that was amazing. That was a really interesting moment."' Or as Danny Fields puts it, 'You'd be surprised at how many rock'n'roll husbands have punched their wives in the face.' Pamela Des Barres was not Jim's wife, though, merely a supportive friend. Maybe so, says Danny, but 'One of his weapons was to turn on people. To bring you in, then push you out over the cliff.'

Jim's bad behaviour became such a feature of nights at the Whisky, suggests Des Barres, that it was almost expected. 'At first, when The Doors were coming up, and Jim was a gorgeous god, he was treated with deference and love and respect, and then the local people who got used to him being around, he was just like all of us, hanging around. Then he got more and more drunk and destructive.'

The crowd became inured to his spoiling things. 'He would climb up onstage with whoever was up there and interrupt their set and grab their microphones and pull his pants down and all those things that he did.' She says Mario the owner would 'get on the mike and say, "Jim, get off the stage."' When Jim ignored him, Mario would repeat the command: '"Jim, if you don't get off the stage, we're going to have to shut down the sound." But he wouldn't get off. So he said, "Jim, you better get off. We're gonna turn off the lights." And he [would] finally turn off the lights in the club to get him off-stage and then carry and drag him off.'

Would he fully expose himself? I asked.

'Yeah,' said Pamela.

At the Whisky?

'Yeah. He would do that. And he shoved the microphone down in his trousers, and expected the poor guy to sing through it.' She burst out laughing. Then quietened down again as she recalled the guy she first knew, compared to the drunken loser he became.

'He was funny and he was deep, and things had meaning for him. He cared. But then I watched the disillusion of this person. I watched him fall apart through the years. It was very gradual, but I remember one night coming out of the Whisky and he was trying to sleep in the gutter in front of the Whisky. He was curled up and he was trying to sleep in the gutter. He didn't even know where he was. People were step-ping over him. That's what had happened to his mystique . . .'

Another blast from Jim's past, Mary Werbelow, also recalled seeing Jim around this time. Speaking with her hometown newspaper, the *St. Petersburg Times*, in 2005, she claimed that she and Jim had maintained contact, albeit in limited form, since their breakup. 'I'd see him when he really needed to talk to someone,' she said. The last time had been during the making of *The Soft Parade*, when Mary recalls Jim telling her, 'The first three albums are about you. Didn't you know that?' To spare his feelings, clearly raw, she didn't ex-plain that she'd never really listened to any of his records. She had heard The Doors on the radio, but she had never been to one of their shows, nor actually bought an album. She said he once even asked her to marry him, but that she had refused. 'It was heartbreaking. I knew I wanted to be with him, but I couldn't.' Wise Mary always did know better than any of Jim's other girls. By early 1969, Mary had left L.A. for India, where she planned to study meditation. Jim never saw her again.*

As this was all happening, a new Doors single was released. The second track to be lifted from the *Soft Parade* session, 'Wishful Sinful', became their first not to make the US Top 40 since 'Break On Through (to the Other Side)' two years before. A whimsical, pretty pop ditty, it sounds like it was recorded in 1964, compared to the new hard rock that was now sweeping the country – on heavy radio rotation at the time were 'Crosstown Traffic' by Jimi Hendrix, 'Rock Me Jupiter Child' by Steppenwolf, 'Pinball Wizard' by The Who, and newest and most scintillating of all to young American rock fans, any track you liked – they were playing them all – from the just released *Led Zeppelin* album. Zeppelin had played a week of shows at the Whisky in January and Jim had been there for at least one of them. Friends say he was put off by what he saw as the unnecessarily histrionic vocals of Robert Plant, and unimpressed by Jimmy Page as a guitarist, but this sounds suspiciously like sour grapes. Zeppelin were now on their way to replacing The Doors as the coolest band in America. He especially hated it when chicks like his old friend Pamela Des Barres began raving about them. Even

---

* Copyright © *St. Petersburg Times*, 2005.

more so when it became clear she was now Page's numero uno girlfriend whenever Zep were in town.

Jim didn't care, he said. Instead he and his ever-faithful entourage were now more in thrall to a new show that had recently opened at the Bovard Auditorium at USC. The latest work from the New York-based the Living Theatre, a renowned experimental theatre company founded in New York in 1947 by the then 21-year-old, German-born actress, writer and director Judith Malina with her partner, Julian Beck, an American poet and painter, aged 23. The abiding philosophy of the company was based, it claimed, on the work of the French playwright Antonin Artaud, in particular on what he called 'The Theatre of Cruelty' – specialising in staging what these days would be termed multimedia productions, which work to dismantle the 'fourth wall' between the actors and the audience. Jim had read about and become entranced by them when he learned of their pioneering productions throughout the 1950s and early 1960s, in which they adapted works by favourite writers of his, Bertolt Brecht, Jean Cocteau and William Carlos Williams.

Having been arrested several times for 'indecent exposure', the outlaw troupe had spent the past few years mainly touring Europe, where they became the darlings of such equally self-absorbed countercultural 'icons' as Keith Richards, Lindsay Kemp and Salvador Dalí. Eventually, though, the novelty wore off and in 1968 the Living Theater returned to America and began staging what was to become its most famous production, simply titled *Paradise*. A semi-improvisational show, as always built around full audience participation, it included a centrepiece in which several actors of both sexes recited a long list of current social taboos, most especially public nudity, at the same time as taking off their clothes and moving among the audience, who may or may not have felt like doing the same. Because of this, the show had attracted equal measures of critical acclaim and public notoriety in Europe. None of which deterred either Malina or Beck from continuing to tour the show now they had arrived back in America. The purpose of the play, Beck explained in an informal address at Yale University some weeks before, was to uphold the idea of, as he put it, 'That madman who inspires us all, Artaud', and of 'the non-civilized man'. He added: 'Our work had always striven to stress the sacredness of life.'

Jim certainly thought so, and became so enchanted by the play he bought tickets for himself and all his friends – especially the ones like Tom Baker and Michael McClure who he felt would be most impressed by the experience – to go several nights in a row, throughout February, making sure he was in the front row for every performance he could get to. Jim came away each night determined to bring some of this 'reality' into his own performances with The Doors. As Jac Holzman puts it, 'When he went to the Living Theater he was seeking.' Now he wanted to 'try it out onstage'. The idea seemed a little far out but, hey, man, this was The Doors, right? There were *supposed* to be far out . . . right?

But as Ray Manzarek would describe it to me, almost poetically, more than 40 years later, 'What *played* in L.A. just didn't *fly* in Florida.' And without any of them knowing, least of all Jim, who was so blind drunk he could barely remember the next day what had happened the day before, when the singer tried to apply some of his recently acquired ideas to

The Doors' own 'more challenging' performances, this time it really would be the end . . .

The band's biggest, most lucrative tour yet was scheduled to begin on 1 March, in Coconut Grove, Miami, at the Dinner Key Auditorium, a converted seaplane hangar with low wooden rafters and a wobbly wooden stage. The band had originally been booked to play the Convention Hall, but the local promoters – two brothers named Ken and Jim Collier, of Three Image Productions, who also owned a karate club – had made the band a better offer to play the Auditorium: a guarantee, on the basis that it held more people, of $25,000, against a maximum possible turnover of $42,000.

'The place had not been used for years for anything much,' recalls Vince Treanor. 'It was old, dirty and *hot*.' What nobody knew until they had arrived and begun setting up the equipment was that Three Image had taken out all the seats, thereby swelling the 7,000 capacity to a crowd almost that twice that size, with hundreds more finding ways of sneaking into the rickety old building undetected. It was a ferociously hot, swelteringly humid afternoon and tempers ran high as Siddons argued with the Collier brothers over the arrangements.

Calculating that the Three Image cut for the show would now amount to more than $75,000, Bill insisted on renegotiating the band's own percentage. But, according to Vince, 'the brothers laughed at him'. In the end, Bill told them the band would not play at all, that he was cancelling the show for breach of contract. 'However, this did not seem to bother the brothers too much,' says Treanor. They asked Bill where the equipment was. 'Bill replied: "At the Auditorium, I assume."

The reply was frightening, "No, it is in our truck. If you ever want to see it again you will play."'

Jim, meanwhile, was having his own problems just getting to the gig. He had intended to fly from L.A. to Miami with Pam, but they had had another huge bust-up on the way to the airport and Jim had ordered her to get the fuck away from him, telling the driver to take a now screaming, hysterical Pam home. By the time he got to the check-in desk he had missed his flight, so he went to the bar and began drinking, waiting for the next flight. Sweet-talking the pretty air stewardess into keeping the drinks coming on the plane, when it stopped at New Orleans he went into the bar there and promptly got even more drunk, causing him to miss his second plane of the day.

By the time Jim finally staggered into the venue, Siddons had, on the one hand, what Vince describes as a band 'angry that Bill had been so foolish as to make a deal with a proven cheat', and, on the other, a now heavily bearded, slovenly Jim Morrison, sporting a leather hat with a skull and crossbones on it, so clearly out of his gourd on whisky and beer he could barely stand up straight. But it was too late to do anything about it now. The only option was to do the show and get the hell out of Dodge as fast as they could, they decided.

The moment they hit the stage, though, it was clear this was going to be one of *those* shows. The band stepped up into 'Break On Through', but in a weird reprise of his improvised ranting on the then unknown 'Rock is Dead' Jim decided to treat everybody with his own unique way of saying hello: 'Yeah!' he roared. 'Now looky here! I ain't talkin' about no revolution. And I'm not talking about no demonstration. I'm talkin' about having a good time. I'm talkin' about having a good time this summer. Now, you all come out to L.A. You all get out there. We're gonna lie down there in the sand and rub our toes in the ocean and we're gonna have a good time.'

The band still vamping the intro behind him are not yet alarmed, maybe this is Jim just revving up for one of those rare nights when he actually entertains the audience. Then Jim leans into the mike and begins jigging around: 'Are you ready? Are you ready? Are you ready? Are you ready? Are you ready? Are you ready? Are you ready? Are you ready? Are you . . . ah, ah, ah . . . whew, whew, whew, whew . . .'

Finally he begins to sing a recognisable verse and the band finish the song with a flourish. The audience, now over 13,000 strong, go crazy, or try to but most can barely move, they are squeezed in so tight; many just holler and scream. The band kick into 'Back Door Man' and Jim yells, 'Fuck! Louder! Come on, band, get it louder, come on! Yeah, baby! Louder! Yeah! Yeah!'

This time though the rambling breaks the song in half, as Jim goes into a verbal tailspin. 'Yeah, hey! Yeah, hey! Suck me, baby. You gotta . . .' He begins to howl like a wolf. 'Hey softer, baby. Get it way down. Softer, sweetheart. Get it way down low. Soft, soft, soft, soft, soft. Sock it to me. Come on softer. Hey, listen, I'm lonely! I need some love, you all. Come on. I need some good time lovin', sweetheart. Love me! Come on. I can't . . . I can't take it without no good love. Love, I want some lova, lova, lova, lova, love me sweet. Come on. Ain't nobody gonna love my ass! Come on!' At which point sections of the audience start to laugh.

The band tries to re-establish some gravitas by ploughing

into 'Five to One' but again Jim gets so carried away he takes things way too far, at the end of the second verse stopping to tell the audience: 'You're all a bunch of fuckin' idiots! Lettin' people tell you what you're gonna do! Lettin' people push you around!' There was some more laughter but the mood quickly changed as it became clear the singer was not joking around. 'How long do you think it's gonna last?' Jim demanded. 'How long are you gonna let it go on? How long are you gonna let 'em push you around? How long? Maybe you like it. Maybe you like being pushed around! Maybe you love it! Maybe you love gettin' your face stuck in the shit! Come on! You love it, don't ya! You love it! You're all a bunch of slaves. Letting everybody push you around!' Now he was yelling at the top of his voice, taunting them: 'What are you gonna do about it! What are you gonna do about it! What are you gonna do about it! What are you gonna do about it! What are you gonna do about it! What are you gonna do?'

The mood lifted slightly when in a prearranged stunt Jim's new pal Lewis Beech Marvin, heir to the Topanga supermarket family fortune, came onstage holding a live lamb, passing it gently to Jim while he made his speech about respecting animal rights and not killing and eating animals – the irony lost on the majority of the crowd, who were unaware of Jim's predilection for eating meat of any variety. As Jim handed the lamb back to Lewis he slurred into the mike, 'I'd fuck her but she's too young!'

The rest of the show continued in similarly chaotic fashion. When Jim asked for a cigarette hundreds arrived on the stage, thrown by the audience. When he refused to sing the hits the band tried improvising around him, on something that appeared to be called 'Away in India' – though the band didn't get it, a pained reference to Mary Werbelow's recent departure. Other times he simply stood and rapped with the people in the crowd, as far as he could see them above the harsh stage lights, which bathed the whole arena in stark black and white hues. Then he gave them 'Celebration of the Lizard', the band struggling to bring any feeling to the occasion, angry and freaked out as they were by the whole fucked-up trip at this point.

After Jim finally acquiesced and counted the band in to 'Light My Fire', it looked like they might get away with this one after all, and Ray and Robby and John all exchanged re-lieved looks that seemed to say, 'Only five more minutes then we're out of here.'

Then Jim got an even better idea. Recalling his recent drunken visits to the Living Theater show, he invited the whole audience up onto the stage, yelling, 'No limits! No laws! Come on, come on! Let's do it!' Then he began to take his clothes off. 'Take off your clothes,' Vince Treanor recalls Jim announcing. 'Let's see a little skin around here! Let's get naked!' Standing out of range of the mike, he joked to kids in the front, asking if they wanted to see his cock.

'Vince, don't let him take his pants off!' Ray yelled at Vince, who now ran up behind Jim. 'When I got behind him I slipped my fingers through his belt loops and twisted them down,' Vince says now. 'Now even if Jim tried to pull away, we were hooked together. I put my elbows on my hips and lifted. This pulled his pants up higher on his waist. So high that I think his voice went up a couple of octaves. I stayed that way for a long time.'

Meanwhile, however, large sections of the audience, now in a complete frenzy, began stripping off their clothes and hurling them around the auditorium. 'How they got the clothes off I don't know because there was no room to move,' says Vince. 'My guess is that of the 13,000 people in that room, probably 8,000 had absolutely nothing on at all. Many of the others, mostly boys, removed their shirts. Most of those retaining their clothing were girls.'

At which point the first policeman walked onstage. Followed by the two Collier brothers, both of whom were now starting to panic too. 'For some ridiculous reason, he grabbed the officer's hat. The audience loved that. The cop was startled and began to put his hand up to ward off the gesture but he was too slow. In one sweeping motion, Jim threw the hat into the crowd. The kids cheered even louder with that.'

Ken Collier, the older of the bothers, told Jim: 'Someone's going to get hurt!' Jim sneered: 'We're not leaving until everyone gets their rocks off!' But by now hundreds of kids had mounted a platform to the rear of the stage, which was starting to collapse, taking John and his kit with it. According to Vince, 'It was at this point that one of the brothers walked up to Jim, who was standing at the mike stage centre, and violently shoved him offstage into the crowd.'

It was now the front of the stage began to falter too, from all the people trying to climb upon it. In desperation Vince and some of the crew tried holding the huge stage amplifiers in place, to prevent them from falling on the people below. 'We wanted to lay them down on their back but fortunately things didn't get that far. I could see Jim heading for stairs and then go up. I didn't see more as things were getting frantic with kids still trying to climb on the stage from both front and back.'

He yelled at the others, 'Get off, the stage is collapsing!' They wasted no time doing what they were told, scrambling through the now crowded stage, and got to the stairs as pandemonium broke out, followed by the policeman who had been foolish enough to join them on the stage. Out of breath and still roaring drunk in the dressing room afterwards, a smiling Jim apologised profusely to the cop for throwing his hat and the cop seemed happy to accept the apology. Out in the arena, Vince helped heap the discarded clothes into a pile he reckoned to be five feet high and at least eight feet wide. With Jim still burbling about the Living Theater, and what a great art performance the show had been, the rest of The Doors were able to finally shrug it off. The very next they would all be on vacation in Jamaica for a few days, until the tour proper started a week later in Jacksonville.

Three days later Jim was sitting around on the beach smoking a joint the size of a banana when Bill Siddons called him with the news. The Dade County Sheriff's Office had just issued a warrant for his arrest on four counts: lewd and lascivious behaviour (a felony); indecent exposure (a misdemeanour); open profanity (misdemeanour); and public drunkenness (misdemeanour). Jim was dazed, couldn't believe what he was hearing. Was it the fucking joint, man? What did he say? Bill spelled it out. If guilty, Jim could be sentenced to five years' hard labour. Meanwhile, all public performance permits for The Doors had been revoked. The rest of the tour was cancelled.

The party was over.

Talking to Ray about it all those years later, he insisted he was unrepentant about the Miami show, even though the fall-out would eventually serve to crush The Doors. I asked how he had felt that night, seeing the energy Jim and the Doors were creating together get so completely out of control . . .

Ray said, 'Yes, it did seem that way. It was never like that for *us*. We *knew* where it was going. We *knew* what was happening. There was no place it couldn't go that we couldn't control it. I mean, it's not as if our music was out of control, or *Jim* was out of control. If Jim was out of control at all it was only because he was *drunk*. But the *ideas* he presented to the audience were terrifying. I think that's what it was all about. And the intensity with which the musicians developed his ideas was terrifying! Because it wasn't a good time. It wasn't the happy Beatles. It just wasn't. It wasn't the Stones playing the blues and that sexy, magic Mick just prancing around the stage. It just wasn't that. It was something else, something that we'd never experienced before. And it was like, *what the fuck are these guys doing?* And as you say, *where is it going?* Am I in the presence of *insane* people? Is everyone in this auditorium *going to go insane?* Well, *yes!* For an hour and a half to two hours, allow us to take you into a place of madness, a place of insanity, a place where Dionysus, that goddamn Greek god of *passion*, of *madness* and *drunkenness*, will *preside* over the evening's presentation – and we will no longer be in control, *none* of us in this room. That was a Doors concert . . .'

Nevertheless, I said, this surely was something else. In Britain, members of The Beatles and the Stones had been arrested for possession of drugs. But The Doors were now getting arrested for what they did onstage. By policemen with guns, who would beat you with clubs, lock you up for years. 'I get nervous,' I said, 'just reading about that stuff, let alone experiencing it first hand in 1969 . . .'

He laughed. 'Well, thank you for your concern. We weren't worried about that, though. The object of a Doors concert was, in essence, as Jim once said, "We perform a musical séance. Not to *raise* the dead, but to palliate the dead, to ease the pain and the suffering of the dead and the living." And in doing that, we dove into areas that were deeply, deeply Freudian, and psychologically deeply Jungian at the same time. So we were merging both Freud and Jung, which might seem impossible but it happened onstage, and really upset the establishment. There was just something about the power in the music, and that insane sexuality of Jim Morrison, that drove the establishment right over the edge.'

Processed by years of selling the myth of Jim Morrison and the legend of The Doors to generations of younger media folk, Ray was on automatic pilot now, I could tell. Speaking to others who were there at the time, though, and were forced to suffer the long-drawn-out fallout from Miami, one gets a very different picture.

'Bedlam, just total craziness' is how Robby Krieger remembered it in an interview with *Guitar World*. 'I remember Jim just rolling around in the midst of all those people and I was wondering if we would ever get out of there.' Even so, he says, none of them had any idea just how badly the whole thing would blow up over subsequent weeks and months. 'No, hell no! Okay, the concert was fucked up, and we didn't finish, but nobody was angry, nobody asked for their money back. And the cops were friendly – they sat around drinking beers with us after the show. Nothing happened until a week later, when somebody decided to make a stink about it. Some politician decided to make their career at our expense. Then it fucked everything up. We couldn't play anywhere for a year. The Hall Managers' Association basically banned us.' As Bruce Botnick observed wryly, 'The people weren't coming for his poetry or anything like that [any more]. They were coming for the event, and Jim in some respects was giving it to them. They came for chaos – we give you chaos!'

Overnight, the bookings stopped, with concert promoters across the country scared off by the threat of arrests and lawsuits and the destruction of venues and equipment. Of people's lives. AM radio also stopped playing Doors records. In the more conservative Southern states, including Florida, Doors albums were even removed from shelves. Not everyone took it that seriously, of course. *Rolling Stone* had a lot of fun with the whole shebang, publishing a specially made-up Wanted poster of Jim and headlining their review of the Miami show as 'Jim's Organ Recital'.

It was left to Bill Siddons to try and make sense of the situation. At least, at ground level. He admits to being shocked, not really knowing what to do, except watch the ground quake under Jim's feet.

'Yes, watching how Jim suffered because of the Miami incident and because, you know, his mission in life was to make you question your own values and standards and get to a higher place because of it. He was dragged down into the dirt because he was trying to provoke an audience to think beyond putting one foot in front of the other, and he was just dead drunk when he did it and he fucked up. And the deep South of our American culture crucified him for it. And it was *very* disheartening to Jim. It broke his spirit, because he was facing going to jail for years and years over an artistic expression.'

He sighs and continues. 'Miami was the breaking point. I think Jim really re-evaluated what the hell he was doing. Although they did continue working together for a couple more years, at least another year, that's really what made him decide he was moving to Paris and focusing on screen-writing and being a writer and a poet, and the rock'n'roll madness was something he'd . . . he had . . . You know, for the first few years he was the master. He was the ringmaster. Then all of a sudden it was taken out of his hands and he was fighting for his life. And he just kind of went, "I can't do that any more. I don't wanna do that any more."'

Or as Jac Holzman puts it, 'Jim was now in another world, he had separated from the rest of us because he had to . . .'

SEVENTEEN

Can You Give Me Sanctuary?

It wasn't quite over. The worst part of the trip had only just begun. But it was already hard to see how The Doors could come back from this. Jim turned himself into the Los Angeles office of the FBI on 3 April, where he was formally arrested, made a signed statement and was released on $5,000 bail the following morning. The Doors were supposed to have been appearing at the Memorial Auditorium arena in Dallas that evening, but, like all of their 21-date tour, the show had been cancelled when local promoters were forced to bow to pressure not to allow 'objectionable rock bands' onto their stages. There had also been a high-profile mass demonstration held at Miami's huge Orange Bowl football stadium on 23 March, under the heading: Rally for Decency, to which the recently elected President Richard Nixon sent a public letter of support. The place was less than half full, but that didn't matter. The TV news was filled with images of people 'showing their support' for a better, decent America and an end to 'disgusting' groups like The Doors and in particular the new rock Antichrist, Jim Morrison.

Jim seemed to lap it all up. Still convinced that the media avalanche over Miami was a storm in a teacup that would soon blow over, he revelled in his latest guise as outspoken rock rebel, secretly relieved that he wouldn't have to take part in the lengthy tour he had been dreading for months. 'Jim did say to me at one point that he hated the later years of concerts because all people wanted to see was him to get on the stage and freak out,' says Bruce Botnick. 'He loved The Doors. He didn't like being, as he described it to me, the monkey with the organ grinder. And [with] the guy grinding – he had to dance. It completely blew his mind, because he was moving on intellectually. He wanted to go and do a concert and not have to freak out.'

The rest of the band, though, was in complete disarray. For now, with little else to do but await the outcome of Jim's arrest, they all retreated into domesticity: Robby was now living full-time with Lynne; John had just a bought a house on Lookout Mountain for him and Julia; and Ray still had Dorothy. Even when Jim was with Pam the divide between singer and band was there for all to see. Pam had grown to hate the other Doors: for taking Jim away from her; for being more important to everyone around Jim than her; the way the other Doors' old ladies looked down their noses at her for being the crazy fucked-up chick on drugs that wasn't helping keep Jim sane. On their shared Jamaican vacation, the three couples had hung together, leaving Jim alone in his old plantation house high on the hill. Pam hadn't come along but the others didn't want Jim around anyway, not alone and brooding, looking for something to do.

As far as they were concerned Miami was not just a

one-off. Jim had been upping the ante with his wilfully antag-
onistic performances, both on and off the stage, for months,
years now. Miami had been less of a crazy one-nighter, more
like the brittle icing on a very foul-tasting cake. Even Ray had
to admit that The Doors were now out of control. Despite the
bravado he would display in the ensuing years, at the time, he
confessed, 'I was afraid . . . lost.' He said that when he looked
in Jim's eyes now 'I would see both of them. Jim and Jimbo.'

John, by his own admission, was torn between frustration
with Jim and relief that he wouldn't have to put up with more
shows like Miami. Not for a while, at least. Maybe never.
Robby offered a knowing shrug. Jim, he said, 'knew he was
pushing authority as far as it could go. We really did have the
sense that we had pushed the system to the edge and finally
they were pushing back.' Did Jim's unpredictability actually
contribute to how good the music finally sounded, though?
Or did it just get in the way, finally? "Well . . . we'll never
know, really,' Robby replied. 'It could have gone either way. I
think just the fact that Jim really was like a crazy genius, you
know? That's just how he was. We couldn't change it, you
know? So . . . what you saw is what you got.'

What The Doors got in the summer of 1969, however, was
to almost vanish off the rock radar. When *The Soft Parade*
was finally released in July it barely scraped into the US Top
10, peaking at No. 6 for one week only, and didn't make it
anywhere near the UK charts, nor several other countries
where just a year before *Waiting for the Sun* had finally broken
through for them. The preceding single, 'Tell All the People'
– which, with its flat Morrison vocal, had started life as a
radical call to arms, inviting the people to 'get your guns', but

ended as the kind of overproduced mush some anonymous, middle-ranking Las Vegas crooner might consider classy – was also a flop, becoming the worst-selling Doors single yet.

Bruce Botnick, who would eventually become the only person outside the four band members to work on all The Doors' albums, still frowns when he recalls the convoluted mess of *The Soft Parade*. At root, he says, Jim simply wanted 'to do the songs that intellectually could tell a story. He wanted to do his poetry. They wanted to do the same thing, the other guys. They wanted to perform more and let it grow. I mean, there's no telling if that had been allowed to happen whether Jim would have continued on his downward path, and whether he would have lived. There's no way of knowing. But obviously, you know, that album, in particular, was drudgery for everyone. And I would like to think it was hardest for Paul [Rothchild], because he was trying to uphold the image and, I think, today he'd probably look back, if he was here and just talking about things, that what he knew now he would have said, wait a minute, guys, this is nuts. Let's not try so hard. Let's get back and do things that make you feel good and make you happy. If it's not working today, we'll do it tomorrow. But that isn't what happened. We were making pasta through the pasta machine. It was hard.'

There had been just four shows since Miami, all painstakingly shoehorned into the space around the release of the album, in a belated attempt to drum up some publicity. But one of these was in Canada (at the PNE Garden Auditorium in Vancouver on 19 June) and one in Mexico (at the Forum, in Mexico City) on 27 June. The only shows they were able to see through in the United States were in Chicago and

Minneapolis in June – but only with the provision that The Doors agree to a new contract with what Jim called 'a fuck clause': that is, a special clause that would make The Doors directly responsible for any damages arising from obscene or inflammatory language or actions during their performance. Hardly the 'free artistic expression' Jim had long stood for.

The only real opportunity The Doors had to show off material from their new album came via a specially filmed performance of seven songs in New York for the Channel 13 TV documentary strand, *Critique*. Presented by the writer Richard Goldstein, who had first interviewed Jim for *New York* magazine during sessions for *Waiting for the Sun* the year before, considering the anti-Morrison climate of the moment it was a brave stab at re-presenting The Doors in a more accurate cultural context; less as off-the-rails pop stars, more as serious underground artists working in the rock medium. Introducing the band, Goldstein noted: 'To some critics, Morrison is guilty of gross excess. They see him as a sort of latter-day Isadora Duncan but without a bosom worth baring. But when the timing and the tempo are right, Jim Morrison can transform rock into something more than words and music, something magic.'

The programme then cut straight to The Doors playing live in the studio, performing an extended medley of numbers, beginning with 'Tell All the People', before segueing seamlessly into 'Alabama Song (Whisky Bar)' and 'Back Door Man'. With barely a pause, they then leant into the louche, thin, pop-by-numbers of 'Wishful Sinful'. A 25-second break followed for tuning up, then Robby began strumming the chords to 'Build Me a Woman', which was so low key hardly anyone noticed when Jim, slurring, rhymed 'Sunday trucker' with 'motherfucker'. Instead it evolved into the kind of languorous, non-event blues The Doors would increasingly fall back on in order to try and disguise Jim's waning powers as both singer and performer.

To their credit, the band, shorn of a live audience to pump them up, kept the tempo bubbling on a low heat throughout, demonstrating just what great players they had become in their years together. Robby was bearded and trim in denim shirt and dark glasses; Ray, supercool in smart-but-casual jacket and very long hair; John, moustached and intense, huddled over his drums, refusing to make eye contact with the cameras. Jim, meanwhile, looked like the drunk in the doorway of the Whisky the patrons have to step over. His beard was now so thick and bushy he looked less like the American Mick Jagger and more the scruffier little brother of Charles Bukowksi. His eyes, when they weren't closed, were sunk so deep in his head he looked positively manic, windows so dirty you could no longer see through them. In his nondescript brown jacket and loose white shirt he also appeared heavier than most people still pictured him; his voice was thick with booze and smoke, and his tongue swollen with self-medication and lies.

The only number on which Jim seemed to wake up long enough to really want to join in was on the otherwise unbearably open-ended 'The Soft Parade', which went on so long it descended into self-parody, Jim hopping from foot to foot like an old tramp shuffling around a back-alley campfire. Coming after the agonisingly cringe-worthy 12-minute interview (actually filmed the morning after the live performances), it belied everything Goldstein had just said about transforming rock into magic. This was rock as walking dead man, the caterwauling of a musical zombie begging to be put out of its misery. It would not have to wait long.

Jim sat on the edge of the stage along with the rest of the band for their interview, his far-gone eyes hidden behind huge Bible-black shades, his face receding almost visibly by the second into the out-of-control beard and badly sculpted hair, as he smoked a cigar and blathered unconvincingly about being a rock shaman and 'that whole trip'. Sounding and looking as alert as any other chronic drunk first thing in the morning, he has subsequently been praised for prophesising the advent, in the near future, of music made by 'one person [in a room alone] with a lot of machines, tapes, electronic setups, uh, singing or speaking, using machines . . .' But it's a rare moment of clarity in an otherwise sphincter-clenching interview. Poetry is mentioned, as are politics. But most of the audience had fallen asleep by then, safe in the assumption that they would not be missing anything remotely exciting.

Whoever this was mumbling into his beard and hiding behind his absurd indoor sunglasses, he seemed far removed suddenly from the figure Pamela Des Barres recalls that 'toyed with people. He played with them, he toyed with them. He was almost like a puppeteer, I think in some ways. He wanted people on his side and he would try and control their little environments. It was all a game. A lot of it was a game for him, I think.' But that had been before Miami. Now the game had changed and Jim seemed to be the one whose strings were being jerked around.

The only interview of real substance Jim Morrison gave in

the wake of the Miami debacle was to Jerry Hopkins, then the L.A. correspondent for *Rolling Stone* and one day destined to co-author the first substantial Morrison biography, *No One Here Gets Out Alive*. Accompanying The Doors to their show in Mexico City – originally to have been held at the city's largest bullring, the Plaza Monumental, but downgraded at the eleventh hour to the much smaller Olmos Forum club, after government officials became nervous at the prospect of so many young fans attending such a potentially incendiary event (the city had been experiencing its own firebrand student protests that summer) – Jerry became the first writer to really bond with Jim. A few years older than the singer and just as smart and adventurous, Hopkins recalls now: 'Everyone in the band was sure [Jim] was going to end up at the infamous Raiford prison, chopping weeds beside the Florida highways, getting butt-fucked, the lot. As you describe it, I guess Miami *was* the end. Let's not forget that 1969 was also when Woodstock was trumped by Altamont. After Miami, he did what he could to erase the familiar image of Morrison the lizard king, grew his beard, got fucking fat, and wore camouflage clothing instead of the hide of unborn horse. This was the Jim I knew. I liked him.'

Hopkins recalls how Jim had asked him to swap rooms at the hotel, which he did, only for Pam to start ringing his room, 'which was Jim's plan all along'. On the night of the first show, Jim and Jerry travelled together in a white limousine while the other three travelled together in a black limo. As they arrived at the venue and the other three members of The Doors climbed out of their limo, the hundreds of fans gathered outside began cheering and screaming. But Jim and

Jerry's exit from their limo was greeted by indifference. The fans simply didn't recognise Jim, still heavily bearded and looking nothing like the huge 'Young Lion' portrait of him that hung outside the venue's front doors.

Hopkins spoke to Bill Siddons about the beard and Bill admitted he'd asked Jim to shave it off but Jim had refused. As well as the show, the band planned to stay in Mexico for the week. Hopkins accompanied Jim on trips to the Indian pyramids and the Anthropological Museum. Jerry recalls Jim as being quiet, friendly, 'using his high school Spanish to communicate with the local fans'. Inevitably, Jim found a woman to be with: as Hopkins put it, 'one of the "presidential groupies", the band of mainly American women that had attached themselves to the president's son'.

Hopkins's subsequent piece for *Rolling Stone* – later reprinted in his excellent *The Lizard King* – comprised several interviews Jim gave him over the period in Mexico and the following days and weeks back in L.A. By this stage, says Jerry, 'Jim Morrison was more than an acquaintance and less than a friend. Ours was a relationship that developed when we found ourselves drinking in the same crummy Los Angeles bars.' After Mexico, 'He invited me to film screenings and poetry readings and took me to my first topless bar.'

The portrait that emerged was one of the most revealing of Jim Morrison's career. Hopkins began by pointing out that, far from seeing his career crumbling in the wake of Miami, as far as Jim was concerned things were looking up. He had recently finished co-writing a screenplay, said Jim, with Michael McClure, and had just signed a deal with a book publisher for his first book of poetry. He even had his own rose-tinted yet strangely revealing take on all the stage busts he and The Doors had endured over the past few months, from New Haven to Miami.

'You can do anything as long as it's in tune with the forces of the universe, nature, society, whatever. If it's in tune, if it's working, you can do anything. If for some reason you're on a different track from other people you're around, it's going to jangle everybody's sensibilities. And they're either going to walk away or put you down for it. So it's just a case of getting too far out for them, or everybody's on a different trip that night and nothing comes together. As long as everything's connecting and coming together, you can get away with murder.'

Jim also offered to discuss the merits of 'alcohol as opposed to drugs', explaining that 'on a very basic level, I love drinking'. He couldn't conceive, though, of simply sticking to soft drinks. 'It just ruins it for me.' There was a long pause and then he added, 'Getting drunk . . . you're in complete control up to a point. It's your choice, every time you take a sip. You have a lot of small choices. It's like . . . I guess it's the difference between suicide and slow capitulation.'

He also articulated again his belief that rock was now officially dead. 'The initial flash is over. What used to be called rock'n'roll – it got decadent . . . It became self-conscious, involuted and kind of incestuous. The energy is gone. There is no longer a belief.'

Certainly the rest of The Doors now feared for the future, though for far more pragmatic reasons. The Doors documentary – titled *Feast of Friends* – which Paul Ferrara, Frank Lisciandro and Babe Hill had filmed over much of the previous year, had finally been finished and screened for them and they were not impressed. With so much film shot over a six-month period, of concerts, of offstage happenings, interviews and casual cut-ups, the end result – 45 minutes of wincingly 'arty' movie collage, of which 15 minutes were devoted to a live performance of 'The End' – was so dire the band were furious. Ray summed up the consensus in his memoir: 'There were some great shots . . . but it was a jumble . . . as if decisions as to form and content had been made under the influence of some new, stupid drug.' Too short for a feature film, too short even for an hour-long TV special, 'I couldn't bring myself to say what I really thought' of the film to Jim.

Instead, the oddly shaped non-movie, non-TV doc, began to be entered into a number of film festivals around the country, beginning with the Second Atlanta International Film Festival, which Jim and Frank Lisciandro personally attended in June, and where they were presented with something called the Golden Phoenix award in the documentary section, aka the thanks-just-for-showing-up prize. Jim and Frank were seated with the makers of Atlanta TV commercials, and passed the time drinking half-pint glasses filled with expensive white wine. By the time a drunken Jim stood up to receive his award, he made a show of offering his hotel room key to the blonde model acting as podium eye-candy. The Oscars this was not.

Nevertheless, *Feast of Friends* would come to assume unexpected historic significance as the years blew by like a gale and subsequent generations craved footage, real-life moving images of Jim Morrison and The Doors – at their peak.

When, in the bitter aftermath of Miami, when projected income streams had suddenly run dry in the wake of the entire tour's cancellation, and there was no prospect of any of the dates being rearranged, for the foreseeable future anyway, Bill Siddons had informed Ferrara, Hill and Lisciandro that the film project was being put on hold indefinitely. When they went crying to Jim, we've put our hearts into this, blah, blah, blah, Jim claimed he knew nothing about it. Another decision made that Jim had not been consulted on, only this time he made far less fuss. Jim was too fucked up with fear about what would happen when Miami came to court. He did, though, suggest taking whatever footage they had and turning it into a shorter film, more underground, man, yeah. He even wrote them a personal cheque for $5,000 to help them do it, renting a room above Pam's Themis store where he and Frank and the guys would smoke weed, drink beer and put together what they now increasingly saw as less a documentary about The Doors and more an art study that focused on Jim Morrison, Renaissance man.

After the initial screening of the film in L.A., when it was made clear that the rest of The Doors disowned it, the 'faux Doors', as Ray derisively dubbed them – Jim, Paul, Babe and Frank – took it in hope to the San Francisco Film Festival, where it drew little attention as a filmic work other than for Jim Morrison's having come along personally to support it. According to Paul, Miloš Forman approached Jim to ask if he'd ever considered acting. But the Czech director was yet to make his first American film and Jim was only vague in his response. Francis Ford Coppola, then a 30-year-old fellow grad of UCLA was also there, trying to drum up interest for his next film project, *The Rain People*, starring Robert Duvall and James Caan, both of whom would also feature in his *The*

Godfather two years later. Coppola also saw Jim as a possible star of one of his many projects, an idea unfulfilled until he used 'The End' in such evocative style a decade later in *Apocalypse Now*.

Jim returned to L.A. suffused with the idea of starting a new career in film. 'He told me he wanted to start a new religion,' says Judy Huddleston. 'But first he wanted to be a movie star.' With The Doors not up to anything else for the time being, Paul Ferrara suggested they shoot some footage of Jim as a kind of screen test, built around Jim's still sketchy idea for a ten-page script called *The Hitchhiker* – which, as they began shooting improvised 'scenes' and Jim couldn't be bothered to actually write more pages, turned into something they called *HWY: An American Pastoral*.

With Jim footing the bill, Ferrara rented a 35mm Arriflex movie camera and bought several thousand feet of colour negative film, and he and Babe and various other hangers-on flew up to Palm Springs and began shooting randomly. Back at the motel, also paid for by Jim, after the first day's filming they each took a handful of THC, synthetic cannabis, and began shooting an improvised interview scene with Jim. This was the first recorded occasion of Jim telling the 'true' story of when he was a little boy seeing the accident on the road and the dead Indians, the same audio that later turned up on *An American Prayer*. The following morning, still high, they drove up to Tahquitz Falls, at the top of a canyon, where they found a waterfall to shoot a heavily bearded Jim swimming around wearing his black leather pants.

One of the final scenes of *HWY* would be Jim in a phone booth – by the bus stop in front of The Doors' office, across the street from the Phone Booth, the strip club they would all go to – making a call, which was also later transplanted to the posthumous *An American Prayer* album. Michael McClure was on the other end of the line, helping Jim get back into character as The Hitchhiker, telling how he'd just killed someone, but that it was 'no big deal, you know'.

The filming ended back in L.A. with them getting their friend John Patk to let them go up onto the roof of the 9000 building on Sunset, where they filmed Jim walking along its parapet. It was at night and you could see the twinkling landscape, Jim doing his highwire act as several dozen onlookers watching from the street below all held their breath. There were several other scenes shot then and later, the most memorable of which involved Jim driving his 'blue lady' Mustang, which was used years later in the DVD documentary *When You're Strange*. Jim also included a song co-written by Paul and his chick Georgia called 'Bald Mountain', and some music under the driving scenes in the Mustang.

The final released version was given its first official showing on Sunset Boulevard in early 1970, under the heading: *HWY: An American Pastoral: By Jim Morrison, Frank Lisciandro, Paul Ferrara and Babe Hill*. The placed was packed with friends, hangers-on, and reviewers. Some people walked out halfway through. Others thought it was great and told Jim it reminded them of something by Antonioni, who had just done *Zabriskie Point*. Most, though, didn't know what the hell to make of it, including the rest of the band, who were still waiting for the great Doors documentary they'd been promised – and helped finance – so long ago.

All the while the furore over Miami refused to die down. No matter that nudity at rock concerts had become almost de rigueur by the late Sixties. On Broadway, *Hair*, the self-styled 'American Tribal Love-Rock Musical' that featured nude scenes, anti-Vietnam rhetoric and the burning of an American flag (still then technically illegal in the US), had been a main-stream hit for a almost a year at the time of Miami. Kenneth Tynan's deliberately provocative *Oh Calcutta!*, featuring ex-tended nude scenes written by Samuel Beckett, John Lennon, Sam Shepard, Edna O'Brien and others, was already in pro-duction and would open Off Broadway at the Eden Theater on 17 June. A month later the movie *Easy Rider* would open in theatres across America. The album *Unfinished Music No. 1: Two Virgins*, released the previous November, featured a full-frontal nude picture of John Lennon and Yoko Ono as its cover. (Though Apple Records' American distributor, Capi-tol, had refused to release it, so Tetragrammaton released it in the US inside a brown paper bag.)

Everyone got naked these days, wobbled their bra-less tits around or let their hairy cocks hang down, what was the big deal here, man? It seemed to come down to the fact that Jim Morrison was using his cock as a taunt, waving it around like a burning American flag. It didn't matter whether he had actually got it out or not – and to this day there has never been a shred of evidence, photographic or anecdotal that he did – the media said he did, which was the same thing. And as we now know, but were then only just discovering, it wasn't actually about the feelings of the people who were at the show in Miami, but the thoughts and angry ideas of those that only heard about it afterwards. Something would have to be done.

Someone would have to pay. And there was only one person capable of satisfying that bloodlust: Jimbo.

It was now that Jac Holzman stepped in with his own plan to rehabilitate the public image of The Doors. 'It was not over before Miami but it could have been over after Miami,' he tells me now. 'John was disgusted. They didn't know what to do. They were being blacklisted in large auditoria around the country and they said, "What are we gonna do?" I said, "Time to make another record. Go into the studio. Work out your demons in the studio." And *Morrison Hotel* came out of that. Not the easiest record but it was stuff that Jim was comfortable with and there was some really fabulous material. So that was the right thing for them to do, because I knew this was gonna blow over eventually and they would go out on the [road] again.'

First, though, Jac suggested they should play two special high-visibility shows in L.A., from which they would extrapolate a live album – a kind of feel-good bridging exercise to get the people and the press back onside again, and show the promoters what they'd been missing during the on-going ban. 'Which became the backbones of *Absolutely Live*.'

For two nights – Monday, 21 July, and Tuesday, 22 July – The Doors would take over the Aquarius Theater on Sunset Boulevard, where *Hair* was then playing, and put tickets on sale for just two dollars a pop.

'That was an incredible performance,' Holzman says now. 'We had to come up with stuff to rehabilitate them but not to look like they were being rehabilitated. I remember the advertisement that I wrote for the concert, which was: "It's time for L.A.'s band to see them in L.A." And it was a thank you from Elektra and the tickets would only be two dollars and of course they disappeared immediately. And it was a wonderful evening. They had a great time.' He goes on: 'See, I wanted them in front of a friendly audience again. Because they had been really shaken and I thought they would get their sea-legs back more quickly if they were in front of a friendly audience, and the only way I could guarantee that was to produce the concerts ourselves . . .'

In the weeks that followed the Aquarius shows, the band got to play three further concerts, in San Francisco, in Eugene, Oregon, and Seattle Pop, where they appeared on the same bill as Led Zeppelin. But any hopes of this being the start of a more widespread return to touring in the US were quickly dashed when projected shows in Toledo, Philadelphia, San Diego and New York were 'rescheduled'. Meanwhile, *Feast of Friends* was still doing the rounds of various film festivals, being shown to half-bored, half-ecstatic crowds in places as far apart as Edinburgh, Santa Cruz, New York and San Diego. Jim put in a personal appearance at the latter, in August, with Michael McClure also appearing, discussing *The Beard*.

But if the band were thwarted out on the road, work in the studio on the projected live album was going no smoother. Rothchild, now heavily into cocaine and at his most tunnel-visioned, was insisting the group come and overdub the many dozens of parts the producer had identified as inadequate, either because of malfunctioning equipment or simply because he thought they should have played better.

According to Vince Treanor, 'Paul was not satisfied with the stage performance. The gospel according to Paul, "You cannot be human onstage." So he brought the tapes, the masters, from the recording machines, into the studio and then did overdubs of little places where he didn't like what Robby had done. Little places where Jim wasn't quite as clear as Paul wanted him to be in the lyrics. Some little thing that Paul didn't like . . . a drum phrase. Everybody was a victim, it wasn't one of them it was all four had to get their dibs in there. But it was during that session that Paul introduced the cocaine. I was appalled. I got out of there . . .'

The Doors played their final show of 1969 on Saturday, 1 November, at a large, anonymous hockey arena in Nevada, the aptly named Ice Palace in Las Vegas, where the crowd are good humoured but have little or no interest in hearing anything from *The Soft Parade* and only really come alive as John cracks open the start of 'Light My Fire'. Jim, though, has more pressing things on his mind and sleepwalks through the show. A week later he was obliged to turn himself into the Dade Count Public Safety Department in Miami, where he was officially arrested, gave them The Doors' office in L.A. as his home address and entered a not-guilty plea. The presiding judge, Judge Murray Goodman, set the bond at $5,000 and 20 minutes later Jim was free to go – on condition that he return for the start of his obscenity trial, now set for Monday, 27 April 1970.

Advised by his lawyer, Max Fink, to keep his head down and his nose clean in the months leading up to the trial, two days later Jim was in trouble again with the law during a Continental Airlines flight from L.A. to Phoenix, to see the Rolling Stones in concert – coincidentally at the Veterans' Coliseum, where Jim was permanently banned from appearing. His crime this time: getting drunk and out of control and harassing airline staff and other passengers. Both Jim and his travelling companion, Tom Baker, were arrested by US Marshalls as soon as they stepped off the plane at Sky Harbour International Airport and were charged with the federal offences of 'assault, intimidation, threatening a flight attendant, interfering with the flight of a transcontinental aircraft and public drunkenness'. When a knife was then found on Tom, there was no doubt about their next stop, and the pair were driven straight to the city jail, where they spent the night. Frank Lisciandro and The Doors' latest publicist, Leon Bernard, who had also boarded the flight with them, were free to go on to the Stones show, which they did, post-haste.

The trouble had started when during a delay in take-off Jim had lit a small cigar even though the non-smoking signs were still on. Told to put the cigar out, Jim and Tom, sitting tall and high in First Class, and with the whole world at their feet, as far as Jim is concerned anyway, begin to act up, ordering the overwrought stewardesses to bring their drinks faster, throwing food around and behaving like spoiled – and furiously drunk – children. When Tom Baker then began trying to fondle the stewardesses, the captain was called in to deal with them. Captain Craig Chapman was a typically stone-faced senior US airline pilot and not to be fucked with. Informing both Jim and Tom that they were to be served no more alcohol, the minute he returned to the cockpit the recalcitrant pair began harassing the stewardesses again, trying to trip them as they walked down the aisles, throwing empty glasses at them. Which was when the captain came back and told them they were both under arrest.

According to Tom Baker, speaking years later, it was all

'You never knew which Jim was going to show up,' said
Paul Rothchild, 'Jim or Jimbo'. (Getty Images)

On trial in Miami, August 1970. (Getty Images)

                                        sexy
Deep dark American night
~~————————————~~
Dark sad endless ~~night~~

innaugurated by silence
winter sadness in the calm cars

Winter photography
Our love's in jeoppardy (2)
Sit up all night
Talking smoking
Count the dead, & wait for morning
Will warm names & faces come again
Does the silver forest end?

Motel money murder madness
Change the mood from glad to sadness

Corruption of power
Masters working
Holy endless monastic~~ism~~
escape to caves

Jim's final days in Paris. Handwritten scrap from one of his many notebooks.
(Nils Jorgensen/REX)

Jim's friends from the Rock and Roll Circus, Patrick Chauvel (left) and Sky Eyes, Vietnam, 1969. (Patrick Chauvel)

An American prayer. The three 'other' Doors and a picture of their fallen idol. LA, 1978.
(Mark Sennet/REX)

The defaced grave of James Douglas
Morrison, Père Lachaise Cemetery, Paris.
(Getty Images)

WHEN THE MUSIC'S OVER TURN OUT THE LIGHTS, FOR THE MUSIC IS YOUR ONLY FRIEND UNTILL
THIS IS THE END THE ONLY END MY FRIEND
THE END

Ray and John on Sunset Boulevard, 1979. (PA Images)

Top right and below right Keeping the
fire burning, The Doors of the 21st Century
with Ian Astbury as front man.
(Getty Images)

Left Ray, Robby and Jac Holzman, 2012. (Getty Images)

Below left In concert with Dave Brock, 2011. (Startraks Photo/REX)

one of Jim's jolly japes which went horribly wrong, but, he insisted, for all the right reasons. 'He handed me a bottle of whiskey and waved a fistful of choice front-row tickets around. He planned to stand outside the auditorium and randomly hand them out to young fans who couldn't afford a ticket, saying, "This is courtesy of your old pal Jim Morrison. Enjoy the show." He felt this would be a good-natured and harmless way to upstage Jagger and company.'

The following morning, Max flew into town, where he arranged with Bill Siddons, also in town for the Stones show, for the pair to be bailed on $5,000, with an arraignment set for 24 November. Driving back to the airport with Max and Bill, Jim was told that, if he was convicted, the charges carried a $10,000 fine and a possible 10-year jail sentence.

The next day Jim was back in the studio with The Doors recording material for their next album, provisionally titled *Hard Rock Café*, later changed to the almost mocking *Morrison Hotel*.

The big idea for the album this time was the same as everyone else's in late 1969, to get The Doors 'back to their roots'. Two months earlier the second album from The Band – the roots rock revivalists who had earned their spurs backing Bob Dylan through his last significant tours in 1966 – had been released and now sat at No. 2 in the US charts. The most frequently played 'rock' record on the radio was their single, 'Up on Cripple Creek'. The Beatles, having ditched the orchestrated superpop of *Sgt. Pepper* in favour of a return to their roots with the earthy rock of the final album they recorded, *Abbey Road*, released in the US in October 1969, and preceded by the pointedly retro 'Get Back' single, also appeared to be signalling the way back to a more 'real' state of musical mind. While Bob Dylan retreated so far back into the history of rock he'd ended up releasing an album so square – *Nashville Skyline* – critics found it hard to believe he wasn't putting them on.

The Doors, though, had a more pressing need for a return to simpler, less bombastic music than that which Paul Rothchild had coerced them into on *The Soft Parade*. Simple blues and balls-out rock was all Jim Morrison could now manage. He simply didn't have the attention span – or the voice – any more for anything more sophisticated or time-consuming. Nevertheless, the sessions were uphill all the way, says Bruce Botnick.

'Some of it was real tough, yeah. That was a concentrated effort to get away from *Soft Parade* and back to the roots. But even then that was a struggle . . . Many was a time when Ray, in particular, would go into Jim's poetry book, see something interesting, do some editing, and sit with the other two guys and they'd come up with an arrangement. Jim might have a smattering of a melody . . . I mean, it still kept going but it just wasn't that block of creativity from Jim . . .'

Paul Rothchild, meanwhile, might have been ready to accept that the experiment of *The Soft Parade* had not proved a hit, but he deeply resented having to try and work with a Jim Morrison that had always been a loose cannon in the studio, but at least in the past had also been able to come up with songs, lyrics and melodies, and been able to sing them well too. Now he was simply a dishevelled drunk, as far as Paul could tell.

It was getting to the point where he couldn't stand the

sight of Jim any more. 'Morrison looked ugly,' he told Jerry Hopkins in *The Lizard King*. 'He was unhappy with his role as a national sex symbol, and after the Miami trial he did everything in his power to obliterate that. He gained enormous weight; he grew a beard.' Paul had 'grown tired of dragging the Doors from one album to another, especially an unwilling Jim, and he had virtually dried up. Two out of three times Jim would either not want to work or would go into the studio drunk. He would intentionally disrupt things – never fruitfully. Most of my energies were spent trying to coordinate Jim with the group.'

Bill Siddons recalled one session where Jim came into rehearsals and drank 36 beers. 'The situation was dire,' Ray would confess. He and the rest of the band had come to realise at last that 'Jim was an alcoholic.' Ray tried to qualify it by pointing out that as far as he knew 'a genetic predisposition to alcoholism ran in his family. It was hard to tell him to clean up his act.' Nevertheless, attempts were made. One afternoon during the *Morrison Hotel* sessions, Ray, John and Robby drove Jim over to Robby's father's house and sat him by the pool for 'a chat'. According to Ray, 'We told him, "This is seriously affecting us all now as a group, and you physically." Jim says, "I know. I drink too much and I'm trying to quit." Which was a rare admission. We told him we'd help. Jim said, "Thanks. Now let's go get some lunch at the Lucky-U. I want some funky Mexican food and a drink." That was Morrison. The romantic poet who wrote "I woke up this morning, got myself a beer." A real "Fuck you!" line. Unfortunately that was the reality. Jim's attitude was always, "Look out, man, I'm hell-bent on destruction." We couldn't moralise. We figured he might emerge from the spiral, but working with Jim in the studio was the only way we knew how to transcend his problem.'

The result was, paradoxically, the most 'up'-sounding Doors album of them all. Opening with 'Roadhouse Blues', featuring the wailing harmonica of an uncredited John Sebastian and the ass-tight bass of veteran rockabilly star Lonnie Mack, here were Jim and the band opening up to where they were at in a way that is both fun and faintly disturbing. It would become the band's new show opener and road anthem throughout the coming months as they returned fitfully to full-time concert commitments.

Other new tracks worth the wait included 'Peace Frog', a funky hunk of L.A. shimmy that found Robby punching out one of his most memorable riffs as Jim scatted wildly about 'Blood on the streets . . .' of New Haven, of Chicago, on a river of sadness, and of fantastic L.A., the lyrics for which Paul Rothchild found in a rough poem headed 'Abortion Stories' in one of the notebooks Jim had left lying around the studio while he disappeared to the Phone Booth for drinks with Paul and Babe and the gang. Other highlights were 'Blue Sunday', a tremulous love song to Pam, or maybe Judy, or maybe Eve, or maybe that chick he'd fucked the other night after the Whisky when he couldn't get it up, not even when she bared her ass and pushed butter into it with her pretty little fingers. It didn't matter; the song was tender and sweet. 'Queen of the Highway', one of the last truly great Morrison/ Krieger numbers, electric jazz piano, snake-hipped guitar, patty-cake percussion and Jim's voice, honeyed again, suddenly, his lyrics exquisite, showed just what The Doors were still capable of, where they might yet go, if they could only keep their singer from setting himself on fire.

Others were repurposed or older tracks, the most lovely, 'Indian Summer', a moment of quiet transcendence constructed from the dying embers of 'The End', as if Jim had chosen to love his brothers and sisters instead of killing his father and fucking his mother. 'Waiting for the Sun', revisited from the original 1968 sessions, was now dated yet still moving enough to hold sway on an album bubbling and rippling with new hope.

Others still were wonderfully wrought facsimiles of great tunes The Doors might have come up with all on their own had they the collective willpower to still accomplish such feats but here were cut and shut together with great skill by Paul Rothchild, whose perfectionism was nevertheless once again driving them all slowly mad. 'Land Ho!', another dated-sounding piece, an 'ironic' take on the traditional sea shanty, filled up four minutes of the listeners' lives they would never get back. 'Ship of Fools', yet another variant on the riff to 'Break On Through (to the Others Side)', could equally have turned up on either of the first two Doors albums. Jim 'borrowed' the title and subject matter of 'The Spy' from Anaïs Nin's novel *A Spy in the House of Love*, in which the heroine, Sabina, plays deliberately dangerous games of desire, intoxicated by the principle of pleasure for its own sake, Jim knowingly crooning about 'your deepest, secret fears', and as such it is one of the most truly autobiographical songs on the entire album.

As Pamela Des Barres notes, in his personal relationships with women, Jim always 'demanded the leeway. He was not going to do anything for anybody. He was sort of a hedonist, I would say, and he was going to do whatever he was going to do, and either you accepted that or you were not in his life. That's the kind of person he was. He never got to grow up. He never got to grow up and fix his ways.'

Time, never their friend, was now running out for Jim and The Doors. When the singer and his so-called friend Tom Baker failed to turn up for their scheduled court appearance in Phoenix on 24 November, sending Max Fink to register their joint not-guilty plea instead, Judge William Copple went ahead and set the trial date for 17 February 1970, in the US District Court in Phoenix. With the Miami trial date set for just two months after that, Jim was looking at a potential combined jail time of over 13 years.

EIGHTEEN

The Witching Hour

The beginning of 1970, the start of a whole new decade, was supposed to have been a time of renewal for The Doors, for America, for the entire free world. Instead it just felt like the Sixties gone bad. America was still waging war in Southeast Asia. Britain was still crumbling while Europe remained aloof. In rock, the dream as personified by Woodstock in August 1969 – an event from which The Doors were pointedly absent, because, according to Bill Siddons now, 'They exclusively headlined and did not want to be one of many', but which Robby Krieger once explained away as being because they thought it would be a 'second class repeat of Monterey Pop Festival', a decision they came to regret – had turned into the nightmare of the Rolling Stones' free outdoor show at Altamont Racetrack in December, where an 18-year-old, Meredith Hunter, was hideously stabbed and clubbed to death by Hell's Angels.

In the same period, the Manson murders and subsequent arrests had turned L.A. from fun-loving and free into a paranoiac's paradise. People – affluent music and movie people especially – now carried guns in their cars. With cocaine and heroin replacing weed and acid as the drugs *du jour*, the new 'heavy manners' under which America in general and L.A. in particular operated made Jim Morrison's antics in Miami and elsewhere seem suddenly, weirdly, in tune with the times. Blood on the streets of fantastic L.A., baby . . .

Nevertheless, the signs, at least for The Doors, were encouraging. When Henry Diltz shot the photographs that would be used on the cover of the new Doors album, he at least had a for once clean-shaven Jim to shoot and try to make look pretty. By now the working title of *Hard Rock Café* had been passed over in favour of the much more obviously commercial *Morrison Hotel*. Side One would still be billed on the sleeve as *Hard Rock Café* – and Side Two as *Morrison Hotel*. The band had found a real-life Morrison Hotel, in the skid row section of downtown L.A. (1246 Hope Street, to be precise), to go with the real-life Hard Rock Café at 300 East 5th Street, and Diltz photographed them at both locations, going 'guerrilla' to get the shots when the owner of the actual Morrison Hotel refused permission for them to shoot inside his hotel, getting the band to hurriedly pose when the manager's back was turned.

In fact the real reason why Jim had taken to shaving again – albeit temporarily – was because his lawyer, Max Fink, had talked him into it, so that he would look the part of the successful, clean-cut young musician when the trial for 'interfering' with the flight to Phoenix came up in February. As it transpired, this nearly put the nail in the coffin of the case when a clean-shaven Jim turned up in court with Tom Baker – who had recently grown a full-length beard – and the stewardess got the two of them mixed up, with the result that Jim was the one found guilty of all charges, rather than Baker, who had been the real perpetrator. It took several weeks for Fink to persuade the court of the mistaken identity, during which time Jim and Tom fell out after Baker refused to stand up and admit the truth to the court. It all came to a predictably drunken head during a party at Elektra celebrating the opening of a new office in West Hollywood, when Tom accused Jim of being a hypocrite for 'financing the very authority you claim interest in overthrowing'. Jim's response: to shove Baker over a desk and proceed to start smashing the new office up. Eventually bundled into the back of a limo, Steve Harris yelled at the driver: 'Get him the hell away from here!' Jim and Tom rarely spoke again.

With the Miami trial now put back until August, The Doors were relatively free to roam the country again. By the time *Morrison Hotel* was released to their best reviews since their first album three years before, The Doors had announced their arrival back onto the American concert stage with four shows over two sold-out nights at the Felt Forum in New York. A 4,000-capacity adjunct to Madison Square Garden, chosen because of its resemblance to the more 'intimate' feel of the Aquarius Theater in L.A., where they had turned in such great shows the previous summer – rather than the colossal chasm of the Garden itself, deemed too reminiscent of the faceless Miami show for comfort – these shows would again be taped by Rothchild, still searching for the perfect Doors performances for their projected live album.

Billed as the Roadhouse Blues Tour – a shrewd move designed to signal the new, bolder, hard-assed direction The

Doors were now moving in, as far away as possible from the flatulent overproduced *mélange* of *The Soft Parade* and much more in tune with the born-to-be-wild mood of American rock in the wake of the game-changing success of the movie *Easy Rider*, the surprise success story of the year, and the gimlet-eyed take-no-prisoners-style Seventies rock, as best exemplified by Led Zeppelin and other wilfully wrongheaded road warriors. The Felt Forum shows were, like the Aquarius shows six months before, a seeming triumphal return to form. At least, while the party mood lasted. Which, for Jim, was never quite long enough any more.

Jim now travelled with his own entourage separately from the rest of the band, and when his mood altered from set to set no one was sure any more what the cause was, though Ray and John and Robby could always hazard a pretty accurate guess, depending on just how fucked up their singer was. On coke, he could still be a defiant presence, ready to play for longer than contracted to, making with the jokes and the moves, giving it his all, or what was left of it. On booze and downers he would be verging on the incoherent, 'just holding on to the mike some nights', as Ray would later recall.

Reviews were varied. 'Mr. Morrison has had trouble before when the police of other cities found his performances variously lewd, lascivious, indecent and profane,' began the piece in the *New York Times*. 'But by the standards of the Off Broadway stage, Mr. Morrison's performance is fairly tame. Saturday he kept his clothes on and made no gestures that could offend.' But the *Village Voice*, early adopters of the Morrison mystique, went for the kill, describing an offstage sighting of Jim a few nights later at a John Sebastian gig at the

Bitter End club as 'a shadow of himself, with his face grown chubby, his body showing flab, his once shoulder-length hair receding into his forehead.'

It was also in New York that Jim renewed his relationship with Patricia Kennealy, the pretty red-haired occultist he had become fascinated by the previous year. Patricia had made sure to stay in touch, but as with all Jim's women, no matter how significant, he was not a consistent presence in her life. But when he was with her, she felt like he was all hers. Pam had joined Jim in New York, which meant getting together with Patricia was difficult, but, of course, Jim found a way, grabbing her at the after-show party in the Penthouse Suite at the Hilton, whispering into her hair, as she later put it, 'I want to fuck you.' Patricia looked at him: 'Well, call.'

He did, the very next afternoon, begging to come over to her apartment. When he arrived, recalls Patricia, he ripped her clothes off and dragged her to the bedroom, where they spent the rest of the day making love and talking. The next time Patricia saw Jim was later that night, at a party at Jac Holzman's apartment, where Pam was also in attendance and where, to Jim's mounting horror, she and Patricia spent most of the time talking. Jim's witchy affair was about to take a sharp turn, something he seemed to welcome, almost as if it were a dare. Then, suddenly, without even the perceptive Patricia expecting it, two nights later, after Pam had left for L.A., Jim turned up at Patricia's door very excited. His boots covered in snow, he took her into the living room and gave her a little box. When she opened it she was stunned to find a small, exquisitely beautiful antique ring. Overcome, Patricia found the finger it fitted the best and put it on; then, as she recalls, the two lovers sat on pillows and sang to each other, at Jim's bidding. Shyly at first, then with mounting gusto, Patricia sang for Jim a 16th-century love song: '*Westron wynde, when wilt thou blow / The small raine down can raine / Cryst, if my love were in my armes / And I in my bedde again . . .*'

Jim, enthralled, enchanted, relieved to be out of the rock'n'roll maelstrom and into something far, far away, spent the rest of the night there. And the next night and the next . . .

There were six more Roadhouse Blues shows in February, all around the release of *Morrison Hotel*. Much better received than its two predecessors – *Creem*'s editor, Dave Marsh, described it as 'the most horrifying rock and roll I have ever heard. When they're good, they're simply unbeatable', while *Circus* announced it as 'possibly the best album yet from the Doors . . . good hard, evil rock' – it had gone gold within three weeks, reaching No. 4 in the US, their best chart position for two years. This was despite the lack of a recognisable hit single from the album: 'You Make Me Real' was issued to American radio stations, but in an era when singles were becoming increasingly frowned on by 'serious' rock fans, the stations hardly played it, favouring instead deep cuts from the album like 'Peace Frog' and 'Roadhouse Blues', which only made the band prouder. They were hip again and resisted suggestions that 'Waiting for the Sun' was a hit waiting to happen.

There were 13 more Doors shows around the United States throughout the spring and early summer, with Paul Rothchild turning up to record several of them. Quality varied so much not just between shows but between numbers in the set that the band could go from world-conquering giants for half a set in Boston to teetering on the brink of self-destruction again in Baltimore, where Jim was so drunk he could barely bring himself to move his lips. Even when they were good there were problems. At Cobo Arena in Detroit, on 8 May, they played brilliantly for more than four hours – the encore of 'The End' alone lasted almost an hour, with Jim improvising madly – yet found themselves banned from ever playing there again because they had overrun the curfew time set by the Teamsters union. A promoter cancelled a show in Salt Lake City less than 24 hours before showtime after he had attended the previous show, in Boston, where the promoters had pulled the plug when the band overran and Jim could be heard loudly describing them as 'cocksuckers'.

Even the publication by the notable New York publishing house Simon & Schuster of Jim's first book of poetry – an amalgamation of his two self-published volumes from the previous year, with the conjoined title, *The Lords and The New Creatures* – was overshadowed, at least for the singer, by the fact that no one – *no one* – outside *Rolling Stone* even mentioned it in passing. Jim bemoaned his lot to Michael McClure, saying he knew this would happen, that no one in the poetry community would take it seriously because it was by him, a rock singer. McClure could only concur. 'He was right,' he said, shrugging.

Maybe Jim should have stuck to his vanity publications. His original self-published volume, *The Lords: Notes on Vision*, comprising mostly his UCLA journal jottings – 'all games contain the idea of death,' ran one typically epigrammatic line – came in 82 cream-coloured parchment paper pages, enclosed in an azure blue box held together by red string, with the title embossed in gold leaf. His second privately published edition, *The New Creatures*, came in a more orthodox 42 pages of pale-yellow, glossy paper, bound between hard brown covers, the title again in gold leaf. Much to Jim's dismay, the amalgamated edition produced by Simon & Schuster used one of the 'Young Lion' shots – whereas the originals bore more recent fully bearded portraits. The originals also gave the author's name as James Douglas Morrison and referred to him as a poet and filmmaker, while the new single-volume edition listed him more recognisably as Jim Morrison, made clear reference to the fact that he was the singer in The Doors and called his fans 'kids'. Only the dedication remained true: 'To Pamela Susan'.

The poems themselves are in that late-Sixties, underground L.A. style that echoed the Beats yet contained all the snapshot buzzwords of the counter-culture – the kind of thing that, on the one hand, his fellow Hollywood lowlife Charles Bukowski really did lift to new heights of charismatic maleficence, with his stark, unpunctuated poems and broken-bottle prose, and which, on the other, Beat survivors like Michael McClure had a tendency to overplay into nothingness, just more weed-blown head music. Jim's poems stumble between the two, sometimes from one line to the next. Yet there is something there, just out of reach – in one so young, for a poet – enticing enough to warrant further investigation. Had he lived and written more . . .

The other area Jim was still intent on breaking into was film. *HWY* had given him some cachet, even if it was clear to serious moviemakers that this was more UCLA student polemic than accomplished film art. He was also still hoping it would entice mainstream Hollywood into casting him in starring roles, in the kind of vehicles that had just made Peter Fonda and Dennis Hopper such huge stars in *Easy Rider*. It looked like his wishes had all come true when Jim Aubry, former head of programming at CBS TV, now president of MGM, decided, after just one meeting, that 'Jim Morrison's going to be the biggest motion picture star of the next 10 years. He's going to be the James Dean of the Seventies.'

A development deal had been done and Jim had worked off and on with McClure throughout March and early April on a shooting script for his still unpublished novel, *The Adept*. The film would star Jim in the title role and would be co-produced between his own new company, HiWay Productions, and St Regis Films, run by Aubry's trusted lieutenant, Bill Belasco. McClure told Jerry Hopkins, 'We turned out a script that was longer than the novel. It looked like somebody shot the manuscript of *Moby Dick* out of a cannon.'

Meanwhile, Jim was now meeting with film directors to discuss possible mainstream acting roles, such as Sam Fuller, a heavy-drinking maker of low-budget genre pictures whose own career had begun to falter – he'd made just one movie in the past five years, the execrable *Shark!*, starring Burt Reynolds – but after he and Jim got on just a little too well, MGM wisely decided against greenlighting any further collaboration. Next up was Ted Flicker, who'd enjoyed a run of innovative for the times TV hits – including *The Man from U.N.C.L.E.*, *The Andy Griffith Show* and *I Dream of Jeannie* – and had made his debut as a movie writer with the 1966 Elvis Presley vehicle, *Spinout*, and as a director in 1967 with the satirical cult hit, *The President's Analyst*. But by the end of April, The Doors were back on the road, going out for two weeks at a time, returning to L.A. just long enough for Jim to come down again, then heading off once more. This went on until June, by which time the heat had gone from the project and everyone involved was doing something else. No one came out of it happy. Aubry, who thought he was getting the new James Dean, was now talking to a pudgy guy with a huge unkempt beard and permanent midnight eyes; McClure saw his and Jim's *Moby Dick*-sized masterpiece cut down to 90 thin pages and retitled *St Nicholas*, after the lead character; and Jim . . . well, Jim was into something else.

And so were the rest of The Doors.

'The boys did not hate Jim,' insists Vince Treanor. 'The boys did not dislike Jim. The boys wanted Jim to be part of the group, but they couldn't take the trouble that Jim was causing. They couldn't take the loss of [so many] performances as a result of his behaviour. They couldn't take the loss of all the record sales. They couldn't deal with the loss of radio time. The censure that went down, the newspaper articles, the pastors and the righteous ministers with their boyfriends in the closet that got up and were saying how terrible The Doors was and how perverted Morrison was. The whole thing. They didn't want to deal with that kind of bad, negative, horrible publicity.

'As Jim got more out of control . . . the roomful of gunpowder waiting for somebody to light a match, Ray himself became more alienated and isolated from him. Now Ray never disowned him, but he never did what we all should have done, which was to say, "Look, asshole, smarten up, you're wrecking everything!" But in the end, Ray never stood up to Jim and said, "Okay, man, toe the line, or else! Because let me tell you, fella, we don't need you. Remember Amsterdam?" That's all he had to say.' Vince says that Jim once told him, '"People wanna see me drunk onstage." I said, "Nobody wants to see you do that. They want to see a Doors performance. They do not want see you lumbering around the stage drunk, forgetting your words and putting on a show where you stand there babbling nonsense. Put on a Doors show, sing Doors music, stop the nonsense because it's only gonna hurt!"'

Others also tried to help but it seemed futile. When Bob Greene, the band's accountant, tried to talk Jim into buying a property – just as the others had already done two years before – in order to offset the huge tax bill hovering over his head and also, though it was never spelled out, to offer him some place of his own away from the seedy environs of the Alta Cienega motel or Pam's angry bed, he eventually agreed and a substantial property was purchased on Kings Road, a lush locale just a short drive into the hills above Sunset Strip. But Jim rarely stayed there. Speaking to the online magazine www.doors.com, Jim's bodyguard, Tony Funches recalled: 'The one time I was there with him to pick up some books he wanted before we went on a concert road trip, the place was virtually empty except for the usual "bachelor" fruit crates, and a lamp here and there. Put simply and bluntly, Jim liked living the life of an avant-garde writer-poet, and the simplicity of the Alta Cienega provided that kind of Beat Generation atmosphere. The trappings of "a home" such as Kings Road were not the atmosphere Jimbo saw for himself as a "serious writer".'

There was, however, one place that did seem to offer Jim

a more acceptable form of sanctuary, even if no one took him seriously on those rare occasions when he actually spoke about it. Which is where he found himself one auspicious day in the summer of 1970.

It was Wednesday, 24 June, midsummer's day. In Washington DC, the US Senate had just voted overwhelmingly in favour of repealing the Gulf of Tonkin Resolution: made after the incident in which Jim's father, Admiral Morrison, had fired on North Vietnamese torpedo ships, thus sparking the Vietnam war. The TV news, though, was more focused on the escalating situation in Cambodia, where the Khmer Rouge, led by Pol Pot, were still running rampant, sending American soldiers home, either dead or wounded, by the hundreds.

Around 10 p.m. that night in New York, a different kind of force was about to be joined together. Patricia held Jim's hand fast as they stood before the carved oak table serving as the altar. Surrounded by glowing gold-coloured candles and pink and white peonies streaked blood red, having been 'purified' with drops of salt water and anointed with consecrated oil, and a special prayer having been said, Jim and Patricia, in their black, floor-length robes, were at last ready to begin their handfasting ceremony – the ancient Wiccan term for their wedding.

Patricia, a 24-year-old former go-go dancer and Mensa member, then the editor-in-chief of *Jazz & Pop* magazine, was born in New York City and had lived there all her life. She attended St Bonaventure University, where she majored in journalism, and graduated from Harpur College (now Binghamton University) with a BA in English literature; she also studied at NYU, Parsons School of Design and later Christ Church College, Oxford.

Since Patricia and Jim had begun their on-off affair nearly 18 months before, though, her life had changed. So had his. Now she hoped to rescue him. One of the first significant women rock critics, Patricia had met and written about almost all the great artists of the time. Later, as an advertising copywriter and director at RCA and CBS Records, working personally with musicians like David Bowie, Billy Joel, and Paul and Linda McCartney, she would become a two-time Clio nominee.

But what really singled Patricia out from the herds of other young women that had crowded into Jim Morrison's life these past three years was the fact that she was a Celtic Pagan high priestess and a minister of the Universal Life Church. Twenty years later she would be knighted at Rosslyn Chapel in Scotland, as a Dame of the Sovereign Military Order of the Temple of Jerusalem (the ancient Knights Templar). This was not another crazy rock chick. No druggie groupie giving blowjobs to get backstage. This was the most well-read and learned woman Jim had ever met. She was also the most genuinely far out. As she was about to prove . . .

Writing in her astonishing 1992 memoir, *Strange Days: My Life with and without Jim Morrison*, Patricia recalled the night of her and Jim's wedding in breathtakingly vivid detail, save for the most secret elements, such as the specific prayers recited. The rest of the picture she paints, though, is remarkably clear: of the small cast-iron cauldron set up to burn incense, the Goddess candle and Goddess statue, the athame (a ritual black dagger usually employed in invocations, but on this occasion for another purpose), the sword, water, salt, censer and God statue. She even gives the coven names of the two adepts who officiated at the ceremony: Lady Maura and Lord Brân. Then Patricia describes 'the special things for this particular rite': the Quaich – a broad, shallow, two-handed silver bowl to hold the consecrated wine; an ornate silver chalice; braided red silk cord; Patricia's own wand of willow wood, 'bound with silver and sealed with a bloodstone'; and two Claddagh rings, one silver, one gold.

A circle forms – 'A sphere of blue light not quite visible to the eye, stretching from floor to ceiling along the line of the candle flames' – Jim and Patricia enter and the ritual begins in earnest: the invocation of the Goddess and the God; the censing of the couple, the anointing of consecrated oils; the sprinkling of water and smudging of foreheads with rowan ash; the slipping of the rings onto the point of the black sword.

At which point, Patricia relates in her book, she went to Jim and spoke to him softly so that only he could hear: 'These rings symbolise the Sacred Marriage, the union of the King and Goddess. When we put them on – and later – that's who we'll be for each other, in this circle and after.' She advised him he could still stop if he wanted to, that he was under no obligation at this point, legal or otherwise, that he could even marry someone else in future if he wished to, but that it was 'a valid religious ceremony, and it will create a real bond between us'. She finished by explaining that there would be no until-death-do-us-part. 'Death doesn't part,' she told him. 'Only lack of love.'

It was now-or-never time. Did he want to stop? 'No,' Jim told her. 'Oh, no! I'm sure.' So the ceremony continued through its most intense moments, not least the taking of the athame and making small cuts in the wrists of each party, allowing three or four drops of blood to fall into the wine-filled Quaich. Patricia went first but Jim blanched when it came to his turn. So Lady Maura did it for him then held their two wrists together while Brân bound them with the red silk cord as Patricia recited the handfasting vow. The rest of the ceremony proceeded quickly: the placing of the rings; the unbinding of the wrists; and finally the drinking from the blood-tinted Quaich; and the stepping over the sword, at which point Jim fainted. When Jim came around, Patricia cradling his head and shoulders in her arms, he told her, 'I felt . . . I felt something bigger than anything I ever felt in my *life*.' As he rested more comfortably now, his head in Patricia's lap, she explained that 'coming into the presence of the Goddess for the first time' was 'a very physical thing'.

'You're telling me,' Jim responded. '. . . I never felt anything like it, not even acid.'

'You felt the presence of the lady,' said Patricia.

Over the years since then Patricia, Celtic Pagan wife of Jim Morrison, has been ridiculed, marked out as a psychologically damaged fantasist, or simply called an outright liar. The only thing no one of note has done until now is actually believe her story. And yet it happened as surely as Miami, and is as real as Jim's other affairs with redheaded women of remarkable power. Anyone versed in occult lore or, specifically, the rites of Celtic Pagan ceremonies will vouch for the accuracy of her description of the ceremony she and Jim went through that long midsummer's night in 1970. More challenging, perhaps, are the descriptions she gives of how 'in the candlelight' he looked 'very beautiful and ridiculously young' – this at a time when the ravages of his years of overdoing it had begun to show so much that people he knew well, like Danny Fields, now describe him as by this point 'almost unrecognisable' from the 'Young Lion' portraits of three years before. When Patricia goes on to describe how many times they made love that night – 'with a kind of violent urgency' – it's a statement that stands in stark contrast to claims by others that throughout this period Jim was in fact largely impotent because of his drinking.

Yet none of this is really that hard to understand. Jim Morrison may have become a drunken, floundering fool when it came to the teenage groupies and drug sluts of the Whisky in L.A., but he was still only 26 years old. At that age, a couple of days not binge-drinking and a couple of good nights' sleep can work wonders. As for the bearded, increasingly overweight Jim appearing 'beautiful and ridiculously young' by candlelight to his adoring bride on the night of their wedding, it seems ridiculously churlish not to allow her the benefit of the doubt. Beauty, even to witches, is in the eye of the beholder. Why would the fiercely intelligent, sharply observant Patricia Kennealy be any different?

That Jim Morrison's followers – including, of course, his biggest, most ardent fan, Ray Manzarek – found Jim's latest adventure so far beyond their own imaginings says more about them than about whatever it was Jim and Patricia felt they were doing together in 1970. Jim Morrison, the great, self-proclaimed shaman, a man who invited his audiences again and again to 'let the ceremony begin', who told anyone who would listen in 1970 that he intended to 'start a new religion', who was more widely read than most literary figures twice his age, and certainly more daring in just how far he was prepared to push himself and the mindless thousands that leapt to proclaim him wherever he had walked these past three years – surely it's no stretch of the imagination at all that he might at the very least be intrigued by the invitation to take part in something as deep and meaningful as a Celtic Pagan wedding with a High Priestess? This was the same Jim Morrison, lest we forget, who just then was facing jail time in Miami, was being roundly rejected by his own band, had fled his family, and may still have been concealing his bisexual urges, a prisoner to his own blighted fate, as he saw it at that precise moment. Might he not be more than willing to accept the kind of unreserved love and protection Patricia Kennealy was now offering him – as well as the promise of his being assisted to some magical higher reality too? Why wouldn't Jim Morrison, fighting just to breathe in so many other areas of his life, seek some shelter from the storm?

'I think jealousy and envy come into it too a little bit,' says Patricia, who changed her name legally to Kennealy-Morrison after Jim's death. 'And also people trying to protect their own self-interests . . . "The Ballad of Jim and Pam", you know?' She doesn't give many interviews any more, having been ridiculed too many times and had her real-life role in The Doors' story reduced to one of loony-chick sidebar. Speaking by phone from her home in New York, she sounds remarkably sane, though. Far more so, it might be pointed out, than Ray Manzarek, with his endless Jim-might-still-be-alive ravings, before he died.

Patricia reserves a special loathing for writers like Danny

Sugerman – who started as a 13-year-old fan boy in The Door's office, opening mail and answering phones, and was just 16 when Jim died, yet who leveraged a career out of his supposed close relationship with Jim Morrison, co-opting Jerry Hopkins's original *No One Here Gets Out Alive* manuscript and turning it into the Gospel According to Jim.

'I think in a way, without sounding completely corny and ridiculous, [Jim] was an avatar of sorts,' says Patricia. 'I really do believe that. I mean, people like Sugerman go on about "Jim was a god!" but . . . I think in some respects he really was. He really was something beyond being a normal human person. That, I think, is where the problem lay, because, of course, he was a human person, not a normal one perhaps, but certainly human. And the dichotomy between Jim Morrison and Jim, I think, was what ultimately killed him in the end. The fact he could not bring those two halves together. I think if he'd had more time and if he'd been with *me*, as he was supposed to be when he came back from Paris, and we had been allowed to work that out, I think that would have been . . . certainly a tremendous help in resolving that fatal dichotomy.'

She also understandably resents those who assume she somehow coerced Jim into the wedding ceremony. Jim knew exactly what he was doing, she says. Partly because she had talked him through the whole thing first, partly because 'he was so learned and so informed and so well read about that sort of thing. I mean I had never met *anybody* who'd read the kind of stuff that he had and I was always quite proud of myself when I could point out something to him that he hadn't thought about before necessarily, consciously anyway.

Or a book that really bore upon the situation that he hadn't read and that I could bring to his attention. I think that was one of the things that he really liked about the relationship. That we could communicate on that kind of a level.'

She points out that Jim – and, as he would tell me, Ray – saw Doors concerts 'as rituals. And [Jim] consciously strove to make them so. If you read stuff that he said about this, he's really open about it when he gave interviews in those days and talked about what he was trying to do. And I think, by and large, he succeeded, except that it just began to consume him and hurt him and he didn't . . . because he was an addict, because he was an alcoholic, he couldn't manage to get away from it all. It was just coming after him and bringing him down from behind and basically ripping him to pieces.'

As a result, she says, 'he was really after bigger game than that. He was involved in soul politics. The politics of the spirit, something higher . . . I think, too, that is one of the things that drew him to me, because I have this thing going on in my life, and also the fact that it was Celtic in nature and he being a Scot by genetic descent. I mean, I think this really spoke to him. He had a poem ['As I Look Back'] about it where he calls it mystery Christianity: the snake in the glen. And the first time we met I had told him a lot of stuff about this. The fact that one of the family symbols of the Morrisons is a serpent, in fact. He thought that was just really cool.

'So, yeah, I think that really kind of opened a whole new view to him. He hadn't really ever considered all this before as being anything real. He'd read about it obviously. He was so well informed about just about everything really. So he knew a little bit about it. But then I was able to tell him so much more about it and I think, you know, to make it real on a very, very personal level. Here's somebody not entirely unattractive who he can have these amazing conversations with about all this *really* good stuff, and I think that was a big draw for him.'

She puts down his obvious physical decline to 'the pain. It was the pain he was having to deal with. He really had put on a mask – you know, Jim Morrison: The Mask. It began as a mask, something that he was doing consciously onstage as a dramatic theatrical sort of thing, which he was very much into. But then I think what happened was the mask got stuck to his face. And he couldn't get out from behind it. And *that* was what he was trying to escape from with the alcoholism and the stupid Jim tricks and all the other nonsense. He really wasn't a jerk, basically. What makes me so angry is that so many of the biographies just continue to paint him as an absolute moron. I mean, the guy had an IQ of 149. I mean, mine is higher but still . . .' She chuckled and you felt for her as her own pain revealed itself. 'Back there . . . there were no maps. It's like, "Here be Dragons!" These were people doing this kind of thing for the very first time. Nobody really had a clue as to how it was going to affect them and how it was going to affect the people around them who cared about them. It was all new and strange and different. And quite dangerous and scary, as well.'

One scary thing Patricia did not tell Jim before he left her a few days after the wedding, to return to L.A. in preparation for his trial in Miami, was that she was pregnant with his child. In what she calls his 'cosmic stupidity' he had pulled out her diaphragm one night while they were making love, as if – yet again – daring the universe to punish him with the direst consequences; the universe, yet again, obliging him. It would be months before Patricia felt able to tell him.

Meanwhile, rather than return to L.A., Jim flew to Paris with The Doors' publicist, Leon Barnard, ostensibly to begin promotion for what was to be the band's second European tour, in September; in reality because Jim badly needed a change of scene. Things had got too heavy in L.A. Whereas just months before he saw his future in books and film, now he spent time alone, reading, drinking, getting fatter and lonelier and more desperate, dreading the thought of going back on the road with The Doors, all of whom now barely made eye contact with him whenever they were together.

Jim loved Paris in the summer. The city and its long history of art and literature, of bohemian bistros and civilised café society, of wine and poetry and long dissolute nights among opium eaters and absinthe addicts, whores and intellectuals, all spoke deeply to the romantic in him, that soft-eyed boy who still lurked somewhere beneath the layers of fat and cynicism, who still thought there might be a place for someone like him, someone other, somewhere. Surely. Not that Jim was ready to rent a garret and starve for his art. He and Leon had checked into the George V, the city's most luxurious hotel, from which Jim could safely survey his alcoholic dreams without having to resort to anything really nasty or street level.

He was also expecting to meet up with Pam, who had left for Europe on another of her 'shopping trips' weeks before. But Pam was not in Paris: she was busy enjoying her own befuddled reveries, hanging out with her heroin-dealing boyfriend, the Count de Breteuil, at a villa in Tangiers owned by Paul and Talitha Getty. Instead, Jim reacquainted himself with Agnès Varda and her husband, Jacques Demy, real-life Left Bank filmmakers who were as passionate about art and film, about life, as Jim longed to be. Visiting the set of Demy's latest film, *Peau d'Âne*, starring Catherine Deneuve and Jean Marais, Jim revelled in the opportunity to spend time in such illustrious, strictly non-rock'n'roll company. François Truffaut was also visiting the set that day, out in the Loire Valley, and Jim lived it up in style over lunch, downing three bottles of wine and exalting in the company.

Days later, Jim and Leon flew down to Tangiers, still looking for Pam. But she and the Count had already fled to de Breteuil's own family villa in Marrakesh. While Pam was permanently smacked out, she couldn't care less where Jim was or what he was doing. Just as long as she had the smack, and she knew she always would while she was with the Count. Never mind that he would slap her around sometimes, treat her like a cheap junkie whore and tell her so. Just as long as she had the smack . . .

Back in Paris, Jim's credit cards were starting to fail and he was forced to check out of the George V and settle for a cheap room in a mice-infested slum hotel in the Latin Quarter. One of the British music papers reported seeing Jim backstage at the Pink Floyd show in Hyde Park on 18 July. But Jim was no longer enthralled by London, finding its streets suddenly dark and grey, its people unfriendly to young Americans, and he was no fan of rock festivals any more, either. And with his money running out and his trial in the US looming, he flew back to L.A. at the end of July and tried to prepare himself for what he knew would be the debacle of Miami.

Jim knew something was up when Judge Hoffman denied Max Fink's petition to introduce the concept of 'contemporary community standards' as the major plank of Jim's defence. A 63-page document that Fink had taken weeks to piece together, drawing on sources as disparate as the Swedish art-house melodrama *I am Curious, Yellow*, from 1968, to *Midnight Cowboy*, John Schlesinger's powerful drama about the misadventures of a male prostitute in New York, which had just won three Oscars in 1970; taking in the art of Michelangelo and Gauguin; and citing the 1st, 8th and 14th Amendments of the US Constitution. Jim later said he knew he was done for when the judge simply disallowed that any of it could be used in his defence.

What discouraged Max Fink even more was when he discovered the good judge was readying himself for a difficult re-election campaign later that year and was clearly intent on making the Jim Morrison case an example of his strong leadership qualities. In his book, Jerry Hopkins relates how Max Fink discovered that all 17 of the prosecution's witnesses were either employees of or related to someone who worked for the prosecutor's office or local police department, Fink suspected the cards Jim was being dealt came from a loaded deck.

The trial began on 6 August and consisted of 23 days' worth of court appearances spread over the next two months. There was surprisingly little publicity about it in the US press. Even *Rolling Stone* declined an invitation from The Doors' office to attend the trial and write about the case. The fans, too, seemed to lose interest fast. According to Mike Gresham, then working as a trial publicist for The Doors, 'The first day, a hundred kids showed up at nine in the morning. Second day it was forty. Third day it was twelve.'

None of the other members of The Doors showed up either. Nor even Pam, who was back in L.A. but still hanging on the Count's every word. In the US illegally, Jean de Breteuil was busy dealing heroin to the Sunset Strip in-crowd. It was a whole new downered-out drug scene and everyone seemed to be in for the long haul. According to Eve Babitz, writing in *Esquire* years later, Pam's 'idea of the diet to be on while Jim was in Miami going to court was ten days of heroin. Every time she woke up she did some, so she just sort of slept through . . .' Meanwhile Jim sat passively, drawing sketches of the jurors or openly reading a book, as if he were above it all. As if he already knew what the outcome would be and was ready for it. (He did and he wasn't.)

In the middle of the trial, on 28 August, Jim was required to fly to England, to get ready for The Doors' appearance at the Isle of Wight festival the following night. Inspired by the 'happenings' at Monterey Pop and most recently Woodstock, the Isle of Wight festival was Britain's version of the same, except it was not free – a fact which angered hundreds of radical hippies, who proceeded to tear down the fences that surrounded the site and turn the event into a logistical fiasco. A year earlier Bob Dylan had headlined the show, making his first live appearance for three years, dressed in an all-white suit, and looking and sounding like he'd aged ten years since his last public appearance. Members of both The Beatles and the Stones had attended that show. The 1970 follow-up was supposed to be equally right on, brother. There was a huge sense of anticipation about the appearance of The Doors, who had not played in Britain since their London shows exactly two years before and were co-headlining with Jimi Hendrix. The fact that they had been forced to cancel the rest of their European tour dates – which were to have included the prestig- ious Montreux festival on 31 August – when Judge Hoffman refused to reschedule Jim's court appearances around the tour only added to the sense of occasion. For The Doors, having the tour blown out was an almighty bummer, forcing them to stake all they had on this one show. For the fans it simply meant this really was something not to be missed. Also on the feel-good bill were such equally significant members of the rock cultural elite as The Who, Miles Davis, Free, James Taylor, Joni Mitchell and many others. Everything was set for this to be another do-or-die Doors show. As far as the other members of the band were concerned, all they needed was for the real Jim Morrison to show up and all would be well in their world again.

Only Jim didn't show. Nor, inexplicably, did the other Jim – the one called Jimbo that everyone hated. Instead the Jim Morrison who appeared onstage at the Isle of Wight festival that night was someone only previously glimpsed through the gloom long after the show was over. Not the Jim who ranted and raved at audiences, offering to get naked for them and start a revolution, nor even the Jim who hung on to the mike for support as he slurred his way through songs, forgetting the words. This was . . . a dead man. It wasn't a help that The Doors didn't get to go onstage until almost two o'clock in the morning. Nor that the experimental moviemaker Murray Lerner was filming the event. Jim barely even responded to the music, sleepwalking his way through a funereal perfor- mance in which his eyes remained almost constantly closed and his mouth barely moved, one that so angered the rest of the band when they came offstage that John threw down his sticks – not for the first time – and stormed off.

Robby Krieger later called it 'one of the worst shows that I remember. Jim was so bummed about his trial and he was just going through the motions.' It hardly helped that The Doors were followed onto the stage by The Who, who performed the set of their lives, all too aware of the lasting significance the event was likely to have.

Vince Treanor describes the Isle of Wight non-performance as 'probably one of the worst shows' he's ever seen. 'Joni Mitchell was there and god knows how many other brilliant performers and here's Jim standing up there like a bloody limp dish-rag, hanging over that mike stand, with his foot on the mike base. It was like he was glued in place. Somebody had poured a poultice on him and it froze, you know? There was no emotion in the singing. There was no movement of his body. Terrible, terrible! Shameful . . .'

It was the beginning of the end for The Doors. 'After the Isle of Wight,' Vince now reveals, 'the decision was, "We'll never play onstage with you again." So the question was: how are we gonna get income? And the answer was: *we* are going to perform. We don't need Jim. So the spectre of the future was already hanging over them. You know? He just blew it.'

Forty-eight hours later Jim was back in court in Miami, even less animated or apparently interested in what was going on around him. When Mike Gresham told him he'd found a girl who said she had overheard the judge tell friends at lunch he was going to 'throw him in jail', he barely responded. Gresham made a last-ditch attempt to track the girl down and persuade her to come back and give evidence about what she had heard, thus triggering an application for a mistrial verdict, but the young woman in question didn't want to know. Instructed not to offer her money for her assistance, or try and persuade on moral grounds, he tried the only other thing he could think of. 'I asked, "Want to meet Jim Morrison?" She said no – and that's the last we saw of her.'

Jim returned, horribly depressed, to the Miami courthouse on 30 October to receive Judge Hoffman's verdict. Bizarrely, Jim was found innocent of the charges of public drunkenness and of lewd and lascivious behaviour, but guilty of the charges of indecent exposure and open profanity. The judge gave him the maximum punishment he was allowed to under state law: a $500 fine – and six months in Raiford Prison, one of the hardest jails in the country. He was put on $5,000 bail and ordered back for sentencing in November.

Patricia had visited Jim during the latter stages of the Miami trial and told him she was pregnant with his child. He told her he didn't intend to become a husband or father but that he would pay for and hold her hand through the abortion. Patricia says she expected that reaction but it's hard not to feel for her. Then Jim turned to her and said, 'You know, it'd really be an incredible kid.'

But Patricia was wise to Jim's games. His self-delusions. They spent a drunken night together then she went home to New York and had the abortion, alone, without Jim, in November.

NINETEEN

Killer on the Road

Time was short. Jim was scared. The Doors had already decided to go on without him. Even Elektra was now hedging its bets. The question was how? When? No longer, why?

Max Fink had immediately launched an appeal against the verdict in the one-sided Miami case. He felt Jim still had a chance of escaping jail time. At the end of the trial, the prosecution had not been able to secure even one eye-witness account of Jim actually exposing his penis onstage; not even one photograph. They only had the outrage of the 'solid citizens' who had testified against Jim to go on. Nevertheless, a guilty verdict had been reached and the fear was that the appeal would merely grant Jim more time to get his things in order, to prepare himself for the ordeal ahead. One of the State of Florida's biggest prisons, Raiford was where death row prisoners went to get the electric chair. This was no candy-ass correctional facility, this was the real deal. Jim's head would be shaved, he would have to share a cell with at least one other inmate, and he would be in for a crime considered beneath contempt by the more hardcore prisoners:

indecent exposure. In their eyes, that made him either a fag or a near-rapist, maybe both. The fact he was a rock musician would not have helped either. Long-haired degenerate, pretty boy, Jim was a cellblock bitch in the making.

Everyone else, meanwhile, was also naturally looking at it from his or her own point of view. For the three other members of The Doors, Jim had singlehandedly fucked their career for over 18 months. It wasn't just Miami. It was everything. If Miami had been a one-off, or just symptomatic of a bad patch, they could have rallied around Jim, seen it through with him, all for one and one for all. But it was never one for all with Jim. There was only ever him. And us. Unable to tour for most of 1969, now things had eased up, promoters' paranoia overcome by dollar signs in the wake of the renewed success of their recording career with *Morrison Hotel*, The Doors still suffered from Jim's lack of engagement, from his apparent determination to sabotage their comeback with a pathetic, indifferent performance one night, followed by a raucous, over-the-top, pathologically unsound display the next. The Isle of Wight fiasco had been the last of many last straws. Now the son of a bitch was going to jail and the band was supposed to do what? Hang on? Still? Hadn't they just done that for nearly two years? If they didn't do something now, maybe they'd never get another chance. Jim would go to jail, get beaten and butt-fucked, and come out even worse than before. *Even worse? Are you fucking kidding me, man? How much worse could this shit actually get?*

Jac Holzman at Elektra, for so long the cool head, the smart cookie, the one with the vision thing who could see round corners and always knew what move The Doors should make next, even Jac was now thinking of a Plan B. The long laboured-over double album, *Absolutely Live*, had been released in July and despite being a fascinating trawl through the more together aspects of The Doors' live show as it had now become – including 'Celebration of the Lizard' and extended firecracker versions of gemstones like 'When the Music's Over' and 'Break On Through (to the Other Side) – had become the worst-selling Doors album yet. Less than a quarter of a million copies sold, just enough to scratch the US Top 10 for one week then nosedive out of the charts again. Paul Rothchild, who had spent so long running around the country taping Doors shows – at least ten by the end of his marathon jaunt – then burning the candle at both ends in the studio trying to make it work, now disowned the album completely. The band simply weren't strong enough, musically, to hold up an entire double live album, he complained. They weren't really about the music, not onstage, where he had no control over the takes, but a theatrical experience, a rock'n'roll cabaret. 'It should have been a movie,' he concluded bitterly.

With The Doors' contract with Elektra set to expire, and Jim making no secret of the fact that he was ready to talk to other record labels, even though he seemed to have little or no interest left in salvaging The Doors' career anyway, Holzman acted quickly. He put together an unprecedented deal that gave them back Elektra's share to their song publishing, plus a hefty advance for one final album for the label.

'It was an enormous gamble financially because their lawyer, who was not my favourite guy, he tried to see if he could sign the band to Columbia also, but [the band] wouldn't let him. Because they recognised that they had an obligation to me. But he, the lawyer, said, "They're not entitled to it but we'll let Jac have it *if* he gives back the 25 per cent of the publishing he has." They had 75, I had 25. And I gave it back. He said, "He'll never do it", and I did it. I made a calculation in my mind that was not a mathematical one. That is, if the album is a bomb I gave away the publishing and I don't have all the records on one label. If the album is great and I give away the publishing, I've got all of the albums for the foreseeable future, and if it's a success I will have no problem re-signing them.'

In need of money and a deep-down reassurance that their careers as rock stars weren't quite over yet, Jim and the rest of The Doors were happy to sign, and rehearsals for a new album began fitfully as the Miami verdict came in and threw the whole thing into a tailspin again.

Meanwhile, to give Elektra a safety net, Holzman elected to roll the dice again and put out the first Doors greatest-hits collection in time for Christmas. It was entitled simply *13*, to denote the number of tracks on the album but also, cleverly, as a coded message to the young 'heads' out there that The Doors were still hip, the number 13 being a favourite way at the time for denoting weed and pot – the 13th letter of the alphabet is M, for marijuana – and had become a popular denim patch to sew onto your jacket or jeans. Containing all the chart hits plus all the tracks now considered Doors must-haves, *13* did what it was supposed to and gave The Doors another million-seller. It didn't happen overnight – the album only reached No. 25 in the charts that Christmas, but it remained in the Top 40 for another six months.

Looking back now, Holzman is surprisingly upbeat about

this period in the band's story. 'I think once Miami happened, Miami happened. The only thing is a hangover from the fall-out. And it was going to go on, unless he was acquitted, it was gonna go on for years. But then there were lots of appeals and stuff. I don't think he ever thought he was really gonna go to jail.' Then he adds, somewhat astonishingly, 'But I think he would have loved going to jail.'

Why did he think that, I asked? 'Because it [would have been] a different experience. There's a kind of righteousness about going to jail for your art. I mean, who's gonna screw over a person everybody is looking at? He was probably not in physical danger there and he would have . . . I don't think he would have been sentenced to more than a year and he would have been out in seven months. But he would have had an adventure.'

I am momentarily speechless. Considering the state of mind Jim now appeared to be in, at the end of 1970 – he had now moved into the Chateau Marmont, the same hotel where the comedian John Belushi would overdose and die a decade later, and begun doing so much coke he gave an ounce to a friend and told him to only dole out a gram at a time to him, otherwise he would snort the lot in one go – I find it hard to believe he was anything but terrified at the prospect of going to jail.

'But, no,' says Jac, 'I think Jim . . . in some ways it got too much for him. There were too many expectations of him by so many people and he didn't want to be responsible for those expectations.' Hence the physical transformation into the growling hulk with the big boozer's gut and the skidrow beard? 'Yeah, I think absolutely. Well, I think that was . . . He was just letting go. And not being what people expected of him and he thought they'd pay less attention to him. I mean, he loved it at the beginning. He *loved* it. I remember Steve Harris saying when [Jim] got out of a limousine for the first time he looked like he had done it all his life. Which was a great line and it was true. It was . . . He loved it until they began . . . the adulation and stuff and what they expected of him . . . got a little crazy and he was out testing the limits.'

Jim, though, had reached his limit long before then. Sitting in the Miami courtroom one morning, a couple of weeks after returning from the Isle of Wight, he had been told of the death of Jimi Hendrix, causes as yet unknown, though Jim didn't need to wait for the TV news to figure it out. He had stood at the side of the stage and watched Jimi do his stuff at the Isle of Wight, as drawn to the thunderstorm of his music as he had been distant from his own with The Doors. He had just got back to L.A. in early October when he learned of Janis Joplin's death, for almost identical reasons. Too much booze, too much dope, too much, too soon, of every damn thing, man. Jimi and Janis had both been just 27 years old. Coming so soon after the death that summer – found face down in his swimming pool – of the Rolling Stones' guitarist Brian Jones, also 27, when Jim turned 27 on 8 December that year, he began telling people, 'Brian, Janis, Jimi? You're drinking with number four.' But those around him, including Vince Treanor, had been listening to Jim talking about how he was going to die young for too long to pay attention. 'Jim said a lot of shit, you know? Who listens! When a cow is taking a shit, you don't listen to them moo!' But as it turned out, we should have . . .'

When Larry Marcus, a veteran scriptwriter, hooked up with Jim at Jim's bungalow at the Chateau, Marcus tried to pitch him an idea for a movie about a rock star who causes a huge outrage onstage at London's Royal Albert Hall, based on Jim's Miami incident. Jim, coked out and in fear for his future, nearly threw him out. He didn't want to have anything more to do with rock'n'roll, he told him. But Marcus, being a canny Hollywood operator, kept pitching ideas to Jim until one finally hit home. As Marcus told Jerry Hopkins, it was to be a movie about 'a human being who wanted to vanish from the world and become zero'. Marcus added: 'I had a feeling that was a very crucial metaphor for how he felt about himself.'

Danny Fields says he feels Jim's depression was self-perpetuating, blaming his outburst and mean-spiritedness on the fundamental fact of being, as he puts it, 'A fat kid who was gorgeous for two years. And then, don't forget, and I've said this a thousand times, when the drinking started going into his cheeks on his face, when the beer was showing up in body fat, he was losing the looks, and he knew it. And he was pissed off when people would shove a picture of him . . . you know that Adonis picture of him? He didn't look like that any more. He hated that picture as much as he hated anything in his life, I'm sure.'

Eve Babitz recalls seeing Jim around this time at a party at the Los Angeles abode of Atlantic Records' chief, Ahmet Ertegun. It was the night of the November 1970 moon landing. She recalls reacting badly to 'a rather gross story about midgets in India' that Ahmet was telling. 'Jim rose to his feet and bellowed, "You think you're going to win, don't you?!

Well, you're not, you're not going to win. We're going to win, us – the artists. Not you capitalist pigs!'" The room instantly descended into embarrassed silence. Until Eve piped up: 'But Ahmet is an artist, Jim!', then ran to the bathroom and locked herself in. She recalls Jim following her there, and telling her, 'You know, I've always loved you.' She also recalls how Jim then went back to Ahmet and apologised profusely. 'But it was too late; by then he was too fat to get away with it.'

Years later, John Densmore would wax lyrical to me about how 'We wanted to be successful but we wanted to make a statement too, about the times we were living in, and if that took breaking the mould and doing things different we were up for it. We were excited by it. We were kind of like pushing the envelope artistically.' But he was thinking of earlier times. As Bruce Botnick put it when we spoke, '[John] loved the music, he loved being a part of The Doors, and what the message was. [But] it got convoluted. It got changed by circumstances and what people came to see. You know, it became a sideshow rather than an event to go hear The Doors.'

A sideshow Paul Rothchild, for one, was no longer prepared to deal with. He is sitting at the control desk at Sunset Sound, in November, the band gathered again in the same room where they made their first two incredible albums, but instead of feeling perhaps like they've come full circle and are ready to do some good work again, Paul puts his head in his hands in despair. With Jim and the band barely speaking any more, ideas for new material have been slow to hatch. There are some unformed blues jams, which Rothchild hates, the more so since he realises they are there because Jim's voice is now so shot he can no longer sing anything without growling;

a sketch for a song called 'L.A. Woman', another blustering blues that in its early stages sounds so hammy Rothchild can hardly bear to listen to it; a few basic electric-piano chords overlaid by Robby's gimmicky take on 'Ghost Riders in the Sky', a kitsch old yarn about a cowboy who has visions of red-eyed, steel-hooved cattle thundering across the sky, being chased by the spirits of damned cowboys, *'trying to catch the Devil's herd across these endless skies'*, which the band have half jokingly dubbed 'Riders on the Storm' but that Paul has already dismissed out of hand as 'cocktail jazz'; and a couple of demos even the band are unconvinced by – an early, acoustic 'Hyacinth House', which sounds like second-rate Crosby, Stills, Nash & Young, and one track titled 'Latin America', originally written for inclusion on the soundtrack to Michelangelo Antonioni's 1970 film *Zabriskie Point* but which had been rejected in favour of music from Pink Floyd and the Grateful Dead.

Hitting the playback button, Rothchild told them: 'You know what? I can't do this any more. This isn't working. This music is . . . awful. You produce it. I can't.' 'We were giving Paul a preview and he was bored,' Ray later recalled. 'We played the songs very badly – no chi, no energy. We didn't want to be back in Sunset and Paul couldn't bring us back to life. In that instant he was right.'

Speaking now, Bruce Botnick reveals for the first time an additional factor behind Paul Rothchild's decision to bow out that has never been written about before. The producer had just completed making Janis Joplin's last album, *Pearl*, and was still devastated by her death (the singer had actually died the night before she was to complete her final vocal performance on the track eventually released as an instrumental, 'Buried Alive in the Blues') – not just because he knew Janis as friend, but because the two had become lovers during the making of the album.

Says Bruce: 'He had just come off of making *Pearl* and he was in love with her [Janis]. I mean, really, physically and emotionally, he was deeply in love. They had a really great thing and she had just died and that was too much for him. And he just didn't have the strength to go in to try to save it one more time. Maybe if he was still on a high with *Pearl* and Janis was still alive . . . I have a lovely picture of the two of them, arms around one another, smiling. He said the greatest producer line I've ever heard. Where he realized he was really falling in love with her. I mean, just off the deep end. And he said, "Janis, I can't tell you how much I love you and all I want to do is be with you. But if we do that we're not gonna get a record. So it's best if we fuck on tape". That's the greatest producer line ever. And they did. They fucked on tape. Then when the album was done and then she died, it just destroyed him. So that's one of the reasons, I think, that he had a very difficult time getting into this.'

It hardly helped, adds Bruce, 'when Paul would go to the rehearsals [and] Jim wasn't there at all, in spirit. You know, he didn't want to know. He couldn't get himself up for it. Paul thought, well, maybe the best way to get them into it would be to take them into the studio and see what happens. I convinced them to go back to Sunset Sound, where we did the first two albums. And we got set up. The first song they started playing was 'Riders on the Storm', and within a few minutes of it being played Paul put his head on his hands and said, "I can't do this any more. It's gonna be too hard. I can't do it."' Looking at Bruce, he said, 'You should make the record with them. You know what to do.'

They all went out for dinner to talk about it. 'We went down the street to this Chinese restaurant, the Moo-Ling and [Paul] proceeded to lay it out. That he didn't have the strength any more or the desire. Then after dinner we all went back to Sunset Sound and they said, "What are we gonna do?" And I thought to myself, well, why the hell don't we do this ourselves? I said, "Where do you feel the most comfortable?" They said, "In our rehearsal studio". I said, "Great. I'll get some recording equipment from across the street at Elektra and we'll do it." And that was it. Plain and simple.'

All these years later, Jac Holzman makes another startling admission. 'When Paul Rothchild quit, I was secretly pleased. I never would have fired him. But I would have . . . I don't know what I would have done. But when Paul quit, that meant they were free. And I just let them figure it out for themselves. I mean, my god, they had six albums with a master, and Paul got better and better and better, but Paul needed something fresh himself. He did *Pearl* with Janis and the two of them fell madly in love with each other. And that would have been an interesting relationship to watch. But he was ready for something different.'

With the addition of Elvis Presley's regular bass player, the sublimely skilled Jerry Scheff, and Leon Russell's rhythm guitarist, Mark Benno, work on the new album, now titled *L.A. Woman*, suddenly kicked into gear and the whole thing was completed in a week. As a result, John Densmore would later describe it as 'the first punk album', mistakes and all. It was certainly unlike anything The Doors could have produced under Paul Rothchild.

Bruce set up his eight-track mobile equipment on Bill Siddons's desk in the first-floor office, with a specially rigged-up intercom microphone over his head to communicate with the band, playing in the basement, and he recalls the sessions with greater fondness than any since *Strange Days*. 'Because it was just the five of us, plus the addition of a bass player and guitar player, we didn't have any bones to pick with one another. Just let them be them, capture the performance and say, that's good, come on up the stairs and hear it. Do one take, you know, two takes. And then if they hear it and go, "I think we can do another", go down and do another one. Great. That's good, guys. Let's move on, until we'd finish a song or two in a day. Finish them! It was a great experience.'

Even John Densmore began to enjoy himself. 'I used the same drum kit I had on the first record,' he would later tell *Classic Rock* magazine. 'It was like going back to the metaphorical garage in Venice where we started. I told Ray, I wanted to get the feeling Miles Davis had on *Live at Carnegie Hall*, where you could make a mistake, but you went for passion.'

There was certainly plenty of that evident in the finished grooves. Passion and a genuine sense of spontaneity on record, at last. Bruce: 'I remember Ray going into Jim's book and seeing "Texas Radio" and going, "I think we can do something now." The four of them talked about it. Jim went away for a couple of hours and in that couple of hours the guys came up with that arrangement and created the music, and we recorded it. Jim came back and he overdubbed it and that was it. Probably five, six hours altogether, from nothing to something . . . They were very good at doing something like that because they still had that spark. It was good. It was fun.'

Jerry Scheff: 'I can still see Jim standing at his microphone. A little heavy in his "fade into the background" clothes, hair and beard enveloping his face. He didn't want to be there. He didn't want the spotlight any more.' Jim, he says now, was simply one of 'the most unassuming and easy to be around' singers Jerry had ever worked with. 'He had an almost invisible ego without being standoffish: almost unaffected. Ray had a good strong sense of who he was, what he had to contribute musically. I never felt any kind of power trip from him. Easy to work with. Same thing with Robby. John was almost passive-aggressive. He showed that by hardly communicating with me at all. Hello and goodbye were pretty much the extent of our dealings with one another . . .'

Mark Benno's main recollection, he said, was of a band and singer 'on a roll. [Jim] reminded me of a wild gorilla at the sessions. One day he stopped the session and took me to lunch. He ordered oxtails and drank Jack Daniel's out of the bottle. When we got back Jim had me show Robby a lick I was playing, and we used it on 'L.A. Woman'. From there, it was a jam right through the album. We worked the tunes up on the spot, and did very few takes. We never saw anyone but each other, which kept distractions to a minimum, and kept Jim from feeling inhibited, which I don't think was a problem for him anyway!'

Whereas Rothchild had winced at the decline in Jim's voice, Botnick saw it more as 'kind of a maturity. I remember when Sinatra got to that place and point with his voice, and Jim used to talk about Sinatra a lot because he loved Sinatra, and he noticed the change in his voice as well, when he became a man, with some experience. You can hear in Jim the spark that inspired him initially, and you can hear the tired old man. Because he lived in three years more than most people lived in 30 years.'

Jim was already 'talking the whole time' about going to Paris when the album was finished, says Bruce. Consequently, there was a real sense that this might actually be the last Doors album. 'This could have been it. We knew that. But we didn't expect it to happen the way it happened.'

Singing into his stage mike, a gold Electrovoice-676-G, Jim did most of his vocals facing a sign he'd hung on the wall that read: 'A clean slate is an empty slate'. For others, he crouched in the doorway of the toilet, having already pulled the door off its hinges. Said John in 2010: 'If he kept his alcoholism out of the studio everything worked great. He was in trouble, yeah, he was, but without the world around him, everything else went away.'

Not quite everything. Interviewed halfway through the sessions by a writer from the *Village Voice*, Jim admitted that these days, 'I don't read or write much. I don't do much of anything. But I will get back in the saddle. I've just been kind of lazy. I go through cycles of non-productiveness, and then intense periods of creativity.' When asked about his weight gain, he jived: 'Why is it so onerous to be fat? Fat is beautiful. I feel great when I'm fat, I feel like a tank you know? I feel like a large mammal, a big beast. When I move through the corridors or across the lawn, I just feel like I could knock anybody out of my way. It's terrible to be thin and wispy – you could get knocked over by a strong wind.'

Knocking back vodka and orange, he went on: 'You gotta get smashed and make a fool of yourself in a public place. You gotta get eighty-sixed [barred] from seven nightclubs. That's the Irish thing. I hang around mostly with the Irish and the Italians.' He then offered to arm-wrestle the journalist.

He was more serious, though, when interviewed the same week by the *L.A. Free Press*. 'There seem to be a lot of people shooting smack and speed now. Alcohol and heroin and downers – these are painkillers. Alcohol for me, because its traditional. Also, I hate scoring. I hate the kind of sleazy sexual connotations of scoring from people, so I never do that. I like alcohol; you can go down to any corner store or bar and it's right across the table.' In reality, though, Jim's consumption of cocaine and, latterly, occasional snorts of Pam's heroin were competing with the alcohol for ultimate control of his metabolism. In the end, they would fight it out to the death.

The finished *L.A. Woman* was a similar patchwork between inspired, truthful beauty and poisoned-chalice nihilism and despair made over to appear more like wonder. The opening track, 'The Changeling', came direct from another of Jim's old journals, and with its chuntering riff and blowsy vocal seemed like a possible hit single. As it turned out, it was Robby who again came up with the goods in that department, with his romping sing-along, 'Love Her Madly', another of his my-chick-is-crazy numbers. 'Hyacinth House' was a much improved, less dainty version of the demo Rothchild had rejected. Jim and Robby had first come up with the idea while tripping at Robby's beautiful new beachfront house in 1969, eyes rolling like pinwheels at the sight of the hyacinths blooming round the swimming pool.

'Latin America' was now retitled 'L'America', though no further work was done on the original track, save for some phasing Bruce did on the drums and Jim insisting on overdubbing a single word: a lustily bellowed 'Fuck!'

One evening, after burning their way through John Lee Hooker's 'Crawling King Snake', a number they had been slinging around in their live set for years, chosen here primarily as a filler track, just to keep the vibe going, Jim then led the band through an almost entirely improvised new jam he called 'Been Down So Long', a run-of-the-mill blues holler in anybody else's hands – title lifted from the American folk singer Richard Farina's 1966 novel, *Been Down So Long It Looks Like Up to Me* – here elevated into a defiant, eyes-slitted yell in the darkness, as the threat of jail time in Miami came crawling back to the forefront of Jim's mind . . . '*I said, warden, warden, warden / Won't you break the lock and key!*'

Also recorded at the same heady session – what came to be known by Bruce Botnick as 'blues day' – was the most impressive of the lot, Jim's low-slung cat-mewling groover, 'Cars Hiss By My Window'. Ray recalled: 'Jim said it was about living in Venice [Beach], in a hot room, with a hot girlfriend, and an open window, and a bad time. It could have been about Pamela Courson. Certainly, the lines 'Can't hear my baby, though I call and call' seemed to reference Pam, who was now living in Paris, hopelessly embroiled in heroin.'

Incredibly, an even better song was recorded at the same session, the title track, 'L.A. Woman'. Ostensibly another blues, this time revved up to the max, with added jazz flourishes on the keyboard to add another time-space dimension to it, 'L.A. Woman' was in many ways the ultimate Jim Morrison road song. With both the man at the wheel and the lights of his 'city of night flashing by like bullets just missing his head'. Lyrically, this was another of Jim's typically literate inspirations, though he wasn't just riffing on the titles of old books now; he was distilling the voices of some of his favourite, most culturally embattled writers, into words he could truthfully call his own. The obvious literary touchstone was a Los Angeles novelist, John Rechy, whose 1963 stream-of-consciousness novel *City of Night*, Jim had devoured at UCLA. But inside the verses, in their neon-blitzed images of girls hidden in Hollywood bungalows, cops in cars outside topless bars, the whole stinking city thing run on 'motel, money, murder, madness', lies the voice of another L.A. chronicler, John Fante, who indented his love of Hollywood with lines like: 'So fuck you, Los Angeles, fuck your palm trees, and your high-assed women, and your fancy streets. Los Angeles, give me some of you!' According to Ray, 'We dug our teeth into that song. It was all about passion and hauling ass. It felt like we were on Route 101, on the road from Bakersfield to San Francisco. You can hear our enthusiasm. Welcome to Los Angeles!'

Jim spent the night of 8 December 1970, his 27th birthday, at the Village Recorders studio in West L.A., taping poetry for a solo album, accompanied by John Haeny, then chief engineer and senior staff recording engineer at Elektra's own studio. Haeny had occasionally assisted Paul Rothchild and Bruce Botnick during Doors sessions, ensuring equipment functioned and that there were ample recording supplies. Although notoriously wary of strangers, Jim never seemed guarded around Haeny, perhaps because Haeny never seemed awed by Jim, sensing that his manipulative tactics were a type of test: that those who took the bait failed, thus inviting even more derision and taunting from Jim. Haeny, inured to rock star trappings and the gleam of fame and fortune, simply viewed Jim as one of the many musicians he was charged with recording, and as a result Jim felt at ease around the engineer.

Jim was particularly fond of John's Siberian Husky, Nikki – the dog that is glimpsed in the promotional film for 'The Unknown Soldier'. When, early in 1969, Jim asked John if he'd mind recording some of his poetry with him, they completed a session together at Elektra's studios late on a Sunday afternoon.

Writing in 2013 on his website, www.johnhaeny.com, John recalls: 'Other than reading, Jim played a bit of piano, accompanying himself on 'Orange County Suite' and also giving the piano a good whack from time to time for dramatic punctuation. David Anderle, the Head of Elektra West Coast A&R, and a mutual friend was present and helped with the tape logs. I'm sure David was there because it's David's handwriting on the tape box logs. This recording is known as the "Elektra Tapes" or some call them the "Echo Tapes". Since these recordings were primarily a demo I recorded them in stereo because of the piano and also because I used a bit of live reverberation chamber on Jim's voice to make things sound a bit more polished.'

No more was said about Jim making a poetry album, though, until almost two years later, when Jac Holzman approached Haeny to enquire if he'd be willing to go into the studio again with Jim for more recordings of his poetry. With

Rothchild out of the picture and Botnick still busy constructing the new Doors album, a delighted Haeny accepted and
began making arrangements, even though he did not actually
sign a contract with Elektra until 31 December 1970 – over
three whole weeks after the sessions – finally accepting $1,000
for his services.

Haeny had collected Jim from the Chateau Marmont hotel
on the afternoon of 8 December, dropping by Jim's favourite
liquor store – Monaco Liquor – to buy a bottle of Bushmills
Whiskey as a birthday present for him. Rothchild had once
confided to Haeny that the key to accessing Jim's loosest and
most fruitful studio efforts was Irish whiskey. Writing on his
website, John recalls: 'It was my plan to document Jim reading his poetry on his journey from cold sober to that locked
room where his drunken Irish poet lurked. Although we never
discussed it, I had an overwhelming feeling that Jim knew
exactly what I was up to and was happy to go along with me.'

John says that Jac Holzman had told him Jim had left The
Doors and was looking to pursue new interests. 'Sometime
later, when I asked Jim that question directly, he simply said
he had left The Doors to focus on his poetry and never elab-
orated further. Jim seemed exceedingly comfortable with his
decision and I never saw any reason to press him further. I
figured that the time had come for him to move on, most
certainly out of the public eye. Being in the public eye took a
tremendous toll on Jim. That was obvious to everyone who
knew him. This is one of a few things those of us who knew
Jim can agree on.' Speaking now, though, Jac denies Jim ever
officially left The Doors. 'No, he had not left the band . . . But
I don't think he ever wanted to be in a band of that kind of

popularity any more and I think he was looking at what else he could do, and to do that he had to get out of town.'

Friends dropped in and out of the Village poetry sessions, including Frank and Kathy Lisciandro, and as Jim grew more and more tight from the booze, he encouraged the onlookers to participate. Eventually Jim began slurring and staggering and, after he had fallen down twice, they called it a wrap.

Back in the so-called real world, in order to help promote both the new *13* compilation and the more sprawling live double, *Absolutely Live*, the reluctant band were persuaded to take on some concert dates in December. According to Vince Treanor, this was only after Jim went 'begging the three guys and Bill Siddons for another chance'. He says this is one aspect of the story that never gets written about: despite outward appearances and all Jim's utterances about wanting to move on from The Doors and become a full-time poet and moviemaker, the fact is he was desperate for another chance at the limelight. He couldn't handle being found guilty in Miami and getting ousted from the group as a live performer at the same time. 'If [Jim] wanted to be this poet, if [he] wanted to retire from the rock scene, why did [he] want another chance?' He points out that the Isle of Wight show had been Jim's 'chance to break, right there. He could have walked away and The Doors would have ended with the disaster of the Isle of Wight. But no, no! "Guys, I can do it. Guys, I can keep it together. Don't worry, I'll prove it to you!" Oh, *really* . . .'

The dates went on sale and the band limbered up with a show, three days after Jim's 27th birthday, at the State Fair Music Hall, in Dallas, Texas. Speaking to me years later, Ray insisted this could have been the start of a reborn Doors, that they were still 'relishing the hysteria. It was a controlled hysteria. Syd Barrett said that it "Set the Controls for the Heart of the Sun'. That's where we were going. Deep into sun. Directly into that orb, that golden orb. And we will *die* with madness or absolute joy. One or the other. That's the object of our performance. To play with *all* the passion you can possibly muster. And after you've opened the doors of perception you can muster a lot of passion. Because you realise that your passion is infinite. That you are infinite. That we're all infinite. We're in *outer space*. We're on this little *blue marble*, it's spinning around the sun, 365 days, to inscribe an arc around the sun, and we're all in outer space. Holy shit! It's terrifying! And yet *we*, as these innocent little things dancing on planet Earth, can make it absolutely joyous. So that's what we would do. We would walk a tightrope, a tightrope between joy and absolute terror. And have just the most fantastic time doing it . . .'

By the end of that little rant I didn't know if Ray was talking about Texas or just talking. He'd been doing it for so long it was as if he no longer knew how to stop. By all accounts the Texas show was fairly mediocre, one of their phoned-in performances, but at least Jim was moving around again. More slowly, like an old man surveying his vegetable patch, growling and snorting and yowling and playing around, almost talking to himself. But they played the set without anyone being arrested or Jim falling over or insulting anyone. They even tried out some new material on the audience: a decidedly gloomy, 15-minute attempt at 'L.A. Woman', and a more spirited go at 'The Changeling', where Jim for some reason chose to sing the song in a disturbingly ill-fitting scat. There were also stiff performances of both 'The WASP' and 'Love Her Madly'. They even got to preview two new songs that would prove pivotal on their next album, including one, 'Riders on the Storm', which both Ray and John would later tell me they thought could have been a signpost for where The Doors might have gone, musically, in the future – if they'd had a future.

It was inspired by a line from the poem 'Praise for an Urn' by Hart Crane, about 'delicate riders of the storm', melded with Jim's now almost obsessional hitchhiker imagery from his own *HWY* project. As Ray put it, 'It gave Morrison the lyric for the last song he ever sang on planet Earth with the Doors. An insane killer, a lunatic, he's going to do something bad. Give him a ride, why don't you? But when the end comes you realise Jim's singing a beautiful, romantic song: *"Girl you gotta love your man / Take him by the hand / Make him understand . . ."* He was singing that for Pam.'

'Yeah, we were kind of excited by that,' John told me. 'But, you know, Jim's self-destruction caught up and . . . we played "Riders" live, first time ever, and we thought, wow, maybe we could be this sort of cool, jazzy band.' By now, this constituted a successful show for The Doors. And at the end of it, after deductions, the band walked away $25,000 better off (a little over $150,000 in today's money).

Then the following night in New Orleans the whole shithouse went up in flames. The venue was the inauspiciously named The Warehouse, a bare-bones, 30,000-square-foot music venue on Tchoupitoulas Street, in uptown New Orleans, close to the banks of the Mississippi River. The Warehouse had only opened for business as a rock venue less than a year before but was already established as the cool place for bands like the Grateful Dead to hang loose in. It seemed the perfect spot for Jim's second comeback show with The Doors. Instead, it became their funeral pyre.

The set had begun well enough. Jim was already drunk and still out on his feet from the night before. But the band ambled through a couple of songs at half-throttle without any above-average concerns. Then something happened to Jim, as he appeared to just give up the ghost. Not like at the Isle of Wight where he simply snored through the whole thing; more like a man leaving his clothes on the beach and wandering slowly into the sea. He began missing lyrics – whole lines, then verses and choruses. He had done that before but that had been drunken infelicity; this was almost . . . deliberate. As though it was the only way left to him to get across whatever message it was he badly needed to send. A wounded or disabled person signalling for help.

He clung to the mike, tried telling a story or two, a joke maybe, one whose punchline not even he could get to. The crowd, normally so out of control at a Doors concert, stop what they're doing and begin to low, like cows at approaching danger. Something is clearly not right: this is no longer theatre, not even of the Grand Guignol variety. This is suddenly, horribly, frighteningly *real*.

Recalling that night in a 2010 interview with *Classic Rock*'s Max Bell, Ray said, 'He just lost his energy completely. He was so dissipated. His voice got lower and lower and he ground to a halt. He was empty. This wasn't like when he comes to the studio wasted and can't deliver, but then there's always tomorrow . . . This was final.'

Panicking, the band cut the set short and launched into 'Light My Fire', their ace-in-the-hole showstopper guaranteed to make everybody, even Jim at his latest all-time low, come back to Earth, surely. But Jim just sat on the drum riser, staring into space, as though he could no longer even hear the music, let alone remember the words. Furious, John kicked him in the back and Jim slowly, unsteadily, groped his way through his stage-blindness to the mike again. He appeared to try to sing one last time, but couldn't manage it, couldn't seem to find the way back into the song, just couldn't . . . fucking . . . SHIT!

He picked up the mike and began ramming it into the stage, once, twice, three times, four, five . . . it goes on and on until the band stop playing, the crowd recoil and the mike stand breaks right through the wooden stage floor. With the broken feet of the mike stand stuck deep into the stage, Jim snapped the shaft of the stand from its base, then hurled it like a spear right into the heart of the crowd. Pandemonium broke out as people ran to avoid the debris. Then Jim Morrison strode off into the wings for the very last time, never to be seen onstage, with or without The Doors, again.

'I was standing over in the corner of stage left,' recalls Vince Treanor. 'Bill Siddons was behind me. Jim had left and John took his drumsticks and threw them on the floor. He said, "That's it. Never again." And he walked off. Robby unplugged his guitar and uncharacteristically dropped his cord on the floor, and he unslung his guitar and just held it by the neck and walked off. He was the first one offstage. Then Ray and then John almost together.'

'Jim was just terrible,' John would tell me. 'It was pretty

tragic . . . I was very proud of how good we were live in the early days. We were just – phew! We could take anybody on! But I was very glad that I talked them into getting off the road, after that New Orleans show. Where it was clear we were *ruining* what we had created live.' In another interview with an Australian journalist, he added: 'Jim was one of those kamikazes, who had creativity and self-destruction in the same package, damn it. That's what I loved about him [but] it was real hard with the self-destruction.'

Backstage, Vince says now, 'There was a sort of a shocked silence except for John. John said, "Never with the asshole *ever* again." And that was it. Bill didn't say anything. Nobody said anything. Bill then walked past me and the mike shaft of course was somewhere. Why somebody was not killed that day I don't know. I could not explain to you how that missile, that spear, did not get somebody. And it would have been their upper body. The way he threw it was just like a spear, just like a javelin. He just threw it right through the air and just – bing!'

The rest of the proposed dates were cancelled early the following morning, including four shows at Madison Square Garden in January. Arriving back at The Doors' office in L.A., Vince was greeted by Bob Greene. 'He looked at me and said, "This is it, kid. That was the end." That was how swift that decision was made.'

On 9 February 1971, in the middle of one of the hottest periods ever recorded in California, The Doors and Botnick began mixing *L.A. Woman* at Poppi Studios, Motown's West Coast outlet. The same day the San Fernando Valley experienced its fiercest earthquake for 30 years: 6.6 on the

Richter scale; 65 people killed; over 50 million dollars' worth of damage. Unfazed, Jim laid down a harmony vocal to 'Hyacinth House' and, with the quake in mind, suggested they preface 'Riders On The Storm,' with a thunderstorm sound effect. He then added a final whispered overdub to the track, barely audible, yet adding a wonderful effect that is almost subliminal. It was to be the last thing he ever recorded.

Speaking to me in 2012, John mused on what he called 'the Cult of Morrison'. He sighed. 'You know, substance abuse came in pretty strong. It's interesting, though, that somehow, even with all that, *L.A. Woman*, for example, and Jim clearly was an alcoholic by then, it just shined. I don't know what . . . there was some *pact* unspoken that when we were alone together, the whole world was outside and we still created really great stuff. Not to be self-serving but, you know, I *love L.A. Woman. L.A. Woman* and *Strange Days* are it, for me.'

'You know, I never heard the album [until it was finished],' says Jac Holzman. 'I was asked not come to the sessions. I usually came to some sessions and I would stay an hour and then I would get out. And I was concerned. Not because I didn't think the boys could do it with Botnick. But because Rothchild had told me there weren't any songs. That worried me. He said it was lounge music. And then when I went over to hear the album and I went into what my staff used to call the Great Listen, eyes closed, intensely, pad in my hand – on which I wrote nothing, I wrote nothing at all, I said, "It's just perfect and the single is . . . 'Love Her Madly'." They all said, "No, the single's 'The Changeling'." I said, "No, guys, it's 'Love Her Madly'." And that went back and forth and I stayed out of it. I left it to Siddons to make it happen and he did and of course it was a giant hit.

'But it was the best album they made. I think it's . . . the first album is one of the greatest first albums of all time. But the last album was really poignant. And 'Riders on the Storm' just was the perfect, I don't know, totem for that album. It was just terrific. I was thrilled with the record. Absolutely thrilled. I told them: "Don't change a thing." I was so relieved. I was in tears I was so relieved.'

Jac's business acumen was as astute as ever and 'Love Her Madly' became the first Doors single to become a sizeable Top 10 hit when it was released in March, dragging *L.A. Woman* in its comet trail also into the Top 10. Yet all was not well. At the photo shoot for the album cover, Jim had to be propped up on a bar stool, barely able to sit up straight up, he was so out of it, a bottle of Bushmills at his feet. 'In that photo you can see the impending demise of Jim Morrison,' Ray would later observe. 'A psychic would have known that guy is on the way out. There was a great weight on him. He wasn't the youthful poet I met on the beach at Venice.' Nevertheless the sleeve designers, Wendell Hamick and Carl Cossick, came up with an innovative idea for a rounded corner cover and a cellophane window. The band's supposed frontman may not have looked at his best any more but the cover to *L.A. Woman* would become The Doors' most memorable: a dark, red-wine-coloured sleeve behind which a yellow inner sleeve displayed a woman crucified on an electricity pole.

Jim, now feeling like he'd been crucified on the cross of trying to break on through whatever it really was he thought he was trying to do the day, he wrote those lines, now looked to climb down, as quietly as possible. To silently escape to some other place far enough away from this – from L.A., from Miami, from himself – to be able to remember whoever the hell he thought he was supposed to be.

Pamela had left for Paris again after the Miami verdict came in, to be with Jean de Breteuil and his deliciously unstamped-on heroin once again. She had returned briefly to be with Jim at Christmas, but in the wake of New Orleans Jim was in no shape to hold on to her. In February, just days after the mix of the new album had been completed, she had flown back to Paris, to the Count. To her drugs and her own form of escape to the wilderness. When Max Fink informed Jim that the next time the court met in Miami to consider his appeal, it seemed likely it would demand his passport, Jim made up his mind. He would leave for Paris too. Someone suggested he try London. But Jim wasn't convinced. When Max explained that France had no extradition treaty with the United States, he knew what he had to do. Whatever way the cookie finally crumbled in Miami – and chances were, Jim was going to jail, the question was just for how long – they wouldn't be able to reach him, take him back and shave his hair, grease his arse and make him swallow his punishment whole if he was now living in Paris.

The rest of the band, meanwhile, were still quietly making music, though not with Jim any more, jamming in the basement again while Bruce Botnick kept the eight-track running upstairs. Off the back of *L.A. Woman*, Elektra had paid them a significant advance for another two Doors albums. The band would insist this was simply a way to keep busy while Jim took his planned 'sabbatical' in Paris. But Vince Treanor points out that Jim didn't even know they were in the studio and wonders if, after New Orleans, they began to talk to each other, and feel they could do it themselves.

The last time Jac Holzman saw Jim Morrison was at an Elektra party at the Blue Boar restaurant on 3 March. 'He was unusually quiet. I could feel finality hanging in the air.' As the meal ended and Jac said goodbye to Jim, the two men hugged each other. 'And then he turned somewhat awkwardly and walked away. I watched and wondered if I would ever see him again.' He sighs when I remind him of it. 'Yeah. I didn't think he was coming back to the band. It had nothing to do with his dying or not. I just didn't think he'd come back to do this. But it was a poignant and somewhat disturbing moment.'

A couple of weeks before Jim left for Paris, he was over at the Elektra offices, as he tended to be whenever he had nothing else to do, and Jim never seemed to have anything else going on any more, and he bumped into Paul Rothchild. 'I heard the door open and felt this large man entering,' the producer recalled in *Follow the Music*. 'I didn't recognise him. Then I was tapped on the shoulder, and I turned around and this large person who looked like Orson Welles' younger son, said "Hi, Paul". I said to myself, "Holy fuck! *This is Jim?*"'

TWENTY

La Mort blanche

Jim flew TWA Ambassador Class, from LAX to Paris–Le Bourget, arriving on the morning of Thursday, 15 April 1971. He had been due to fly a day earlier but had driven to LAX with the usual gaggle of hangers-on, heartbroken at having to wave goodbye to their meal ticket, and, predictably, got so drunk with them in the airport bar he missed his flight.

This time, though, Pam was actually there to meet him and the unhappy couple checked into a luxury suite at the George V together. Writing home sometime later, Jim described the grand old hotel as looking 'like a red-plush whorehouse'. This had more to do with the fact that at around $400 a night Jim could simply not afford to stay there long. Within days Jim and Pam had moved into a $65-a-night room at L'Hotel, on the Rue des Beaux-Arts, considered cool since Mick Jagger had once stayed there. But even that was stretching the budget. With The Doors playing so few concerts since Miami – barely 40 concerts in two years – and with Jim having been forced to request advances in lieu of future record royalties, he was broke. As soon as advance orders for *L.A. Woman* came in he'd tapped up Bob Greene for more advance money to finance his Paris sojourn.

For once, Pam's extended time away from Jim in the city of smack yielded positive results when, through a passing acquaintance with the French model and starlet Elizabeth Larivière, she was able to rent a luxury third-floor, three-bedroom apartment at 17 Rue Beautreillis, in the pretty Le Marais district. The same week Jim and Pam moved in, *Newsweek* ran a cover story headlined 'War against the White Death', an in-depth piece about the tsunami of heroin from Indochina, sparked by the Vietnam War, that was now flooding Western Europe and America, via Paris and Marseilles. It was no coincidence that William Friedkin, about to become Hollywood's hottest director, had just finished shooting the final Parisian scenes for his Oscar-winning smash, *The French Connection*, its international heroin-dealing villain, Alain Charnier, based on the real-life, Paris-based trafficker Jean Jehan, of whom Assistant US Attorney General James Drucker would say, in 1973, 'He wasn't a drinker and didn't cheat on his wife the way most of these guys do. His one big fault is that once in a while, he would import 50 to 100 kilos of pure heroin.'

It was the main reason Pam had virtually moved to Paris full time. As any street corner junkie could tell you in 1970–71, Paris was now the smack capital of the so-called civilised world. Not just any smack either, but the purest, most lethal, the world outside Southeast Asia had ever seen. And nowhere more so than in the all-night clubs that Pam and the Count and their vampiric circle liked to frequent: most especially, the notorious Rock and Roll Circus, on the Left Bank.

Working as a barman at the club was a 21-year-old freelance war photographer, Patrick Chauvel. 'The job at the Rock and Roll Circus was to pay my trips back and forth to Vietnam,' he tells me now from his apartment in Paris. 'I started in '67 with the Six-Day War. And then I went to Vietnam in '68. In Vietnam I was 18. That was more or less the same age as the American soldiers, so it was okay.' He says Jim became a regular face at the Circus that summer. 'He came very often. The Rock and Roll Circus was one of those clubs where all these kinds of people would come in and out.'

Visitors in the recent past had included Keith Richards and Mick Jagger, Jimi Hendrix and his entourage, and various members of Led Zeppelin. But Jim cut a somewhat more modest figure, sitting in the semi-darkness, without the glitz and party atmosphere that always surrounded those other stars. The Doors had sold a lot of records in France, too, but they had never performed there, and whatever public profile Jim Morrison enjoyed was all based on the 'Young Lion' look of four years before.

'I remember not recognising him at all when someone pointed him [out] to me,' says Patrick. 'Because he was like fat and had a big beard and didn't at all look like the image I had in my head of him. He'd come in and sit on a couch, separate to the other clientele. He didn't dance or make a big noise. I remember him coming in once three nights in a row. He came often and there were times when I didn't see him but it was a big club on two floors, full of French stars. He wasn't the only big star in the club.'

The Rock and Roll Circus was also a hotspot for professional gangsters and big-time drug dealers, says Patrick. 'A lot of drugs, yes, a very free time for sex, a lot of jealousy and tension. The nightclub scene was heavy – gangsters and very bad cops. There were a lot of fistfights inside, which wound up on the stairs and in the street. There was a gunfight outside the club. I used to carry a bayonet for protection. Crazy but necessary. There was a triangle of these places – the Circus', which shared a large building with the Alcazar, 'La Bulle and Le Sherwood. All heavy.'

The Circus didn't get going usually until after midnight, but Patrick recalls many occasions when Jim would show up earlier than that, chatting to the staff, as he threw back double vodkas. 'I remember a few conversations, you know, at the table. He just didn't care. One of the things I heard him say is like, he just thought his fans were idiots. I don't remember his exact words but it was something like, "If I represent the image of my fans, or my fans represent my image, I mean, it's horrible. They're idiots." He just wanted to cut away from his fans. He did everything to get away from them. He was like writing stupid poems. They were very bad. I mean the ones I read were *bad*. It was like ridiculous.'

Patrick recalls how sometimes, as the night wore on, Jim would decide to treat the whole club to his poems, an echo of all those nights in American dives like the Whisky when he would get up and tell everyone they were niggers. 'Yeah. He would sometimes just stand up and just scream them through the ceiling. Everybody would shut up and listen . . . It was a lot about Vietnam. He was very upset. He'd be silent then he'd get up and say something really loud. You could see in his eyes, he had something important he wanted to say with a lot of energy, but it wouldn't get past his mouth. It went through his eyes for a moment. That was it. He was fed up. He was not in a good place. But do you know? It was the same time there was this play called *Hair*. It was sort of the same area. There was [Parisian *Hair* star] Julien Clerc and [French rocker] Johnny Hallyday, all these people were going to the club. A lot of people were talking about Vietnam and I was coming back from Vietnam . . . everybody was like in a half dream, half reality.'

It was Patrick that introduced Jim to Sky Eyes. With his running fantasy about his childhood soul being invaded by the spirits of dead Indians on the highway, and his other obsession, the truly free man who walked his own road, no matter how far it removed him from the society of other men, Jim became instantly besotted with the red-skinned army deserter. Sky Eyes, whom Patrick had first befriended in Nam, had deserted to Amsterdam, 'through what they called the Jesus pipeline'. Patrick had gone to get him back, the plan being to try and find him some work in Paris. 'He was this huge half-breed Apache who was in the First Cavalry and this guy had a hard time adapting and he was always talking with Jim. Oh, a lot.'

Jim even wrote a story based on a true tale Sky Eyes had told him of his childhood, growing up the son of a Scottish engineer working for Texaco who had discovered oil in the San Carlo reservation, where he met Sky Eyes' Apache mother. He married her, they had two kids together, then he killed himself in a car collision, drunk-driving, when the children were still little. 'And so the mother suddenly found herself in a white area alone with two kids, a simple Indian. So she went back to the reservation and when Sky told this story – and how he was brought up in the reservation – to Jim, I remember he tried to make up a small story about that.'

He says Jim, when drunk, also talked of plans to remake the *Hair* story as a real-life adventure, how he wanted to replace Sky in Vietnam, 'which is exactly the story of *Hair*, except the guy [Claude] in *Hair* doesn't do it on purpose. So at one moment, Jim said, "I will replace you! I'll go and say my name is Sky Eyes . . ."' He breaks into laughter. 'But he was a fat drunk guy so . . .' Did Patrick think Jim was just drunk or was he remotely serious? 'Well, when he was drunk he was really serious. The fact is, Sky looked at him and said, "You would last about five minutes in the jungle. You don't need the Vietcong to finish you, just the weather." They were laughing but sometimes, you know, they would burst into tears. And everybody was completely stupid. I mean, it was like . . . There was a lot of emotion, you know, about this. And a lot of good music and girls and alcohol. So it was like a metaphor of what was happening in Vietnam. It was really strange.'

Jim's health was poor, had been for a while. Nine months earlier doctors feared he had pneumonia: his temperature was sky high and he had begun sweating profusely when walking just a short distance. Some of that, though, was to do with the tremendous amount of weight he had put on in a short time. Part of it was to do with his heavy drinking and smoking and drug taking. And part of it, as Patricia Kennealy put it, because of 'the pain he was having to deal with'. Now in the humid spring weather of Paris he became asthmatic. He was also victim to sudden bursts of uncontrollable hiccupping. Looking for dry heat to clear out his lungs, Jim and

Pam took the train to Toulouse, 360 miles south of Paris. From there they continued after a few days on to Andorra, then Madrid, Granada and finally Morocco, where they had both enjoyed themselves in different ways and with different travelling companions the previous summer.

By the time they had returned to Paris, on 3 May, Jim and Pam seemed to be more like a regular couple, enjoying showing the Super-8 home movies they had shot on their travels. Jim had even lost a little weight and shaven off his beard, and he was looking tanned and reasonably healthy again. Within days, however, Pam was back seeing the Count, often for days and nights at a time, lost in her sweet junk delirium, as Jim brooded alone in the apartment. But he couldn't stand to be alone and soon went looking for company. It was now he began to go to the Rock and Roll Circus more regularly. The club's then manager, Sam Bernett, recalled, 'Every time Morrison came in he was high, or drunk; in an abnormal state.' When things got too 'abnormal' Sam would find himself in the odious position, as so many club managers before, of ordering Jim to leave. It was on one such occasion, just four days after Jim had returned from Morocco, that a young Frenchman named Gilles Yepremian first met Jim, as he was being thrown out of the club for throwing tables and chairs around.

'He was totally drunk. Nobody recognised him,' Yepremian would recall nearly 40 years later. 'I got a taxi and we drove down the Seine. At the lights Jim saw some policemen and he rolled down the window and shouted, "Fuck the pigs!" So the driver kicked us out. I got another taxi and Jim was so pleased he tried to tip the man hundreds of francs. He was laughing uncontrollably. I didn't know where he lived so I took him to the apartment of my friend Hervé Muller.'

Muller, who lived with his girlfriend, Yvonne Fuka, was gobsmacked when he opened the door to find The Doors' singer standing there, holding on to the doorframe for support. 'Hervé! Meet Jim Morrison,' Gilles told him. 'He'll have to stay with you.' They led the staggering semi-comatose figure to the bedroom, where he promptly passed out on the bed. Ten hours later Jim was awake again and suddenly in fine fettle. Thanking his newfound best friends for their kindness, he treated them to a long boozy lunch at Bar Alexandre, on Avenue George V, a familiar haunt where the waiters indulged him no matter how drunk and out of order he got because of the sizeable tips he would always leave. On this occasion, Jim knocked back several large Bloody Marys as Yvonne Fuka took pictures, followed by a whole bottle of Chivas Regal whisky. By the end of the afternoon he was back to picking arguments with other diners and becoming increasingly loud and obnoxious. As Gilles, Hervé and Yvonne struggled to get him to leave the bar, he collapsed in a heap on a bench opposite the restaurant shouting, 'I don't wanna go away! Where are you taking me?'

'When he was sober he just looked like an American student on holiday,' remembers Gilles. 'Very quiet and shy. Once he became drunk he was a madman.' Not enough to frighten off his new friends entirely, though. Later that month Jim brought Pam with him to dinner at Hervé's and Yvonne's apartment. Invited to choose some music from their record collection, Jim plumped for Buffy Sainte-Marie, the half Canadian, half Cree Indian folk singer he'd first discovered on the soundtrack to Mick Jagger's first movie, *Performance*. Sitting there, baked on strong hashish and the rich red Corsican wine Yvonne served them, digging Buffy and maybe beginning to remember who they thought they used to be, Jim and Pam got excited by the idea of driving down to Marseilles, the French Mediterranean coastal port where Yvonne told them you could find the best Corsican wine.

Still high on the idea the next day they did exactly that, but this time the trip was a disaster as Jim had his passport and wallet ripped off by local street hustlers expert at relieving drunk American tourists of their valuables. Forced to wait for two days for the American Embassy to forward him a new passport and for Bob Greene to wire him some more cash, they flew on to Ajaccio, on the west coast of Corsica, where Pam zoned out on some of the seaside smack she'd been able to score in Marseilles – then, like Paris, in the death-rattle throes of its biggest heroin invasion ever. The only hassle about travelling around France this way, they now realised, was that neither of them could speak French. When they returned to Paris a week later, Pam hired a pretty 19-year-old blonde French-Canadian girl named Robin Wertle. 'My job included everything from getting a cleaning lady, typing letters, calling America, buying furniture, a typewriter for Jim, and making arrangements for him to show his films,' Wertle recalled. But Jim never did get around to showing any of his films. He was too busy telling himself how much he adored his new life in Paris to look back on what was.

Hervé Muller next saw Jim on 11 June, at a performance of Robert Wilson's then in vogue play, *Le Regard du Sourd* (*Deaf Man's Glance*), at Théâtre de la Musique. Alain Ronay,

Jim's old UCLA buddy, now also living in Paris, had turned up during the interval. After the show the three men headed for a cocktail bar named Rosebud. But Jim started to get hassled by fans, an unusual occurrence in Paris and, suddenly ill at ease, he insisted they move on to La Coupole. Somewhere along the line Pam showed up, accompanied by two 'weird' guys – 'minets bizarres' – none of them had met before, and found themselves being led to various smack dens favoured by Pam in the Saint-Germain area of the city, before finally ending the evening in the small hours drifting incoherently from the Café de Flore, to Les Deux Magots, and eventually Brasserie Lipp, joined by a crowd of Eurotrash flotsam and jetsam and self-appointed 'artistic' dopers.

Hervé Muller never saw Jim Morrison again.

In a letter home to Frank and Kathy Lisciandro, Jim idealised his and Pam's situation in Paris, urging his friends to join them. 'There's a room for you here.' He also wrote a postcard to Max Fink. 'Dear Max, it's a beautiful spring in the 'City of Love'. Just got back from Spain, Morocco & Corsica – Napoleon's birthplace. Take a vacation! The women are great & the food is gorgeous. Love, Jim x.'

At the end of May, Jim even phoned The Doors' office in L.A., ostensibly to say how much he dug the finished copy of *L.A. Woman* they had just sent him, but in reality to try and gauge the temperature of his relationship with the band, see if his absence had made their charts grow any fonder. Pulling the short straw, he got John on the phone. 'He'd just got the finished album,' Densmore told Max Bell in 2010. 'Jim told me what a great place Paris was, and he said he was definitely coming back to L.A. He didn't know when. He said good things about the band. He sounded happier than when he left.' What neither John nor anyone else from The Doors' office had felt the need yet to tell Jim was that they were already halfway through recording a new album, and lining up their next major tour, too.

'It was in that spring,' says Vince Treanor, 'when Bob Greene called me in and said, "Say, Vince, you wanna check the equipment and dah dah dah . . . You're gonna start work in . . ." August, I think it was, or end of July, or early August. And we got all the equipment checked out and got everything tested and got everything together for a road trip. Then we went into rehearsal. Well, of course, that was business every day. We were over there doing the rehearsals, during which Bruce Botnick had his portable board and his recording machine and he would tape the rehearsals, and they could listen to that . . . Here's all these things going on behind Jim's back. Bill [Siddons] of course is not going to spill the beans. He was still employed by the other guys so he couldn't say much or he'd be looking for another job. But everybody knew that Jim was out. That was the thing. And everybody knew that [the album they were working on while Jim was in Paris] was the threat that was being carried out. "Jim, we will never go onstage with you again. Only in the studio." But they never dreamt that the consequences were going to be as they were.'

Back in Paris, in June, Jim had hooked up again with Agnès Varda and Jacques Demy. 'I wasn't like a private friend where he'd come and have dinner on his own,' Varda recalls. 'It was always in company. He sat in my kitchen in what's supposed to be his time of craziness [but] he was okay. I didn't bother him, and I wasn't constantly bothered about him.'

Still trying to catch a thrill, Jim and Pam flew over to London, in June, checking into the Hyde Park Hotel, which Jim disliked, mainly because it was another drain on his rapidly dwindling finances. London, generally, was a drag. More so when he realised Pam had only suggested the trip after she'd discovered the Count was going to be there that month. He had been given the keys to Keith Richards' and Anita Pallenberg's lavish flophouse at No. 3 Cheyne Walk, in Chelsea, while the Stones guitarist was away at Villa Nellcôte, in the south of France, working on the next Stones album, *Exile on Main St*. Jean de Breteuil was now using his superior-strength smack to keep three prominent ladies dangling: Pamela, Jean Paul Getty Junior's wife, Talitha, and Mick Jagger's former girlfriend, Marianne Faithfull. In her autobiography, Faithfull describes de Breteuil as 'a horrible guy, someone who had crawled out from under a stone. Somehow I ended up with him. It was all about drugs and sex.'

Also in London again was Michael McClure, who recalled getting arrested in Soho with Jim for being 'drunk and disorderly'. Released after a summary fine the next day, the two amigos jumped into a London taxi and demanded to be driven to the Lake District, a northern region of England known for its natural beauty and more than 200 miles from London – and had the police call on them again. 'I guess taking a taxi all that way isn't done ordinarily,' said McClure.

Jim had better luck when Alain Ronay accepted his invitation to join them in London. 'I moved them to the Cadogan Hotel, near Sloane Square,' Ronay, who now lives in Los Angeles, told the writer Max Bell in an extraordinary piece published in *Classic Rock* in 2010. 'It was a happy time. No paparazzi. I never saw Jim sign one autograph. We went to the theatre, did all the usual things. I returned with them to Paris and moved into the apartment. Pam had her own life entirely. She wasn't always around, but for the whole of June I lived with Morrison, practically 24 hours a day. I won't deny he was a dark and complicated person, or that Pam was a basket case. But strike the fact that Jim was despondent, or drug-addicted, or terminally depressed. He was living his dream, and that had nothing to do with rock. He was delighted at the success of *L.A. Woman*, but his pleasure lay elsewhere.'

That was certainly the impression he liked to give his French friends. Alone back in the Le Marais apartment though, he still fretted over what would happen in Miami. If the final appeal failed, as seemed likely, he would either have to go back and do his time in one of America's toughest prisons – or never go home again. Something he was now beginning to consider seriously.

Sitting alone one afternoon drinking whisky at the Café de Flore, Jim tuned into two young American buskers shambling their way through Crosby, Stills, Nash & Young's latest hit, 'Marrakesh Express'. They couldn't believe their luck when they suddenly found Jim Morrison joining them on the street, trying to sing along. Inspired as only one very drunk, un-happy man can be, Jim excitedly arranged for them to join him in a small local studio, used primarily for producing radio jingles, where they recorded a handful of woefully un-dercooked tunes, with one notable exception: Jim's poem to Pam, 'Orange County Suite'. When he left, the engineer at the session gave Jim the tape box, on which Jim drunkenly scribbled a band name, Jomo and the Smoothies. Jim tossed the box into a plastic carrier bag from the La Samaritaine department store, then carelessly left it at the apartment of yet another newfound best friend, Phil Dalecky, telling him he'd pick it up another day. He never did and these days you can find the recordings on the Internet under the title, *The Lost Paris Tapes*.

In the last week or so of June, Jim hit a new low. The Count was back in Paris – but shacked up with Marianne Faithfull – and though he was still happy to supply Pam with all the smack she wanted, she was definitely not welcome to stay with him. In a more hateful mood than usual, she now sat around the Rue Beautreillis apartment, snorting heroin and berating Jim for not getting on with more writing. He had come here to be a poet, hadn't he? Well, where was all the great fucking poetry, man? Or was that just more bullshit? Earlier in his stay, Jim had frequented the famous writers' bookshop-cum-salon, Shakespeare and Co., near Notre Dame. Now he simply sat in bars or outside cafés, staring into a glass. One day at the end of June, escaping Pam by walking the short distance to the beautiful Place des Vosges, he slumped on a bench and wrote what would be his last poem, 'The Sidewalkers Moved'. 'Join us at the demonstration,' he wrote, thinking back to the Paris riots of 1968, while staring blindly into his own unimagined future.

Jim's health had grown worse again. He was coughing up blood, feeling feverish. Pam dragged him to an America doctor, who prescribed him asthma medicines, but Jim already had his own medicines: whisky, vodka, beer, wine. Plus coke, weed, hash and, increasingly, now Pam was around more, little tastes here and there of the China White the Count was selling her. Pam later told friends he did it to keep her company, 'snorting lines off his credit card'. Vince Treanor can't disguise the disgust in his voice at such stories. 'That stupid bitch he was with. She was a heroin addict right from the start. It was she that introduced him to that particular recreational facility.' As Vince puts it, that's when 'things went from *badder* to *worser*, you know?'

In one of the last letters Jim would write, dated 28 June, he told Bob Greene, 'Paris is beautiful in the sun, an exciting town, built for human beings. Speaking to Bill [Siddons] a while back I told him of our desire to stay here indefinitely.' He waxed lyrical about the plans he and Pam now had to purchase an old property; they pictured themselves living in an old church, perhaps, he wrote. Someplace where Jim didn't have to be a rock star any more and really could become a poet. Getting to the point, Jim asked Greene 'for a sort of financial statement in general. Also a copy of the [Doors] partnership agreement.'

Almost out of money, he urged Greene to place Themis in the care of Pam's sister Judy and her husband. 'We'd like to be completely clear of any involvement.' He also asked Bob 'to organise new credit cards . . . we could use them made out in both our names'. And to please send him a cheque made out for $3,000 (about $17,500 in today's money). 'House bills are catching up,' he plaintively explained. Movingly, Jim also asked if Bob could make sure his dog, Sage, was well looked after. 'Send Judy 100 bucks for the dog.' It was Jim's goodbye letter to his old life.

On 1 July 1971, the day before Jim died, he and Pam had a very loud, very public row in a neighbourhood restaurant near their apartment, observed at close quarters by two German students who were sharing their table. Pam stormed off and Jim went for a long, despondent walk, before finally settling into a chair at a table for one at the bar Le Mazet, in the Saint-Michel district, where he was spotted by an American fan: Jim, alone, surrounded by people, drinking white wine and eating a croque-monsieur.

Alain Ronay, who had been staying with Jim at the apartment, had now moved out, escaping to the less melodramatic atmosphere of Agnès Varda's house on Rue Daguerre, where she was now working with the director Bernardo Bertolucci on dialogue for his next film, to be called *Last Tango in Paris*. The film, starring Marlon Brando, and released a year later, was about a deeply troubled American, exiled and close to death in Paris, and newly obsessed with an anonymous young Frenchwoman, played by a beautiful, red-haired young actress named Maria Schneider. When it was later suggested that the storyline was in some way inspired by Jim Morrison's last, choking days in Paris, nobody associated with the film denied it.

On Friday, 2 July, Jim spent his last morning strolling around a sunny Le Marais with Alain Ronay. Jim bought some jewellery for Pam. Despite it all, she was the only woman he really felt he didn't have to be someone else around, someone good. Pam may have been a junkie, a sponger, a take-take-taker, but at least she knew who Jim really was. Knew he had never really been there for her and never would, yet accepted that as part of the unspoken bargain they had made somewhere back down the road, back when they both felt sure they somehow had a choice in the matter.

Jim and Alain stopped for lunch at Ma Bourgogne, the same traditional bistro that Jean-Paul Sartre and Simone de Beauvoir had once sought refuge in. But Jim wolfed down the rich Alsace-based food too quickly, sparking another strenuous bout of hiccups. They spent the rest of the afternoon strolling around, picking up some newly mended boots for Jim at an old-fashioned cobblers' on Place de la Bastille. These days Alain Ronay recalls a relaxed Jim, walking around, taking in the sights and smells of what was still then one of the more low-rent districts of Paris, the houses old, the shops and bistros even older. In reality, though, Jim was down, uneven, lost. They stopped off for the inevitable beers at Café du Phare, one of the Bastille's oldest cafés, from where it was just a short walk up Rue de la Roquette to the Cimetière du Père-Lachaise, the beautiful cemetery Jim had visited recently and told Pam wistfully he would like to be buried in someday.

When Alain got up to leave for a dinner date with Varda, a clearly agitated Jim begged him to stay, to not leave him alone like this. 'One more short beer! Come on! Do it for an old friend.' Alain reluctantly stayed for 'one more beer'. Regarding his friend closely as they drank their final beer together, Alain recalled in *Classic Rock* not being able to stop staring at Jim's face, which had suddenly appeared to grow dark, almost black in the summer glare. Noticing his look, Jim demanded: 'Well? What did you see?'

What happened next has since become one of the most celebrated mysteries in rock. Pamela Courson would later claim she and Jim went out for dinner at a Chinese restaurant, then on to the cinema Action Lafayette to see an old movie Alain had recommended: *Pursued*, a 1947 film-noir Western with

Freudian undertones set in New Mexico and starring a still-young Robert Mitchum and the beautiful Teresa Wright. Set at the turn of the century and told in flashback, the story centres on Mitchum's character, whose family was wiped out when he was a boy. Jim couldn't get into it though; the movie was badly subtitled and after drinking all day and night he was coming down and needed a pick-me-up, and Pam was so stoned she kept nodding out, so they left early and walked back to their apartment.

The following afternoon, however, in her official police statement to officer Jacques Manchez, as translated by Alain Ronay, Pam would claim she had been too ill to go out so Jim had dined alone at a Chinese place on Rue Saint-Antoine, and had washed the meal down with several glasses of beer. After that, she said, Jim went on to the cinema alone, returning home around 1 a.m. She said Jim then built a fire, as was his habit, despite the summer heat, and started drinking whisky. She said she recalled him sitting at his desk, trying to write in one of his spiral-bound notebooks that would later become known as the 'Last French Notebook'.

She later added a further detail to this version of the story, when she told it to close friends back in L.A., which she did not make in her official police statement: that for the third day running Jim then snorted a line of Pam's heroin from a small mirror. According to her official version, she and Jim then kicked back to watch some of the Super-8 home movies they'd made on their travels that spring. Pam told Manchez, referring to Jim not by name or even as her lover, but simply as 'my friend', that he had 'appeared healthy and seemed very happy. But I noticed there was something not quite right about him. Later we played some records that I found in the bedroom and we played music for two hours lying on the bed. I think we fell asleep about 2.30 but I can't say when exactly. The record player turned itself off.'

Manchez asked her: 'Did you have sex with the deceased?' She replied: 'No, we didn't have sex last night. About 3.30 a.m., I think – there isn't a clock in the bedroom – my friend wakes me with the noise of his breathing. He was so noisy I got the impression he must need help. I wanted to help my friend. I asked him, did he want a doctor? No. He said he was okay, and he was going to take a hot bath. He got in the bath and then he called me because he felt sick.' She added: 'I took him in an orange saucepan, and my friend threw up the meal he'd eaten and I noticed some blood clots.'

She went on, as though reciting her lines: 'He is sick three times. Third time it's just blood. I tipped the pan into the basin, then I washed it. Now my friend says he feels strange. "But I don't feel ill enough for you to call me a doctor. I feel better now. It's over. Go to bed!" he tells me. "I'm gonna stay in the bath, and I'll be in with you later." I thought he seemed better, because he'd been sick, and his colour had returned, so I went back to bed feeling reassured. I don't know when I went back to sleep, but I woke up later and realised my friend wasn't in bed with me. I ran to the bathroom and saw he was still in the bath with his head back as if asleep. He had blood round his nostrils. I thought he must be ill, or he's unconscious. I tried to pull him out of the bath but it was impossible for me. At that point I called Mr Ronay and he came with Mrs Agnès Demy [Varda], and they called the police station for me.'

So much for Pamela Courson's official police statement. But this is what she later told Alain Ronay. That Jim had returned that night and started listening to Doors albums, specifically *Waiting For The Sun* and the track 'Not To Touch The Earth'. She and Jim both snorted smack, which the Count had told her was 86 per cent pure: roughly four times the strength of regular street-bought heroin. She said they both began crashing out around 3 a.m. The rest of the story stuck close to the 'official' version she'd given the cops. She later told Ray that at one point she'd thought she heard Jim calling out to her: 'Pamela – are you there?' How she'd rushed to the bathroom only to find him already dead. Then phoned Alain and Agnès, in a panic. For the record, it should be stated that neither the admirable Varda nor the staunch friend Ronay have ever believed the rumours about Jim dying at the Rock and Roll Circus, and have always maintained a consoling certainty in Pamela's version of events.

All of which would form the backbone of what the rest of the world believed to be the story of Jim Morrison's death for the next four decades. Poor old Jim, found in a bathtub by his loving spouse, dead of a heart attack, aged just 27. And not a word of it true . . .

Here's what really happened.

At around 1 a.m., a shitfaced Jim had slunk into the Rock and Roll Circus, slurring his hellos to the pretty blonde cloakroom girl, before taking the stairs very carefully down to the basement club, where he went to the bar and ordered a bottle of vodka. 'He was with some friends who I didn't know,' the club's manager, Sam Bernett, told *Classic Rock*. 'He was expecting people to bring him some stuff for Pamela. He was often in there doing that, or going to little cafés and dealers in the streets in Saint-Germain. He was waiting. He drank, talked, I listened but I wasn't always next to him. I bought him drinks. About 2 a.m. two guys came and then for 20 minutes he wasn't at the bar. He disappeared.'

According to Patrick Chauvel, also there that night, Jean de Breteuil – the Count – maintained his own side room at the Circus from which he would deal heroin. 'When you were going down those steep stairs from the cloakroom, into the club, there was a small room halfway down on the left filled with cushions, just cushions everywhere, and he was there. So it was like a club in the club. You would go left and voila! And then after you would go down and listen to the music completely . . . on drugs, you know? He was like a guru – all the girls slept with him, once or twice. It was like sleeping with Jesus, or something. You know?' he chuckles, 'It didn't count!'

The real names of the 'two guys' Jim 'disappeared' with that night have never been discovered. But they were ru-moured to be nicknamed Le Chinois, (The Chinaman) and Le Petit Robert (Little Bob). Both were working that night for the Count. When Sam Bernett was alerted to the rumpus developing in the ladies' loo, he banged on the door. 'Anyone there?' But there was no reply. Not even the sound of someone moving around inside. *Rien.*

In an extraordinary interview given to Max Bell of *Classic Rock* magazine in 2010, Bernett recalled: 'I called my security guy to smash the door open and inside was Jim. Sitting on the loo with no reaction, like he's sleeping or knocked out, his trousers slightly down. He was sitting with his head forward and his arms down – like a dead guy, actually. I shook him. I looked at his face, still no reaction.' His skin was grey, his eyes closed, with blood foaming under his nose and around his mouth and beard. Bernett leaned forward and tried shaking him by his shoulders, shouting at him to wake up – but nothing. 'I told the girl to get a doctor. I had a friend, a customer there every night – he was in the club. He came, looked at Jim and started a little check-up.' In his 2007 memoir, *The End: Jim Morrison*, Bernett recalls the doctor 'held Jim's head back, raised his eyelids, opened his mouth, took his pulse, and put his ear to his chest. He looked for marks and traces on the body and the arms. A quick and professional examination. His diagnosis was just as precise: "This man is dead." Apparently the victim of cardiac arrest. The doctor was no fool and spoke about a fatal overdose.'

With onlookers now starting to gather, Sam ordered the toilets to be cleared, began telling customers it might be best for them to leave the club early that night. Panicking, Bernett went to call the police and ambulance services. But before he could get to a phone, he was stopped in his tracks by The Chinaman and Little Bob. 'He's not dead,' Bernett recalled them telling him. 'He's just fucked up. Don't call the police, don't call his family. We take him home, we know where he lives.' Bernett was in a state of shock, couldn't quite believe his ears. 'I said, "That's impossible! We have to call the police and the medical people." "No!" they say. "Forget it. We'll take him and we'll use a back door."'

With the Circus sharing the building with the Alcazar, a transvestite cabaret, there was a private connecting door situated at the back of the Circus cloakroom. It was decided to get Jim's body out the back way, via the Alcazar. There then followed a macabre, Chaplinesque scene with the two drug dealers fumblingly trying to drag the dead body down the corridor. The Chinaman was a big guy, more than able to carry such deadweight. Little Bob was smaller, less able, and kept dropping his end of the body. Even when they swapped, with the Chinaman carrying the head-end, Little Bob had to keep stopping for a breather.

The eventually got the body out to the street door opposite the Rue de Seine and the entrance to the Circus. 'The Alcazar had closed,' says Bernett. 'The cabaret was over, apart from a few people who looked to see what was happening. They took him to the apartment. I was told this. They put him in the tub and waited an hour and a half before calling the paramedic. Pamela was in the apartment, out of her mind, screaming. Completely stoned . . .'

According to Patrick Chauvel, who was also there that night and a witness to this grizzly scene, Jean-Marie Rivière, who owned the Alcazar and was 'a king of the Parisian music halls and night club scene', now got involved. 'He spoke to several guys, including me, and said, "We've got a problem here." They called in a doctor and asked us to stay around and, to make the [story] shorter, we had to take him out of there because if they find Jim Morrison dead in the club, that's the end of the club. They all just wanted to keep it real quiet. It was an embarrassment so they took him via the tunnel between the clubs, which connected the cloakrooms, and up the stairs to the backstage street door. The boss was afraid of having a doctor or a newsman say anything, so they evacuated Jim, *et voilà*, into the car.'

And he helped? 'Yes, I helped carry him in a blanket. I can't say one hundred per cent that he was dead, but he wasn't moving. That's for sure. Yeah, I thought "This is bizarre", but I'd just come back from Vietnam. I'd seen a lot of weird things. Anyhow, he was then put into the back seat of a Mercedes. I don't know who drove the car. They took him home, is what they told me. I didn't see the car leave, no. I helped put him in and then went back inside the Circus. They wanted everything to look as normal as possible. I remember they put him into the back seat very gently and that's why I thought he might still be alive. I saw that shape, that heavy shape . . .'

Later that night, Sam and Patrick and a few others, like Cameron Watson, an American club DJ then in Paris to escape the draft to Vietnam, had little doubt in their minds about what had happened that night. 'Well, everybody knew you could get drugs in the clubs. That was not a big thing,' says Patrick. 'But that week somebody brought some drugs that was pretty strong, I think. Because [Jim was] not the only guy who died in Paris in the weeks [that followed]. There was like a stronger dose, or whatever. It was pure or something and I think, I'm not a specialist, but I think what happened is when you put the same dose but the drug is stronger, then you've got your problem. So I think [Jim] just overdosed not by taking more, but by taking a more pure drug than the usual way.'

The fact that he had also spent the whole day and night drinking beer, wine, whisky and vodka also took its toll. The connection was less well known in 1971, but a small mixture of alcohol and even the lowest-grade heroin can prove incredibly toxic, often fatal. As for what happened next, back at the apartment on Rue Beautreillis, only one man seemed to hint that he knew more than was good for him – and he killed himself, sticking a shotgun in his mouth and pulling the trigger, in front of a roomful of people at a party held – bizarrely – at the same Rue Beautreillis just a few months later.

What now seems certain is that Pam, true to form, was more concerned with saving herself than worrying about Jim, when the men burst into her apartment at around 3 a.m. Junkies stratify their lives clearly and without pause for doubt: first, above anything else, comes the junk. How much they have, how little, how safe it is to use, how unsafe. What the chances are, as specifically as possible, of them being busted, or even worse, left without any gear? Pam's first thought when she saw the two breathless henchmen dragging Jim's body in, wrapped in a blanket was: Have they come to steal my heroin? Or, worse, have they come to bust me, or rape me, then steal my heroin? Initially she gave little thought to Jim's prone and apparently unconscious body – she had seen him carried home like that by complete strangers too many times before for that to even flicker on her radar. Screaming, she began to run around the apartment, 'cleaning up', that is, hiding the detritus of another night spent chopping lines, snorting lines, spilling lines, then chopping and snorting some more. The stuff was everywhere, the nuclear fallout of the fulltime, blood-oath junkie.

When the two men, in their broken English, made it clear they were friends of the Count's, that they were here to help, she began, slowly, still woozy and still plenty wary, to calm down and force her brain into gear. When they began undressing the casually slung body on the floor, though, a new sense of foreboding overtook her.

What the fuck were they doing?

The two men carried the now naked body over to the bath, laid it in the tub, and began to run the hot-water tap. They then dragged Pam into the adjoining room and began to tell her what to do. The hot water was to disguise the cause of death. She would wait two hours, then phone the paramedics. The two men would be sitting outside in their car watching for the paramedics' arrival. Her story was simple: she knew nothing. Jim had spent the night with her, he had taken a bath when she went to bed. When she woke up this is how she found him – and called the paras. Got it? And while she was waiting to do that, she should clean the fucking place up. The cops would not take kindly to finding all this shit about the place . . .

Pamela, lost, alone, stoned immaculate, did as she was told. With the finely attuned sense of survival that only the most devout heroin addicts have access to, she instantly calculated that this was her only chance of making it out of this mess alive. Thanks a fucking bunch, Jimbo . . .

According to Marianne Faithfull's 1996 memoir, *Faithfull*, Pamela phoned Jean de Breteuil, whom Marianne was in bed with, at around 6 a.m. 'We were staying at L'Hotel. Suddenly Jean had to leave. He slammed out the room. He didn't come right back. He returned in the early hours very agitated. I was fucked up on Tuinals. For no reason he beat me up. I asked him, "Did you have a good time there?" He replied: "Get packed, we're going to Morocco."'

By lunchtime they were on a plane to Marrakesh, where

they took refuge with the Count's mother, at another notorious international jet set hangout, the Villa Taylor, in Tangiers. Marianne had never seen the Count in such a state. Not even after the death of Janis Joplin nine months before, when de Breteuil had actually boasted about being the guy who'd sold her the fatally strong heroin that killed her. As Faithfull writes in her book, de Breteuil was 'scared for his life. Jim Morrison had OD'd, and he had provided the smack. He saw himself as dealer to the stars. Now he was a small time dealer in big trouble. Jean took me to Tangier. It was a disaster. We were horribly strung out. In a panic before he left Paris he got rid of all his drugs.'

Another guest at the Villa that evening was the noted musicologist Roger Steffens, who a week later wrote an extraordinary letter home to his family, dated 9 July, in which he observed: 'The Countess's son, Jean, the handsome 21-year-old jet-setting playboy who inherits his late father's title this November, arrived unexpectedly in Marrakesh last Saturday.' He went on to explain how the visibly shaken Count had arrived with a clearly distressed Marianne Faithfull. 'The pair had just come from two violent days in Paris, which began with an auto crash, included an attempt by Jean's best friend to slash his wrists and culminated in a call from another old girlfriend of Jean's, Pamela Courson, who was staying in Paris with her husband [sic] Jim Morrison, lead singer of The Doors. She begged Jean to rush over to her place, and when he arrived they found Morrison dead in the bathtub of an apparent overdose of drugs. All these being too much, Marianne and Jean hopped a plane for Marrakesh, and a peaceful, retreating week.'

Retreating, yes. Peaceful, no. Speaking over 40 years later, Steffens recalled how 'Jean and Marianne seemed very high and spaced out as they recounted the story. They were very upset! I met Jean through his mother, the Countess de Breteuil, second wife – and first love, though a commoner – of the late Count. Jean was the apple of his mother's eye, but in reality a profligate drug-dealer who left a long trail of disasters in his wake.' Quite so. Among them, Janis Joplin, Talitha Getty (who would die, in Rome, of a heroin overdose just 11 days later), Pamela Courson (who would also died of a heroin overdose, back home in L.A., less than three years later), Jim Morrison of course. Even himself: before 1971 was over, Jean de Breteuil, too, would die in Tangier of a massive heroin overdose.

This was the end. *Finis*. And it was much, *much* worse than anyone, least of all The Doors, could ever have imagined.

TWENTY-ONE

The Calm Calculus
of Reason

Jim Morrison had barely felt the heroin slide down the back
of his throat before the lies began. Barely time to feel the first
heatwave of nausea and pleasure envelope his fat, sweaty body
before the vultures began circling, shitting from on high.

The cleaners had just arrived at the club around eight
o'clock that morning, slopping out the toilet floors and sluic-
ing away the blood and semen, urine and puke, on the walls,
the usual morning-after-the-night-before scene for the Circus's regular *nettoyeurs*. Around the same time, Pam was
doing some *nettoyage des toilettes* of her own, phoning Alain
Ronay, at Agnès Varda's house. 'Please call an ambulance. I
think my Jim is dying,' she tells them knowing Jim has been
dead for at least three hours. 'He is in the bath. He has blood
around his nose. Please call for me.'

As Varda would later recall, 'Pamela called my house and
I answered. I called for the firemen – *les pompiers*. In an accident you always call them, they are the first assistance, like
paramedics. I told them: "Go right away to this address. There
is a scene there where maybe someone is out of life." Ronay

gave the exact address. We went together, we arrived, and the fireman said, "It's too late – he's already dead."' Next on the scene was Varda's family doctor, Dr Max Vasille, whom she had also phoned. 'But it was hopeless.'

The first official on the scene was Alain Raisson. Now living in Rio de Janeiro, he recalls arriving at the apartment with his usual team of five. 'We carried him onto the bed to do cardiac massage,' he says. 'We tried to revive him and failed. It was a short, intense, very real and brief encounter.' The official police doctor, who arrived a few minutes later, was astonished when told he was examining the corpse of a 27-year-old. 'He looks much older. I would have said a 57-year-old!' the doctor exclaimed. But the doctor was not young either, struggling against the Paris heat. Soon all of Paris's most affluent citizens would flee the city for their summer vacations. The doctor was in no hurry to ask awkward questions. It seemed obvious what had happened, and, without any of the surviving relatives pushing for more detail, he was happy to sign away the death as being from 'natural causes'. Autopsies were not as a rule performed in France unless there was a suspicion of murder. The doctor advised the death had been caused by heart failure, possibly brought about by respiratory problems. *'Affaire classée.'* Case closed.

By nine o'clock that Saturday the street outside Jim's and Pam's apartment was choked with police and onlookers. Yet Alain Ronay had managed to push through to take Pam to a nearby undertaker's office and, later, to arrange to pick up an official death certificate at the Town Hall, which caused the Commissioner of Police handling the matter great consternation. Pam flushed away her entire stash before calling the paramedics, who she knew would bring with them the cops. She had been cool, done what she'd been told, or else. More mysteriously, she had also set fire to a bundle of Jim's letters and notes, his scrawled two-line poems and small-hours elegies. When the Commissioner of Police arrived on the scene and saw the small fire burning in the grate, he demanded to know why she had done that. She answered, in her small, sing-song, stoney-woney voice: 'They mustn't read this stuff, this stuff!'

The only note she ever admitted to keeping was the one that contained the disturbingly self-aware lines: 'Last words, Last words. Out.' Followed by a space and then: 'Regret for wasted nights & wasted years / I pissed it all away / American Music.' A truth teller then right to the end, my friend.

Now it was a slow, sunny Parisian Saturday. That night, the Rock and Roll Circus and the Alcazar opened as normal. As did La Boule, Le Sherwood, and all the other late-night hiding places for the night-bound and drug-serene. Although no one working at the Circus was allowed to breathe a word, everybody was talking about it under their breath. Earlier that day, in the dying moments at La Bulle, those still awake told of seeing Cameron Watson, who was the night owl DJ there, being approached by two heavy-set, swarthy-looking men. Watson immediately cut the music and announced through his microphone: 'Ladies and gentlemen, Jim Morrison has died tonight at the Rock and Roll Circus.' There was a moment of ill-prepared silence, then he put another record on and people again began to dance. By that night word on the street was that the Corsican mafia had offed Morrison.

A hit man had been sent up especially from Marseilles to silence the crazy American. Others told of seeing Jim beaten to death, maybe stabbed, in a street fight with the Count and his heavies. Still others said they'd heard from reliable sources that he had committed suicide. That they had seen it coming for weeks.

As the years passed, these rumours assumed even more outrageous shape. There was a huge blood-soaked knife found in the bathroom. He'd been shot twice in the head. There were strange bruises on his body. (The latter was given credence by the amount of times the body was dropped during its tortured journey from the ladies' toilets of the Rock and Roll Circus and up the three flights of stairs to his apartment.) Today you can even buy books that claim Morrison's death was the work of the CIA, as part of a covert campaign to reclaim youth culture, administering fatal drug overdoses first to Brian Jones, then Jimi Hendrix, Janis Joplin and now Jim Morrison. Also on the list were John Lennon, Bob Dylan and Mick Jagger. A decade later the same claims would be made about the tragic death from cancer of Bob Marley.

But the most sickening and absurd claim of all, and the one that has persisted the longest, was that he had not died at all; that Jim Morrison had faked his own death in order to escape the trappings of celebrity. This overlooked the fact that Jim had already forced The Doors to plan for a life without him, long before he died. That, in fact, he had already begun to live a life as far away from the famous Lizard King of L.A. as possible, so grossly overweight and heavily bearded few who passed him in the street recognised him any more anyway. That no one *cared* any more, man, what the fuck he did next.

As was French custom, his body was placed in a coffin and laid out on a long table in the bedroom. The next day was Sunday and the day after that was a French holiday, so there was nothing else to be done anyway, they were told. Somebody from the undertaker's would be by every few hours with large blocks of dry ice so that the decomposing body wouldn't begin smelling too bad too quickly. Also contrary to the stories that have been passed down ever since, Pam did not spent the night alone with Jim's body. 'She stayed at my place and she went back to the apartment in the day', according to Agnès Varda. 'People were with her at all times. The *secrétaire* [Robin Wertle] was there. The police and the undertaker had keys to Rue Beautreillis.'

With the Count having vanished in a puff of pure Moroccan, and Jim lying dead on a bed of ice at the apartment, Pam spent the weekend reliant completely on the goodwill of Varda and Ronay. There were a couple of attempts to try and phone home but it was the 4 July weekend in the United States and no one was in The Doors' office. Pam had dialled back so far from the other members of the band she didn't even have their home numbers any more. She determined to wait until Tuesday, when everybody would be back at work after Labour Day, and phone Bill Siddons. But on the Monday, 5 July, Clive Selwood, who ran Elektra's London offices, phoned Bill at home. 'Three journalists have called me and asked if Morrison is dead,' he told him down the crackling phone line. Bill tried to shrug it off, assuring Clive the Jim-is-dead rumours did the rounds regularly in America. Maybe they had just spread to London? But Clive was not so sure. The journalists in question had not been long-haired, pot-smoking music press bozos. These were serious newspapermen.

Bill spent the next six hours trying to phone Pam in Paris. He finally got her on the phone at around 9 p.m., French time. She blurted out the news and became hysterical. Bill promised to fly over immediately. She was to hang on, hold it together. For Jim. 'I got to the apartment on Tuesday morning while all the local workers were in the cafés drinking their coffee and brandy,' he recalled in 2010. 'Pam was alone. She was coherent but totally distraught. She'd hit the wall. I cooperated as best as I could. I was only 21. I had no tools to deal with this. We ran round the city all day. She filed a report at the American embassy ['The Death of an American Citizen Abroad' forms] and we went to the funeral house.' Bill denies later stories that he ordered a more expensive white ash coffin for Jim to be buried in. He says he simply took Pam's explanation for Jim's death at face value. 'All I know is Pam told me he died of a heart attack. She simply said, "I went to check on him and he was no longer with us."'

Speaking now from his office in Sherman Oaks, Bill recalls it as a trip into the unknown, 'before telex, before fax!' Still just 21 years old at the time, trying to calm Pam down long enough to make arrangements for the funeral and keep his own feelings in check was an almost impossible task. 'I lost someone that I just loved as a person. I mean, as much as a handful as Jim was in so many ways, he was a brilliant talent. The smartest guy I ever met, and a really good soul. He drove people crazy – intentionally. And I saw it, so it didn't drive me crazy. So it was incredibly difficult to do. At the same time, there was no question: I was going to do . . . to be the support system that was needed in the moment. And I went to Paris, sat down with Pam, told her: "I am here on my own volition. I'm not here representing the other guys. I'm here to help you with anything you need to do. Let's make this as painless as possible. Let's work together in making this happen."

'And she accepted it for what it was and . . . you know, we did everything together for the next three days until we flew home. I understood her values. She told me that Jim wanted to be buried in Père-Lachaise and she told me the conversations of how it had happened. And I just went, "Okay, let's make it happen", and we did what we had to do.' One thing Bill was intent on doing, he explains, was avoiding the media circus that had surrounded the similarly sordid deaths of Brian, Jimi and Janis over the past year. 'Pam and I just . . . we talked about it and she said, "I don't want it to be like Jimi and Janis." I said, "It won't be. We are gonna bury Jim as an American poet." We didn't tell the French authorities anything about [it], we didn't say rock star singer. We said American poet. Same thing with the Père-Lachaise people. Fortunately The Doors were not huge over there. And we were able to get it done before the media even found out about it.'

According to Agnès Varda, though, 'When people say that Bill Siddons organised Jim's funeral at Père-Lachaise – no, he did not. I did that. I helped with all the arrangements. It wasn't easy getting a foreigner into Père-Lachaise. Anyway Jacques and I organised with Alain. There was no priest. It was all done quickly and properly. Just normal. Is it lucky to have been there? Would you love to have been there? The man was dead! I wish he were still alive. He cannot be replaced. *Voilà!*' While according to Alain Ronay, 'I buried Morrison in Père-Lachaise. It was my idea. I was the only person at the funeral parlour. I picked the site. I went alone. Agnès had nothing to do with it. Bill Siddons can't take credit. Can he speak French? Give me a break. Enough already.' What Siddons's arrival did do, he agrees, is take care of Pam. 'She had no money and she was losing control. Agnès was good to her. Agnès drove me to the funeral. Pam wanted Jim buried in L.A. for God's sake! What? And have bus tours stopping every two hours?'

Now Paris's second most popular tourist site – after the Eiffel Tower – at the time of his initial interment on 7 July, Jim's grave was unmarked, and listed in the cemetery directory as Douglas James Morrison, the name Pam had given the police in order to try and disguise who he really was. A few days later a black metal plaque was placed there, with the singer's name given this time as 'Morisson [sic], James Douglas'. It was stolen two years later and replaced by another, smaller stone plaque, with the surname again spelt incorrectly. When this too was stolen, the cemetery authorities decided to mark the grave. By then the gravesite was smothered in graffiti, at first in chalk then soon with paint and spray cans, indented by morbid slogans and lines from Doors songs. In 1981, the Croatian sculptor Mladen Mikulin made a special bust, which he placed over a new gravestone to commemorate the tenth anniversary of his death; the bust was defaced mercilessly over the years, smothered in graffiti and littered with cigarette butts and empty beer cans. It was finally stolen in 1988. Mikulin made another in 1989, which was also soon stolen. And finally there was a bronze portrait of Jim, set up in 2001. But that didn't last long either before 'fans' first defaced then stole it. In the early Nineties, Jim's now retired father, Steve, consulted with E. Nicholas Genovese, Professor of Classics and Humanities at San Diego State University, to produce a flat stone for the grave. It came with a beautiful bronze plaque with an inscription in Greek: KATA TON ΔAIMONA EAYTOY, meaning 'according to his own daemon' – aka 'guiding spirit'. Or in simple but to-the-point words of a lifelong military man and, now, heartbroken father of a son he would never quite understand yet wished, finally, to honour: 'True to Himself'.

One detail nobody disagrees with is that Bill Siddons never took the opportunity to view Jim's dead body. This would become the lynchpin of all the he-faked-his-own-death guff that still bubbles around Morrison's legacy. Says Bill with a wry chuckle: 'The only thing I doubted about my decision is that I went, "Yeah, I guess *technically* I should have looked at the body." But I loved this man. My dad died a few years before, and when he died I walked into the funeral home and the casket was open and I just went, "Argh!" I was only 14 or something and my mother ran to the funeral director, got him to close the casket. I *never* want to see somebody that I loved dead. I want to remember them as I remember them. I was there for Jim as my friend. I wasn't there to be The Doors' manager doing something for The Doors' career. I was just doing what I needed to do for Jim and I did and I never re-gretted any of that.'

More aggravating, he suggests, is how 'Ray took great ad-vantage of the fact that I hadn't insisted on seeing the body. I knew Pamela. There was never a doubt in my mind about Jim's death. I slept in the room with his casket. I knew that there wasn't somebody else in there. I saw the anguish in Pam. I knew she wasn't a very talented actress. There was just absolutely no doubt. And the fact that Ray chose to exploit the myth . . .' He sighs heavily. 'Okay, it's your myth. I disagreed with it but . . .'

The funeral ceremony was perfunctory, modest, *weird*, Bill says. 'I travelled with Pamela and the secretary, Robin Wertle, to the cemetery. Ronay and Varda followed separately.' There were four unnamed pallbearers, arranged as a courtesy by the undertakers. 'Everyone was distraught but it was a nice little goodbye ceremony. Pam said some words', reciting from one of Jim's last poems, 'The Severed Garden', and then they left. Ready to begin the rest of their lives. Or not, as the case may be . . .

The same week, the newspapers reported the death of Louis Armstrong, who'd died in his sleep from a heart attack, aged 69. Publicity surrounding Jim's death was strangely muted by comparison. Bill had issued an official press statement the day he and Pam got back. It read: 'I have just returned from Paris, where I attended the funeral of Jim Morrison. Jim was buried in a simple ceremony, with only a few friends present. The initial news of his death and funeral was kept quiet because those of us who knew him intimately and loved him as a person wanted to avoid all the notoriety and circus-like atmosphere that surrounded the deaths of such other rock personalities as Jimi Hendrix and Janis Joplin. I can say that Jim died peacefully of natural causes – he had been in Paris since March with his wife [sic], Pam. He had seen a doctor in Paris about a respiratory problem, and had complained of this problem on Saturday – the day of his death. I hope that Jim is remembered not only as a rock singer and poet, but also as a warm human being. He was the most warm, most human, most understanding person I've known. This wasn't always the Jim Morrison people read about – but it was the Jim Morrison I knew, and his close friends will remember.'

Two days later, however, Britain's then highest-profile weekly music paper, *Melody Maker*, was still denying the rumours of Jim's death. Based on a phone call a reporter from the United Press agency had made to Pam the day Bill arrived in Paris, in which she insisted that Jim was alive but staying at a special clinic outside Paris, to convalesce, news of his death took much longer to sink in than it should have. Several newspapers around the world ran with the story, ignoring Bill Siddons's statement. On 8 July, the day after the funeral, the cover of a French magazine, *Pop Musique*, declared: 'Jim Morrison n'est pas mort' (Jim Morrison is not dead).

When Patricia Kennealy got the news of Jim's death, she immediately flew to Paris. She found the soil around the grave surrounded by shells, with a wooden plaque with Morrison's name on top of it. She knelt there alone with her thoughts, silently vowing to Jim to remain true, no matter what.

All the time Jim had been away in Paris, she says now, 'It was agony. It was absolute torture. I did not know how I was going to manage. Frankly, I didn't think I'd ever see him again because he would die. I honestly believed that it was going to kill him. And, as we see, it did. But you hope against hope when you care about someone. When you're in a relationship with someone. When you're *married* to someone. I mean, you do what you do, you know? People have asked me, "He was very brutal to you from time to time." I say, "Yeah, he was. But that wasn't *him*." Maybe that was me making excuses, but I never believed that that was *him*. And other people have said the same. I mean there were so many different Jim Morrisons, I think anybody that ever knew him for kind of a significant degree has their own Jim that they saw. I like to think I got the best of it, frankly, because that's just what I have to think.'

Patricia, who would change her name legally to Kennealy-Morrison shortly afterwards, remains bitter towards Pamela Courson. 'I mean, both of them told me they had no sexual relationship whatsoever from about 1969 onwards . . . I think what it was, was that they imprinted on each other before he became famous and it was very easy and comfortable for both of them. I mean, basically they competed with one another to be more stoned and more drunk and more outrageous and more horrible to one another. It was a very, very sick relationship. He told me that himself when we first started going out. He said, basically, "it was a poisoned relationship, half pity and half habit". And I think that really kind of sums it up. He knew it. It wasn't that he was being stupid about it. He knew exactly what was going on. But he didn't, because of the addiction, because of the alcoholism, he didn't have the strength to entirely get out of it. I think his best shot at that, honestly, came when he met me.'

Patricia claims she and Jim had already made plans for his return to America; that he was going to leave Pam and come and live with her in New York. 'He had been in Paris telling his lawyer to set up some kind of alimony programme for [Pam] so that when he got back he could just give her a pay-off and make her go away. And that's what he was telling me as well. So unless he was lying to Max Fink, the lawyer, and also to me, I think that that's what would have happened. He [Jim] was asking me to look for studios in New York and engineers because he wanted to record stuff solo without The Doors.'

Back in L.A., a week after Jim's death, Bill began phoning round, giving everyone the news. Asked for their memories of being told of their singer's death, over 40 years later, all three Doors told me, as Ray put it, 'On a certain level, it was not a surprise. Yes, there are some stimulations to alcohol and a freeing of inhibitions. But there's an addictive quality to it also and I think poor Jim fell victim to the addictive side of alcohol. That's the great tragedy of Jim Morrison, that he did die at 27, as did Janis Joplin at 27, and Jimi Hendrix at 27 and Brian Jones at 27. Brilliant young people, some of them die young and it's a great tragedy.'

Robby: 'It was still a terrible shock, because we never thought *that* would happen, you know, really. Most of things [Jim] did were for show, dramatic or whatever. But he obviously never killed anybody, or went that far. But, yeah, it was a surprise. I always thought he'd live to be 100. Be one of those drunks that drinks a bottle of whisky every day and lives to be 90.' He paused, sighed. Then added cheerfully, 'He was lucky he didn't meet his end sooner.'

John: 'I don't wanna blame his demise solely on fame. Certainly, there was the drink, as they say in Ireland. And then there's genetics, growing up in a military family that moved around from base to base, so that you don't have a lot of roots. I loved him for his words. He would just talk his words to me and I'd hear rhythms. And I was rather tortured by his self-destruction. But that was it. That was the card I was dealt, that band.' He added ruefully: 'Jim knew I disapproved of his self-destruction, that's for sure. More than anyone else in the band.'

Speaking in *Follow the Music*, Paul Rothchild recalled how he was sitting at home in Laurel Canyon when he heard the news. 'And I had no feeling. I was numb. Then my first thought was, "Well, he finally made it over. I hope he's feeling good now." To [Jim] the exploration of death was another and maybe the ultimate high.' 'The End', he said, was 'almost a love song to death'.

In his memoir, Jac Holzman recalls how he had spent the 4 July weekend entertaining friends at his house, which he had recently moved into and named 'Tranquility'. His partner, Ellen Sander, had recently moved out, taking their unborn baby with her. Jac was struggling with his own demons but he tried to keep his guests entertained with funny stories about Jim Morrison. The time he'd squirted a fire extinguisher all over the studio at Sunset Sound. The time he'd pissed Ed Sullivan off mightily. The times he'd show up at Jac's house unannounced and sit with his young son, Adam, the two of them playing happily together for hours. He told 'all the stories I knew about Jim Morrison. I talked about him for hours.'

When he got to his office that Monday morning and took the call letting him know Jim had died, he says it affected him more than the death of his own father. Jac's father had been old. Jim was young, just 27. Like Jimi and Janis. He resolved that Elektra would do better by Jim and The Doors, no quick albums or 'any of that kind of sordid nonsense'. Jim Morrison was 'the great seeker,' he says now. His presence in Jac's life had changed everything, helped make him a multimillionaire, given Elektra a whole new identity; a whole different story to tell the world. Jac would never forget that.

Not one given to sentimentality, Vince Treanor says one of the big unspoken emotions among the rest of The Doors on learning of Jim's death, however, must have been guilt. 'Everybody knew that Jim was on a ten per cent grade – and he had no brakes. Everybody knew it. The problem was, everybody also knew that nobody could do anything about it. That was number one. Number two . . . They're rehearsing all summer and finally [that summer] they have the in-house rehearsals, in the theatre rehearsals and we were off on the road. But when the shock came [of Jim's death] it was like, "What? What? What?"' He says that when Bill phoned to say Jim really was dead, 'Everyone went crazy. *Everybody went crazy.* The three boys stopped *everything.* It was, "Don't talk to me." They weren't together. They stopped rehearsals. They just came apart at the seams. They were really broke up about it.'

Other friends on the scene, like Pamela Des Barres, simply could not get her head around the news, almost refused to believe it. 'I saw [Jim] right before he went to France. He looked healthier than I'd seen him in a long, long time. He was in a convertible with a couple of friends. He saw me walking down the street, I was on a commercial audition and he just pulled up right in front of me on La Cienega and said, "Baby, you so sweet, and healthy." He said, "I'm going to France, and I'm going to start over. It's good". He was upbeat. And I really felt so happy that he was going to do something good for himself. He was going to write his poetry, he was really into his work and then he got there.'

She says that her first thought after hearing of his death was for Pam. Despite the crack-ups, the freak-outs and hate trips and fighting in the street, she still believes that 'He was in love with Pamela Courson and that was it. He toyed and played with everybody because he could, because of the world we lived in, because it was there for him to fiddle with. He was curious and he wanted to tamper with everything. And he could, he was Jim fucking Morrison and he was a kid. He was a child. And of course he's in this playground and he's going to fuck around with it, but he was really in love with her.'

Since Jim Morrison's death in 1971 the story of The Doors has continued, but only through wish-fulfilment. A kind of phantasmagoria of Ray Manzarek's avuncular fairy stories, given added resonance by the plethora of reissued albums, endless live compilations, box sets, limited editions, books, movies, documentaries, Internet conspiracy theories, music press whodunits, and generations of rock musicians and fans who can't help but fall in love with the idea of Jim Morrison and the age-old fantasy he still conjures up for them. Today, despite the brilliantly researched, wonderfully evocative biographies, the Kindle-only record-straighteners, the kiss-and-tell memoirs from former lovers and friends, the online now-it-can-be-told memories of those still alive to tell the tale, at least as they lived it – despite all that, less is known about Jim Morrison and The Doors than ever before.

In the acclaimed 2009 documentary *When You're Strange*, the depth of what we don't know about The Doors is revealed as staggering, unending, almost infinite. No, Jim did not die in a bathtub. But the story that he died that way is still told today just like the tale of Red Riding Hood. It doesn't begin to uncover the truth, and it's not meant to. Quite the reverse, in fact. No, Jim Morrison was not Christ-like or given to prophetic visions. No his poetry really wasn't that good – yet.

But the *idea* of Jim Morrison – that grows more glorious, more precious, more removed from reality by the year. And who wants to spoil the kids' fun by telling them there is no such thing as Santa Claus? Certainly not Ray Manzarek, Robby Krieger and John Densmore. And who could blame them? After all the shit Jim put them through, practically destroying their careers when they should have been at their peaks. Something, paradoxically, he only redeemed himself for by dying so young and so 'mysteriously'. His death, so young, so tragic, so apparently inexplicable, guaranteed The Doors a glorious afterlife they almost certainly would not have attained had Jim lived. They had already planned for a life without Jim, something they would, ultimately, not be able to do, as they would soon find out. But he would have been gone by then, staying in Paris and trying to become that poet he always talked so much about. That filmmaker he still hadn't given up becoming. In the end, appalling though it seemed to be at the time, Jim Morrison was the singer's last great gift to The Doors. They would never work again without him. They would never *need* to work again without him.

Never mind the deeply troubled, immensely intelligent, utterly pretentious, irresponsibly generous, sexually gregarious, possibly repressed, possibly abused-as-a-child, irrefutably talented, brazenly forthcoming, immensely insulting, handsome-as-a-matador-in-his-prime real-life person that was James Douglas Morrison. Never mind the books he quietly read, the sweet love he secretly made, the men he surrounded himself with who were never his equal, the cronies and the fawners, the groupies and the hangers-on, and how much he despised them for what they were but hated himself more. Never mind all that shit, man. Let's get him onstage with the band again, man, one more fucking time. For the road! Get yourself up one morning, get yourself a beer and let's roll, baby, roll. Fuck, yeah! Go, Jimbo, go!

The last time Ray spoke to me, by phone from his home in Napa, some months before his death in 2013, when he surprised me by agreeing to appear on a BBC TV documentary I was helping make, by telling me I could take his words and 'Do what you want, man. Be free! That's how Jim wanted it!', he said, 'You know what, I don't think as word-men we ever find that vocabulary, because music is totally ephemeral. How can words describe a musical sound? It can only be *like* something. You know, Robby's guitar could scream like a banshee, but it was *like* a banshee. It wasn't a banshee, it was screaming like a banshee, sliding up and down, this slithery snake of that bottleneck guitar of his. So there's no words . . . Music is totally ephemeral. It's pure vibration, that's all it does. It only deals with vibration, which is what made sense for it, in its placement in time, in the Sixties. The Sixties were a time of increased, heightened vibrations, due to psychedelic substances. And due to the fact that we were all so lucky to be there. We were the result of our parents winning the Depression and winning World War Two, and we were the fruit of their Herculean effort. They sent us to school and said go and get education, and, I mean, we did!'

You knew what he meant even if you didn't.

I asked him where he thought *Strange Days* fitted into The Doors' canon. I was writing a magazine story about the album, which I considered one of their best, alongside *L.A. Woman*, but Ray was so on-message all the time he barely listened to the questions, just gave you his rant, his practised spiel, except coming from him, you knew the crazy motherfucker actually meant it, which was astounding, when you thought about it, after all these years.

And he said, 'I never rank them. I don't *rank* the albums. I don't see them the same way that other people see them. I see this body of work – from the first song on the first album, to . . . all the way from 'Break On Through' to 'Riders on the Storm'. It's our work; it's our creation. It's like your children; we're like parents. We've created these little things and they live now without our help at all. Once we record them they become immortal and I couldn't even possibly rank them. You know, some of the songs, in artistic terms, work better than some of the other songs. Some of them are more profound than some of the others. But even "Hello, I Love You" works perfectly as a Top 40 ditty, which is why we created it. We said, "Let's write a Top 40 song", you know? Let's write something real light and three minutes and fun and light, something Top 40. And out of it came, 'Hello, I Love You'. You know, so the preconceived plan was to write a Top 40 song and it worked – boom! It was the first No. 1 song we had.'

For Ray, the music of The Doors was always the real story, the real trip. 'It becomes a journey. It's a psychic journey. You can enter into Doors-world and be taken on a long psychic journey through all manner of thought and all manner of being, and all types of consciousness.

And if Jim hadn't died, would it have carried on . . .?

'Well, think of it this way. 'Riders on the Storm' is the beginning of a new Doors direction. That's where it was going to go. Unfortunately it never got to go there. Now here's the tragedy of The Doors. They never got to complete that journey. That narrative will always be open-ended. And it will never be completed. It would have taken, oh god, another *decade* to complete that journey. At *least* another decade. But that's the tragedy of it. But we have what we have. We danced with Jim while he was here. We have the creations of his literary mind and we're all better off for it.'

He was on a roll now and it was a trip just hearing it. 'And it's open now. The mantle can be passed to the next generation, the next band that wants to come along and take over The Doors slot, it's wide open. And I heartily encourage any band that wants to go in that direction. Please do, I'd love to hear some new Doors music. And that would encompass classical, jazz, of course a rock'n'roll foundation, blues, and then it's got to have some Flamenco in there too. It's got to have a sense of Spanish. And I was planning that after Spanish we would go into adding some oriental things, some Japanese and Chinese.

'And a perfect example of that is *on* the album *Strange Days*

– 'I Can't See Your Face in Your Mind'. It has a very oriental overtone to it. That's one of the directions we *never* got to explore. I'm playing the marimba, an actual marimba, without playing the mallet backwards. So it's wood hitting against wood. And you can hear that in the background. Listen to the marimba in there, it combines both a Latin American and an oriental sound and note selections. And that's where it would have gone.

'*Plus*, it would have gone, what we would have done, is gone into where John and Robby and I took it in *An American Prayer*' – the superb posthumous, spoken-word album The Doors released in 1978, which reactivated their career, alongside the recent use of 'The End' in the brilliantly mind-altering *Apocalypse Now*, the movie made by another ex-UCLA visionary named Francis Ford Coppola – 'in which there would have been a combination of poetry and musique concrète and sounds of the time, sounds of the street, and music and rock'n'roll and like that. It would have just continued to grow. It would have expanded and it would have left . . . perhaps it might have become too complex but it would have left the basic power, the basic simplicity, of The Doors – live at the Whisky A Go Go, as I like to call our first album. We would have expanded and gone further and further into performances . . . performance art onstage is what it would have become. And we never got to do it – shit, man! Fuck! That pisses me off . . .'

He paused, but only for a microsecond. Then, happy, began again. 'So, you know, unfortunately we never got to grow into all the things we could have. But it was a great burst [of energy]. As Jim said, "That year we had a great visitation of energy." And that year for The Doors lasted from 1965 to the summer of 1971.'

Right on, Ray. Right on through to the other side, man. Yeah!

Epilogue: Stoned Immaculate

After Jim Morrison's death, The Doors tried in vain to carry on, almost as if nothing had happened. They had already recorded their first album without him while Jim was in Paris. According to Bruce Botnick, 'it wasn't to be an album. It was to work up some stuff with the hope that Jim was gonna come back, and there will be an infusion and these new ideas that the guys have been working on will meld with what Jim was doing and there would be an album. So . . . it became an album out of the default of Jim's passing.'

Perhaps so, but the fact they had done so much work on *a Doors album without Jim Morrison* underlines just how far they were already down the road of working without their singer. Maybe they *were* hoping Jim would come back. But they certainly weren't relying on it. And what were they supposed to do in the meantime? After Miami, after the Isle of Wight, after New Orleans, after everything, and now the guy's run away to Paris and doesn't know when he's coming back and will probably end up going to jail if he comes back anyway?

No, fuck that. Who could blame them? What other option did they have? Hadn't they let the whole thing drift long enough? Now it was their turn to front up and do something. As Ray said, 'We were back in the studio the day after we heard he'd died.' He'd added that going back to work so quickly was a good way of dealing with the trauma of losing their friend. The fact that *Other Voices*, as they wincingly titled their first album without Morrison, was released just three months after his death shows just how far advanced they already were with the recording at the time of his death, and how determined they were to carry on without him, no matter what. Jim dying was the only part of the plan they hadn't bargained for.

The result was an album that was neither fish nor fowl; characterless and plain. Produced by Bruce Botnick and recorded, again, as live in the basement of The Doors' office on mobile equipment, the album is as exciting as it sounds: The Doors *without* Jim Morrison. The Stones *without* Mick Jagger. The Velvet Underground *without* Lou Reed. The pen without ink. Just the three of them, Ray and Robby sharing the vocals in place of Jim. The only track that really jumps out is the lengthy, far-out jazz-rock of 'Ship w/Sails'. Built around a jam that Robby and John had worked up, with added percussive flourishes from the Afro-Cuban master percussionist Francisco Aguabella, as an instrumental it could have been something extra-cool by Santana. Unfortunately, once Ray's overwrought vocals and half-baked lyrics have been added to the mix it becomes more like second-rate Doors.

'None of the songs on *Other Voices* are from Jim. That was the missing quotient,' agrees Botnick. 'It was Robby trying to sing. Ray doing his thing. And all of a sudden they had to stand up and write music. But it didn't have any of the danger or any of the theatre that Jim brought to it. You've got to realise, musically, they were still The Doors. They just didn't have Jim's melodies or words to play off of. But all the arrangements, all the musicality was the three guys. So it's not surprising that when you heard *Other Voices* or albums after that, that you still heard The Doors. You just didn't hear Jim.'

In which case, wouldn't it have been better to simply forget the whole thing? Either get a plausible replacement in to sing or simply record under another name? 'Elektra could have forgiven the contract. The guys could have said, you know, we can't make any more records as The Doors, we're sorry, Jac. And he would have said, "I understand. No problem. Keep the money." I'm sure that would have happened.'

Does Bruce think, in retrospect, they should have done that? He paused. 'No . . . No, I don't think so. I think it was . . . unlike other bands I'm glad they didn't go out to find somebody else to be in Jim's leather pants, you know?'

It must have felt very strange, though, making a Doors album without Jim?

'Totally! Totally strange. Without Jim there wasn't really – quote-unquote – The Doors any more. [But] I think it was important that they do those records on their own so that they could break up totally, and Ray could do his thing, and Robby could do his thing, with John, with The Butts Band, and they can move onward. Robby's made six . . . ten albums as a solo performer. Some of it's vanity stuff, but he's constantly doing something. But he's not singing, he's only playing. He doesn't have a singer. It's an instrumental band.

And John has done an album. Tribal Jazz was the name of his band . . . If you look at other bands, did they continue after one of their main people died? For the most part, no. Look at Queen after Freddie Mercury died, they stopped.'

Except, of course, The Doors didn't immediately stop. When *Other Voices* was released in October 1971, they went out on the road. And it was a disaster. With the album stalling at No. 31 in the charts and the band basing their new live set almost entirely on material from *Other Voices*, it was, if anything, an even sadder end to the live career of The Doors than the debacle of New Orleans. But then this was 1971 and the concept of it being better to burn out than to fade away had yet to be considered.

Vince Treanor, who did the tour with them, is still aghast at the memory. 'It makes me wonder why in hell they were so damned anxious to change the music when they went on the road [with] *Other Voices*. Why didn't they listen to the audience, when the kids applauded the lights off the ceiling every time they played a Doors piece and the silence was thunderous when they played this other crap.'

In fact, after the tour was over, they went back straight back into the studio to have another go at making a plausible Doors album without Jim. Bruce Botnick had now bailed though and they were left to their own devices. The result, *Full Circle*, was full of good-timey get-up-and-dance guff and contrived acid-funk that made The Doors sound like what they were, adrift without a rudder, grasping at straws, up shit creek and other clichés.

'When they came back [after Jim's death] and they decided they wanted to record as a trio, I agreed to do that simply because I wanted to show them that it wasn't just Jim,' says Jac Holzman now. 'We made two records. The first one sold about 300,000, which made its money back. The second one did less well. And then they realised that they couldn't do it without Jim. And I wasn't interested in anybody else taking Jim's place.'

In fact, Holzman had tried to hook them up with an English vocalist, Howard Werth, whose London-based band, Audience, had recorded four art-rock albums for Charisma between 1969 and 1972, the later two released in the US by Elektra. When the band broke up in 1972, Holzman suggested the three Doors look into auditioning Werth as the new singer of The Doors.

'That's how I understand it,' says Werth now. 'The Doors were looking for a new singer to replace Jim Morrison and I met up with them in London at this lovely little summerhouse down by the river. We rehearsed a couple of days and it was working quite well. They tried a couple of other people out as well. I remember singing songs like 'Light My Fire' and 'Riders on the Storm' and some others. I wasn't really a huge fan at that time, actually. So I wasn't really au fait with a lot of their stuff. Then at the end they said they'd be in touch but that was the end of it. I spoke to them at their hotel a couple of times but then it didn't happen because Ray Manzarek's wife, Dorothy, was expecting their baby son, Leo. So he decided he couldn't deal with it any more and he went back to California.'

Werth says there didn't seem to be much in the way of a plan beyond simply 'looking for a replacement for Jim Morrison. Then if it worked they'd probably do some more recording, then organise a tour. But it just wasn't meant to be.' Other singers under consideration in the summer of 1972 included Iggy Pop – a big Jim Morrison fan – and Joe Cocker, then widely regarded in America as one of the finest singers of his generation. Unfortunately, the former was about to go in the studio with David Bowie, then in full-on Ziggy Stardust mode, and the latter was still in the full throes of heroin addiction. At the same time as they were rehearsing with Howard Werth they had also set aside a few days to work with another young British talent, named Kevin Coyne, whose unique blues voice and superior skills as a lyricist would have made an intriguing choice.

'They went to London,' recalls Botnick. 'They gave me a call, said, "We want you to come over. We're putting together a whole different thing." Then the day before I left I got a phone call saying, "Ray's quit the band, come anyway. We're gonna go to Jamaica, we'll do reggae!", which was The Butts Band.'

With Ray bailing out, Robby and John took the bull by horns and consigned the name The Doors to history. Whatever they did next, they decided, would be new and fresh, and have nothing to do with The Doors. With Elektra having recently become part of a much larger group of companies, WEA (Warners, Elektra, Atlantic), Jac Holzman was no longer there either to help guide them on a day-to-day basis, so the remaining Doors were now cast into unfamiliar territory – 'out in the street', as John told the journalist John Tobler in a 1974 interview with *ZigZag* magazine. As they struggled to plot a course without Holzman, their captain, or Jim, their magnetic north, Ray's return to the States abruptly closed off their creative outlet, and for gigging musicians like John and Robby downtime represented nothing less than slow, torturous death.

Rather than regroup in the US, they resolved to dig in and make a go of it in London, and so began the survivors' first post-Doors project. John and Robby auditioned local musicians over the course of four months, trying to play it cool so as not to intimidate the line of punters with stars in their eyes and ambitions to become the next Jim Morrison. As in their previous search with Ray, they found no one viable. It wasn't until Davy Harper, a roadie who split time between them and Traffic, introduced them to the singer Jess Roden that the flicker of hope first sparked. Roden was 24, recently of critically praised but commercially unsuccessful Bronco, and a well-known face on the London recording scene who had lent his talents as singer and/or guitarist to albums by Mott the Hoople, Sandy Denny, John Martyn and others. Seasoned, charismatic and gifted with a versatile range that wrapped easily around blues, rock and soul, it was impossible to deny how effortlessly Jess gelled with the loose grooving they laid down, his harmonies dovetailing smoothly into Robby's, and his stage presence charismatic and confident. Even better, Jess was hungry. Wanted it.

The project with the ex-Doors could not have arrived at a better time, but before leaping in headfirst, Jess had a few stipulations of his own. First and foremost was the understanding among all parties that he was not interested in primping his hair, throwing on leather pants and playing the new Lizard King. The Doors were over, as far as Jess was concerned, as he told a journalist in a 1973 interview: 'I am a singer, not a showman. I'm not a sex symbol and that, I believe, is the difference [between Jim and him]. I'm here to sing, not create news stories. When I joined, Ray Manzarek had left and we just came together for an album. From the first day I met them they said they wanted to start afresh . . . a whole new effort.'

Even better, Jess brought his own material to the table and he introduced them to the two other musicians to round out the project – bassist Phil Chen and later keyboardist Roy Davies. The new band was complete; all that remained was to find a new name. Where John and Robby's last project boasted a name steeped in mystic potency and literary gravitas, their new band settled on a name far closer to the way they actually felt. They decided on the schlocky Butts Band, a ham-fisted attempt at irony that played them as down-and-out losers, starving for work. Such a jokey name stood in blinding contrast to Ray's evolving fascination with mysticism and ancient pagan cults. With Ray out of the picture, however, John and Robby slipped loose of the inscrutably cryptic fetters that had constrained them for so long working with Jim and Ray.

In 1974, with the players in place, they wasted little time getting their ideas on tape, holing up in London's Olympic Studios to cut the first half of what would become their eponymous debut, *The Butts Band*. With Jess as the face of the new band, they built the core sound around the guitar. Robby's leads on 'I Won't be Alone Anymore' and the reggae-influenced 'Pop-a-Top' were full of his newfound swagger, as was his work on the Jess-penned 'New Ways'. Despite John's insistence that their sound be distinct from the Doors, 'Baja Bus' strongly evoked their musical past. But if any song captured the easy creative flow of the new outfit, it was the smoking live take of 'Kansas City', which perfectly show-cased Robby's extemporaneous chromatic brilliance. No one had ever talked about the guitarist of The Doors in the same way they did the guitarist of The Who or Led Zeppelin. Now Robby was showing them what they'd been missing.

As the first wave of advance copies took flight to the music press, early buzz classified the sound as heavily weighted towards reggae, which was understandable, although inaccurate. Such pigeonholing stemmed squarely from Phil's having been born and raised in Jamaica and the band's having recorded the latter half of the album there. Moreover, Phil received an album credit for 'reggae guitar'. Bob Marley had released both *Catch a Fire* and *Natty Dread* in the past year, albums that reset the dial on what a white rock audience found palatable. Eric Clapton had just enjoyed his biggest hit for years with his version of Marley's 'I Shot the Sheriff'. By 1974, reggae was the coolest music in the rock world. Even hairy rock behemoths like Led Zeppelin had dabbled with reggae (on 'D'yer Maker', from their 1973 album, *Houses of the Holy*). For The Butts Band to make it their musical calling card was about as far away from The Doors as you could get and in keeping with contemporary trends. This was not the groovy, tripped-out Sixties any more, they seemed to be saying, but the streetwise new Seventies.

In June 1974, with their album on the shelves, The Butts Band began gigging around London, supporting The Kinks at the Palladium. Roden quickly established his dominance on stage, promptly disabusing anyone of the notion that he was a minor player in the legacy of The Doors. The modest US tour that followed proved equally encouraging. Their gig at

Max's Kansas City, in New York City, drew a curious gaggle of Doors fans, critics and industry types who were equally impressed with the vibrancy of the Butts. By then the band had added Michael Berkowitz as a second drummer and showcased new material such as 'Sweet Danger'. The wheels, however, were about to fall off.

While the musicians had initially committed to convening every few weeks, either in the US or in London, the logistical briar patch of five musicians collaborating eight time zones apart would eventually prove too much. Long before Skype and email, such an arrangement offered awkward, costly and impersonal solutions to the larger problem of a band needing to be in the same room to create together. John and Robby eventually dissolved The Butts Band and re-formed it with the Americans Michael Stull and Alex Richman, both on vocals and keyboards, along with Karl Rucker on bass.

Jess, who was already signed to Island records, owed one more album to that label and formed the Jess Roden Band. Meanwhile, Roy opted to stay with his former band, Gonzalez, a sprawling, 20-man collective that gigged around London in the early Seventies. Phil went back to session work, although his role in the story of the Doors was not yet finished.

The new Butts Band pulled back on the jazz influence of their debut and released a 1975 follow-up called *Hear and Now* that saw them double down for an old-school soul record, in line with their Blue Thumb/ABC label mates The Four Tops. That record would fail to engender much love in Doors fans, however, falling well short of the ambitious promise of their debut. Soon thereafter, The Butts Band quietly drew to a close. Robby and John might have achieved rock star status in The Doors but they were studio musicians at heart; they simply wanted to play music that turned them on. Without somebody else's creative vision, their substantial talents withered amid unoriginal songwriting and poor business decisions.

With a better name and some reliable management who got what they were all about, who knows what might have occurred? They arguably blew a golden opportunity by letting go of Bill Siddons, who recalls representing The Butts Band's earliest incarnation, until the musicians baulked at his request for the standard 15 per cent commission (something he'd never enjoyed with The Doors, where as a young, inexperienced hired hand he had initially been happy to accept a salary). Looking back now, he recalls telling them, 'Hey, guys, I've given you five years of my life. I've saved your ass 20 times. It's time to pay me appropriately.' Instead, they opted for 'a Hollywood manager' who they felt had a better track record, sacrificing a mentor who had proven himself a valuable ally, simply to shave off a few commission points. A few years later, after The Butts Band had become just a footnote in post-Doors lore, Siddons would rise to prominence shepherding the careers of Van Morrison and many others.

Meanwhile, back in Los Angeles, Ray had set to work on his own solo album, thematically inspired by his interest in Egyptology and in thrall to the King Tut exhibition which had recently taken America by storm. The album, *The Golden Scarab: A Rhythm Myth*, revealed Ray's determination to try and recapture some of Jim's mystical lyricism, infused with his own passionate interest in sun worship and the cryptic secrets of ancient Heliopolis. John's prediction that Ray would carry the Doors' sound forward proved true, and in fact, Ray enlisted the Doors sideman Jerry Scheff to play bass, along with the guitarist Larry Carlton and virtuosic jazz drummer Tony Williams.

Although neither outfit was commercially successful, critics favoured John and Robby's post-Doors direction over Ray's, with some accusing the keyboardist of relying on slavish, Morrisonesque vocal stylings to make a bridge back to The Doors, songs like 'The Moorish Idol' and 'Oh Thou Nectar Filled Form: A Little Fart' containing all the impish humour of early Morrison but none of the gravitas. The two projects – Ray's solo efforts and The Butts Band – offered a preview of the musicians' path in the decades to come: Ray, unable to relinquish The Doors' bequest to the ages, swathed himself in the lyrical trappings and sonic pastiche of vintage Doors, while John busied himself in low-key side projects that sounded little like his old band, although the two would soon clash in a nasty battle between their competing visions of The Doors' legacy. Both then and now, Robby just wanted to play.

By the time of the US Bicentennial, however, fans disappointed in the post-Doors output would have cause to celebrate. In 1978, it was announced that new Doors material would soon be released, in which a reunited Ray, Robby and John would provide original music for a recently discovered cache of Jim's spoken poetry. More than a crass repackaging of old material (although those days weren't far off), or a hastily scrubbed soundboard recording from an old live show, this new album offered a scintillating promise – fresh, studio-quality recordings of legitimately new Doors music.

Getting the new music out to the public, however, would prove anything but simple.

Following his 27th birthday recordings with John Haeny, Jim had left his notebooks with Haeny and sometime that month, March 1971, he asked the engineer to drop them off at The Doors' office. He was planning on going to Paris to work on the poetry, Jim explained, so on 12 March Haeny dropped off both the notebooks and a copy of their first demos. The plan was for Haeny to meet the singer in Paris to resume work in a few months, but by then Jim was dead. Those demos, found among his belongings in Paris, eventually resurfaced as the infamous bootleg, *The Lost Paris Tapes*.

To protect the second session from getting into the wrong hands, Haeny retrieved the tapes from the Elektra vaults and kept safe watch over them for several years, during which time Max Fink, now representing Jim's estate, threatened to order the sheriffs to forcibly confiscate them. Haeny was unmoved. 'I told Max to go ahead and try,' Haeny writes now. 'If he did I would deliver a pile of ashes and he could figure out if they were the ashes of the real recordings or not. They stayed quiet after that and never challenged me again.' Years later, Oliver Stone would make the same request for his upcoming Doors film, and Haeny's answer was still the same – no.

Robby reached out to Haeny at some point around 1976 to inquire about the tapes and Haeny agreed to play them for the three musicians – and only those three – on condition that he be allowed to play the tapes through in their entirety, without stopping, and that if they were ever used commercially, it would only be towards the completion of the poetry album. Without any real leverage of their own, they consented. The experience blew their minds. It was the first time they'd heard new verse from their bandmate in five years. All agreed that these 'lost' tapes offered an unparalleled opportunity to bring Jim's poetry to the public in a unique and vibrant way, but before they could significantly take the idea forward, a number of sticky legal complications would see some unlikely players added to the mix.

Complicating the situation were the terms of the recently settled litigation concerning Jim's estate, the control of which was essentially divided into two equal parts – Jim's father, Admiral George Stephen Morrison, retained approval rights over anything autobiographical, while Pamela's father, Columbus 'Corky' Courson, retained creative control over Jim's artistic body of work. After Jim's death, Pam went into tailspin, retreating into full-time heroin addiction. With Jim's financial affairs unsettled until 1974, she was forced to scratch a living as best she could. Jerry Hopkins speculates that she turned tricks at various times to get the money together to feed her habit. Others, however, recall a lost, lonely woman who was fucked up by drugs and the memory of Jim's death, and her passive-aggressive role in it.

Danny Fields recalls visiting Pam with friends not long after she'd returned from Paris. 'We went to make a courtesy call to Pamela, who was grieving. And it was kind of spooky. But she was coherent, and she sat and we poured condolences on her. We didn't ask her for what happened, except she sort of verified he was dead in the bathtub and the police came . . . Okay. She had this nasty mutt. I don't know where this dog had been the whole time that they were away or what. And this dog was . . . I love dogs. But this dog was being unlovable, big time – to me. Just grabbing and growling and trying out the teeth on the leg and stuff like that. And then it jumped up on me. She [Pamela] said, "That's Jim." I looked in the eyes of the dog and he vomited on me. Yes. And then jumped off and walked away. I swear, I mean, you couldn't make this up. And we said, oh dear, well, yeah. And then [Pam] reiterated that this is how he is now. She said, "He's living in that dog now."'

Pam finally overdid it and was found dead on her couch, on 25 April 1974. The few people that still spoke to her on any sort of regular basis say she had recently taken to saying how much she was looking forward to seeing Jim again soon. Her family tried to get her buried at Père-Lachaise, next to Jim, even listing it as the place of burial on her death certificate. In fact, her cremated remains are now interred at Fairhaven Memorial Park in Santa Ana, California, in a cardboard box. The plaque reads: 'Pamela Susan Morrison 1946–1974', though, of course, she never did marry Jim and has no legal right to the Morrison family name. When the fortune Jim had left her finally came through, it went instead to her parents, Columbus and Penny Courson, something Jim's parents later contested, which led to additional legal battles.

In order for *An American Prayer* to be completed, The Doors would have to come to some form of agreement with both Corky Courson and John Haeny. Corky viewed the Doors with withering disdain, blaming Jim Morrison for his daughter's death. The Doors for their part had little affection for Jim's junkie girlfriend, and even less for her father, the retired school Principal, who now owned a percentage of everything they had recorded with Jim. Haeny, wary of The Doors from the get-go, eventually introduced Corky to his own attorney, John T. Frankenheimer, fearing that Corky would be out of his league in any dealings with Elektra or their legal team. As Haeny explained in 2013 on his website, 'Individually I had always found the Doors both charming and reasonable, even warm and funny. But collectively there emerged what I called "The Doors Mentality".' Meaning they would be tougher to deal with, more business-like.

In addition to Haeny's tapes, The Doors and Frank Lisciandro contributed material, including the now famous phone call Jim placed to Michael McClure, saying that he'd just killed a guy in the desert. That call appears on 'The Hitchhiker'. There were also tapes of Jim and friends drinking in a Palm Springs motel room, which yielded the tape of Jim describing his vivid childhood memory of seeing the Indians in the fatal car crash at the side of the highway. This story appears in the track 'Dawn's Highway'.

Interestingly, one of the highlights of the album, the live version of 'Roadhouse Blues', was actually a back-up plan to the band's initial decision to use a live version of 'Gloria'. Corky, as a former academic, solemnly discharged his obligations as curator of Jim's poetry and in his view 'Gloria' was both sexist and wholly inappropriate in view of his daughter's demise. Without Corky's approval, 'Gloria' could not appear on the album. Instead, Haeny scoured the Elektra vaults and found a ferocious version of 'Roadhouse Blues' that is now one of the most downloaded songs in The Doors' catalogue.

While Jim had envisioned his poems read against a musical backdrop, the project never progressed far enough for him to articulate what sort of music he had in mind. As he had never invited the band into the project, it was hardly a foregone conclusion that his own bandmates would provide the soundtrack, and yet the poetry needed music. It was Haeny who first proposed that The Doors provide that music, and much to his surprise they declined. He explains, 'I presumed that it had been such a long time since they had played together that they were understandably apprehensive about going back into the studio again.' They eventually agreed to compose new music for Jim's poetry, and with Frank Lisciandro brought in to assist, production resumed.

The resulting album represented a complex, balanced effort that drew heavily from Jim's life with and without The Doors. Jim's verse, reverently curated by Corky, received a thoughtful presentation befitting an established poet, and with so many of Jim's confederates collaborating on the details the finished product was a much more mature, polished, *groovy* extension of Jim's artistic vision than anyone could have hoped for. 'I believe Jim would be pleased,' says Haeny today. 'Jim would have understood our motivation and appreciated our dedication and heartfelt handling of his work.'

When it was released, Elektra arranged a massive listening party in New York City, offering 3,500 lucky fans an exclusive opportunity to hear a full advance playback of the album. Tickets were awarded via a lottery that attracted 16,000 entries. Record company executives were licking their fangs when the crowd refused to leave without at least one more listen. A few hours south, in the blue-collar city of Philadelphia, a séance was held to commune with Jim, presided over by someone claiming to be a credentialed medium. While Jim failed to materialise, participants were stunned when an irritable black cat slinked from behind a curtain and hissed at the would-be occultists before retreating back into the shadows.

Commercially, Elektra's gambit paid off big time – *An American Prayer* would eventually go platinum (although not until 2001). More important, it went a long way to reactivating interest in both Morrison and The Doors, a process that had begun when Francis Ford Coppola had used 'The End' over the opening shots of his classic 1979 Vietnam saga, *Apocalypse Now*, and culminated in the September 1981 *Rolling Stone* cover story, complete with the headline over an early 'Young Lion' photo of Jim that read: 'He's hot, he's sexy – and he's dead!'

Not all of the material from the birthday sessions was used, and Lisciandro, who declined Jim's invitation to recite some of his poetry at that session, would later comment, 'I have a hope that more of the poetry from that night's reading will someday be released, and if it is released, I think it should be without Doors music, maybe without any music at all. Jim Morrison was one of the best poets of his time. That's not only my opinion but it is also the judgement of teachers and poets in America who use Jim's poetry in the classroom. I don't know if he was a "visionary poet"; maybe all great poets are visionaries.'

Not all of Jim's acquaintances appreciated his poetry, however; Judy Huddleston says, 'People try to say he was poet. A lot of poets I know look at [his poems] and are like, "Please! Get over it!" Some of them are better in songs. Some of them are sophomoric, I guess you'd call them, or just embarrassing – on a real poetry level. Some of them I just go, oh dear!' she laughs.

Ever the showman, Ray Manzarek announced to the media that the band had convened their own séance, that a medium had channelled the spirit of Jim and advised that upon completion of the record Jim's soul had fulfilled its purpose and was now free to move to another plane. Back here on Planet Earth, however, The Doors' comeback was just warming up. 1998 saw the publication of *No One Here Gets Out Alive*, the first comprehensive account of the life of Jim and the history of The Doors. A collaboration between Jerry Hopkins and the former Elektra intern Danny Sugerman, *No One Here Gets Out Alive* offered nothing but a ripping yarn which read like one of the ancient Greek myths that had once inspired Jim. Heroic tales of excess, effusive paeans to Jim's prodigious talent and graphic accounts of Bacchanalian revelry burst from its pages, taking the breathless reader up to Jim's ignominious death in a French bathtub.

The problem, according to Jim's closest friends, was that it was an overblown exaggeration that bore little resemblance to the singer, obscuring some facts while inflating others, all in the service of building the mythology of Jim. In his fascinating 2013 eBook, *Behind Closed Doors*, Jerry Hopkins explains how his original book – written in the wake of the success of his earlier biography of Elvis Presley, an idea Jim had given to him – became inflated by Sugerman's own teenage fandom of Jim, but says that without his sponsorship the book might never have been published. As John Densmore noted in his 1990 memoir, *Riders on the Storm*, 'With Sugerman as the religious zealot and Manzarek as St. Paul the crusading has worked.'

Hopkins recalls how 'in the summer of 1971, with the Elvis

book on the presses, Jim, to whom the book was dedicated, died in Paris, prompting [my book editor] Jonathan Dolger to ask if I'd like to write a book about him. I said yes and, after interviewing about 200 people in the US and Europe – many of whom expressed surprise that I wanted to write a book about Jim Morrison – I submitted a manuscript about three inches thick. Jonathan asked me to shorten it to about an inch and a half. By the time I did that, Jonathan believed interest in Jim had waned and he rejected the manuscript. That was the first of 30 rejections before Warner Books took it, on the third submission. I might add that several I approached for interviews while researching Jim's book said the same thing I'd been told about Elvis: "What do you want to write a book about him for?"'

The result both glorified and extended the legend of Jim Morrison – and deliberately left open to question of whether or nor Jim had actually faked his own death. Published less than a decade after his death, for many wide-eyed young Doors fans this was a tantalisingly plausible prospect. 'You know, that kid was 17 years old when Jim died,' says Vince Treanor now. 'And he's saying, "I am Jim Morrison's confidant?" Come on! You know, the relationship between a 27-year-old man and a [teenage] boy is subject to some scrutiny. Especially when Jim was on the borderline anyway. He didn't really care what happened [any more].

'And as far as Danny's relationship with the group, they really didn't want him around. He used to come over to the office and hang around. I never figured out how and why they ever fell in with Danny, except that after Bill [left] where else did they have to go? Danny, I think, made propositions and they at least knew him . . . He kissed everybody's ass in that place . . .'

The passage of time, and the accounts of others, would dislodge more information throughout the years, offsetting many of the claims in the book. Nevertheless, *No One Here Gets Out Alive* introduced a new generation to the music of The Doors, unwittingly setting the table for the next wave of Doors fever. Sugerman died in 2005, aged just 50, of lung cancer. When Hopkins tried to publish a specially revised account of the story in 2011, submitting the manuscript to the band who had given their approval to the hagiographic original, they rejected it.

In the spoken piece on *An American Prayer* called 'The Movie', Jim asks the listener, 'Did you have a good world when you died? Enough to base a movie on?' The answer for Jim was 'Yes', courtesy of Oliver Stone's controversial 1991 blockbuster, *The Doors*, which made Hopkins's and Sugerman's book appear dry as old bones by comparison. Starring the white-hot pair of Val Kilmer as Jim and Meg Ryan as Pamela, *The Doors* focused almost entirely on the evolution of Jim from starry-eyed poet to loathsome train wreck. Stone had actually unsuccessfully pitched the script to Morrison himself prior to his death, and without a living Jim to bless the narrative Stone spun a trippy rock'n'roll fantasy that, while rooted in fact, achieved wild cinematic vibrancy through what Jim's friends have described as an unfairly broad artistic licence. Through spot-on set dressing and a *tour-de-force* performance by Kilmer, however, Stone chronicled Jim's tragic descent from pouty-faced, leather-panted sexpot to narcissistic, self-sabotaging drunk while pushing the band and Pamela

Courson into impotent supporting roles, reducing the talented and often mercurial musicians – the architects of The Doors' sound – to slack-jawed neophytes basking in the glow of the increasingly insufferable frontman.

Val Kilmer gave the performance of a lifetime, channelling Jim's appearance and mannerisms with unsettling accuracy, even turning in vocals so dead-on that many assumed he was lip-synching. He wasn't. Paul Rothchild estimated that Val had nailed '80 per cent' of Jim's persona by the time production began, and Paul helped the actor fill in the rest with deep dives into the nuances of Jim's singing, his idiosyncrasies, and subtle mannerisms and expressions.

While the surviving Doors had been offered on-set roles as advisors, ironically it was Ray who walked away from production after creative differences with Stone that would boil over into a venomous hatred of the director decades after the movie's release. The co-producer Sasha Harari had originally taken the project to the surviving Doors and Jim's estate (managed by the families of Jim and Pamela), and the project had nearly imploded in a disagreement between the Morrison and Courson families. The iconic producer Bill Graham was brought in to broker a deal and eventually the rights for the movie were secured. Ray, however, got spooked when Stone stepped on board as director, which Harari would note was baffling when one considers that Stone's vision for the story very closely tracked Ray's own post-1971 storytelling.

Vince Treanor recalls running into John during the filming of the movie. With Paul doing the sound and John and Robby on the set, Treanor knew that it was inevitable that he would bump into them at some point. When he finally did, John pulled him aside and said, 'You know, Vince, what happened was never really a fair thing. I wanna take care of you.' The next day, John handed Vince an envelope containing a cheque for $3,000, which Vince assumed was 'sort of a conscience thing. John was always a good guy.'

While both Robby and John served on the film in an advisory capacity, both would eventually distance themselves from the finished product, categorising it as overblown, exaggerated and at times untrue. Robby stated, 'I think when you see the Oliver Stone movie – I'm amazed how good Val Kilmer did – but, you know, the problem with that movie is that the script was kind of stupid. It doesn't really capture how Jim was at all.' John, too, disagreed with the movie's gravitational pull.

Siddons didn't even need to see the film, forming his conclusion after reading the script. 'I went, "This is terrible. This is one side of an incredibly rich and complex individual. It's mean-spirited." I just didn't like it.'

Patricia Kennealy-Morrison also served as an advisor to the film and played a small but ironic role as the priestess who marries Jim and the Patricia character. She would eventually express profound regret over her participation in the movie and the way Stone portrayed Jim, telling me, 'If Oliver had only stuck to this story instead of the way he chose to go, he could have made the *Lawrence of Arabia* of rock'n'roll movies, and he didn't. He chose to make a stupid wet dream music video and I will never forgive him for that. Not so much for what he did to me, which is horrible enough and I will kill him if I ever get my hands on him, but for what he did to Jim. He made Jim look like a buffoon. You do not care that the character is dead at the end of the movie, and that's something I will never forgive him for.'

These days an acclaimed novelist, Patricia was so affronted by the Stone movie she was compelled to write her own, more accurate account of her relationship, in the book *Strange Days: My Life with and without Jim Morrison*. She was not the last person to create an artistic response to the movie. Lisciandro also felt that Stone had landed substantially wide of the mark. While Stone had nailed the styles and look of the time, he missed the defiance and rebellion that fuelled that early generation of Doors fans. Lisciandro would subsequently gather a group of Jim's acquaintances and record them offering their own views of Jim – far more even and supportive – for a 39-minute documentary and excellent accompanying book, both titled simply *A Feast of Friends*. Jim's occasional girlfriend Judy Huddleston, who knew Jim on a level that relatively few ever could, found the movie to be harsh and one-sided, saying, 'I think [Jim] looked like a real buffoon. An asshole. I mean, he had his bad moments but he wasn't that screwed up, or that unlikeable. The thing is, he still was likeable. Except for when he was being really mean . . .'

Ultimately Oliver told his version of the story of the Doors – it was never intended as a documentary – and while the artists themselves must admit that the story and many of the events are rooted in truth, it must also be conceded that in order to package such a complex and sprawling narrative into a 140-minute film, certain artistic liberties were warranted. According to Stone, at a high level, the movie isn't just about Jim or The Doors, explaining, 'It's movie stars, too, and writers, poets . . . anybody that something tragic happens to, it elevates them. Jack Kerouac died young, Hemingway shot himself, F. Scott Fitzgerald had a miserable, drunken second half to his life. There's charisma to it, and an element of the macabre.'

It was also hard to deny certain Christ-figure comparisons invoked by this dramatic account, obscured by the passage of time, of a prophetic, longhaired mystic, with a hazy and unimportant childhood whose legend and myth reach full potency only in his early death. Besides, moviegoers didn't care about accuracy. Riding on the strengths of Stone's name and Kilmer's preternatural performance, moviegoers pumped over $9,000,000 into the coffers on opening weekend alone. The film would go on to top $35,000,000 in the US.

During this renewed wave of popularity, the Doors steadfastly resisted any offers to reunite, reinforcing the anti-materialism platform that stretched back to the Sixties. It would have been easy to cash in, playing private concerts, reunion gigs, tributes, etc., but 15 years – over twice as long as their recording career with Jim – would pass after the sessions for *An American Prayer* before the surviving Doors would share a stage again, at their 1993 induction into the Rock and Roll Hall of Fame. That this would be the band's second official reunion proved only slightly more buzz-worthy than the musician chosen to perform their induction – Pearl Jam's Eddie Vedder, then one of the hottest rock stars in the world.

While Jim had established a reputation for turning up incapacitated for gigs, even missing them on rare occasions, Eddie Vedder bore no such stigma. It was therefore surprising when the Pearl Jam singer pulled a no-show for the band's first rehearsal for the induction ceremony. Even more disconcertingly, Eddie missed the second rehearsal as well. He finally arrived, explaining that he had elected to drive from Seattle to L.A. and was pinned back by torrential north-west rainstorms. His rehearsal time was therefore reduced to listening to The Doors on the drive down, but he nevertheless made it in time for The Doors' big moment.

For his speech, Eddie discussed how the four members of The Doors had each been drafted into the US military in 1966, detailing the various ploys they respectively used to avoid service. Ray had actually enlisted before realising that the service was not his cup of tea, and Vedder pointed out that he swallowed tinfoil balls to simulate tumours in his chest. Robby, said Eddie, pretended to be gay, while he claimed John opted for the bat shit crazy routine – all of which worked. Jim reportedly obtained a category 'Z' exemption, which nobody really understood, but he had apparently convinced the recruiting staff that the US Armed Forces were far, far better off without James Douglas Morrison.

Vedder then pointed out something that few might have realized, saying, 'It amazes me to see all these songs and all these records within the period of '67 to '71. Six records.' By today's standards, a new album every two years is par for the course. To consider Vedder's point – that in four short years, the Doors had released six ambitious, world-beating albums packed with anthems, rockers, ballads and psychedelic head-trips – underscored the special phenomenon the four musicians had created. Vedder then ceded the podium to Ray, Robby, John and Jim's sister, Anne Cherney.

Although Ray would later dismiss the Hall of Fame accolade as inconsequential (telling the San Diego music journalist

George Varga, 'It doesn't mean a whole hell of a lot one way or another. It's just an honouring'), he delivered the longest speech of the four, at one point appearing to wave off a stage manager who tried to cut his speech short, and ending with a reading from *An American Prayer*. At the end, Robby and John thanked their families, while Anne thanked the audience for honouring Jim.

The Doors' honorary post-induction jam remains one of the RRHOF's enduring high points, as the Eddie Vedder-fronted band blazed through 'Roadhouse Blues', 'Light My Fire' and 'Break On Through'. Eddie's absence at rehearsals had not impaired his preparation one iota. Since that moment, no other vocalist performing with any or all of The Doors would ever bring the same unshakeable authenticity to the role as Eddie Vedder.

The next reunion came four years later, with the release of the boxed set *Orange County Suite*, when the three musicians collaborated to provide additional music for the song 'Orange County Suite', which Jim had recorded with John Haeny in 1969, on both vocals and piano. By 1997, Jim had been dead for 26 years – almost as long as he had lived, and Elektra believed the pumps were primed for a new retrospective, issuing four discs of live tracks, outtakes, demos, covers and alternate versions of songs, from the sprawling, 17-minute psychedelic opus 'Celebration of the Lizard King', from a 1970 show, to the 12-second 'Adolph Hitler', captured at a late show that same year at the Boston Garden. Like earlier compilations, this collection would also receive platinum certification, which is no small feat in view of the patchy quality of the material. Bootlegs of many of these shows had been floating around for years, including the 1994 bootleg, *The Lost Paris Tapes*, which included a nearly nine-minute version of 'Orange County Suite', so fans in the underground tape trading network would have been deeply familiar with this song long before the boxed set.

In 2000, VH1 brought The Doors together – again – for a star-choked edition of their massively-popular *Storytellers* series, where artists are invited to play stripped-down versions of their hits before an intimate studio audience, sharing the stories behind the songs. For vocals, the network invited a posse of mainstream rock's frontmen *du jour*, including The Cult's Ian Astbury ('Back Door Man', 'Alabama Song', 'Wild Child'), Stone Temple Pilots' Scott Weiland ('Break On Through', 'Five to One'), Jane's Addiction's Perry Farrell ('L.A. Woman'), Creed's Scott Stapp ('Roadhouse Blues', 'Riders on the Storm', 'Light My Fire'), Train's Pat Monahan ('Love Me Two Times') and Travis Meeks, from Days of the New ('The End').

Accompanied by the bassist Angelo Barbera, from Robby's solo band, The Doors played a nearly two-hour show, with Ray discussing some of the covers they chose in the early days, while John described the songwriting process that saw 'The End' morph from a sparse ballad to the sprawling, iconic head-trip that would end up on wax. While each of the guest musicians offered reverential versions of their songs, few were as effusive as Weiland, who would claim, 'The track seemed to come to life on its own, no tricks involved, just great players and a lot of raw emotion. That weekend will stand out for me as one of the highlights of my musical life.'

During the post-set Q&A, the band were asked if they had

considered heading back out on the road, to which Robby teased, 'We haven't ruled out that possibility.' Indeed, the raucous *Storytellers* experience seemed to blindside the band, reminding them that before the lawsuits and movies there was the music. And what timeless music it had proved to be. To receive the homages of men who sold records in the millions and who occupied the magazine covers of the day placed their contributions in a thrilling new context and it proved strong enough to keep the band together long enough to contribute new material to the Doors tribute album, *Stoned Immaculate: The Music of the Doors*.

While the album enjoyed generally positive critical reception, The Doors again parted ways thereafter, and many journalists and observers would speculate that The Doors' reunion streak had at last come to an end. There had been the release of a glut of live albums – both official and bootleg – as far back as 1983's *Alive, She Cried*. Elektra would officially release four live albums, and the band would eventually form Bright Midnight Records, through which they released over 30 albums and nearly 100 hours of previously unheard material recorded with Jim. With this announcement and with the preponderance of demos flowing through the terabytes of the Internet, it had finally appeared that there was no more blood in the stone.

And yet if the story of The Doors suggests any immutable rules, it is to never say 'never'.

The band did have one final reunion in them. Unfortunately, it would arrive at the tail end of one of the most acrimonious and embittered periods in the band's history. In 2002, Ray and Robby recruited The Cult's frontman, Ian Astbury, to join a new version of The Doors, with Angelo Barbera on bass. They called themselves The Doors of the 21st Century, and according to John the arrangement was simply capitalising on the band's re-emergence into mainstream culture. John wanted no part of the Doors of the 21st Century, or whatever they called themselves.

The band soldiered on without John as they prepared for their debut show, in September, recruiting the Police's drummer, Stewart Copeland, to replace John, and in doing so infusing the band with a supergroup mystique. The inclusion of Copeland – a musician entirely too familiar with band dysfunction – would suffice to quash any speculation that this project was intended as the 'new Doors'. Quite the opposite. Joining the recent slate of all-star collaborators, Copeland, bringing his own storied legacy to the mix, would, if anything, underscore how different this new project would be. *Billboard* reported that Densmore's non-participation was due to a bout of tinnitus. Further confusing the issue, *Billboard* additionally stated that, according to the band's website, the three remaining Doors were planning not only a US and European reunion tour in 2003, but a new studio album to follow. John was not about to sit quietly at home and let it all go down without a fight.

Copeland would eventually pull out of the reunion after an injury and Ty Dennis, also from Robby's solo band, was brought in for their debut gig, which was followed by a number of TV appearances in the US. But the party was soon to be disrupted by their old drummer, whose vision of The Doors' legacy cut a sharp contrast with that of Ray and Robby. John's opposition stemmed from the agreement reached by the four original Doors in 1969, when they rejected Buick's offer of $75,000 to use 'Light My Fire' in a TV commercial. Consistent with this position, sometime around 2003, John rejected a new $15,000,000 offer from Cadillac to license the band's music. Ray and Robby, well up for it, were reportedly incensed that John rejected it out of hand, referring back to the Buick incident.

Fans, however, rarely care about things like 40-year-old agreements and multi-million-dollar advertising deals; they want to see their favourite bands playing together and consequently John was simply viewed as the guy preventing the Doors reunion. The Internet bristled with glib accusations that Densmore was being petty or, worse, that he was the greedy one. Nonetheless, Densmore stood immovable and in February 2003 he filed an injunction against the Doors of the 21st Century, asking the courts to bar the band from using the Doors name and logo.

A judge initially dismissed Densmore's request for an injunction against his bandmates, but that dismissal was later reversed and from that point onward, the Doors of the 21st Century were doomed. Jim and Pamela's families joined John's lawsuit as co-plaintiffs, and in July 2005 he and the Morrison estate prevailed, winning a permanent injunction against John and Robby from using The Doors' name without him. Undaunted, they renamed themselves D21C and later Riders on the Storm. Ultimately however, they settled on Manzarek–Krieger. The order additionally allowed them to bill themselves as 'former' members of the Doors, so long as the distinction was clear that they were not passing themselves off as a new version of their old band.

In 2007, as the lawsuit ascended the appellate channels of the California court system, Densmore was reported to have said, 'I play with Jim. If there's someone of that level, okay. I'm not gonna join them with Ian. That's not to dis Ian, he's a good singer, but he's no Jim Morrison. Eddie Vedder? My God, there's a singer.' The bitter feud lasted six years, during which time both sides expressly left open the possibility of a future reunion, although by then their relations had suffered serious damage.

'My perception is that Ray was so obsessed with building the myth that he got lost in it,' says Bill Siddons. On the other hand, as the *de facto* spokesman for the band, Ray was forever invited to comment on the importance of The Doors and on the mystique of his tragic frontman. Moreover, despite the struggles and conflicts that marred the band's final months, Ray had always considered Jim a brother and his posthumous remarks bore an air of fraternal duty. Would the band enjoy the esteem they now do without the tireless efforts of Ray Manzarek for over four decades? Probably not, according to Siddons, who admits, 'Looking back, almost 50 years later, the Doors are still an important force in the music business, in art and poetry, and you have to give Ray a lot of credit for it.'

Bruce Botnick agrees, stating, "[Ray] was a great story-teller. And he was quite prone – and I used to kid him about it – to enhancement. It's like when you make a movie out of a true-life story . . . I'll never forget during the making of the movie *The Doors*, I was talking with Oliver Stone about it and he had made one scene in the movie which was really a composite of about three or four incidents that had happened in real life, because no one incident by itself was cinematic enough. So Ray would do that, just on a daily basis. He would turn almost every little thing that happened to The Doors into cinema.'

Like Siddons though, Botnick is quick to credit Ray's un-flagging enthusiasm as the main reason The Doors legacy burned as brightly as it did, decades after the band had stopped making music. 'If it wasn't for Ray,' Botnick says, 'the flame wouldn't have continued burning. Without a doubt he was the cheerleader and kept The Doors out there, good, bad or indifferent. He did keep it out there, and he deserves a lot of respect for that.'

Ray and Robby toured off and on for the next few years, with dates across North America, Europe and even the Middle East. Barbera left in 2004, replaced by none other than Phil Chen. Astbury was next to part ways with the group, to take part in a Cult reunion. Fuel's former frontman, Brett Scal-lions, took over as the new singer for Riders on the Storm, as they were called in 2007. Eventually they even brought in Dave Brock, a Jim Morrison impersonator from a local Doors tribute band. Ever the optimist, Robby justified the choice by insisting, 'I think when people come to see Ray and I, they want to see us do the Doors music as it should be done, so why not use a guy who is really an expert? He knows the songs better than we do, really.'

In 2010, the outgoing Florida governor, Charlie Crist, an admitted Doors fan, awarded a posthumous pardon to Jim Morrison for public indecency and open profanity charges relating to the 1969 Miami concert. Because Jim died while in the middle of his criminal appeal, Governor Crist rea-soned that Jim's presumption of innocence remained intact, pending final adjudication. Because Jim never got his final day in court, and at the governor's urging, the Florida Board of Executive Clemency voted to pardon Jim, four decades after his conviction.

Not all agreed with the gesture. CNN reported that 'Morrison's widow, Patricia Kennealy Morrison', had opposed the pardon and quoted her as saying, 'Since the original charges and trial were a publicity stunt to begin with, it doesn't surprise me in the slightest that the pardon should follow in those footsteps.' She also told CNN that because Jim had committed no crime, a pardon was therefore an improper vehicle for clearing his name because the very process implied that Jim had done something wrong. She urged that an expungement – which would erase the arrest from public records – was the only just resolution of the case.

It would be the 2011 documentary *Re:Generation* that would bring the surviving Doors together for one last time. With their legal differences resolved and wounds relatively healed, the three agreed to collaborate with the latest hot-as-a-pistol producer Skrillex on a movie that paired DJs and producers with artists from different genres. Their contribution, called 'Breakin' a Sweat', was a head-scratching, bland chunk of overproduced club music, bearing zero resemblance to anything the three men had released before. Obscured by the heavy-handed machinations of Skrillex and a dizzying patchwork of samples of male and female vocalists, one wondered how a listener would identify the three brilliant musicians, toiling away somewhere in the background. That this collaboration stands largely forgotten serves the higher interests of all parties involved.

Robby and Ray had begun plotting a Doors 50th anniversary tour in 2016, but those plans vanished on 20 May 2013, when Ray, suffering from bile duct cancer, died in a clinic in Rosenheim, Germany, with Dorothy and his brothers at his side. John would issue a statement that he felt 'totally in sync' with his 'musical brother', adding that 'There was no keyboard player on the planet more appropriate to support Jim Morrison's words.' Robby simply offered, 'I'm just glad to have been able to have played Doors songs with him for the last decade. Ray was a huge part of my life and I will always miss him.'

As Ray told Kris Needs for *Clash* magazine, back in 2007, 'That's what we hope to do, even more than the bands, just the young people walking the street thinking, "Where did I come from? Why am I here? What am I doing with my life? I know some day I'm gonna die, where do I go after I die?" Hopefully we can help you along with those questions: the idea of freedom and if you can find a freedom for yourself in The Doors' lyrics and music.'

Notes and Sources

The vast majority of interviews for this book were carried out by me personally, with the assistance of my trusty aide-de-camp Joe Daly also helping out with a couple. These include the following people: Jac Holzman, who also kindly gave me permission to quote from his splendid 1998 memoir, *Follow The Music: the Life and High Times of Elektra Records*; Bruce Botnick, who kindly and generously allowed me into his home (via Skype) more than once, and who introduced me to . . . Bill Siddons, who like Jac and Bruce simply does not do interviews about The Doors anymore but again kindly made an exception in this case.

Also, the one and only Danny Fields, who again took the trouble to speak to me more than once; the exceptional Patricia Kennealy-Morrison, who kindly gave me permission to quote from her superb memoir, *Strange Days: My Life With And Without Jim Morrison*; the brilliant and beautiful Eve Babitz, who insisted on standing while she spoke, and also very kindly gave me permission to quote from some of her numerous writings.

Similarly, the great Jerry Hopkins, who was as honest in his answers as he has been all his life in his outstanding journalism, and gave me permission to quote from his brilliant now-it-can-be-told insider account, *Behind Closed Doors*, and *The Lizard King: The Essential Jim Morrison*; Judy Huddleston, who didn't flinch from discussing some very sensitive memories, and also kindly gave me permission to quote from her moving memoir, *Love Him Madly: An Intimate Memoir of Jim Morrison*; Vincent Treanor III, who gave it to me straight, and kindly gave me permission to quote from his extensive online writings on the subject of his life with The Doors. And Dennis Jakob, whose fascinating memoir, *Summer With Morrison*, his publisher R. Merlin kindly gave me permission to quote from

Also, the always marvellous Pamela Des Barres, the frank and generous Patrick Chauvel, Evert Wilbrink, Jerry Scheff, Jess Roden, Howard Werth, and a handful of others who would prefer not to be named here but whose contributions helped inform this book.

Some other sources that were extremely helpful include *Classic Rock* magazine and, in particular, its estimable chief, Scott Rowley, who arranged permission for me to quote extensively from their powerful 2010 dissection of Morrison's last days in Paris, authored by the legendary Max Bell. Sam Bernett, who agreed to speak to me for the book but later had a change of heart but kindly offered no objection to my request to quote – in English – from his compelling 2007 French-language memoir, *The End: Jim Morrison*. Also Jeff Kitts, who gave permission to quote from the extensive 2008 interview with Robby Krieger in *Guitar World*. Nicolas Lejeune who kindly gave permission for me to quote from his interview with Franck Lisciandro for *Feast of Friends*, the French Fan Club of The Doors. And Alison Burke, who arranged permission for me to use the 2005 interview with Mary Werbelow originally published in the *St. Petersburg Times*.

Also, the marvellous John Haeny, who kindly gave me permission to quote from his eye-opening account of the *American Prayer* recordings, which can be found in full at www.johnhaeny.com

My original interviews with Ray Manzarek, Robby Krieger, and John Densmore, were originally conducted for *Classic Rock* magazine in 2012. Ray also kindly agreed to more than one interview, including being filmed at his home for the BBC4 documentary that I co-wrote, *When Albums Ruled The World*. Speaking with John and Robby was an especially insightful experience, more than anything serving to underline just what a deeply intelligent, incredibly nuanced group of people the four Doors were. And how fortunate the rest of the world was that they managed to make such great, timeless music in such a relative short space of time.

There are also some excellent books that I found useful in helping put the pieces of the Doors story together, and which I have occasionally quoted briefly from. Of these the most strikingly real are Ray Manzarek's 1998 memoir, *Light My Fire: My Life With The Doors*, and John Densmore's 1990 autobiography, *Riders On The Storm: My Life With Jim Morrison And The Doors*.

Ray of course was the great facilitator, in terms of the thousands of retellings of the story of The Doors he happily gave over the years. But in his book he puts it all down in a way that both perfectly mirrors the way he liked to remember things – with that special golden glow we all warmed to – and actually sounds musical, too.

John's book acts as the ideal yin (shade) to Ray's yang (sun). In many ways, John Densmore had the best view in the house, not just at Doors shows, but everywhere they went. As he demonstrates in his marvellous book, which I urge you to read, he more than anybody that ever knew him had the most realistic view of Jim Morrison, and his strengths and weaknesses. If Jim had been half as strong as John he might still be here now.

I urge you to also seek out the great Stephen Davis's superb 2004 book, *Jim Morrison: Life, Death, Legend*. A wonderful piece of work, as you would expect from this exceptional rock chronicler.

Other books which proved exceptionally interesting include: *Break On Through: The Life And Death Of Jim Morrison* by James Riordan & Jerry Prochnicky; *No One Here Gets Out Alive* by Jerry Hopkins and Danny Sugarman; *A Feast Of Friends* by Frank Lisciandro; *Flash Of Eden* by Paul Ferrara; *The Doors Unhinged* by John Densmore; *The Doors* by The

Doors and Ben Fong-Torres; *The Lords: The New Creatures: His Original Published Poetry* by Jim Morrison; *Nico: The Life & Lies Of An Icon* by Richard Witts; *Linda McCartney: The Biography* by Danny Fields; *Faithful* by Marianne Faithful and David Dalton.

I was also assisted by my regular subscriptions to the following newspapers and magazines: *The Times, Classic Rock, Mojo, Rolling Stone, Billboard*, and from the archives, *L.A. Times, Esquire, The Village Voice, Creem, Cashbox, NME, Melody Maker, Sounds, Guitar Player, Guitar World* and several others.

There are also some online resources definitely worth a mention that were always interesting, even when they didn't yield quotes, but certainly in terms of colour and background: not least, www.doors.com, www.doorshistory.com, www.thefreedomman.com, www.waiting-for-the-sun.net. There are many other good ones. You could spend the rest of your life looking at great Doors sites on the net. Happy hunting.

If I have inadvertently missed mentioning and giving credit to anyone, I will happily correct, with thanks, in future editions.

Index

INDEX

INDEX

INDEX